THE BEST

AMERICAN

MAGAZINE

WRITING

2019

THE BEST AMERICAN MAGAZINE WRITING

2019

Edited by Sid Holt for the American Society of Magazine Editors

Columbia University Press   New York

Columbia University Press
Publishers Since 1893
New York   Chichester, West Sussex
cup.columbia.edu

Library of Congress Cataloging-in-Publication Data
ISSN 1541-0978
ISBN 978-0-231-19001-5 (pbk.)

Columbia University Press books are printed on permanent and durable
acid-free paper.
This book is printed on paper with recycled content.
Printed in the United States of America

Cover design: Nancy Rouemy

Contents

Adam Moss

Introduction

I grew up during the golden age of magazines. It was the late sixties. I was eleven. My parents were charter subscribers to *New York* magazine, and I remember flipping through one of the early issues, which I had picked up out of boredom, and finding myself unexpectedly excited. The magazine was sardonic, a little bratty, and very smart, and I, an ordinary misfit with outsized curiosity, didn't take long to realize it was much more entertaining than television (which had been occupying all of my downtime; for a budding adolescent with nothing but downtime, that was a lot of television). The writing in *New York* was showy and funny. It had what I later understood magazine people called "voice"—also swagger and, crucially, confidence. And because that was my first experience with magazines, those were properties I associated with the form. The writers—Tom Wolfe, Gloria Steinem, Jimmy Breslin—were in many ways big names, almost as big as their subjects: Richard Nixon, Leonard Bernstein, and Joe Namath, to name a few. I eagerly awaited each new piece of cultural assassination (that's what this kind of magazine did at the time), and when a new issue arrived, I would cackle at the sarcastic headlines on the cover, feel connected to the thrilling counterculture that was going on outside my personal purview, and grow, issue by issue, more sophisticated.

But it wasn't just *New York*. My parents were friends with an ad guy who used to get magazines for free, and they were piled high in his den: *Rolling Stone*, *Ramparts*, *Harper's*, and *Esquire*. To a new magazine fanboy like me, his house was like a private toy store. *Esquire* was even more electric to me than *New York*— and I would sit in the corner during my visits and devour it, reading Michael Herr on Vietnam and Nora Ephron on breasts, hers and others, mesmerized by the covers which were perfect expressions of antiestablishment poster art. I could list some examples of its genius, but if you are reading this book and therefore a lover of magazines, it is likely that that is unnecessary—you know every great *Esquire* cover.

Magazines then were at the epicenter of the culture, and you know that because if you are a certain generation—mine, give or take—you recognize that period as the golden age. And when the times shifted and the Vietnam War ended and Watergate came and went and Jimmy Carter became president, the times got boring and so did magazines. And the people who grew up with these magazines and learned to love them because their countercultural swagger was so alluring began to look back at this era through a fog of mist: these magazines would never return again. Nor, by the way, would their youth.

Eventually I would become an editor first at *Esquire* and then at *New York*, and I would have the opportunity to pore over the back issues of both those magazines, and you know what? There was a lot of greatness there, but in retrospect it all seemed a little sophomoric. Much of what was published was crap.

·　　　·　　　·

I came of age as an editor during the golden age of magazines. It was the early eighties, and I was in my twenties. I worked at *Rolling Stone* and *Esquire*, and instead of covers skewering the establishment, magazines were full of movie stars and the covers were bright and sexy and fun. Reagan was president, and people did a lot of coke. Mostly, though, there was a lot of money oozing around, and magazines were thick and smelled of perfume and confidence, with big expensive photo shoots and big expensive stories. Editors (not me, but still) traveled around in town cars and went to a lot of parties, and the whole world of magazines seemed romantic, not just to those who worked in them but to readers as well. Magazines were glitz and fizz and buzz. And if you were a certain age and came of age flipping through these huge tomes of fabulousness, you would pine for them when they went away, which, of course, they did.

And you know what? A lot of what was published was crap.

•   •   •

I started a magazine during the golden age of magazines. It was the late eighties now, and I was thirty. The magazine was called *7 Days*—I doubt you remember it, but it came along around the same time as a great, satiric magazine you probably do remember called *Spy. Spy* was mean and fun and fit the times like a glove. But there were plenty of other start-ups because everybody wanted to fund and make and read magazines. There was *Egg* and *New York Woman* and *Fame*. Annie Leibowitz took a picture for *Vanity Fair* of all the new editors of all the new magazines. There were more than twenty of us.

And you know what? Nearly every one of those magazines went out of business.

•   •   •

It took a while for magazines (there were still plenty) to dig themselves out of the recession that had done the damage, but eventually they dug until another recession hit, and then they climbed back from that, too. In the meantime, there was 9/11 and the Iraq War. I became editor of the *New York Times Magazine* and, later, *New York*. Times changed again. Barack Obama became president. Magazines became more optimistic, and business was good; magazines were still flush. A lot of journalism was published, some wonderful, some not. And a great big story was emerging that was irresistible to cover: the racing pace of new technology and its effect on all corners of life. Magazines wrote about the miracle of the internet, and at first the coverage was giddy—after all, journalism feeds on change, and there was plenty of change to write about.

But then some of that coverage got a little darker. It was hard for magazine journalists not to notice that the internet was having some pernicious effects and was beginning to upend some industries that were getting closer and closer to their own. First music, then television, then newspapers. The internet was changing people's reading habits, but even more dangerous (to magazines) was the threat to the financial lifeblood of most journalism—advertising—as big technology companies like Google and Facebook began to draw dollars away, leaving media without any means of support. This was serious business.

And magazines began first to shrink and then, in many cases, disappear altogether. Recessions and zeitgeists come and go, but this was a different order of change: category killing, apocalyptic. Lovers of magazines began to smell the stench of retreat, an erosion of that confidence that sustained the form for so long. Websites began to proliferate, many of them written by youngsters who were willing to work for bupkis in the general wreckage. Journalism was becoming . . . listicles! And to many—probably many of you—this turn of events seemed terribly depressing.

Recently, I left my job at *New York*. I happened to be part of an exodus of many editors of my generation. And perhaps predictably because of my and my colleagues' advanced ages and long tenure in this business, the news of our departures was met in some circles with this refrain: an era was over. And not just that. Some seemed to suggest that the entire age of magazines was pretty much kaput.

.   .   .

Yet perhaps because I was implicated in all of this doomsaying, I feel obliged to correct the record. And so here's what I have to say about that: I am writing these words during the golden age of magazines. I know that sounds disingenuous, but I very nearly mean it. During this same period that magazines have been felled by so-called disruptions to their business, homegrown digital journalism and digital distribution of journalism that originated in print has flourished. And there is so much journalism now published on the web that an open-minded reader, one not reflexively resistant to change, has to notice that some of it is really very good. Digital journalism has many magical attributes—it can live in real time, it invites interaction with its readers, and almost anybody can play on their own platforms, which is bringing a lot of new talent into the fold. But most important, it's where much of the audience is, and that audience is enormous, way bigger than it has ever been for magazine writing. Magazines have largely adapted to the internet by using it to reach more people, and as a result most magazines have seen the audience for their stories increase exponentially. In some cases the internet has inspired more colloquial means of expression, and that's often good for journalism, too, shaking up story forms. Voice, that powerful magazine tool, is vigorously employed, sometimes to good effect and sometimes not, but really, that was always the case.

Perhaps more interesting, where once the only canvas for magazines was the printed page, now that's not at all true. Beyond digital, there's audio, and some of the most interesting journalism being perpetrated today is in nonfiction narrative podcasts (like *Slate*'s sensational *Slow Burn*). There's video, and some of it is marvelous as well (see the videos made by a digital magazine called *Topic* that swept the video categories at this year's National Magazine Awards). There are live magazines—there's even a touring magazine show (stories kind of enacted on stage) called *Pop-Up*. Social media has become a journalistic platform as well—when we at *New York* published a story a couple of years back on Bill Cosby's accusers, our website went down, and we refashioned the entire story into serial Instagram posts and published it that way. It worked great. Snapchat publishes magazine editions for their young readers that are constructed from an entirely original magazine language. Innovation, which has always driven the magazine as a genre and art form, is exploding.

Oh, I know. If you love print—and I do—there's plenty to be wistful about. Magazines on paper are not going away altogether, but there will certainly be fewer of them, and they will be more expensive. And I won't argue that a long and glorious magazine era isn't ending; it's just that all endings are also beginnings. After all, if the old model of television hadn't died, you would never have gotten streaming and then you wouldn't have . . . the golden age of television, which is I guess what we're in now because nobody remembers that that's what they used to call it when Milton Berle wore a dress on *Texaco Star Theater*.

The point is, it's very easy to romanticize the past, but one person's memory lane is not like another's. Also, if you get my drift, most golden ages weren't so golden anyway. Plus: what use are golden ages anyway, especially in journalism (which, yes, loves to declare them, but that's another story)? Journalism is about the now. And the now is pretty astounding. So I'd advise magazine nostalgists to get with the program. The entire point about magazines is that they are supersensitive to their times. That's what's so wonderful about them.

Which brings me to this volume.

Herein is a collection of the best American magazine writing last year, and it has been carefully culled: I can promise you there is nothing crappy within. It can stand up to the best writing in magazines of any year. Like all magazine writing, it is very much a reflection of its period, and this period is interesting for journalism. As I write this, Donald Trump is the president of the United States. The Mueller report has just been issued, and among its many attributes is the confirmation that much of the hard-hitting journalism of the past couple of years has been exceptionally on target. Trump is barely mentioned in these pages, yet that spirit of aggressive (and confident) journalism animates much of the content. There's Franklin Foer's investigative essay on Paul Manafort, originally published in *The Atlantic*. Also Ben Taub's "Shallow Graves," about the ISIS aftermath in Iraq (*New Yorker*); Nahal Toosi's inquiry into the ethnic slaughter in Mynamaar (*Politico*); Mark Arax's "A Kingdom From Dust" (*California Sunday Magazine*), about the secretive farmer who has remade California's landscape, not for the better; and Hannah Drier's "The Betrayal," a story about an MS-13 gang member who turned evidence for ICE and was then betrayed by it. This story was copublished by *ProPublica* and *New York*; in another development of these times, partnerships between nonprofit investigation outfits and magazines are proliferating, animated (as all these pieces are) by the imperative that sees journalism (properly, I think) as a critical bulwark against all sorts of malfeasance. Magazine journalism didn't always matter. I do think it does now.

Some of these entries deal more directly with the big news of the year. For instance, you will find two groups of entries that deal in large part with the Brett Kavanaugh confirmation hearings: Caitlin Flanagan's series of articles from *The Atlantic* and Doreen St. Félix's collection from the *New Yorker* (St. Félix, by the way, rose very much as a talent shaped on the internet—and she is just one especially gifted example of many). And in this year of increasing focus on criminal justice, it is fitting to see not one but two features written by present or past felons: "Getting Out," by Reginald Dwayne Betts, and "This Place Is Crazy," by John J. Lennon, the first from the *New York Times Magazine* and the second from *Esquire*. The Betts essay is one of the strongest and most poignant I've read in many years.

I won't list all of the entries—you can find them in the table of contents. Read them, and then see if you still feel nostalgic for a time that's passed. The golden age is now. But then, isn't it always?

Acknowledgments

This edition of *Best American Magazine Writing* collects articles honored by the American Society of Magazine Editors at the presentation of the National Magazine Awards in March 2019. The Best American Magazine Writing series began in 2000 and has been published by Columbia University Press since 2005, but the history of the National Magazine Awards dates to the early 1960s, when ASME and Columbia University founded the program as a counterpart to the Pulitzer Prize. More than half a century later ASME continues to sponsor the awards in association with the Columbia School of Journalism.

The first National Magazine Award—there was only one award presented in the first four years of the program—was presented to *Look* in 1966 for "its skillful editing, imagination and editorial integrity, all of which were reflected particularly in its treatment of the racial issue during 1965." Look at the time was one of the largest general interest magazines in the United States, with a circulation of more than 7 million, but from the beginning ASME strove to honor a broad range of publications. The same year *Look* won the first National Magazine Award, three magazines—*Ebony, Grade Teacher,* and *Scientific American*—were presented Certificates of Special Recognition, and nine received commendations, including the *New Yorker* for "its flair for dramatic innovation as demonstrated by its publication of Truman Capote's 'In Cold Blood,'" *Time* for "its well researched, expertly written and balanced series of 'TIME Essays,'" and *Vogue* for "its effective use of color in editorial pages."

In 2019, the *New Yorker*, *Time*, and *Vogue* were again among the National Magazine Awards honorees, but the categories in which they were finalists go far toward explaining the changes that have overtaken both the awards program and the very nature of magazine journalism in recent years. Both *Time* and the *New Yorker* were nominated in Reporting, a category that was first introduced in 1970 (and that the *New Yorker* has won on thirteen separate occasions), but the *New Yorker* was also nominated in Website and Podcasting. And *Vogue* was a repeat finalist in Video—work, let alone a category, unimaginable to magazine editors in 1966. Yet despite these changes, the purpose of the awards has remained the same: to advance the practice of journalism by recognizing excellence, enterprise, and innovation.

The articles collected in *Best American Magazine Writing 2019* evince these three qualities while demonstrating the enduring power of magazine journalism. What makes magazines special? Deep reporting, informed analysis, stylish writing, a distinctive point of view. This collection begins with examples of extraordinary reportage, continues with often-provocative commentary and opinion, and concludes with the kind of service journalism and feature stories rarely found outside the pages—print or digital—of a magazine. Some of these stories address subjects readers in 1966 would have recognized: racism, political corruption, foreign-policy blunders. Others reflect unforeseen changes, both the good and the terrifying: new demographics, #MeToo, climate crisis. But each bears the distinctive stamp not only of the writer but also of the editor who assigned it.

This year the editors of 275 publications entered the National Magazine Awards. Fourteen hundred entries were received. Half of the entries were published in print; the others were either a combination of print and digital content or digital only. The nearly 300 judges were assigned preliminary reading in mid-December then met at Columbia University in mid-January to choose five finalists in twenty of the twenty-two categories and seven finalists (because of the number of entries) in Reporting and Feature Writing. The judges then chose the winner in each category. After the judges finished their work, the National Magazine Awards board, composed of current and former ASME officers, veteran judges, and representatives of the Columbia Journalism School, reviewed and sanctioned the results.

Sixty-seven media organizations received nominations in 2019, led by the *New Yorker* with nine. The *New Yorker* also received the most awards—four—nearly sweeping the narrative-journalism categories by winning Reporting, Feature Writing, Columns and Commentary, and Public Interest. Each of the winning publications received a copper "Ellie," modeled on Alexander Calder's stabile *Elephant Walking*, which has been the symbol of the National Magazine Awards since 1970, when the recipients of the first four awards—*Look*, *Life*, *Newsweek*, and *American Machinist*—purchased it from Calder and gave it to ASME. The National Magazine Awards are now familiarly known as the Ellies as a result. There is more information about the judges, the finalists and the winners—as well as links to honorees in categories such as Video, Podcasting and Social Media—to be found at http://ellies2019.org/.

Hundreds of magazine journalists make the Ellies possible. Among them are the editors in chief who choose to enter the awards; the assistant, associate, and senior editors who organize the submissions; the judges who receive dozens of stories to read the week before the year-end holidays begin then fly to New York in the middle of January (when visitors to Columbia can feel the wind whipping off the Hudson River) to spend two days reading, debating and voting in sometimes cramped classrooms; and the reporters, photographers, story editors, and art directors who wait hopefully for the announcement of the finalists and winners then go back to work, regardless of the results. All of them deserve our thanks.

The ASME board of directors is responsible for overseeing the administration, judging, and presentation of the Ellie Awards, which include not only the National Magazine Awards but also the ASME Award for Fiction and the ASME Next Awards for Journalists Under 30. The sixteen members of the 2018–2019 board—all of whom were the editors in chief of well-known print and digital publications—are listed at http://ellies2019.org/. The success of the 2019 Ellies was especially the work of the president of ASME, Christopher Keyes, who, despite his responsibilities as the editor in chief of *Outside*, was willing to tackle each new challenge. I also want to acknowledge the contributions of Jim Nelson, the former editor in chief of *GQ*, who, long before he joined the ASME board, helped contemporize the Ellies.

As director of operations at ASME, Nina Fortuna is largely responsible for the day-to-day running of the Ellies. Everyone who knows anything about the National Magazine Awards knows that Nina is the first person to ask when questions need to be answered. I also want to express my gratitude to my colleagues at the MPA—the Association of Magazine Media—especially Patty Bogie and John DeFrancesco, for their invaluable assistance. ASME is also thankful to Steve Coll, the Pulitzer Prize–winning reporter who now serves as the dean and Henry R. Luce Professor of Journalism at the Columbia Journalism School, and Abi Wright, the executive director of professional prizes at Columbia, for their continuing support of the National Magazine Awards.

On behalf of ASME, I want to thank John Avlon for hosting the presentation of the 2019 awards. Now a senior political analyst at CNN, John was for many years a member of ASME and frequently served as a National Magazine Awards judge when he was editor in chief of the *Daily Beast*. I also want to thank David McCormick of McCormick Literary for representing ASME as our literary agent. The editors of the Best American Magazine Writing series at Columbia University Press are Philip Leventhal and Michael Haskell. Philip's enthusiasm for the work represented in this book is always a source of inspiration. Michael's editorial skill and gentle determination ensures that the book not only reads well but gets printed.

This year for the first time, *Best American Magazine Writing 2019* includes interviews with two of the award winners, the *New Yorker*'s Ben Taub and *McSweeney's* Claire Boyle. I want to thank Eric Sullivan, senior editor at *Esquire*, and Karolina Waclawiak, executive editor, culture, at *Buzzfeed*, for conducting the interviews—and for giving readers of this book new insight into the work the Ellies are intended to celebrate. Both Eric and Karolina also serve as awards judges, so I am doubly appreciative of their contributions to ASME.

In his introduction to this book, Adam Moss explores the timeless appeal of magazine journalism. As the editor of *New York* and, earlier, the *New York Times Magazine* and *7 Days*, Adam set the standard for both print and digital journalism and won more than forty National Magazine Awards. In recognition of his accomplishments, ASME this year elected him to the Magazine Editors' Hall of Fame. I want to thank Adam for writing the introduction but most of all for decades of incomparable magazine making. Yet the last word as always belongs to the writers who graciously consented to the publication of their stories in *Best American Magazine Writing 2019*. Their work makes winners of us all.

THE BEST
AMERICAN
MAGAZINE
WRITING

2019

ProPublica, copublished with *New York*

FINALIST—PUBLIC INTEREST

ProPublica—*which describes itself as a nonprofit newsroom—partnered with* New York *magazine, the suburban New York newspaper* Newsday, *and the* New York Times Magazine *to publish the three-part series that included this story, "A Betrayal." The series provided an inside look at MS-13—Henry, the subject of "A Betrayal," joined MS-13 as a child in El Salvador—and explored efforts to contain the gang using immigration policy. The writer of the series, Hannah Dreier, joined* ProPublica *in 2017 after three years as the Venezuela correspondent for the Associated Press. She began her career as a reporter for the Bay Area News Group. Nominated for the 2019 National Magazine Award for Public Interest, "A Betrayal" and the other articles in the series, "The Disappeared" and "He Drew His School Mascot—and ICE Labeled Him a Gang Member," later won Dreier the Pulitzer Prize for Feature Writing.*

Hannah Dreier

A Betrayal

I f Henry is killed, his death can be traced to a quiet moment in the fall of 2016, when he sat slouched in his usual seat by the door in eleventh-grade English class. A skinny kid with a shaggy haircut, he had been thinking a lot about his life and about how it might end. His notebook was open, its pages blank. So he pulled his hoodie over his earphones, cranked up a Spanish ballad and started to write.

He began with how he was feeling: anxious, pressured, not good enough. It would have read like a journal entry by any seventeen-year-old, except this one detailed murders, committed with machetes, in the suburbs of Long Island. The gang Henry belonged to, MS-13, had already killed five students from Brentwood High School. The killers were his friends. And now they were demanding that he join in the rampage.

Classmates craned their necks to see what he was working on so furiously. But with an arm shielding his notebook, Henry was lost in what was turning out to be an autobiography. He was transported back to a sprawling coconut grove near his grandfather's home in El Salvador. In front of him was a blindfolded man, strung up between two trees, arms and legs splayed in the shape of an X. All around him were members of MS-13, urging him on. Then the gang's leader, El Destroyer, stepped forward. He was in his sixties, with the letters *MS* tattooed on his face, chest and back. A double-edged machete glinted in his hand. He wanted Henry to kill the blindfolded man.

For years, the gang had paid for Henry's school uniforms, protected him from rival gangs, and given his grandmother meat for the family. In exchange, Henry had delivered messages and served as a lookout. Then the gang started asking him to come to shootouts, to help show strength in numbers. They also beat him for thirteen seconds—an initiation ritual—and asked him to choose a gang name. He eventually settled on Triste, the Spanish word for "sad." What you become when your parents abandon you as a toddler and go to America and leave you behind in a slum.

Henry hunched over his notebook, oblivious to the kids around him. Now he was twelve, standing in the coconut grove, and it was time to complete the final initiation rite. He took the machete. It was sharper, with more teeth, than the one he used for chores at home. El Destroyer traced his index finger on the trembling man to show Henry where to cut: first the throat, then across the stomach.

"Your first killing will be hard," El Destroyer told him. "It will hurt. But I've killed thirty-four people. I'm too tired to do this one." He said the devil was there in the grove and needed fresh blood. And if Henry didn't kill the man, the gang would kill them both.

So, to live a little longer, I had to do it.

But now, Henry wrote, he wanted to escape the life that had followed him from El Salvador. If he stayed in the gang, he knew he would die. He needed help.

He tore out the pages and hid them inside another assignment, like a message in a bottle. Then he walked up to his teacher's desk and turned them in.

A week later, Henry was called to the principal's office to speak with the police officer assigned to the school. In El Salvador, Henry had learned to distrust the police, who often worked for rival gangs or paramilitary death squads. But the officer assured Henry that the Suffolk County police were not like the cops he had known before he sought asylum in the United States. They could connect him to the FBI, which could protect him and move him far from Long Island.

So after a childhood spent in fear, Henry made the first choice he considered truly his own. He decided to help the FBI arrest his fellow gang members.

Henry's cooperation was a coup for law enforcement. MS-13 was in the midst of a convulsion of violence that claimed twenty-five lives in Long Island over the past two years.

President Trump had seized on MS-13 as a symbol of the dangers of immigration, referring to parts of Long Island as "bloodstained killing fields." Police were desperately looking for informants who could help them crack how the gang worked and make arrests. Henry gave them a way in.

Under normal circumstances, Henry's choice would have been his salvation. By working with the police, he could have escaped the gang and started fresh. But not in the dawning of the Trump era, when every immigrant has become a target and local police in towns like Brentwood have become willing agents in a nation-wide campaign of detention and deportation. Without knowing it, Henry had picked the wrong moment to help the authorities.

·   ·   ·

Henry had tried to escape MS-13 before.

From the day he joined the gang, he was part of an operation that trafficked in a single product: violence. Other criminal enterprises attract members who want to get rich and who sell drugs or women or stolen goods to achieve that aim. Violence is a tool for carving out territory and regulating the marketplace. MS-13, by contrast, was established by Salvadoran refugees in Los Angeles who were seeking community after fleeing civil war. The gang offers a sense of security and belonging to its members, who kill to strengthen the group and move up the ranks. Members sometimes sell marijuana and cocaine, but major cartels have been uninterested in partnering with the gang because purposeless violence is bad for business. MS-13 kills in large groups to minimize betrayal, and it uses machetes, a weapon even the poorest can afford.

In his first few years running with the gang in El Salvador, Henry witnessed more than a dozen murders. He learned how soft skin feels when you slice into it and how bodies, when they are sprayed with bullets, look like they are dancing. Then, in 2013, a shaky truce between MS-13 and the rival gang Barrio 18 broke down. The country's slums became as dangerous as any war zone. One afternoon, when he was fifteen, Henry was playing cards in an abandoned lot when he got a call from a stranger. The voice on the phone told him that if he did not leave the country within twenty-four hours, he would be disappeared—along with his grandparents. To protect his family, Henry set out that night to join his mother and father on Long Island. Before he left, his grandfather made him promise he would use the new start to break with the gang.

Henry made the journey north through Mexico stowed away in the back of a livestock truck. Some 200,000 unaccompanied children from Central America have shown up at the U.S. border since 2013, and nearly 8,000 continued on to Long Island, most to join parents who had settled there years earlier. The suburbs have proved an ideal landing spot—close to low-wage work around New York City and filled with illegal basement apartments. By the time Henry arrived, so many Salvadorans were living in Suffolk County that El Salvador had opened a consulate in the town of Brentwood, the only foreign government with an office on Long Island.

Henry entered the United States legally, turning himself over at the border and pleading for asylum. He was granted release pending a final hearing that could be years away and sent to join his mother. He didn't recognize her when she ran up to him at JFK Airport, clutching welcome balloons; in all the time she'd been gone, she had never sent him a photo. As they headed to her apartment, he learned that she had long ago separated from his father. He soon became acquainted with her abusive boyfriend, who one day threw hot cooking oil at her head, landing her in the hospital with third-degree burns. His father helped Henry lie about his immigration status and age to get a job in a factory, where he worked twelve-hour shifts punching perforations in toilet paper for nine dollars an hour. On payday, he handed over almost all his earnings to his mother, who expected him to pay for rent and groceries.

That summer was the loneliest time Henry had ever known. Unable to speak English or navigate the bus system, he barely left the house except to work. His father sometimes sat next to him on meal breaks at the factory, but Henry didn't know what to say, and his father didn't seem interested in talking. He found the wide, empty streets of Brentwood eerie after the crowded slums of El Salvador, and he was unsettled by the misty weather. His mother worked late, so he was often on his own. At night, as he sat in the dark watching horror movies, he couldn't help but miss aspects of the gang—never being bored, always having backup.

All that changed when he enrolled at Brentwood High in the fall of 2014. The school—one of the largest in America, with 4,000 students—felt like a fortress, ordered and welcoming and safe. The overhead lights were brighter and the walls whiter than his schoolhouse in El Salvador, which had been ringed with fencing to stop pigs and chickens from wandering through. Posters on the wall advertised spirit rallies. At orientation, Henry learned that the school had swimming pool and a music program. He had never touched an instrument before.

His classes were filled with so many recent arrivals from Central America that they were taught in both English and Spanish.

The kids talked about soccer and teachers and tried out their shy English on each other at lunch. One friend was struck by the long hours Henry had to work after school and how reluctant he seemed to talk about his childhood in El Salvador. Another liked his funny, street way of talking; he nicknamed her Curly, and that became what everyone in school called her. "He would always want to know how things were going with me, like he was a brother," she says. "He would get really serious, and we would think up crazy things to do to make him laugh."

Henry loved every minute of his freshman year: buying sandwiches at the deli with his friends, playing soccer in the park. One friend gave him an old bike so he could get around more easily; others came to visit him at his second job at a car wash. An uncle started to show an interest in him, taking him fishing off the piers at dawn. Noticing that his nephew was friendly and curious, he warned Henry to steer clear of MS-13, which had already established itself on Long Island. "I told him don't let them become your friends, but don't let them be your enemies either," the uncle recalls. "Because that would be seeking death."

Henry knew how to pick out the gang kids at school—red shirts and bandannas for the Bloods, yellow for Latin Kings, royal blue for the Crips, light blue and white for MS-13. At first, Henry had worried that El Destroyer's crew would find him: He knew membership in MS-13 is for life, no matter where you move. But as his freshman year passed and no one from his old life recognized him, he began to relax. Maybe it really was possible to start over.

·   ·   ·

His new life began to fall apart at the start of his sophomore year, when Henry saw El Fantasma. The boy, a shot-caller in the gang back home, had enrolled at Brentwood High that fall. One day, he confronted Henry in the cafeteria. He ordered him to attend a meeting in the woods that afternoon, to receive his punishment for failing to report in.

In El Salvador, cutting ties with the gang would have landed Henry on a kill list. But in the suburbs of Long Island, MS-13 had softened its rules. Here, recruits didn't have to commit a murder to join the gang. Members could socialize with outsiders, and a beating would do for punishment. After school, Henry found more than a dozen boys waiting for him in the woods. There was El Monkey and El Satanico and El Big Homie—willowy teenagers in the midst of growth spurts, with pierced ears, gelled hair, and skinny jeans. They punched and kicked Henry until he curled up into a ball on the ground, then continued for a drawn-out count of 13. "The blows came from all sides like rain," Henry would later recall. "I had wanted to change, and I'd been succeeding for months at that point. But that's when it ended."

Henry felt guilty about breaking the promise he'd made his grandfather. But it was also a relief to fall back into his old ways. The gang on Long Island had the same rituals and spoke the same slangy Spanish he'd grown up with. Like any good franchise, MS-13 was comfortingly familiar.

In the United States, MS-13 is organized into small subgroups called cliques. Its emphasis on social rather than criminal bonds has helped the gang persist without a powerful central leader or a steady source of income. On the East Coast, the highest regional level is the "New York program"—middle management put in place by bosses in El Salvador and Los Angeles to oversee unruly cliques, including a dozen on Long Island. At Brentwood High, the main clique is known as the Sailors. Henry began wearing the white plastic rosary they favored and picked up Chicago Bulls gear, which the gang wears because bullhorns evoke the devil, a central figure in MS-13's symbology. He identified himself to new recruits as *Triste, Sailors, New York*, like a soldier stating his rank and chain of command. He was low on the totem pole: his main duty was to ensure that the clique's thirty or so members were respected in the school. He learned how to turn a mechanical pencil into a weapon by replacing the eraser with a razor blade and how to threaten boys who tried to get close to the Sailors' girl-friends. "If you want to stay aboveground, it's better you stay away from her," he warned them. It worked every time.

Back in El Salvador, the gang was led by veterans hardened by decades of violence. On Long Island, the Sailors were led by a pair of teenage brothers who lived with their mom and kept the gang's cache of machetes, swords and hatchets buried in their backyard. They navigated the neighborhood on dirt bikes and met up at McDonald's and worked long hours at normal jobs. They created a hangout in a mulchy clearing in the woods, where they spray-painted tree trunks with stick-figure devils and laughing clown faces. One day, they hoisted an old mattress on a stump to make a lean-to and drew the outline of a naked woman on the fabric. Dues were ten dollars a week. In Facebook group chats, they talked about girls and Clash of Clans, their favorite multiplayer game. They also shared news of friends and enemies getting arrested in Long Island or murdered back in El Salvador. One wrote: "Did you see El Black, El Funny, El Flash and the others have fallen?" Another said: "I miss El Bad Boy."

That Christmas, his mother, who had been increasingly dis-tant, left to live in a domestic-violence shelter without saying goodbye. Henry moved in with his uncle. He texted the Sailors to tell them how he felt abandoned, once again, by his parents. "We're your family," one responded, "and we'll never abandon you." Henry was comforted, but he knew that his relationship with his gang friends could crumble the moment he did anything to make them question his loyalty, no matter how simple the transgression—even being slow to answer a text message.

One afternoon in English class, Henry caught the eye of a girl who had been feuding with the Sailors. She scowled at him, and he responded by flashing the signs *M* and *S* with his hands. She folded her hand into a *B* for Bloods. After class, Henry told the gang leaders what she had done. They seemed conflicted. The girl was just fifteen, with long hair and a wide-eyed expression. Then again, they told Henry, *hasta el peor demonio se viste de ángel*: Even the worst demons hide in angels' clothing. They decided to keep an eye on the girl. If she kept testing them, she would have to fall.

•　　•　　•

By the summer of 2016, the Sailors and other cliques were starting to return to their violent roots. They began selling marijuana and getting into street fights. Teenagers who wore yellow or red shirts were listed for death; those who acted like they were MS-13 without actually belonging were listed as well. In the first half of that year, the gang killed three boys from Brentwood High and buried their bodies in the woods.

Henry joined in the fights and sold marijuana, but he didn't want to participate in another murder. In El Salvador, the violence had seemed necessary, a form of survival. In Brentwood, the Sailors wanted Henry to help lure his classmates to their death—kids he knew from homeroom and parties and field trips—simply because they were acting like kids. MS-13 was like any other bunch of bored and anxious and hormonal teenagers at school, only with machetes.

Local detectives who later questioned Henry, as well as his own texts and Facebook messages, confirm that he stayed on the outskirts of the gang, avoiding the most extreme violence. He tried pretending that he had suddenly been put under curfew. "Look man," he texted the leaders one night, "the problem is my uncle is here watching me like a hawk." They backed down that time, but it was clear they were losing trust. "Yesterday, El Delincuente said he thought I was acting like I don't want to be in anymore," he wrote a friend on Facebook. "He said I knew from the moment I joined that the only way out is a coffin. So now you know that if one day I'm not on here, it's because I'm already dead."

As Henry started his junior year, the girl who had flashed a Bloods sign at him was finally placed on the gang's kill list. She had continued feuding with the Sailors, and even according to the softer rules on Long Island, the only punishment for rival gang members is death. One afternoon, a car full of Sailors spotted the girl as she was walking home with a friend. They jumped out and attacked her with bats and machetes. They killed her friend as well, to avoid leaving a witness. She was beaten so badly that police initially thought she had been hit by a car.

The exploding violence on Long Island was almost entirely aimed at kids who were flirting with gang life; in texts, the Sailors were careful to distinguish whether an intended target was a "civilian"—only suspected snitches and rival gang members were marked for violence. The Sailors rarely hurt civilians except by accident: in one incident, they shot a young man at a deli they believed was a rival gang member, and the bullet passed through the man's skull and hit the deli worker behind the cash register.

That fall, not long after the two girls were killed, police discovered the bodies of the three boys MS-13 had buried in the woods. Henry obsessed over the footage of their grief-stricken families on the TV news. He imagined his grandfather crying at his own funeral. He started looking for ways to escape the gang for good, but there seemed to be no way out. He approached U.S. military recruiters in school, eager to join the army, but they told him that he was too young to enlist without a form from his parents. When he called his grandparents and told them he was struggling to get his life back on track, they told him to go to church and confess.

In school, Henry grew increasingly anxious and moody. That day in English class, staring at a blank page in his notebook, he felt he was ready to explode. He hadn't planned to write a confession, but it just poured out—the murders, the beatings, his growing remorse about what he had done in El Salvador. He needed help, and he wanted his teacher to know that he hadn't killed those two girls. She had always seemed to want him to succeed, and he thought of her as a second mother.

Lingering at the door after the bell rang, he saw his teacher discover the pages, noting with confusion that he had signed them "Triste." He saw her cheeks flush and tears come to her eyes. In that moment, the import of what he had done started to sink in. The Sailors were already losing trust in him. If they found out what he had told his teacher, they would surely add him to the kill list.

He stayed away from school for a full week. When he returned, the teacher pulled him aside. She asked him why he had written the pages instead of talking to her. He said he didn't think he could have gotten it out face to face. He had worried she would be mad, but instead she gave him a tender look and said she wanted to help him.

.   .   .

The message calling him to the principal's office came over the intercom while Henry was sitting in class, texting a friend. His classmates teased him as he left, assuming he was in trouble again. But when he got to the office, he was introduced to a stranger in a suit. The Suffolk County police officer who was stationed in the school, George Politis, told Henry that the man was from the FBI. If Henry wanted to help, Politis said, he should tell the man everything he knew, because the FBI could give him a new identity and relocate him far from Long Island.

The stranger asked Henry to come up with an alias for him. Henry chose the name Tony and the last initial *F*, for *federale*. In reality, Tony was Angel Rivera, a Suffolk County homicide detective detailed to the FBI's Long Island Gang Task Force. With his menacing face and air of authority, he reminded Henry of El Destroyer, the gang leader back home. And unlike Politis, Rivera spoke Spanish. Henry decided to trust him. He knew about the witness protection program from TV shows, and he thought this could be his ticket out of MS-13. But Rivera never offered him a formal agreement.

Rivera had spent the previous month questioning gang members rounded up after the murder of the two girls. They either blew him off or grudgingly negotiated to save themselves from years in prison. But Henry faced no charges; he was volunteering to come forward as an informant. He seemed eager to unburden himself. After the initial meeting they spoke only over the phone or via text. Henry tried to answer whenever Rivera reached out, and apologized when he was unavailable. "I'm sorry I didn't answer you quickly," he wrote one afternoon when he missed a few messages. "It's just that I was sleeping because I work nights."

Rivera texted him looking for leads about the gang's plans and for help connecting gang aliases with real names. The exchanges read like debriefings a teenager in a talkative mood might give a probing parent. One night, Henry complained about two fellow gang members. "One told me, 'You've been in this since you were 12 because you liked it, and now you want to leave?'"

Rivera asked for that boy's given name and gang name. He wanted to know if Henry had any ideas about how to catch him breaking the law. "Do you know if he had a gun?" he asked. "Or if he sells drugs? Are they here illegally?"

Henry kept on going with his story, focused on his own troubles. "Another one of them told me, 'You're useless. I don't know why we keep you around. You don't do anything.' And I said, 'If I'm useless, why don't you let me out?' And he told me, 'Quiet, man. We're never letting you out. We're always going to have you, whether you like it or not.'"

Rivera tried to steer the conversation in a more evidentiary direction. "I'm thinking I'd like to catch them with a gun," he wrote. "Or if you know of anything."

"I'll keep you posted," Henry promised.

"Okay," Rivera responded, "but be cool."

After a few days, Rivera got in touch again: "You don't have to worry about that boy any more." Thanks to the name Henry had provided, the boy had been swept up by Immigration and Customs Enforcement.

Since Trump's election, the Suffolk County Police Department has stepped up its cooperation with ICE, targeting suspected MS-13 members for deportation. Shipping suspects back to Central America is easier and quicker than proving they have broken the law; even if suspects have committed no crime, ICE can petition to have their immigration bail revoked. In effect, it is a repeat of the same failed strategy that led to the creation of MS-13. The gang first spread to El Salvador from Los Angeles amid a wave of deportations in the 1990s that sent members like El Destroyer back to Henry's slum. Now, by deporting children who have come to America seeking escape from MS-13, the Trump administration is only intensifying the cycle that drove them here in the first place.

Last year, under Trump, ICE arrested nearly four times more immigrants simply for being suspected of belonging to MS-13 than it did in 2016. Long Island has been the epicenter of the new initiative, called Operation Matador. Trump and Attorney General Jeff Sessions both delivered major speeches in front of the Suffolk police last year and congratulated them on embracing the administration's strategy. Trump also invited the mother of Kayla Cuevas, the murdered girl who had flashed the Bloods sign at Henry, to his State of the Union address in January. In private, some Long Island detectives and prosecutors grumbled about the ICE partnership, saying it hampers efforts to investigate the gang. But as the wave of arrests attracted federal grants, additional staff, and positive national media attention, Suffolk County effectively began to serve as a local arm of ICE, rounding up immigrant kids for deportation.

·　　　·　　　·

Children's advocates on Long Island started to warn teenagers to avoid the cops. "We can't work with Suffolk County police, because any information they have is going to go straight to ICE," says Feride Castillo, who runs a program for at-risk youth on Long Island. "I tell my immigrant kids all the time not to open their mouths—I don't care what they're promising you."

Henry did his part to aid the federal crackdown on MS-13. In addition to the gang members he reported to Rivera, he shared what he knew about the killings and supplied the names of eleven kids who had been marked for death by the Sailors. That spring, the FBI task force arrested the brothers who led the clique on multiple murder charges.

When Henry learned that his grandfather had died in his sleep in El Salvador, he locked himself in his room and spent the night crying, vowing to do better. He scratched his grandfather's initials into the back of his cellphone as a reminder. He started seeing a therapist. At school, he sat in the front of his classes and spoke up more often. He especially liked history class, where he learned about pre-Columbian tribes that extracted still beating hearts from their sacrificial victims.

Now that he had helped the police, Henry assumed his witness protection papers would be coming through any day. When he turned eighteen, he started telling friends and teachers he trusted that he would soon disappear to California. Then one morning in August, as Henry was making lunch for his shift at the toilet paper factory, the *federales* finally came for him. But they weren't from the FBI or the witness-protection program. They were from ICE. The same unit that Henry had helped to arrest members of

MS-13 was now pursuing a deportation case against him, using the information he had provided as evidence.

Confused, Henry told the agents he was already working with the police. He asked them to call Tony. Instead, after interrogating him, the ICE agents put him on a bus. He watched the Long Island streets he knew disappear, replaced by the highrises of downtown Manhattan, then darkness as the bus was swallowed by a tunnel to New Jersey. He was headed to an ICE detention center full of young men suspected of being MS-13 members—the very same ones he had snitched on.

·   ·   ·

At first, Henry was confident that he would be released from ICE custody in time for the start of his senior year. But as the weeks passed, he fell into a routine of sketching anime characters, watching TV, and looking forward to the days when chicken was served in the jail's cafeteria.

One night, as Henry sat in the TV room watching a reality show about aspiring Miami rappers, a half dozen MS-13 members walked up to him, led by a Brentwood High student who had established himself as the gang's leader on the ward. The boy called him Triste and demanded to see his detention memo.

Every inmate rounded up in ICE's antigang raids is given a memo explaining why the government has pegged him as a member of MS-13. Most are short and vague. They list things like school suspensions, Facebook posts, and statements by anonymous informants. Henry's memo is so specific that it amounts to a signed confession. It lists the details that Henry confided to George Politis, the school's police officer. It quotes his account of the murder he committed back in El Salvador. And most damning, it reveals that he informed on the Sailors to the Suffolk County police. "The subject told SCPD that he has recently had contact with the following confirmed MS-13 members," the memo says, listing the names of El Fantasma and another Sailor. Instead of protecting his identity as an informant, the police and ICE had effectively signed his death warrant.

"He's screwed," says John Oliva, a retired member of the FBI's Long Island Gang Task Force who saw Henry's memo. "At the end of the day, that kid is going to become a statistic. If he wanted out, he should have just moved to another town, lived in a basement apartment with ten other people, and started working his way out."

The MS-13 members who were locked up with Henry suspected that he had been an informant. The only way to clear his name and save his life, the boy from Brentwood warned him, was to produce his detention memo. For weeks, Henry tried to put them off. He told them he was waiting for his lawyer to send it, but that wasn't credible for long. When the boys started coming around to his bed at night to ask about the memo, he signed up to work an overnight shift in the kitchen, drinking weak coffee to stay awake until morning, then lying on his bed during the day trying to fall asleep. Every day he waited for the attack to come. Gang members in the jail routinely got into violent fights, splattering the floor with blood until they were broken up by guards known as *tortugas* because their oversize helmets and heavy armor made them look like turtles.

Finally, sitting cross-legged on his bunk with a piece of paper barely thicker than a tissue, Henry once again decided to scribble a plea for help. This time he addressed it to his lawyer, Bryan Johnson, asking him to put together a fake memo he could show the gang.

"I just need a document saying I was questioned by the FBI but didn't tell them anything," Henry wrote. "The members here have said that if I don't show them my memo, they'll know I'm a rat, and that will be the end of me. They'll greenlight the hunt."

He ended with an apology. "Forgive how bad my handwriting is. It's just that I feel very scared right now."

Johnson was rattled by the letter. He couldn't create a fake memo for Henry, but there was a chance he could get him out of ICE custody by appealing to a federal court. The government has a program that gives green cards to people with criminal records who cooperate with investigators. It is especially intended for immigrants who might be killed back home. Henry could qualify, but he would need someone from law enforcement to confirm that his information had been valuable.

.　　　.　　　.

Johnson texted Rivera, asking him to share what he knew at Henry's asylum hearing, which is slated for April 5. Rivera texted back the names of two boys that Henry had helped get arrested. But he refused to testify, citing concern for his own safety. "My job doesn't allow me to do that," he wrote, "especially in my situation being an enemy of MS-13 and several certain individuals incarcerated for murder." The federal prosecutor overseeing the murder cases involving the Sailors also declined to assist in Henry's defense, as did Politis.

The choice to turn an informant like Henry over to ICE has consequences far beyond his individual case. If gang members can't receive protection in exchange for coming forward with information, police will have almost no means to penetrate the insular world of MS-13. School officials who turned Henry over to the authorities were outraged when they learned he had been trapped in a no man's land between the gang and the law. "They certainly were taking advantage of what he had to offer," says Robert Feliciano, the head of the Suffolk County school board. "You can't just do that and then drop him."

Those who work to get kids out of gangs echo that concern. "Anyone in MS-13 who sees what's going on with this guy, they're not going to want to talk to the cops," says Bob DeSena, founder of the Council for Unity, one of the largest gang-intervention programs in New York. "The one thing you never do—the last thing the police want to do—is send a message that if you cooperate with the police, you're not going to get protection and no one is going to come speak up for you. Rivera, if he wasn't full of shit, should pick up the phone and say, 'Look, this guy helped us.'"

In fact, it appears that Henry's case was mishandled at almost every step along the way. Everyone involved places the blame on someone else. The school says it was required by law to tell the police that Henry was in danger. The police, who told ICE about Henry, blame the feds for trying to deport him. The FBI says that Rivera wasn't officially a member of the task force, even though he was working out of the bureau's office. And ICE says that it didn't know that Henry was an informant. It acknowledges, however, that creating detention memos for kids like Henry puts their lives at risk, and it has decided to end the practice. "That memo was not intended for public consumption," says Rachael Yong Yow, an ICE spokesperson. "You do these memos, and then something like this happens."

One of the gang members that Henry turned over to Rivera, meanwhile, has been released by ICE. Unlike Henry, he did not admit to being a member of MS-13, and ICE was unable to prove it. All told, a quarter of the 200 immigrants rounded up in ICE's antigang operation on Long Island last year have been released because of insufficient evidence. So Henry is marked for death and slated for deportation, while the gang members he helped his handler target go free.

"Just for having talked, all this is happening," Henry says. "They were asking for help, and I gave them all these names. So how am I here?"

.   .   .

Sitting across from me in ICE custody, Henry still looks like a boy. His orange jumpsuit pools at his feet, and he has stenciled "Henry" on his shirtsleeve in graffiti-style writing. He's still getting veiled threats from the boys who want to see his ICE memo. The other day, a fellow gang member told him the bosses were sending killers from Los Angeles to take care of a suspected snitch in New York. Another said he had recently used a machete to carve a suspected informant's lips into a gruesome smile, then buried the body near the Brentwood train tracks.

Henry describes the most horrifying moments of his life in a flat, hyperdetailed way, as if he were watching a movie and narrating the plot. Like many children who have witnessed traumatic events, his mind has recorded the minutest details, but there are huge gaps in the emotional content. One day, he tells me about seeing the gang execute a dirty cop in El Salvador who had tattooed the logo of a rival gang on his inner lip. "They were shouting, 'This is what happens when you work with punks from the other gang.' You could see the bullets going into his chest, his stomach, his arms." When I ask how the killing made him feel, he responds by calculating the number of bullets he thought had blasted apart the victim's body: 235.

Talking about his memories actually seems to ease Henry's fears as he imagines what will happen next. If he is deported, anyone who takes him in would be putting themselves at risk. Back in El Salvador, he watched gang members stake out the homes of suspected traitors then kill their brothers and cousins when they stepped outside. Even if he is granted asylum and returns to Brentwood, the gang will likely kill him unless he gets help relocating.

As he waits in the crowded jail, surrounded by gang members who want to kill him, Henry sometimes lies on his bed with his face hidden and cries. He imagines himself strung up in the same sprawling coconut grove where he killed the trembling man. He has resolved that he will not beg or try to bargain as he has seen others do. "Sometimes I feel like a piece of string being pulled from both ends," he says. "Sometimes, I think it would be better to be dead than to have done the things I've done. I know it would be better never to have talked to anyone."

Sometimes, though, Henry tries to imagine a better future for himself. "If someone out there decided to get involved and give me a chance to start a new life," he says, "I would not waste it." He pictures himself graduating from high school and living by the ocean and fishing off a pier with children of his own. His grandmother would live nearby, so she could hang out with his kids. He would work in construction. Or maybe he would join the army and get to travel the world. Whatever gets him away from the gang, and the *federales*, and allows him to live a little longer.

The Atlantic

FINALIST—REPORTING

Paul Manafort is now best known as the convicted felon who chaired Donald Trump's presidential campaign in the spring and summer of 2016, but Franklin Foer argues in "American Hustler" that Manafort's "personal corruption is less significant, ultimately, than his lifetime role as a corrupter of the American system." The National Magazine Awards judges described this comprehensive account of Manafort's life and career as "an extraordinary synthesis" of earlier reporting and new work. Currently a staff writer at The Atlantic, Foer was the editor of the New Republic from 2006 to 2010, then again from 2012 to 2014. He is the author of How Soccer Explains the World: An Unlikely Theory of Globalization and, more recently, World Without Mind: The Existential Threat of Big Tech. The nomination of "American Hustler" in Reporting was The Atlantic's twentieth in the category since 1971.

Franklin Foer

American Hustler

I. The Wisdom of Friends

The clinic permitted Paul Manafort one ten-minute call each day. And each day, he would use it to ring his wife from Arizona, his voice often soaked in tears. "Apparently he sobs daily," his daughter Andrea, then twenty-nine, texted a friend. During the spring of 2015, Manafort's life had tipped into a deep trough. A few months earlier, he had intimated to his other daughter, Jessica, that suicide was a possibility. He would "be gone forever," she texted Andrea.

His work, the source of the status he cherished, had taken a devastating turn. For nearly a decade, he had counted primarily on a single client, albeit an exceedingly lucrative one. He'd been the chief political strategist to the man who became the president of Ukraine, Viktor Yanukovych, with whom he'd developed a highly personal relationship. Manafort would swim naked with his boss outside his *banya*, play tennis with him at his palace ("Of course, I let him win," Manafort made it known), and generally serve as an arbiter of power in a vast country. One of his deputies, Rick Gates, once boasted to a group of Washington lobbyists, "You have to understand, we've been working in Ukraine a long time, and Paul has a whole separate shadow government structure. . . . In every ministry, he has a guy." Only a small handful of Americans—oil executives, Cold War spymasters—could claim to have ever amassed such influence in a foreign regime. The power had helped fill Manafort's bank accounts; according to his recent indictment, he had tens of millions of dollars stashed in havens like Cyprus and the Grenadines.

Manafort had profited from the sort of excesses that make a country ripe for revolution. And in the early months of 2014, protesters gathered on the Maidan, Kiev's Independence Square, and swept his patron from power. Fearing for his life, Yanukovych sought protective shelter in Russia. Manafort avoided any harm by keeping a careful distance from the enflamed city. But in his Kiev office, he'd left behind a safe filled with papers that he would not have wanted to fall into public view or the wrong hands.

Money, which had always flowed freely to Manafort and which he'd spent more freely still, soon became a problem. After the revolution, Manafort cadged some business from former minions of the ousted president, the ones who hadn't needed to run for their lives. But he complained about unpaid bills and, at age sixty-six, scoured the world (Hungary, Uganda, Kenya) for fresh clients, hustling without any apparent luck. Andrea noted her father's "tight cash flow state," texting Jessica, "He is suddenly extremely cheap." His change in spending habits was dampening her wedding plans. For her "wedding weekend kick off" party, he suggested scaling back the menu to hot dogs and eliminated a line item for ice.

He seemed unwilling, or perhaps unable, to access his offshore accounts; an FBI investigation scrutinizing his work in Ukraine had begun not long after Yanukovych's fall. Meanwhile, a Russian oligarch named Oleg Deripaska had been after Manafort to explain what had happened to an $18.9 million investment in a Ukrainian company that Manafort had claimed to have made on his behalf.

Manafort had known Deripaska for years, so he surely understood the oligarch's history. Deripaska had won his fortune by prevailing in the so-called aluminum wars of the 1990s, a corpse-filled struggle, one of the most violent of all the competitions for dominance in a post-Soviet industry. In 2006, the U.S. State Department had revoked Deripaska's visa, reportedly out of concern over his ties to organized crime (which he has denied). Despite Deripaska's reputation, or perhaps because of it, Manafort had been dodging the oligarch's attempts to contact him. As Deripaska's lawyers informed a court in 2014 while attempting to claw back their client's money, "It appears that Paul Manafort and Rick Gates have simply disappeared."

.   .   .

Nine months after the Ukrainian revolution, Manafort's family life also went into crisis. The nature of his home life can be observed in detail because Andrea's text messages were obtained last year by a "hacktivist collective"—most likely Ukrainians furious with Manafort's meddling in their country—which posted the purloined material on the dark web. The texts extend over four years (2012–2016) and 6 million words. Manafort has previously confirmed that his daughter's phone was hacked and acknowledged the authenticity of some texts quoted by *Politico* and the *New York Times.* Manafort and Andrea both declined to comment on this article. Jessica could not be reached for comment.

Collectively, the texts show a sometimes fraught series of relationships, by turns loving and manipulative. Manafort was generous with his family financially—he'd invested millions in Jessica's film projects and millions more in her now-ex-husband's real-estate ventures. But when he called home in tears or threatened suicide in the spring of 2015, he was pleading for his marriage. The previous November, as the cache of texts shows, his daughters had caught him in an affair with a woman more than thirty years his junior. It was an expensive relationship. According to the text messages, Manafort had rented his mistress a

$9,000-a-month apartment in Manhattan and a house in the Hamptons, not far from his own. He had handed her an American Express card, which she'd used to good effect. "I only go to luxury restaurants," she once declared on a friend's fledgling podcast, speaking expansively about her photo posts on social media: caviar, lobster, haute cuisine.

The affair had been an unexpected revelation. Manafort had nursed his wife after a horseback-riding accident had nearly killed her in 1997. "I always marveled at how patient and devoted he was with her during that time," an old friend of Manafort's told me. But after the exposure of his infidelity, his wife had begun to confess simmering marital issues to her daughters. Manafort had committed to couples therapy but, the texts reveal, that hadn't prevented him from continuing his affair. Because he clumsily obscured his infidelity—and because his mistress posted about their travels on Instagram—his family caught him again, six months later. He entered the clinic in Arizona soon after, according to Andrea's texts. "My dad," she wrote, "is in the middle of a massive emotional breakdown."

· · ·

By the early months of 2016, Manafort was back in greater Washington, his main residence and the place where he'd begun his career as a political consultant and lobbyist. But his attempts at rehabilitation—of his family life, his career, his sense of self-worth—continued. He began to make a different set of calls. As he watched the U.S. presidential campaign take an unlikely turn, he saw an opportunity, and he badly wanted in. He wrote Donald Trump a crisp memo listing all the reasons he would be an ideal campaign consigliere—and then implored mutual friends to tout his skills to the ascendant candidate.

Shortly before the announcement of his job inside Trump's campaign, Manafort touched base with former colleagues to let them know of his professional return. He exuded his characteristic confidence, but they surprised him with doubts and worries. Throughout his long career, Manafort had advised powerful men—U.S. senators and foreign supreme commanders, imposing generals and presidents-for-life. He'd learned how to soothe them, how to bend their intransigent wills with his calmly delivered, diligently researched arguments. But Manafort simply couldn't accept the wisdom of his friends, advice that he surely would have dispensed to anyone with a history like his own—the imperative to shy away from unnecessary attention.

His friends, like all Republican political operatives of a certain age, could recite the legend of Paul Manafort, which they did with fascination, envy, and occasional disdain. When Manafort had arrived in Washington in the 1970s, the place reveled in its shabby glories, most notably a self-satisfied sense of high duty. Wealth came in the form of Georgetown mansions, with their antique imperfections and worn rugs projecting power so certain of itself, it needn't shout. But that old boarding-school establishment wasn't Manafort's style. As he made a name for himself, he began to dress differently than the Brooks Brothers crowd on K Street, more European, with funky, colorful blazers and collarless shirts. If he entertained the notion, say, of moving his backyard swimming pool a few feet, nothing stopped him from the expense. Colleagues, amused by his sartorial quirks and his cosmopolitan lifestyle, referred to him as "the Count of Monte Cristo."

His acts of rebellion were not merely aesthetic. Manafort rewrote the rules of his adopted city. In the early eighties, he created a consulting firm that ignored the conventions that had previously governed lobbying. When it came to taking on new clients, he was uninhibited by moral limits. In 2016, his friends might not have known the specifics of his Cyprus accounts, all the alleged off-the-books payments to him captured in Cyrillic ledgers in Kiev. But they knew enough to believe that he could never sustain the exposure that comes with running a presidential campaign in the age of opposition research and aggressive media. "The risks couldn't have been more obvious," one friend who attempted to dissuade him from the job told me. But in his frayed state, these warnings failed to register.

When Paul Manafort officially joined the Trump campaign, on March 28, 2016, he represented a danger not only to himself but to the political organization he would ultimately run. A lifetime of foreign adventures didn't just contain scandalous stories; it evinced the character of a man who would very likely commandeer the campaign to serve his own interests, with little concern for the collective consequences.

Over the decades, Manafort had cut a trail of foreign money and influence into Washington then built that trail into a superhighway. When it comes to serving the interests of the world's autocrats, he's been a great innovator. His indictment in October after investigation by Special Counsel Robert Mueller alleges money laundering, false statements, and other acts of personal corruption. (He has pleaded not guilty to all charges.) But Manafort's role in Mueller's broader narrative remains carefully guarded and unknown to the public. And his personal corruption is less significant, ultimately, than his lifetime role as a corrupter of the American system. That he would be accused of helping a foreign power subvert American democracy is a fitting coda to his life's story.

II. The Young Man and His Machine

In the spring of 1977, a twenty-eight-year-old Paul Manafort sat at a folding table in a hotel suite in Memphis. Photos from that time show him with a Tom Selleck mustache and meaningful sideburns. He was surrounded by phones that he'd specially installed for the weekend. The desk held his copious binders, which he called "whip books." Eight hundred delegates had gathered to elect a new leader of the Young Republicans organization, and Manafort, a budding kingmaker, had compiled a dossier on each one. Those whip books provided the basis for deal making. To wheedle and cajole delegates, it helped to have an idea of what job they wanted in return for their support.

Control over the Young Republicans—a political and social network for professionals ages eighteen to forty—was a genuine prize in those days. Presidential hopefuls sought to harness the group. This was still the era of brokered presidential conventions, and Young Republicans could descend in numbers sufficient to dominate the state meetings that selected delegates. In 1964, the group's efforts had arguably secured Barry Goldwater the GOP nomination; by the seventies every Republican aspirant understood its potency. The attention paid by party elders yielded opportunities for Young Republican leaders. Patronage flowed in their direction. To seize the organization was to come into possession of a baby Tammany.

In Memphis, Manafort was working on behalf of his friend Roger Stone, now best known as a pioneer in opposition research and a promiscuous purveyor of conspiracy theories. He managed Stone's candidacy for chairman of the group. Stone, then twenty-four, reveled in the fact that he'd received his political education during Richard Nixon's reelection campaign in 1972; he even admitted to playing dirty tricks to benefit his idol. Stone and Manafort had met through College Republicans. They shared a home state, an affection for finely tailored power suits, and a deeper love of power itself. Together, they campaigned with gleeful ruthlessness.

Even at this early stage in his career, Manafort had acquired a remarkable skill for managing a gathering of great size. He knew how to command an army of loyalists, who took his orders via walkie-talkie. And he knew how to put on a show. In Memphis that year, he rented a Mississippi River paddleboat for a booze cruise and dispatched his whips to work over wavering delegates within its floating confines. To the Young Republican elite, the faction Manafort controlled carried a name that conveyed his expectation of unfailing loyalty: the Team. And in the face of the Team's prowess, Stone's rival eventually quit the race, midconvention. "It's all been scripted in the back room," he complained.

Manafort had been bred for politics. While he was in high school, his father, Paul Manafort Sr., became the mayor of New Britain, Connecticut, and Manafort Jr. gravitated toward the action—joining a mock city council, campaigning for the gubernatorial candidate Thomas Meskill as part of his Kiddie Corps. For college and law school, he chose Georgetown University, a taxi ride from the big time.

In the seventies, the big time was embodied by James A. Baker III, the shrewdest Republican insider of his generation. During the epic Republican National Convention of 1976, Manafort holed up with Baker in a trailer outside the Kemper Arena, in Kansas City, Missouri. They attempted to protect Gerald Ford's renomination bid in the face of Ronald Reagan's energetic challenge; Manafort wrangled delegates on Baker's behalf. From Baker, he learned the art of ostentatious humility, how to use the knife to butter up and then stab in the back. "He was studying at the feet of the master," Jeff Bell, a Reagan campaign aide, remembers.

By the late seventies, Manafort and Stone could foresee Ronald Reagan's ascendance, and both intended to become players in his 1980 campaign. For Manafort, this was an audacious volteface. By flipping his allegiance from the former Ford faction, he provoked suspicion among conservatives, who viewed him as a rank opportunist. There was little denying that the Young Republicans made an ideal vehicle for his ambitions.

These ambitions left a trail of damage, including an Alabama lawyer named Neal Acker. During the Memphis convention, Acker had served as a loyal foot soldier on the Team, organizing the southern delegates on Stone's behalf. In return, Manafort and Stone had promised to throw the Team behind Acker's campaign to replace Stone as the head of the Young Republicans two years later, in 1979. Manafort would manage the campaign himself.

But as the moment of Acker's coronation approached, Manafort suddenly conditioned his plan. If Acker wanted the job, he had to swear loyalty to Reagan. When Acker ultimately balked—he wanted to stay neutral—Manafort turned on him with fury, "an unprecedented 11th-hour move," the Associated Press reported. In the week leading up to the 1979 Young Republicans convention, Manafort and Stone set out to destroy Acker's candidacy. At Manafort's urging, the delegates who were pledged to Acker bolted—and Manafort took over his opponent's campaign. In a bravura projection of power that no one in the Reagan campaign could miss, Manafort swung the vote sharply against Acker, 465 to 180. "It was one of the great fuck jobs," a Manafort whip told me recently.

Not long after that, Stone and Manafort won the crucial positions in the Reagan operation that they'd coveted. Stone directed the campaign in the Northeast, Manafort in the South. The campaign had its share of infighting; both men survived factional schisms and purges. "They were known as the Young Republican whizzes," Jeff Bell told me. Their performance positioned them for inner-sanctum jobs in the Reagan administration, but they had even grander plans.

III. The Firm

During the years that followed World War II, Washington's most effective lobbyists transcended the transactional nature of their profession. Men such as Abe Fortas, Clark Clifford, Bryce Harlow, and Thomas Corcoran were known not as grubby mercenaries but as elegant avatars of a permanent establishment, lauded as "wise men." Lobbying hardly carried a stigma because there was so little of it. When the legendary lawyer Tommy Boggs registered himself as a lobbyist, in 1967, his name was only sixty-fourth on the active list. Businesses simply didn't consider lobbying a necessity. Three leading political scientists had studied the profession in 1963 and concluded: "When we look at the typical lobby, we find its opportunities to maneuver are sharply limited, its staff mediocre, and its typical problem not the influencing of Congressional votes but finding the clients and contributors to enable it to survive at all."

On the cusp of the Reagan era, Republican lobbyists were particularly enfeebled. Generations of Democratic majorities in Congress had been terrible for business. The scant tribe of Republican lobbyists working the cloakrooms included alumni of the Nixon and Ford administrations; operating under the shame-inducing cloud of Watergate, they were disinclined toward either ambition or aggression.

This was the world that brash novices like Manafort and Stone quickly came to dominate. The Reagan administration represented a break with the old Republican establishment. After the long expansion of the regulatory state, business finally had a political partner eager to dismantle it—which generated unprecedented demand for lobbyists. Manafort could convincingly claim to know the new administration better than anyone. During its transition to power, he was the personnel coordinator in the Office of Executive Management, which meant that he'd stacked the incoming government with his people. Along with Stone and Charlie Black, another veteran of the Young Republican wars, he set up a firm, Black, Manafort and Stone, which soon compiled an imposing client list: Bethlehem Steel, the Tobacco Institute, Johnson & Johnson, Trans World Airlines.

Whereas other firms had operated in specialized niches— lobbying, consulting, public relations—Black, Manafort and Stone bundled all those services under one roof, a deceptively simple move that would eventually help transform Washington. *Time* magazine deemed the operation "the ultimate supermarket of influence peddling." Fred Wertheimer, a good-government advocate, described this expansive approach as "institutionalized conflict of interest."

The linkage of lobbying to political consulting—the creation of what's now known as a double-breasted operation—was the real breakthrough. Manafort's was the first lobbying firm to also house political consultants. (Legally, the two practices were divided into different companies, but they shared the same founding partners and the same office space.) One venture would run campaigns; the other would turn around and lobby the politicians whom their colleagues had helped elect. The consulting side hired the hard-edged operative Lee Atwater, notorious for pioneering race-baiting tactics on behalf of Strom Thurmond. "We're getting into servicing what we sell," Atwater told his friends. Just as imagined, the firm's political clients (Jesse Helms, Phil Gramm, Arlen Specter) became reliable warhorses when the firm needed them to promote the agendas of its corporate clients. With this evolution of the profession, the effectiveness and influence of lobbying grew in tandem.

In 1984, the firm reached across the aisle. It made a partner of Peter Kelly, a former finance chairman of the Democratic National Committee, who had earned the loyalty of lawmakers by raising millions for their campaigns. Some members of the firm worked for Democratic Senate candidates in Louisiana, Vermont, and Florida, even as operatives down the hall worked for their Republican foes. "People said, 'It's un-American,'" Kelly told me. "'They can't lose. They have both sides.' I kept saying, 'How is it un-American to win?'" This sense of invincibility permeated the lobbying operation too. When Congress passed tax-reform legislation in 1986, the firm managed to get one special rule inserted that saved Chrysler-Mitsubishi $58 million; it wrangled another clause that reaped Johnson & Johnson $38 million in savings. *Newsweek* pronounced the firm "the hottest shop in town."

Demand for its services rose to such heights that the firm engineered a virtual lock on the 1988 Republican primary. Atwater became the chief strategist for George H. W. Bush; Black worked with Bob Dole; Stone advised Jack Kemp. A congressional staffer joked to *Time*, "Why have primaries for the nomination? Why not have the candidates go over to Black, Manafort and Stone and argue it out?" Manafort cultivated this perception. In response to a questionnaire in the *Washington Times*, he declared Machiavelli the person he would most like to meet.

Despite his young age, Manafort projected the sort of confidence that inspires others to have confidence, a demeanor often likened to that of a news anchor. "He is authoritative, and you never see a chink in the armor," one of his longtime deputies, Philip Griffin, told me. Manafort wrote well, especially in proposals to prospective clients, and excelled at thinking strategically. Name-dropping never substituted for concrete steps that would bolster a client. "If politics has done anything, it's taught us to treat everything as a campaign," he once declared. He toiled for clients with unflagging intensity. His wife once quipped, according to the text messages, that Andrea was conceived between conference calls. He "hung up the phone, looked at his watch, and said, 'Okay, we have 20 minutes until the next one,'" Andrea wrote to her then-fiancé.

The firm exuded the decadent spirit of the 1980s. Each year, it hosted a golf outing called Boodles, after the gin brand. "It would have to move almost every year, because we weren't invited back," John Donaldson, an old friend of Manafort's who worked at the firm, says. "A couple of women in the firm complained that they weren't ever invited. I told them they didn't want to be." As the head of the firm's "social committee," Manafort would supply a theme for the annual gatherings. His masterwork was a three-year progression: "Excess," followed by "Exceed Excess," capped by "Excess Is Best."

Partners at the firm let it be known to the *Washington Post* that they each intended to take home at least $450,000 in 1986 (a little more than $1 million today). "All of a sudden they came into a lot of money, and I don't think any of them were used to earning the money that we were earning," Kelly said. Senior partners were given luxury cars and a membership to the country club of their choosing. Manafort would fly the Concorde to Europe and back as if it were the Acela to New York. "I must confess," Atwater swooned to the *Washington Post*, "after four years on a government payroll, I'm delighted with my new life style."

The firm hired kids straight out of college—"wheel men" in the office vernacular—to drive the partners around town. When Roger Stone's old hero, Richard Nixon, came to Washington, the wheel men would shuttle him about.

Many of these young associates would eventually climb the firm's ladder and were often dispatched to manage campaigns on the firm's behalf. Climbing the ladder, however, in most cases required passing what came to be known as Manafort's "loyalty tests"—challenging tasks that strayed outside the boundaries of standard professional commitment and demonstrated the control that Manafort expected to exert over the associates' lives. At the last minute, he might ask a staffer to entertain his visiting law-school buddies, never mind that the staffer had never met them before. For one Saint Patrick's Day party, he gave two junior staffers twenty-four hours to track down a plausible impersonator of Billy Barty, the three-foot-nine-inch actor who made movies with Mickey Rooney and Chevy Chase—which they did. "This was in the days before the internet," one of them told me. "Can you imagine how hard that was?"

IV. Man of the World

By the 1990s, the double-digit list of registered lobbyists that Tommy Boggs had joined back in 1967 had swelled to more than 10,000. Black, Manafort, Stone and Kelly had greatly abetted that transformation, and stood to profit from the rising flood of corporate money into the capital. But by then, domestic politics had begun to feel a little small, a bit too unexotic, for Paul Manafort, whom Charlie Black described to me as a self-styled "adventurer."

Manafort had long befriended ambitious young diplomats at the trailhead to power, including Prince Bandar bin Sultan Al Saud, then the Saudi ambassador to Washington. When Bandar attended the 1984 Republican National Convention, Manafort dedicated a small group of advance men to smooth his way. Manafort arranged for Bandar to arrive at the presidential entrance, then had him whisked to seats in the vice-presidential box.

Foreign lobbying had certainly existed before the eighties, but it was limited in scale and operated under a penumbra of suspicion. Just before World War II, Congress had passed the Foreign Agents Registration Act, largely in response to the campaigns orchestrated by Ivy Lee, an American publicist hired by the German Dye Trust to soften the image of the Third Reich. Congress hadn't outlawed influence peddling on behalf of foreign interests, but the practice sat on the far fringes of K Street.

Paul Manafort helped change that. The Reagan administration had remade the contours of the Cold War, stepping up the fight against communism worldwide by funding and training guerrilla armies and right-wing military forces, such as the Nicaraguan contras and the Afghan mujahideen. This strategy of military outsourcing—the Reagan Doctrine—aimed to overload the Soviet Union with confrontations that it couldn't sustain.

All of the money Congress began spending on anticommunist proxies represented a vast opportunity. Iron-fisted dictators and scruffy commandants around the world hoped for a share of the largesse. To get it, they needed help refining their image so that Congress wouldn't look too hard at their less-than-liberal tendencies. Other lobbyists sought out authoritarian clients, but none did so with the focused intensity of Black, Manafort, Stone and

Kelly. The firm would arrange for image-buffing interviews on American news programs; it would enlist allies in Congress to unleash money. Back home, it would help regimes acquire the whiff of democratic legitimacy that would bolster their standing in Washington.

The firm won clients because it adeptly marketed its ties to the Reagan administration and then the George H. W. Bush administration after that. In one proposal, reported in the *New York Times* in 1988, the firm advertised its "personal relationships" with officials and promised to "upgrade" back channels "in the economic and foreign policy spheres." No doubt it helped to have a friend in James Baker, especially after he became the secretary of state under Bush. "Baker would send the firm clients," Kelly remembered. "He wanted us to help lead these guys in a better direction."

But moral improvement never really figured into Manafort's calculus. "Generally speaking, I would focus on how to bring the client in sync with western European or American values," Kelly told me. "Paul took the opposite approach." (Kelly and Manafort have not spoken in recent years; the former supported Hillary Clinton in the last presidential campaign.) In her memoir, Riva Levinson, a managing director at the firm from 1985 to 1995, wrote that when she protested to her boss that she needed to believe in what she was doing, Manafort told her that it would "be my downfall in this business." The firm's client base grew to include dictatorial governments in Nigeria, Kenya, Zaire, Equatorial Guinea, Saudi Arabia, and Somalia, among others. Manafort's firm was a primary subject of scorn in a 1992 report issued by the Center for Public Integrity called "The Torturers' Lobby."

The firm's international business accelerated when the Philippines became a client, in 1985. President Ferdinand Marcos desperately needed a patina of legitimacy: the 1983 assassination of the chief opposition leader, Benigno Aquino Jr., had imperiled U.S. congressional support for his regime. Marcos hired Manafort to lift his image; his wife, Imelda, personally delivered an initial payment of $60,000 to the firm while on a trip to the States. When Marcos called a snap election to prove his democratic bona fides in 1986, Manafort told *Time*, "What we've tried to do is make it more of a Chicago-style election and not Mexico's." The quip was honest, if unintentionally so. In the American political lexicon, Chicago-style elections were generally synonymous with mass voter fraud. The late pollster Warren Mitofsky traveled to the Philippines with CBS News to set up and conduct an exit poll for the election. When he returned, he told the political scientist Sam Popkin the story of how a representative of Manafort's firm had asked him, "What sort of margin might make a Marcos victory legitimate?" The implication was clear, Popkin told me: "How do we rig this thing and still satisfy the Americans?"

The firm's most successful right-wing makeover was of the Angolan guerrilla leader Jonas Savimbi, a Maoist turned anticommunist insurgent, whose army committed atrocities against children and conscripted women into sexual slavery. During the general's 1986 trip to New York and Washington, Manafort and his associates created what one magazine called "Savimbi Chic." Dressed in a Nehru suit, Savimbi was driven around in a stretch limousine and housed in the Waldorf-Astoria and the Grand Hotel, projecting an image of refinement. The firm had assiduously prepared him for the mission, sending him monthly reports on the political climate in Washington. According to the *Washington Post*, "He was meticulously coached on everything from how to answer his critics to how to compliment his patrons." Savimbi emerged from his tour as a much-championed "freedom fighter." When the neoconservative icon Jeane Kirkpatrick introduced Savimbi at the American Enterprise Institute, she declared that he was a "linguist, philosopher, poet, politician, warrior . . . one of the few authentic heroes of our time."

This was a racket—Savimbi paid the firm $600,000 in 1985 alone—that Black, Manafort, Stone and Kelly did its best to keep alive; the firm's own business was tied to Savimbi's continued rebellion against Angola's leftist regime. As the country stood on the brink of peace talks in the late eighties, after nearly fifteen years of bloody civil war, the firm helped secure fresh batches of arms for its client, emboldening Savimbi to push forward with his military campaign. Former senator Bill Bradley wrote in his memoir, "When Gorbachev pulled the plug on Soviet aid to the Angolan government, we had absolutely no reason to persist in aiding Savimbi. But by then he had hired an effective Washington lobbying firm." The war continued for more than a decade, killing hundreds of thousands of Angolans.

V. The Family Business

"Paul's not especially ideological," his former partner Charlie Black told me recently. Many of Manafort's colleagues at Black, Manafort, Stone and Kelly professed to believe in the conservative catechism. Words like *freedom* and *liberty* flowed through their everyday musings. But Manafort seldom spoke of first principles or political ideals. He descends from a different kind of political lineage, and in his formative experience one can see the makings of his worldview.

Back in the sixties, Manafort's hometown, New Britain, Connecticut, was known as Hardware City. It housed the factory that turned out Stanley tools and was a tangle of ethnic enclaves—Poles, Italians, Irish, Ukrainians. Nancy Johnson, who served New Britain in Congress, told me that when she arrived in the city during those years, she couldn't believe how little it interacted with the outside world. "It was a small city and very ingrown. When my kids were in high school, the number of their classmates who hadn't been to Hartford was stunning." Hartford, the state capital, is a fifteen-minute drive from New Britain.

In 1919, not long after the Manaforts emigrated from Naples, the family founded a demolition company, New Britain House Wrecking, which eventually became Manafort Brothers, a force in local construction. When Manafort's father, Paul Sr., ran for mayor in 1965, he was a lonely Republican attempting to seize a blue bastion. But he had the schmoozing gene, as well as an unmistakable fierceness. Paul Carver, a former New Britain city council member and a protégé of the old man, told me, "It was like going to the bar with your grandfather. He would stick his hand out and buy a round of drinks. He knew almost everybody in town." Paul Jr., known as P.J. to his friends, idolized his dad, plunging himself into the campaign, whose success he would decades later describe as "magic." Over the years, he would remain a devoted son. All the partners in his firm came to know his father, running into him at parties that P.J. hosted in his Mount Vernon, Virginia, home. "He was dedicated to him," Nancy Johnson told me.

The elder Manafort's outsize capacity for charm made him the sort of figure whose blemishes tend to be wiped from public memory. But in 1981, he was charged with perjury for testimony that he had provided in a municipal corruption investigation. New Britain police had been accused of casting a blind eye toward illegal gambling in the city—and of tampering with evidence to protect Joseph "Pippi" Guerriero, a member of the DeCavalcante crime family.

Several investigations into the tampering drilled through New Britain's rotten government. The most devastating report came from Palmer McGee, a Hartford lawyer hired by New Britain to sort through its muck. In his findings, he pointed a finger straight at Manafort Sr., calling him the person "most at fault." According to the testimony of a whistle-blower, Manafort had flatly announced that he wanted to hire someone "flexible" to manage his personnel office, a place that would "not [be] 100 percent by the rules." The whistle-blower also testified that he had delivered an envelope to Manafort's home containing the answers to the exam that aspiring police officers had to pass—and that Manafort had given it to two candidates via a relative. Manafort never denied receiving the envelope but insisted that he'd merely asked for "boning-up materials."

A statute of limitations precluded prosecutors from filing charges against Manafort for the alleged crime of test fixing—and ultimately he was never convicted of perjury. But his arrest caused the *Hartford Courant* to compile a list of dealings that reflected badly on him: "Throughout his more than twenty years in public life, he has been the focus of controversy, and several accusations of wrongdoing." The litany includes a complaint with the Department of Housing and Urban Development accusing him of steering contracts to Manafort Brothers, whose stock he still owned while mayor. When investors from Florida built a jai alai arena in Bridgeport—using the Teamsters' pension fund to finance the project—Manafort had "improperly" finagled its environmental permit. His family business had then inflated the fees for its work on the arena so that cash could be kicked back to the Teamsters. (The business admitted to inflating its fees, but a grand jury declined to issue an indictment.) Even before this scandal broke, a former mayor of New Britain blasted Manafort for behavior that "violates the very essence of morality."

Conventional wisdom suggests that the temptations of Washington, D.C., corrupt all the idealists, naïfs, and ingénues who settle there. But what if that formulation gets the causation backward? What if it took an outsider to debase the capital and create the so-called swamp? When Paul Manafort Jr. broke the rules, when he operated outside of a moral code, he was really following the example he knew best. As he later said of his work with his father in an interview with a local Connecticut paper, "Some of the skills that I learned there I still use today. . . . That's where I cut my teeth."

VI. Al Assir

By the late 1980s, Manafort had a new friend from abroad, whom he mentioned to his partners more than any other, an arms dealer from Lebanon named Abdul Rahman Al Assir. "His name kept popping up," Peter Kelly remembered. While Al Assir never rated much attention in the American press, he had a familial connection who did. He was, for a time, the brother-in-law of the Saudi arms dealer Adnan Khashoggi, the middleman used in the arms-for-hostages scheme that became the Iran-Contra scandal. In the early eighties, Khashoggi was worth $4 billion; his biography, published in 1986, was titled *The Richest Man in the World*. At the height of his wealth, Khashoggi spent $250,000 a day to maintain his lifestyle—which reportedly included a dozen houses, 1,000 suits, a $70 million yacht, and a customized airplane, which has been described as a "flying Las Vegas discotheque."

Al Assir was the Khashoggi empire's representative in Spain and a broker of big weapons sales to African armies. He'd ensconced himself among the rich and famous, the set that skied in Gstaad, Switzerland, and summered in the south of France. The London-based Arabic-language magazine *Sourakia* wrote, "The miracle of Al Assir is that he will have lunch with Don Juan Carlos [the king of Spain], dinner with Hassan II [the king of Morocco], and breakfast the next day with Felipe González [the prime minister of Spain]."

Manafort suggested to his partners that Al Assir might help connect the firm to clients around the world. He wanted to increase the firm's global reach. Manafort's exploration of the outermost moral frontiers of the influence business had already exposed him to kleptocrats, thugs, and other dubious characters. But none of these relationships imprinted themselves more deeply than his friendship and entrepreneurial partnership with Al Assir. By the nineties, the two had begun to put together big deals. One of the more noteworthy was an arms sale they helped broker between France and Pakistan, lubricated by bribes and kickbacks involving high-level officials in both countries, that eventually led to murder allegations.

It all arguably began with a 1993 dinner hosted by Manafort in his Virginia home and attended by Pakistan's prime minister, Benazir Bhutto. Bhutto had just returned to power after three years in the opposition, and Manafort badly wanted her business. She knew of him as a skilled manipulator of public opinion, and throughout the meal, Manafort displayed his most strategic, most charming self. One former Pakistani official who attended the dinner told me that Bhutto came away determined to make use of his services. She suggested that Manafort work with the Pakistani intelligence service. Spooks in Islamabad had observed the international rush to hire Washington lobbyists, and they had been clamoring for one of their own.

At about that same time, Pakistan was looking to upgrade its submarine fleet, and European arms contractors raced to hawk their wares. In the end, France's state-owned manufacturer won the contract—and Al Assir was added as an intermediary at the last minute. An ensuing scandal that is still unfolding, some twenty years later, would entangle both Al Assir and Manafort. It entailed alleged kickbacks into the 1995 presidential campaign of Édouard Balladur, apparently arranged by the French defense minister. Al Assir seems to have been a key conduit of the kickbacks. Years later, in 2002, a car bomb went off in Karachi, killing eleven French naval engineers in transit to the shipyard where the submarines were being assembled, along with three Pakistanis. One theory, fervently supported by some of the engineers' families, holds that the bombing was orchestrated by Pakistani officials who were disgruntled that the bribes promised to *them* as part of the deal had never arrived.

Manafort was not a central figure in this scandal and was never charged with any wrongdoing. But as the former Pakistani official told me, "He was an introducer—and he received a fee for his part." Documents show that Manafort earned at least $272,000 as a consultant to the Balladur campaign, although, as Manafort later conceded to French investigators, it was Al Assir who actually paid him. (Balladur has denied any wrongdoing and doesn't recall Manafort working for him. Al Assir could not be reached for comment on this story.)

Manafort and Al Assir were more than business partners. "They were very brotherly," one mutual acquaintance of theirs told me. Manafort took Al Assir as his guest to George H. W. Bush's inauguration, in 1989. When Al Assir and his second wife had a child, Manafort became the godfather. Their families vacationed together near Cannes. Al Assir introduced Manafort to an aristocratic world that exceeded anything he had ever known. "There's money, and there's really big money," a friend of Manafort's told me. "Paul became aware of the difference between making $300,000 and $5 million. He discovered the south of France. Al Assir would show him how to live that life."

Colleagues at Black, Manafort, Stone and Kelly noticed changes that accompanied the flowering of the friendship. Manafort's sartorial style began to pay homage to Al Assir, with flourishes of the European dandy. Suddenly he started wearing unconventional shirts and suede loafers without socks. In the firm's early years, Manafort had been a fixture of the office, a general presiding over his headquarters. But now he frequently flew off to France or Spain, collaborating with Al Assir on projects that remained a mystery to his subordinates, and even to his partners. "Paul went off on different foreign things that none of us knew about," Peter Kelly told me.

Manafort's lifestyle came to feature opulent touches that stood out amid the relative fustiness of Washington. When Andrea expressed an interest in horseback riding, Manafort bought a farm near Palm Beach then stocked it with specially bred horses imported from Ireland, which required a full-time staff to tend. John Donaldson, Manafort's friend, recalls, "He was competing with the Al Assirs of the world—and he wanted to live in that lifestyle."

There were always suspicions among Manafort's colleagues in the firm that he was making money for himself without regard for his partners. Al Assir's occasional appearance in the international press lent these suspicions weight. One deal brokered by Al Assir helped crash a private bank in Lisbon. In 2002, he and Manafort persuaded the bank to invest 57 million euros in a Puerto Rican biometrics company. According to reporting by the Portuguese newspaper *Observador*, Manafort was the lead American investor in the company; his involvement helped justify the bank's investment, despite evidence of the company's faulty products and lax accounting. Al Assir is alleged to have extracted bloated commissions from the deal and to have pocketed some of the bank's loans. Manafort reportedly made $1.5 million selling his shares of the biometrics firm before the company eventually came tumbling down.

Stories about Manafort's slipperiness have acquired mythic status. In the summer of 2016, *Politico*'s Kenneth Vogel, now with the *New York Times*, wrote a rigorous exegesis of a long-standing rumor: Manafort was said to have walked away with $10 million in cash from Ferdinand Marcos, money he promised he would deliver to Ronald Reagan's reelection campaign (which itself would have been illegal). Vogel relied in part on the 1996 memoir of Ed Rollins, a Republican consultant and Reagan's reelection-campaign director. In the book, Rollins recounted a dinner-party conversation with a member of the Filipino congress who claimed to have personally given a suitcase of cash to a "well-known Washington power lobbyist" involved in the Marcos campaign. Rollins would neither confirm nor deny that the lobbyist was Manafort, though his description doesn't leave much uncertainty, and he conceded in an e-mail that "it's a pretty good guess." Rollins admits in his book to being "stunned" by what he heard—"not in a state of total disbelief, though, because I knew the lobbyist well and I had no doubt the money was now in some offshore bank." This irked Rollins greatly: "I ran the [Reagan] campaign for $75,000 a year, and this guy got $10 million in cash."

Manafort has always denied Rollins's insinuation—"old stuff that never had any legs," he told Vogel. And as a practical matter, it's hard to imagine that anyone could stuff $10 million in a suitcase. Still, Vogel found a raft of circumstantial evidence that suggested the plausibility of the tale. When I asked Manafort's former colleagues about the apocrypha, they couldn't confirm the story. But some didn't struggle to imagine it might be true, either. Even though John Donaldson doubts the veracity of the tale, he told me that it persists because it reflects Manafort's ethics. "I know how Paul would view it. Paul would sit there and say, 'These guys can't get access to Reagan. I can get them access to Reagan. They want to give $10 million to Reagan. Reagan can't take $10 million. I'll take the $10 million. They think they'll be getting their influence. Everybody's happy.'"

Another alumnus of Manafort's firm answered my questions about the Marcos money with an anecdote. After the election of George H. W. Bush, Black, Manafort, Stone and Kelly agreed to help organize the inauguration festivities. The firm commissioned a company from Rhode Island to sell memorabilia on the parade route—T-shirts, buttons, and the like. After crews had taken down the reviewing stand and swept up the debris, the alumnus recalled, a vendor showed up in the office with a bag full of cash. To the disbelief of his colleague, Manafort had arranged to take his own cut. "It was a Paul tax," the former employee told me. "I guess he needed a new deck. But this was classic: Somebody else does the work, and he walks away with the bag of cash."

Colleagues suspected the worst about Manafort because they had observed his growing mania for accumulating property, how he'd bought second, third, and fourth homes. "He would buy a house without ever seeing it," one former colleague told me. His Hamptons estate came with a putting green, a basketball court, a pool, and gardens. "He believed that suckers stay out of debt," the colleague told me. His unrestrained spending and pile of debt required a perpetual search for bigger paydays and riskier ventures.

In 1991, Black, Manafort, Stone and Kelly was purchased by the mega-public-affairs firm Burson-Marsteller, the second-largest agency in the world. It was a moment of consolidation in the industry, where the biggest players came to understand how much money could be made from the model that Manafort had created. But nearly as soon as Burson acquired the firm, Tom Bell, the head of its Washington office, began to notice the ways in which Manafort hadn't played by the rules. He'd been operating as a freelancer, working on projects that never went to the bottom line. In 1995, Manafort left Burson. Taking a handful of colleagues with him, he started a new firm—Davis, Manafort and Freedman—and a new chapter, one that would see him enter the sphere of the Kremlin.

VII. The Master of Kiev

During the 1980s and '90s, an arms dealer had stood at the pinnacle of global wealth. In the new century, post-Soviet oligarchs climbed closer to that position. Manafort's ambitions trailed that shift. His new firm found its way to a fresh set of titans, with the help of an heir to an ancient fortune.

In 2003, Rick Davis, a partner in Manafort's new firm, was invited to the office of a hedge fund in Midtown Manhattan. The summons didn't reveal the name of the man requesting his presence. When Davis arrived, he found himself pumping the hand of the Honorable Nathaniel Philip Victor James Rothschild, the British-born financier known as Nat. Throughout his young career, Nat had fascinated the London press with his love interests, his residences, and his shrewd investments. For his fortieth birthday, he threw himself a legendary party in the Balkan state of Montenegro, which reportedly cost well over $1 million—a three-day festival of hedonism, with palm trees imported from Uruguay.

Russian oligarchs were drawn to Rothschild, whose name connoted power—and he to them. "He likes this wild world," Anders Åslund, a friend of Rothschild's, told me. Rothschild invested heavily in postcommunist economies and became a primary adviser (and a friend) to the young Russian billionaire Oleg Deripaska.

Rothschild and Deripaska fed off each other's grand ambitions. Like a pair of old imperialists, they imagined new, sympathetic governments across Eastern Europe that would accommodate and protect their investments. Their project required the type of expertise that Manafort had spent years accumulating. In 2004, Rothschild hired Manafort's new firm to resurrect the influence of an exiled Georgian politician, a former KGB operative and friend of Deripaska then living in Moscow. This made for a heavy lift because the operative had recently been accused in court as a central plotter in a conspiracy to assassinate the country's president, Eduard Shevardnadze. (He denied involvement.) The rehabilitation scheme never fully developed, but a few years later, Rick Davis triumphantly managed a referendum campaign that resulted in the independence of Montenegro—an effort that Deripaska funded with the hope of capturing the country's aluminum industry.

Deripaska's interests were not only financial. He was always looking to curry favor with the Russian state. An August 2007 e-mail sent by Lauren Goodrich, an analyst for the global intelligence firm Stratfor, and subsequently posted on WikiLeaks described Deripaska boasting to her about how he had set himself up "to be indispensable to Putin and the Kremlin." This made good business sense since he had witnessed the Kremlin expropriate the vast empires of oligarchs, such as Mikhail Khodorkovsky, who'd dared to challenge Putin. In fact, the Kremlin came to consider Deripaska an essential proxy. When the United States denied Deripaska a visa, the Russians handed him a diplomatic passport, which permitted him to make his way to Washington and New York.

Manafort understood how highly Deripaska valued his symbiotic relationship with the Kremlin. According to the Associated Press, he pitched a contract in 2005, proposing that Deripaska finance an effort to "influence politics, business dealings and news coverage inside the United States, Europe and former Soviet Republics to benefit President Vladimir Putin's government." (Deripaska says he never took Manafort up on this proposal.)

The Kremlin's grip on its old Soviet sphere was especially precarious in the early aughts. President George W. Bush's democratic agenda espoused an almost messianic sense of how the United States could unleash a new age of freedom. The grandiloquent American rhetoric posed an existential threat to entrenched rulers of the region who were friendly to Russia and who had become rich by plundering state resources. Suddenly, the threat of democratic revolution no longer felt theoretical.

The risks of popular uprising were very much on Rothschild's and Deripaska's minds during the last months of 2004, when they handed Manafort a specific task. Ukraine had descended into political crisis, one that jeopardized business interests they'd already developed in the country (Rothschild had various private-equity investments; Deripaska had an aluminum smelter). They sent Manafort to Kiev to understand how they might minimize the dangers.

Of all Paul Manafort's foreign adventures, Ukraine most sustained his attention, ultimately to the exclusion of his other business. The country's politics are hardly as simple as commonly portrayed; corruption extends its tentacles into all the major parties. Still, the narrative of Manafort's time in Ukraine isn't terribly complicated. He worked on behalf of a clique of former gangsters from the country's east, oligarchs who felt linguistic and cultural affinity to Russia and who wanted political control of the entire nation. When Manafort arrived, the candidate of this clique, Viktor Yanukovych, was facing allegations that he had tried to rig the 2004 presidential election with fraud and intimidation, and possibly by poisoning his opponent with dioxin. He lost the election anyway, despite having imported a slew of consultants from Moscow. After that humiliating defeat, Yanukovych and the oligarchs who'd supported him were desperate for a new guru.

By the time Manafort first entertained the possibility of working with Yanukovych, the defeated candidate had just returned to Kiev following a brief self-imposed exile at a Czech resort. They met at an old movie palace that had been converted into the headquarters for his political organization, the Party of Regions. When Manafort entered the grandiose building, the place was a mausoleum and Yanukovych a pariah. "People avoided him," Philip Griffin said. "He was radioactive."

Manafort groomed Yanukovych to resemble, well, himself. Åslund, who had advised the Ukrainian government on economic policy, told me, "Yanukovych and Manafort are almost exactly the same size. So they are big, tall men. He got Yanukovych to wear the same suits as he did and to comb the hair backwards as he does." Yanukovych had been wooden in public and in private, but "Manafort taught him how to smile and how to do small talk." And he did it all quietly, "from a back seat. He did it very elegantly."

He also directed Yanukovych's party to harp on a single theme each week—say, the sorry condition of pensioners. These were not the most-sophisticated techniques, but they had never been deployed in Ukraine. Yanukovych was proud of his American turn. After he hired Manafort, he invited U.S. ambassador John Herbst to his office, placed a binder containing Manafort's strategy in front of him, and announced, "I'm going with Washington."

Manafort often justified his work in Ukraine by arguing that he hoped to guide the country toward Europe and the West. But his polling data suggested that Yanukovych should accentuate cultural divisions in the country, playing to the sense of victimization felt by Russian speakers in eastern Ukraine. And sure enough, his clients railed against NATO expansion. When a U.S. diplomat discovered a rabidly anti-American speech on the Party of Regions' website, Manafort told him, "But it isn't on the English version."

Yanukovych's party succeeded in the parliamentary elections beyond all expectations, and the oligarchs who'd funded it came to regard Manafort with immense respect. As a result, Manafort began spending longer spans of time in Ukraine. One of his greatest gifts as a businessman was his audacity, and his Ukrainian benefactors had amassed enormous fortunes. The outrageous amounts that Manafort billed, sums far greater than any he had previously received, seemed perfectly normal. An associate of Manafort's described the system this way: "Paul would ask for a big sum," Yanukovych would approve it, and then his chief of staff "would go to the other oligarchs and ask them to kick in. 'Hey, you need to pay a million.' They would complain, but Yanukovych asked, so they would give."

When Yanukovych won the presidency in 2010, he gave Manafort "walk-in" privileges, allowing him to stroll into the inner sanctum of the presidential offices at any time. Yanukovych could be bullheaded, and as his presidency progressed, he increasingly cut himself off from advisers. Manafort, however, knew how to change Yanukovych's mind, using polling and political arguments to make his case. Oleg Voloshyn, a former spokesman in the foreign-affairs ministry, told me that his own boss, the foreign minister, eventually turned to Manafort to carry messages and make arguments regarding foreign-policy priorities on his behalf. "Yanukovych would listen to him," Voloshyn told me, "when our arguments were ignored."

VIII. A Reversal of Fortune

Before everything exploded in Ukraine, Manafort saw the country as his golden land, the greatest of his opportunities. But his role as adviser, as powerful as it was, never quite matched his own buccaneering sense of self. After spending so much time in the company of Russian and Ukrainian oligarchs, he set out to become an oligarch himself. Rick Davis declared their firm to be mostly "in the deal business," according to James Harding's 2008 book, *Alpha Dogs: The Americans Who Turned Political Spin Into a Global Business*. "The thing I love," Davis said, "is that the political elites and the economic elites in every other country but the United States of America are the same." The elected officials and the people "running the elections are the richest people in the country, who own all the assets."

In 2006, Rick Gates, who'd begun as a wheel man at the old firm, arrived in Kiev. (Gates did not respond to multiple requests for comment on this article.) Manafort placed him at the helm of a new private-equity firm he'd created called Pericles. He intended to raise $200 million to bankroll investments in Ukraine and Russia. "It was a virgin market in virtually any industry you wanted to pick up," Philip Griffin told me.

Manafort had always intended to rely on financing from Oleg Deripaska to fund Pericles. In 2007, Manafort persuaded him to commit $100 million to the project, a sum that would have hardly made a dent in the oligarch's fortune. On the eve of the 2008 global financial crisis, he was worth $28 billion.

Deripaska handed his money to Paul Manafort because he trusted him. Manafort repeatedly traveled to the oligarch's Moscow office, where they would sit for hours and tour the business and political horizon of the former Eastern Bloc. Deripaska had become a billionaire in his thirties and acquired the noisy pretensions of young wealth. He wanted to become the global face of Russia, he said. But that would require overcoming the reputation that stalked him, and Manafort could help. In 2001, before Manafort and Deripaska met, the World Economic Forum in Davos had withdrawn its invitation to the oligarch as a court examined his alleged misdeeds in the course of erecting his empire. (The case was eventually dismissed.) Five years after the Davos rejection, Rick Davis shepherded Deripaska around the elite confab, taking him to a party brimming with U.S. senators, including John McCain.

For Pericles's first deal, Manafort used Deripaska's money to buy a telecommunications firm in Odessa called Chorne More ("Black Seas," in English) at a cost of $18.9 million. He also charged a staggering $7.35 million in management fees for overseeing the venture.

But months after the Chorne More purchase, the 2008 financial crisis hit, gutting Deripaska's net worth. It plummeted so far that he needed a $4.5 billion bailout from the Russian state bank to survive. The loan included an interest payment in the form of abject humiliation: Putin traveled to one of Deripaska's factories and berated him on television.

As Deripaska's world came crashing down, his representatives asked Manafort to liquidate Pericles and give him back his fair share. Manafort had little choice but to agree. But that promise never translated to action. An audit of Chorne More that Rick Gates said was under way likewise never materialized. Then, in 2011, Manafort stopped responding to Deripaska's investment team altogether.

Deripaska wouldn't let go of the notion that Manafort owed him money. In 2015, his lawyers filed a motion in a Virginia court. They wanted the authority to track down more information on the deal, even though the initial papers for it had been filed in the Cayman Islands. The lawyers had already managed to get their hands on some of the documentation surrounding the deal, and they had extracted a belated explanation of what had happened from Gates. According to a spokeswoman for Deripaska, Gates said that Chorne More had defaulted on a $1 million loan that it had taken out to pay for capital expenditures, allegedly forfeiting the partnership's entire investment in the process. This explanation struck Deripaska's lawyers as wildly implausible. Deripaska began to publicly doubt whether Manafort had even bought the telecommunications company in the first place. "At present it seems that the Partnership never acquired any of the Chorne More entities," his lawyers argued.

All of the papers for the initial deal had included Rick Davis's name. They suggested that he would serve as Manafort's partner, and that shares would be divided evenly between the two. But Davis knew nothing of the Chorne More deal. While Manafort had been putting together Pericles, Davis had been on leave from Davis, Manafort and Freedman, running John McCain's 2008 presidential campaign. Because Davis's connections to Manafort and Deripaska had caused him a public-relations headache at the outset of the campaign, he'd kept a healthy distance from both men. When Deripaska's lawyers asked him about the money he supposedly owed their client, Davis was gobsmacked. He soon discovered that Manafort had also registered a new company—Davis Manafort International—to continue trading on the old firm's name, while cutting him out of consulting fees. Upon returning from the campaign and witnessing the extent to which Manafort had abused his trust, Davis left the firm they had created together.

Deripaska's attorneys had leveled a serious allegation—and true to his pattern, Manafort never filed a response. Those who have known Manafort the longest suggest that this reflects his tendency to run away from personal crises: "He'll get on a jet and fly off to Hawaii—and will come back when everything blows over," an old colleague told me, recalling Manafort's response to a scandal in the late eighties. But it was one thing to hide from reporters; it was another to hide from Oleg Deripaska. Though no longer the ninth-richest man in the world, he was still extremely powerful.

The fact is that by then, Manafort's options were tightly limited: Despite all the riches he had collected in Ukraine, it is unlikely that he could have paid Deripaska back. For years, according to his indictment, Manafort had found clever ways to transfer money that he'd stashed in foreign havens to the United States. He'd used it to buy real estate, antique rugs, and fancy suits—all relatively safe vehicles for repatriating cash without paying taxes or declaring the manner in which it had been earned.

But in the summer of 2014, in the wake of the revolution that deposed Viktor Yanukovych, the FBI began scrutinizing the strongman's finances. Manafort had stuck with Yanukovych as the president had initiated criminal investigations of his political opponents, opened the government's coffers to his cronies, and turned his country away from Europe and toward Russia. He'd stuck with him to the gruesome end, amid growing popular unrest—right up to the slaughter of more than one hundred protesters by government forces on the Maidan. He'd remained faithful to Yanukovych while large swathes of the strongman's circle abandoned him. Perhaps living so long in moral gray zones had eroded Manafort's capacity to appreciate the kind of ruler Yanukovych was, or the lines he had crossed. (He is now being tried in absentia in Ukraine for high treason, although he has denied any culpability from his perch in Moscow.) The previous December, as protesters had gathered on the Maidan, Manafort had texted his daughter Andrea, "Obama's approval ratings are lower than [Yanukovych's] and you don't see him being ousted."

The FBI investigation into Yanukovych's finances came to cover Manafort's own dealings. Soon after the feds took an interest, interviewing Manafort in July 2014, the repatriations ceased. Meanwhile, Manafort struggled to collect the money owed him by Yanukovych's cronies. To finance his expensive life, he began taking out loans against his real estate—some $15 million over two years, his indictment says. This is not an uncommon tactic among money launderers—a bank loan allows the launderer to extract clean cash from property purchased with dirty money. But according to the indictment, some of Manafort's loans were made on the basis of false information supplied to the bank in order to inflate the sums available to him, suggesting the severity of his cash-flow problems. All of these loans would need to be paid back, of course. And one way or another, he would need to settle Deripaska's bill.

IX. The Prize

"I really need to get to" Trump, Manafort told an old friend, the real-estate magnate Tom Barrack, in the early months of 2016. Barrack, a confidante of Trump for some forty years, had known Manafort even longer. When Manafort asked for Barrack's help grabbing Trump's attention, he readily supplied it.

Manafort's spell in the Arizona clinic had ended. It hadn't been a comfortable stay. After having acquired so many properties of his own, he had been forced to share a room with another patient, according to Andrea's texts. Despite his reticence about his private life, he'd spent his days in group therapy—and he claimed that it had changed him. "I have a real self awareness of why I broke down," he texted her.

Still, most of the proximate causes of his breakdown remained in place. Once an indispensable man, he had not been missed in professional circles. He was without a big-paying client and held heavy debts. His attempts to prove his entrepreneurial skills had ended as expensive busts. Because of his biggest bust of all, Deripaska was looking for him. "He has too many skeletons," Andrea had written her sister soon after he had entered the clinic, noting that his work in Ukraine was legally dubious. "Don't fool yourself," she had texted Jessica a few months before. "That money we have is blood money."

She had not forgiven him for his affair. She complained to a cousin about her father's treatment of her mother. "We keep showing up and eating the lobster," she wrote. "Nothing changes." But Manafort's ability to provide lavishly for his family—a role he had always played, whatever his other failings—had in fact changed. The millions he'd invested in Jessica's films were gone; so, too, were the millions he'd blown on her then-husband's real-estate ventures.

With the arrival of Donald Trump, Manafort smelled an opportunity to regain his losses, and to return to relevance. It was, in some ways, perfect: the campaign was a shambolic masterpiece of improvisation that required an infusion of technical knowledge and establishment credibility.

Barrack forwarded to Trump's team a memo Manafort had written about why he was the ideal match for the ascendant candidate. Old colleagues describe Manafort as a master pitchman with a preternatural ability to read his audience. He told Trump that he had "avoided the political establishment in Washington since 2005," and described himself as a lifelong enemy of Karl Rove, who represented the entrenched party chieftains conspiring to dynamite Trump's nomination. In other words, to get back on the inside, Manafort presented himself as the ultimate outsider— a strained case that would strike Trump, and perhaps only Trump, as compelling.

Manafort could write such a calibrated pitch because he had observed Trump over the decades. Back in the eighties, his firm had represented Trump when the mogul wanted to reroute planes flying over Mar-a-Lago, his resort in Palm Beach. Since 2006, Manafort had kept a pied-à-terre in Trump Tower, where he and Trump had occasionally seen each other and made small talk. This exposure yielded perhaps another crucial insight: Trump's parsimony. When Manafort offered Trump his services, he resisted his tendency to slap a big price tag on them; he would provide his counsel, he said, free of charge. To his family, Manafort described this decision as a matter of strategy: if Trump viewed him as wealthy, then he would treat him as a near-equal, not as a campaign parasite.

But Manafort must have also believed that money would eventually come, just as it always had, from the influence he would wield in the campaign, and exponentially more so if Trump won. So might other favors and dispensations. These notions were very likely what led him to reach out to Oleg Deripaska almost immediately upon securing a post within the campaign, after having evaded him for years. Through one of his old deputies, a Ukrainian named Konstantin Kilimnik, he sent along press clippings that highlighted his new job. "How do we use to get whole," Manafort e-mailed Kilimnik. "Has OVD operation seen?" Manafort's spokesman has acknowledged that the initials refer to Oleg Vladimirovich Deripaska. In the course of the exchanges, Kilimnik expressed optimism that "we will get back to the original relationship" with the oligarch.

All of Manafort's hopes, of course, proved to be pure fantasy. Instead of becoming the biggest player in Donald Trump's Washington, he has emerged as a central villain in its central scandal. An ever-growing pile of circumstantial evidence suggests that the Trump campaign colluded with Russian efforts to turn the 2016 presidential election in its favor. Given Manafort's long relationship with close Kremlin allies including Yanukovych and Deripaska, and in particular his indebtedness to the latter, it is hard to imagine him as either a naive or passive actor in such a scheme—although Deripaska denies knowledge of any plan by Manafort to get back into his good graces. Manafort was in the room with Donald Trump Jr. when a Russian lawyer and lobbyist descended on Trump Tower in the summer of 2016, promising incriminating material on Hillary Clinton. That same summer, the Trump campaign, with Manafort as its manager, success-fully changed the GOP's platform, watering down support for Ukraine's pro-Western, post-Yanukovych government, a change welcomed by Russia and previously anathema to Republicans. When the Department of Justice indicted Paul Manafort in October—for failing to register as a foreign agent, for hiding money abroad—its portrait of the man depicted both avarice and desperation, someone who traffics in dark money and dark causes. It seems inevitable, in retrospect, that Robert Mueller, the special counsel, would treat Manafort's banking practices while in Ukraine as his first subject of public scrutiny, the obvi-ous starting point for his investigation. The sad truth is that all of the damning information contained within the Mueller indict-ment would have remained submerged if Manafort had withstood the temptation to seek out a role in Trump's campaign. Even if his record had become known, it would have felt unexceptional: Manafort's misdeeds, in our current era, would not have seemed so inconsistent with the run of global play.

From both the Panama Papers and the Paradise Papers, vast disclosures illuminating previously hidden offshore accounts of the rich and powerful worldwide, we can see the full extent to which corruption has become the master narrative of our times. We live in a world of smash-and-grab fortunes, amassed through political connections and outright theft. Paul Manafort, over the course of his career, was a great normalizer of corruption. The firm he created in the 1980s obliterated traditional concerns about conflicts of interest. It imported the ethos of the permanent cam-paign into lobbying and, therefore, into the construction of pub-lic policy.

And while Manafort is alleged to have laundered cash for his own benefit, his long history of laundering reputations is what truly sets him apart. He helped persuade the American political elite to look past the atrocities and heists of kleptocrats and goons. He took figures who should have never been permitted influence in Washington and softened their image just enough to guide them past the moral barriers to entry. He weakened the capital's ethical immune system.

Helping elect Donald Trump, in so many ways, represents the culmination of Paul Manafort's work. The president bears some likeness to the oligarchs Manafort long served: a businessman with a portfolio of shady deals who benefited from a cozy relationship to government, a man whose urge to dominate and to enrich himself overwhelms any higher ideal. It wasn't so long ago that Trump would have been decisively rejected as an alien incursion into the realm of public service. And while the cynicism about government that enabled Trump's rise results from many causes, one of them is the slow transformation of Washington, D.C., into something more like the New Britain, Connecticut, of Paul Manafort's youth.

Last year, a group of Manafort's longtime friends, led by an old Republican hand named Bill Greener, tried to organize a cadre of surrogates to defend Manafort from the allegations against him, including the worst one: that he collaborated with a hostile foreign power to subvert the American democratic process. Manafort's old partner Charlie Black even showed up for a meeting, though the two had largely fallen out of touch. A few of the wheel men from the old firm wanted to help too. Yet when volunteers were needed to go on TV as character witnesses, nobody raised his hand. "There wasn't a lot to work with," one person contacted by this group told me. "And nobody could be sure that Paul didn't do it." In fact, everything about the man and the life he chose suggests that he did.

The California Sunday Magazine

FINALIST—FEATURE
WRITING

"A Kingdom from Dust" is: a profile of the biggest farmer in the United States, a billionaire who lives with his wife, the "Pomegranate Queen," in a Beaux Arts mansion in Beverly Hills; an investigation of water-intensive agricultural practices; a depiction of the changing lives of farm workers; and a social history of central California. A former reporter for the Los Angeles Times, Mark Arax is the author of four books, among them The Dreamt Land: Chasing Water and Dust Across California, which includes a slightly different version of "A Kingdom from Dust." Arax lives with his family on what he describes as "a suburban farm" in Fresno. Since it was founded in 2014, the California Sunday Magazine has been nominated for thirteen National Magazine Awards and won three. The same organization also produces a "live magazine," Pop-Up Magazine, which now tours the country.

Mark Arax

A Kingdom from Dust

I. The Land Baron

On a summer day in the San Joaquin Valley, 101 in the shade, I merge onto Highway 99 past downtown Fresno and steer through the vibrations of heat. I'm headed to the valley's deep south, to a little farmworker town in a far corner of Kern County called Lost Hills. This is where the biggest irrigated farmer in the world—the one whose mad plantings of almonds and pistachios have triggered California's nut rush—keeps on growing, no matter drought or flood. He doesn't live in Lost Hills. He lives in Beverly Hills. How has he managed to outwit nature for so long?

The GPS tells me to take Interstate 5, the fastest route through the belly of the state, but I'm partial to Highway 99, the old road that brought the Okies and Mexicans to the fields and deposited a twang on my Armenian tongue. The highway runs two lanes here, three lanes there, through miles of agriculture broken every twenty minutes by fast food, gas station, and cheap motel. Tracts of houses, California's last affordable dream, civilize three or four exits, and then it's back to the open road splattered with the guts and feathers of chickens that jumped ship on the slaughterhouse drive. Pink and white oleanders divide the highway, and every third vehicle that whooshes by is a big rig. More often than not, it is hauling away some piece of the valley's bounty. The harvest begins in January with one type of mandarin and ends in December with another type of mandarin and in between spills forth everything in your supermarket produce and dairy aisles except for bananas and mangoes, though the farmers here are working on the tropical, too.

I stick to the left lane and try to stay ahead of the pack. The big-rig drivers are cranky two ways, and the farmworkers in their last-leg vans are half-asleep. Ninety-nine is the deadliest highway in America. Deadly in the rush of harvest, deadly in the quiet of fog, deadly in the blur of Saturday nights when the fieldwork is done and the beer drinking becomes a second humiliation. Twenty miles outside Fresno, I cross the Kings, the river that irrigates more farmland than any other river here. The Kings is bone-dry as usual. To find its flow, I'd have to go looking in a thousand irrigation ditches in the fields beyond.

There's a mountain range to my left and a mountain range to my right and in between a plain flatter than Kansas where crop and sky meet. One of the most dramatic alterations of the earth's surface in human history took place here. The hillocks that existed back in Yokut Indian days were flattened by a hunk of metal called the Fresno Scraper. Every river busting out of the Sierra was bent sideways, if not backward, by a bulwark of ditches, levees, canals, and dams. The farmer corralled the snowmelt and erased the valley, its desert and marsh. He leveled its hog wallows, denuded its salt brush, and killed the last of its mustang, antelope, and tule elk. He emptied the sky of tens of millions of geese and drained the 800 square miles of Tulare Lake dry.

He did this first in the name of wheat and then beef, milk, raisins, cotton, and nuts. Once he finished grabbing the flow of the five rivers that ran across the plain, he used his turbine pumps to seize the water beneath the ground. As he bled the aquifer dry, he called on the government to bring him an even mightier river from afar. Down the great aqueduct, by freight of politics and gravity, came the excess waters of the Sacramento River. The farmer moved the rain. The more water he got, the more crops he planted, and the more crops he planted, the more water he needed to plant more crops, and on and on. One million acres of the valley floor, greater than the size of Rhode Island, are now covered in almond trees.

I pity the outsider trying to make sense of it. My grandfather, a survivor of the Armenian genocide, traveled 7,000 miles by ship and train in 1920 to find out if his uncle's exhortation—"The grapes here are the size of jade eggs"—was true. My father, born in a vineyard outside Fresno, was a raisin grower before he became a bar owner. I grew up in the suburbs, where our playgrounds were named after the pioneers of fruit and canals of irrigation shot through our neighborhoods to the farms we did not know. For half my life, I never stopped to wonder: How much was magic? How much was plunder?

I'm going to Kern County, just shy of the mountains, to figure out how the biggest farmers in America, led by the biggest of them all, are not only keeping alive their orchards and vineyards during drought but adding more almonds (79,000 acres), more pistachios (73,000 acres), more grapes (35,000 acres), and more mandarins (13,000 acres). Even as the supplies of federal and state water have dropped to near zero, agriculture in Kern keeps chugging along, growing more intensive. The new plantings aren't cotton, alfalfa, or carrots—the crops a farmer can decide not to seed when water becomes scarce. These are trees and vines raised in nurseries and put into the ground at a cost of $10,000 an acre to satisfy the world's growing appetite for nuts and fruits.

Agriculture in the south valley has extended far beyond the provisions of its one river, the Kern. The farmers there are raising almost 1 million acres of crops, and fewer than half these acres are irrigated with flows from the Kern. The river is nothing if not fickle. One year, it delivers 900,000 acre-feet of snowmelt. The next year, it delivers 300,000 acre-feet. To grow, Big Ag needed a bigger and more dependable supply. So beginning in the 1940s,

Kern farmers went out and grabbed a share of not one distant river but two: the San Joaquin to the north and the Sacramento to the north of that. The imported flow arrives by way of the Central Valley Project and State Water Project, the one-of-a-kind hydraulic system built by the feds and state to remedy God's uneven design of California. The water sent to Kern County—1.4 million acre-feet a year—has doubled the cropland. But not even the two projects working in perfect tandem can defy drought. When nature bites down hard and the government flow gets reduced to a trickle, growers in Kern turn on their pumps and reach deeper into the earth.

The aquifer, a sea of water beneath the clay that dates back centuries, isn't bottomless. It can be squeezed only so much. As the growers punch more holes into the ground looking for a vanishing resource, the earth is sinking. The choices for the Kern farmer now come down to two: He can reach deep into his pocket and buy high-priced water from an irrigation district with surplus supplies. Or he can devise a scheme to steal water from a neighbor up the road. I now hear whispers of water belonging to farmers two counties away being pumped out of the ground and hijacked in the dead of night to irrigate the nuts of Lost Hills.

I roll past Tulare, where every February they hold the biggest tractor show in the world, even bigger than the one in Paris. Past Delano and the first vineyards that Cesar Chavez marched against. Past McFarland and the high school runners who won five state championships in a row in the 1990s. Past Oildale and the boxcar where Merle Haggard grew up. Past Bakersfield and the high school football stadium where Frank Gifford and Les Richter, two future NFL Hall of Famers, squared off in the Valley Championship in 1947 in the driving rain. And then it hits me when I reach the road to Weedpatch, where my grandfather's story in America—a poet on his hands and knees picking potatoes—began. I've gone too far. The wide-open middle of California did its lullaby on me again.

I turn back around and find Route 46, the road that killed James Dean. I steer past Wasco to the dust-blowing orchards that flank Lost Hills, the densest planting of almonds, pistachios, and pomegranates on earth. This is the domain of Stewart Resnick, the richest farmer in the country and maybe the most peculiar one, too. His story is the one I've been carting around in my notebook for the past few decades, sure I was ready to write it after five years or ten years, only to learn of another twist that would lead me down another road.

.   .   .

Like the wheat barons of the 1870s who lived on San Francisco's Nob Hill, Resnick isn't of this place. He's never driven a tractor or opened an irrigation valve. He's never put a dusty boot on the neck of a shovel and dug down into the soil. He wouldn't know one of his Valencia orange groves from one of his Washington navel orange groves. The land to him isn't real. It's an economy of scale on a scale no one's ever tried here. He grew up in New Jersey, where his father ran a bar. He came to California in the 1950s to remake himself. Welcome to the club. He remade himself into a graduate of the UCLA law school, a cleaner of Los Angeles buildings, a vendor of security alarms, a seller of flowers in a pot, a minter of Elvis plates and Princess Diana dolls, a bottler of Fiji Island water, a farmer of San Joaquin Valley dirt. He purchased his first 640-acre section in the late 1970s and kept adding more sections of almonds, pistachios, pomegranates, and citrus until he stretched the lines of agriculture like no Californian before him.

At age eighty-one, he's gotten so big, he doesn't know how big. Last time he checked, he told me he owned 180,000 acres of California. That's 281 square miles. He is irrigating 121,000 of those acres. This doesn't count the 21,000 acres of grapefruits and limes he's growing in Texas and Mexico. He uses more water than any other person in the West. His 15 million trees in the San Joaquin Valley consume more than 400,000 acre-feet of water a year. The city of Los Angeles, by comparison, consumes 587,000 acre-feet.

Resnick's billions rely on his ability to master water, sun, soil, and even bees. When he first planted seedless mandarins in the valley seventeen years ago, the bees from the citrus orchards around him were flying into his groves, pollinating his flowers, and putting seeds into the flesh of his fruit. He told his neighbors to alter the flight of the bees or he'd sue them for trespassing. The farmers responded that the path of a bee wasn't something they could supervise, and they threatened to sue him back. The dispute over the "no-fly zone" was finally resolved by the invention of a netting that Resnick sheaths around his mandarins each spring. The plastic unfurls across the grove like a giant roll of Saran Wrap. No bee can penetrate the shield, and his mandarins remain seedless.

The control Resnick exercises inside his $4.5 billion privately held company does relinquish to one person: his wife, Lynda, vice chairman and co-owner, the "Pomegranate Queen," as she calls herself. She is the brander of the empire, the final word on their Super Bowl ads, the creator of product marketing. There's "Cheat Death" for their antioxidant-rich pomegranate juice and "Get Crackin'" for their pistachios and "Untouched by Man" for their Fiji water. A husband and wife sharing the reins is rare for corporate America, rarer still for industrial agriculture. He commands his realm, and she commands hers, and he takes care to mind the line. "If he sticks even a toe onto her turf," says a former business partner, "she gives him a look that sends him right back."

Together, the Resnicks have wedded the valley's hidebound farming culture with L.A.'s celebrity culture. They don't do agribusiness. Rather, they say, they're "harvesting health and happiness around the world through our iconic consumer brands."

Their crops aren't crops but heart-healthy snacks and life-extending elixirs. Stewart refers to the occasional trek between Lost Hills and Beverly Hills—roughly 140 miles—as a "carpet-bagger's distance." It seems even longer, he says, if you add in the psychological distance of being an East Coast Jew in a California farm belt where Jews are few and far between. Lynda is making the trip on the company jet more often these days. She's done giving big gifts to Los Angeles museums and mental-health hospitals that name buildings after her and Stewart. The south valley—its people and poverty, its obesity and diabetes—is her newest mission.

In Lost Hills, they call her "Lady Lynda." She shows up in high fashion and stands in the dust and tells them about another charter school or affordable-housing project she is bringing to them. They have no way to grasp the $50 million to $80 million a year that the Resnicks say they are spending on philanthropy. This is a magnitude of intervention that no other agricultural company in California has ever attempted. The giving goes to college scholarships and tutors. It goes to doctors and nurses, trainers and dietitians, who track the weight of workers, prod them to exercise, and wean them off soda and tortillas. As she announces the newest gift, the men and women in the back of the crowd smile and applaud politely and try not to show their faces to the publicity crew she has brought with her to film the event. Many are here without documents, after all.

Seventy-five years ago, writer Carey McWilliams, in *Factories in the Field*, lambasted the "ribboned Dukes" and "belted Barons" of California agriculture. If he were on the scene today, he'd have to add "sashed Queens" to the list. Measuring the reach of the Resnicks, it's tempting to lean on the hyperventilated language of the 1930s: Empire. Kingdom. Fiefdom. Feudal. Today, most everything in this desolate reach of Kern County, save for the oil wells, belongs to Paramount Farming, which belongs to the Resnicks.

But Paramount isn't Paramount anymore. By the decree of Lynda, who once contemplated a bowl of those juicy little seedless mandarins and on the spot named them Cuties, this is now the land of Wonderful.

.　　　.　　　.

It's the summer of 2016, eight weeks before the big pick, and I'm zigzagging across the almonds and pistachios, square mile after square mile of immaculate orchards lined with micro-irrigation systems and heavy with nuts. Of all the wonders of Wonderful, this is the one I find most mystifying. The State Water Project that allowed western Kern County to grow into a farming behemoth has given no water or very little water over the past three years amid the worst drought in California history. If this were any other part of Kern, the farmers would be reaching into the earth to make up the difference. But western Kern has no groundwater to draw from. The aquifer either doesn't exist or is so befouled by salts that the water is poison.

As a consequence, the farmland here, nearly 100,000 acres planted in permanent crops, is completely reliant on the government's supply of mountain water. This is gambler's ground unlike any other in California, and as I drive from hill to dale, examining each orchard, my head spins. *How can this be? No rain in five years. State water dwindling year after year. No water in the ground to make up for the missing government supply. So why hasn't this place gone to tumbleweeds? How can another record crop be sitting pretty on these trees?*

I do all the calculations from the numbers I am able to gather, and I cannot figure out how these nuts are getting enough water. There is a local water bank, a kind of underground lake, that the Resnicks control. In the years of plentiful rains and heavy snowmelt, the bank fills up with more than 1 million acre-feet of stored water. But most of this water has been spent by the Resnicks and other account holders in years two, three, and four of the drought. Whatever remains is not nearly enough to make up for the short-fall of imported water from the state.

Then I get lucky. I come upon a Wonderful field man in a four-by-four truck who listens to my bewilderment and takes pity. As he drives off, he throws a clue out the window. Turn onto Twisselman Road off I-5 and continue west until it intersects with the California Aqueduct. There, he tells me, in the shadow of the state's great concrete vein moving snowmelt north to south, I will find a private, off-the-books pipeline that Stewart Resnick has built to keep his trees from dying. The water is being taken from unsuspecting farmers in an irrigation district in Tulare County more than forty miles away.

No stranger enters this zone unless it's to get rid of a body or dump waste from cooking meth or drown a hot car. Its vastness makes you feel safe and in jeopardy at the same time. I head straight into the glare of the sun shooting over the Coast Range. Through the haze I can see the knoll of the aqueduct come closer. Ever since I was a kid, I have felt its pull—a gravitational presence on the land and in my own story. On a fog-drip night in January 1972, two men walked into my father's empty bar with gloves on and shot him to death. They dumped their stolen car into the canal's black waters and got away with murder for the next thirty-two years. In a valley of dead rivers, each one killed on behalf of agriculture, the aqueduct was the one river still alive. Its artificiality had achieved a permanence; its permanence had created my California.

I pull over into the dirt of a pomegranate orchard, the ancient fruit that the Resnicks have turned into POMWonderful, the sweet purple juice inside a swell-upon-swell bottle. The shiny red orbs, three months shy of harvest, pop out from the bright green leaves like bulbs on a Christmas tree. I study the terrain. This must be the spot the Wonderful field man was describing. Sure enough, cozied up next to the bank of the aqueduct, I see a glint. I get out of the car and walk down an embankment. There before me, two aluminum pipes, side by side, twelve inches in diameter each, slither in the sun.

Where gravity needs a boost, the pipes run atop wooden crates used to pack boxes of fruit. Where the pipes butt up against Twisselman Road, a more clever bit of engineering is required. Here, a crew has dug a culvert beneath the road and hiked the pipeline under the asphalt that divides one field from another. Here, private water jumps from Tulare County to Kern County, but government jurisdictions don't count. On one side of the road and the other, for miles in both directions, the dirt belongs to Wonderful. I stand over the pipes and give them a hard slap. They slap back with the cold vibration of water. Where's it coming from? Who's it going to?

II. The Empire Builders

Water is what led me to Stewart Resnick in the winter of 2003. Back then, the *Los Angeles Times* had a bureau in the middle of California. The bureau happened to be my house in northwest Fresno. I had finished the last chapter of *The King of California*, a book I wrote with a good friend about J. G. Boswell, who owned more land and controlled more water than any other person in the West for most of the twentieth century. He and his forebears from Georgia had dried up Tulare Lake, the biggest body of freshwater this side of the Mississippi, and planted 100,000 acres of cotton outside the town of Corcoran. As it happened, just down the road, on the other side of the lake bottom, Resnick had captured his own body of water, the Kern Water Bank, and planted millions of nut trees on desert scrub. No journalist had written a word about his rise as an agricultural giant, how he had turned public water into private water by grabbing control of California's largest water bank, a project jump-started with $74 million in tax-payer money. The deed had been done in a series of hidden meetings in Monterey. Resnick wanted no part in my story. Each time I called, his secretary hung up the phone.

I waited five years before placing another call to his headquarters. It was the early spring of 2008, and this time his secretary didn't hang up on me. I had in mind a magazine profile on Stewart, the Nut King. "Why not send him an e-mail?" the secretary suggested. A few weeks later, I found myself riding up the elevator of a high-rise on the Westside of Los Angeles.

He sat behind a desk without clutter and stood up to shake my hand. He was a small, trim man, no more than five-foot-five, in his early seventies with thinning silver hair and brown eyes rimmed in pink. The speech of his parents and grandparents, the Yiddish-inflected New York with its humors and cut-to-the-quick impatiences, had not left his own speech in the half-century since he'd come to California. He was dressed in the latest slim-fit style. Arrayed before him were small bowls of almonds, pistachios, and easy-to-peel mandarins, a plate of ground white turkey meat cooked in olive oil, and a glass of pomegranate juice. Everything but the turkey had come from his orchards. He'd been diagnosed with early prostate cancer and had no doubt that the juice was keeping him well. "My health, knock on wood, is good. It gives me the luxury to keep on working. Frankly, I'm having too much fun to think about retiring."

Even if he were inclined to wind down, he had no successor in mind. None of his three children had the slightest interest in taking over the company. Still, he was starting to think about his legacy, and that's why he finally agreed to meet with me. "I've never given an interview to a newspaper or magazine before. I've told them all no. When you're making the kind of money we're making, what's the upside? I'd rather be unknown than known." He had recently read *The King of California*, and that got him thinking. "I'm not going to live forever, even with the massive amounts of pomegranate juice I'm drinking. It might be nice if my kids and grandkids could turn to a book someday and read about what we've built."

He and Lynda were changing the way food was grown in California and sold to the world. If they were farmers, they were farmers who hung out with Tom Hanks, Steve Martin, David Geffen, Warren Beatty, and Joan Didion. They donated $15 million to found UCLA's Stewart and Lynda Resnick Neuropsychiatric Hospital and more than $25 million to the Los Angeles County Museum of Art to build a pavilion in their name. Unlike many other billionaires, they could poke fun at themselves. During the holiday season, they sent out 4,000 gift boxes to their "nearest and dearest friends" filled with their fruits and nuts, along with a card of the two of them dressed in skin-colored body stockings, posing as Adam and Eve. "If only Eve had offered Adam a pomegranate instead of an apple," Lynda wrote, "every day could have been a holiday."

The Resnick story certainly deserved a book, but did he really want me to be the one to write it? Boswell had tried to tear apart a copy of *The King of California* when his secretary asked if he might autograph it.

"Why not we start with an extended interview or two?" I offered.

"Let's meet again in two weeks," he said.

•   •   •

The front gates of the 25,000-square-foot Beaux Arts mansion on Sunset Boulevard magically opened without a guard giving a nod. I exited my car and approached the entrance with its fourteen-foot columns and wrought-iron balustrades. Perched up there, a queen might peek out and utter, "Let them eat cake," Lynda once said. When the mansion was built in 1927, it was known as the Sunset House. I was prepared to knock on the door, but a housekeeper, flanked by two blow-dried dogs, greeted me on the front steps and led me inside. I tried not to stare at the gold that was everywhere: heavy-legged gold furniture, paintings in thick gold frames, gold-leaf carpet, and gold-fringed drapes. From the vaulted ceilings with gold-leaf moldings hung two blown-glass chandeliers. The curtains were made of a fabric woven in Venice and substantial enough that they might finish off a person who happened to be looking out the window in the throes of an earthquake.

There was a majordomo of the house, a butler, a chef, a sous-chef, three housekeepers, a limo driver, and a trio of assistants who worked in the basement, juggling Lynda's calendar and the buying, wrapping, and shipping of gifts she handed out to her Rolodex of "highfalutin people." Stewart had made it clear that Lynda would not be joining us. She had her own book—about her genius as a marketer—going. He had spent the morning on his exercise bike reading *Fortune*. Fresh from a shower, a red Kabbalah string tied around his wrist and a multihued pair of socks covering his feet, he welcomed me. If he had his druthers, he said, he'd still be living in a little ranch house in Culver City. "None of this is my idea. This is my wife. This is Lynda."

Where do you begin with a man of great riches if not the distant places you might have in common? And so I began with slaughter and madness and then moved on to bartenders for fathers.

His grandfather Resnick had fled the Ukraine in the wake of another killing of Jews by Cossacks. The bells in the churches pealed, and out came the villagers with their scythes and axes, believing they had found the reason for their poverty. It was the early 1900s, and his grandfather and grandmother decided to secure passage to America. His father was three years old at the time. They settled in Brooklyn among Jews who had fled their own pogroms, and his grandfather went into the needle-and-embroidery trade. His father met his mother, the cantor's daughter, and they married. When the Depression struck, his parents migrated to Middlebush, New Jersey, where they bought a few trucks and peddled coffee and pots and pans. Stewart was the second of their four children, the only boy. "I sort of remember growing up on a farm," he said. "But we weren't there long." They moved to Highland Park, home to Johnson & Johnson and close enough to Rutgers University to hear the fans screaming at Neilson Field. Manhattan was thirty minutes in one direction; the Jersey Shore, thirty minutes in the other. The borough measured no more than two square miles. It wouldn't even make a couple of sections of his almonds.

His father bought a neighborhood bar and ran it with the same iron fist with which he ran the house. He was short, bull-like, and didn't take crap from anyone. "He was about my size, but he was very tough. He was a big drinker, a big liver who loved the fast life. His bar was a place for guys, Damon Runyon–type guys."

Resnick's pals were all Jewish kids from upper-class families, so it wasn't easy being the poorest one, the one whose father was a gambler and capable at any moment of losing the few comforts they had. Once, he came home from school and discovered the family car gone. His father had lost it in a bet. "He was tough on the outside. But inside he had these weaknesses. Compulsive gambler and alcoholic. Then he'd lose his temper and get the strap out."

Like many billionaires, he didn't have a decent explanation for his fortune. Because he hadn't done it with Daddy's money or what he considered a superior brain, he attributed his wealth to luck and to a simple lesson he had learned early in life. He was thirteen and standing inside the Rutgers Pharmacy on the first day of his first job. The boss showed him a storeroom filled with chemicals tossed here and there and told him to bring order to the mess. He didn't know where to begin. He studied the situation. The stacks of bottles gave him no answer. The boss came back in, saw his do-nothing, and said only three words: "Just get started." He began to move, and the job went quickly after that.

Digging in was its own wisdom, he discovered. Order finds itself through action. *Just get started* became one of his guiding principles.

At Highland Park High, he excelled in math and struggled in English. Upon graduation, he only needed to look across the Raritan River to find his college. The idea was to enroll at Rutgers and study to become a doctor. A year into his studies, an uncle called from California. He had moved out to Long Beach, bought some property, and built one of those new strip malls. The money was too easy. His dad had sold the bar and was adrift. Why not California? Once his parents decided to go, he decided to go, too. He left in 1956. "I never liked New Jersey, but I never knew why. California showed me why."

The making of a billionaire over the next half century was a series of dots that connected in the California sunshine. It was linear, logical, fluid, and quite nearly destined.

He got into UCLA and joined a Jewish fraternity. One of his frat brothers was a wealthy kid whose father ran a janitorial business. He had an industrial machine, hardly used, that scrubbed and waxed floors. Resnick dipped into his savings from his job at a mental hospital and went in half on the machine. "After school and on weekends, we'd clean and wax floors. It took time for the wax to dry. So in that time, we started cleaning windows, too." They named the business Clean Time Building Maintenance.

His frat brother got bored, as rich boys do, and Resnick bought out his half interest for $300. He started cleaning pizza parlors and drugstores. Business got so brisk that he bought two trucks and hired crews. By the time he graduated from UCLA in 1960 and entered its law school, he was bringing home $40,000 a year—the equivalent of $320,000 today. "When I got out of law school, I probably had one hundred people I was employing."

At the buildings he was cleaning, he noticed that no one was watching the front and back doors. With that insight, he sold the company for $2.5 million and went into the security-guard business. It then dawned on him that guards were good, but they had to be paid an hourly wage. Burglar alarms, on the other hand, offered round-the-clock vigilance without coffee breaks. He went out and bought an alarm company. That company led to another company, and he soon owned half the commercial alarm accounts in Los Angeles.

His first wife, the mother of his two sons and daughter, told him she was quite happy living in their $30,000 condo in Culver City. Month after month, she made ends meet on a $1,600 budget. "She was a very frugal lady. She wanted me to put our $5 million in an account, draw interest, and we could live happily on the fifty grand a year."

She didn't understand his drive. He was going to Vegas, hanging out with his own Damon Runyon characters, and making plans to get even bigger. He packed his bags and left his wife and kids. It wasn't a midlife crisis, he told me. He did little, if any, catting around. Then one day, he was trying to find a marketing person and got a call from Lynda Sinay, who worked in advertising. She was in her late twenties, almost a decade younger than Stewart, and the mother of two children. She had recently divorced and wasn't about to settle for a life in Culver City. She was the daughter of Jack Harris, a film distributor, who moved the family to Los Angeles when Lynda was fifteen to produce movies. One of his films, *The Blob*, became a cult classic, and they lived in a house on the Westside with two Rolls-Royces in the garage.

By age nineteen, Lynda had dropped out of college, married a magazine ad man, and opened her own advertising agency. She wasn't content to pursue the usual list of wealthy businessmen as clients. She was aiming to surround herself with famous actors and artists and public intellectuals. She divorced her husband in 1968 and began dating Anthony Russo, who worked at the RAND think tank in Santa Monica with military analyst Daniel Ellsberg. From a safe, Ellsberg had lifted the Pentagon Papers, the secret history of how successive presidents lied to the public to cover up the failings of the Vietnam War. Russo and Ellsberg needed a place to photocopy the 7,000 pages, and Lynda volunteered the Xerox machine at her ad agency on Melrose Avenue. The three of them spent two weeks of all-nighters making copies. When a copy found its way to the *New York Times*, Lynda was pursued by federal prosecutors until they concluded she was more dilettante than radical.

The courtship of Stewart and Lynda went fast. They both knew what they wanted. They married in 1972, and he sold the alarm company for $100 million. He wanted to stay in the customer-service business and heard from his doctor that Teleflora, the giant flower-delivery company, could be bought for a buyer's price. It was Lynda who came up with the idea of "flowers-in-a-gift." Roses are short-lived, she reasoned, but the teapot or watering can that the flowers arrive in is a keepsake. The concept changed the industry. She won a gold Effie, advertising's Oscar.

In the late 1970s, he went looking for a hedge against inflation. His accountant suggested he buy apartments. He could collect the rents while he slept. But he wasn't looking for the monotony of steady. He was in the mood to gamble. On vacation in the south of France, he heard about a farming company called Paramount that needed a buyer for some of its orchards in Kern County. "They were selling 2,500 acres of oranges and lemons and a packing house for a third of their appraised value," Resnick said. "It was simply a place to park some money and have another opportunity." He drove to Delano, the farm town where Chavez and his union had made so much trouble and history. By the time he drove back, he was a citrus grower. "I think I paid $9 million. Look it, I'm from Beverly Hills. I didn't know good land from bad land. But I had some good people helping me."

He and Lynda decided in 1984 to buy the Franklin Mint, the maker of commemorative coins and other kitsch, for $167.5 million. They knew little about the company except it was selling its keepsakes for five times the amount Teleflora was. Shoving aside the coins, they introduced a Scarlett O'Hara doll that, by itself, raked in $35 million in sales. They were pushing plates, costume jewelry, perfume, and model cars. They issued a commemorative medal of Tiger Woods winning the 1997 Masters that offended the golfer. He called it fake junk, sued, and won. Lynda spent $150,000 at an auction to buy the beaded gown and matching bolero jacket, "the Elvis Dress," that Princess Diana had worn on a visit to Hong Kong. The designers at the Mint made a porcelain doll with a tiny replica outfit so precise that it had to be hand-beaded with 2,000 fake pearls. It was a hit. Annual sales at the Mint jumped to nearly $1 billion.

Bankers and their fair-weather financing exasperated Resnick. He hired Bert Steir, a Bostonian with a Bronze Star from the Second World War and a degree from Harvard, to come west and work his deals. The oil companies and insurance companies were looking to unload their farms in Kern County, Steir learned, chunks of earth that measured 20,000 and 40,000 acres. Mobil and Texaco and Prudential Life were willing to practically give the ground and trees away. This is how Resnick became a pistachio, almond, and pomegranate grower. Sitting in his mansion in 2008, he already counted more than 100,000 acres of orchards across five counties. His trees were drinking from the Central Valley Project and the State Water Project, from rivers and irrigation canals and the water bank. "My life is about California. I didn't grow up here, but if it wasn't for California, its openness and opportunities, I wouldn't be sitting where I'm sitting."

No other farmer, not even Gallo, had cornered a market the way Resnick had cornered the growing, buying, processing, and selling of pistachios. He had his hands on 65 percent of the nation's crop. One of the first things he did with his monopoly was kill the California Pistachio Commission, the industry's marketing group, by yanking his funding. He and Lynda wanted to run their own ads for their own brand. The independent growers and processors, no surprise, regarded him as a bully eager to employ teams of lawyers and tens of millions of dollars to force his agenda. A member of the commission, on the eve of its demise, told me, "Stewart wants to be a benevolent dictator. But if he thinks you're defying him, he'll start with, 'Nobody realizes the good I've done for agriculture.' Then he moves on to, 'Do you know who I am? Do you know what I am? I'm a billionaire.' He's got an awful temper he's trying to control through Kabbalah. That little red string is supposed to remind him to count to ten. But his ego—there's no controlling that."

Resnick had heard it all before. He was the bad guy in agriculture for no bigger offense than that he was big. "Look, these farmers go back two, three, and four generations. Me, I'm a carpetbagger from Beverly Hills. But you ask the growers we process, and they'll tell you that year in and year out, no one offers a better price. No one pushes their product harder." It was this persistence and, above all, good timing that explained his bigness. "I'd have to say that fully half of my success has been luck. Now in farming, we're in a unique position. The crops we grow can only be grown in a few places in the world. Still, none of it would have happened without luck."

What he and Lynda had done with the wretched pomegranate was another matter. They planted the first 640 acres, half the pomegranates in the country at the time, knowing there was zero market. Instead of trying to sell the fruit as a piece of fruit, they squeezed its seeds into POMWonderful. If anyone doubted the health benefits of the juice, they spent more than $30 million in research to prove that it fought heart disease and prostate woes. Antioxidants that delivered thirty-two grams of sugar in each serving didn't come cheap: eleven dollars a bottle. Lynda sent the first batches of POM, week after week, as gifts to David Bowie, Rupert Murdoch, and Disney head Michael Eisner. On Oscar night, she handed out free samples to the stars at the *Vanity Fair* party. "Of course, I know everyone in the world," she told one reporter. "Every mogul, every movie star. You have no idea the people on my VIP list who drink it. But that doesn't make people buy a second bottle. They do that because they love it."

A POM craze followed. Stewart and Lynda planted 15,000 more acres and bought a juice plant. "Who would have thought that people would be asking their bartender to fix them a Pomtini?" he said. All of it was Lynda's doing, of course. There she stood in the foreground of the photo that accompanied a *New Yorker* profile titled "Pomegranate Princess." She was wearing a black pantsuit with open-toed silver pumps and a single piece of jewelry around her neck. In the distant background, under the gaze of a ten-foot-tall marble goddess, sat Stewart in a gold-skirted chair, head down. "She wanted to tell the story of the pomegranate," he told me with a touch of sarcasm. "For a long time, she got no credit. Now she's getting lots of credit."

I returned for two more sessions, and then he and Lynda took off to their $15 million vacation house in Aspen, where they were warring with the locals over a housing project for community workers that was blocking their view. By the time they returned to Beverly Hills, he had lost interest in a book about his life, at least one that I might write. I kept my notes and tapes and waited for another day.

III. The Farm Workers

Lost Hills sits on an upslope. This is the closest to hills it comes. Main Street is Highway 46, which slices through the middle of town. At the east end, where the highway meets Interstate 5, the traveler gets a choice. Day's Inn or Motel 6. Carl's Jr., Subway, McDonald's, Wendy's, Love's, or Arby's. None of the sales taxes go to City Hall because Lost Hills isn't a city. It's known as a census-designated place, which is another way of saying that Kern County has every reason to neglect it. Highway 46 shoots past Resnick almonds and takes you straight into town, population

1,938. The tumbleweeds on open ground give you a peek into what Lost Hills looked like before the aqueduct made a river here.

The July sun is a scorcher, and I fuss with the dial on the AC long enough to blow past the town's one stoplight and the aqueduct, too. I'm in another land, an expanse of hard, ugly, cratered-out earth the color of sand. Hundreds of giant praying mantises standing on platforms of concrete are pulling oil from a Chevron field. This is the west end of Lost Hills, the extraction end. The wind kicks up dirt from the reap of oil and almonds, and the dust cloud carries back into town, raining down on the elementary school first.

I park the car and walk in the direction of a scattering of buildings slapped together with stucco and corrugated tin. A meat store, an auto repair, a pool hall, and an arcade pass for a commercial strip. No one is out and about. They're either working in the heat or hiding from the heat. Three dogs, part pit bull, the menacing part, have given up on the shade and lie on the open road. Their tongues loll to their knees. I walk into the supermarket El Toro Loco, and the clerk directs me to the back office, where a tobacco-chewing Yemeni named Anthony Hussein is sitting beneath a photograph of an uncle in his U.S. Army uniform. The uncle died at age twenty-two fighting in Afghanistan. "Talk to me," Hussein says, draining a can of Rockstar. "What do you need to know, sir?"

"What's it been like here during the drought?"

"Drought, no drought, makes no difference. The aqueduct was built with tax money, yes? The aqueduct brings the water, yes? So everybody should have it, right? But this is water for Mr. Resnick. Not the people. When it doesn't come, he finds a way to make it come." He spits tobacco juice into the empty can of Rockstar. "The checks the workers bring in here from Mr. Resnick are the same checks they bring in for years. I cash them the same. Nothing changes. Big fish eat the small fish here. Anything else I can help you with?"

He seems in a hurry. He guides me back into the main store with its displays of fresh fruit and vegetables, meats, cold cuts, and baked goods. The shelves spill piñatas, gloves, hats, pruning shears, and loaves of Bimbo white bread. The wall of Pacifico and sixteen-ounce cans of Bud is rebuilt daily. Vicente Fernández, the king of Ranchera music, is crooning to no one, but it won't be this way in thirty minutes, Hussein tells me. Today is *quincena* day, twice-a-month payday, and he needs me to scram because the workers coming in to cash their checks and wire 25 percent back across the border to families in Guanajuato and Guerrero will wonder if I'm with Immigration and Customs Enforcement. If that happens, they'll go down the highway, and he'll lose the one dollar he takes for every one hundred dollars' worth of their checks. "It's a bad day," he says, shooing me out. "You look like Border Patrol undercover."

I sit in my car and wait in the parking lot. They arrive in Chevy trucks and Dodge vans and spill out in groups of four or five under the sweat-stained hats of the 49ers, Penn State, and the Yankees. Each face wears its own weary. The twenty-year-olds look like twenty-year-olds; the thirty-year-olds, like forty-year-olds; the forty-year-olds, like sixty-year-olds. Summer or not, they're dressed in shirt layered upon shirt and the same no-name dusty blue jeans. Or at least this is what I can glean through the car window. I grab my notebook and walk up to one of the vans.

Inside sits a young man named Pablo. The oldest of five children, he came from Mexico when he was eighteen. He had no papers, like so many others, just an image of what this side of the border looked like. When he was told there were fields upon fields, he did not believe there could be this many fields. That was eight or nine years ago. He lives down the road in Wasco, the "Rose Capital of America," though the roses, too, have turned to nuts. He works year-round for Wonderful. This means he can avoid the thievery of a labor contractor who acts as a middleman between the farmer and the farmworker and charges for rides and drinks and doesn't always pay minimum wage. Pablo prunes and irrigates the almond and pistachio trees and applies the chemicals that cannot be applied by helicopter. He makes ten-fifty an hour, and the company provides him with a 401(k) plan and medical insurance.

He's thankful to the Resnicks, especially "Lady Lynda," for that. "I saw her a few months ago. She is here and there, but I have never seen her up close. She owns this place." He goes on to explain what he means by *own*. Most everything that can be touched in this corner of California belongs to Wonderful. Four thousand people—more than double the number on the highway sign—live in town, and three out of every four rely on a payday from Wonderful. All but a handful come from Mexico. In the Wonderful fields, he tells me, at least 80 percent of the workers carry no documents or documents that are not real. U.S. immigration has little say-so here. Rather, it is the authority vested in Wonderful that counts. It was Lynda who teamed up with the USDA to develop twenty-one new single-family homes and sixty new townhouses on a couple of acres of almonds that Wonderful tore out. The neighborhoods didn't have sidewalks; when it rained, the kids had to walk to school in the mud. Lynda built sidewalks and storm drains, the new park and community center, and repaved the roads. So the way Pablo uses *own* isn't necessarily a pejorative. "When I crossed the border and found Lost Hills, there was nothing here," he says. "Now there's something here. We had gangs and murders, but that's better, too."

He has come to El Toro Loco to cash his check and buy some beer. I follow him inside to a long line of workers that ends at a plastic window where Hussein sits on the other side, working the cash register like a teller at a race track. When it's Pablo's turn, he hands Hussein a check for $437, and Hussein counts out $433 back to him in cash. On the way out of the market, Pablo buys a case of Pacifico. Tonight, feeling no pain, he'll sit in one of the strip clubs in Bakersfield and maybe buy himself a fancy lap dance.

• • •

Across the street, the Soto family has built a new Mexican restaurant named Gabby's that dwarfs every other business on the street with its Spanish Mission façade. The Sotos made a name for themselves in Lost Hills by taking their taco trucks into the agricultural fields. Angelica, one of four sisters, runs the restaurant. She tells me her not-so-silent partner is Lady Lynda, who was so bothered that Lost Hills didn't have a sit-down restaurant of its own that she sought out Angelica. Lynda assisted her with the design and color scheme but otherwise has remained hands-off. "She'll check in every so often to see how business is going. But she doesn't dictate this or that." Angelica would prefer not to get into the details of their financial arrangement. It's been more than a year since the grand opening, and they're still operating in the red. So far, Lynda has shown only patience. A restaurant built by Wonderful for the purpose of making the company town look better from the roadside may enjoy a more forgiving bottom line than, say, the Subway up the road. But that still doesn't mean that most people in town can afford to eat here. "We're still trying to figure out who our typical customer is going to be," Angelica says. For now, she's playing country-western music on the sound system and trying to lure a combination of oil-field workers, supervisors at Wonderful, and travelers driving the last miles of James Dean.

I leave Gabby's and follow a winding concrete path through the new Wonderful Park. The grass is a color green on the verge of blue, and the cutouts for trees are razor etched. The 5.3 acres are so flawless and at odds with the town that the whole thing feels like a movie set. Even the community water tank is painted baby blue with a big sunflower. "You Have Found Lost Hills!!" it says. On the north end sits the Wonderful Soccer Field with its all-weather track, stadium lights, artificial turf, and giant yellow sunburst embossed at midfield. On the south end stands the Wonderful Community Center, where residents are urged to attend thrice-weekly Zumba and core-training sessions, healthy cooking classes, and weekend cultural outings featuring the likes of America's Premier Latino Dance Company.

This is a lot of gestures to unpack, and as I exit the grounds, I keep turning around to get one last look that's true. I don't know how Hershey did Hershey, Pennsylvania, but Lynda is present in every painted sunburst, every planted flower, every blade of grass. The believer and the skeptic do their tussle inside my head. This is a park for the people, to give them a break from their hard lives. Lost Hills finally has something to be proud about. This is an offering of cake handed down from king and queen to serfs. It is one more way to extend the brand. Even Wonderful Park is spelled with the same heart-shaped O that stamps a bottle of POM.

.　　　.　　　.

The compass in my car says I'm headed east, but that means almost nothing inside a province of 15 million trees. Each square-mile section is divided into blocks, and each block counts a precise number of rows. When a farmer's orchards encompass 186 square miles, finding the field man can be a challenge. Section, block, and row don't compute; he has to direct me by cell phone and guideposts. My dust cloud tells him I'm getting close. He turns out to be a kindly religious man whose short hair is dyed the black of shoe polish. I ask him about his delivery of services— pruning, pesticides, herbicides, fertilizer, water—that can be calibrated and timed to enable the smallest unit to achieve maximum yield. Surely, no one does this better than Wonderful?

He explains that Wonderful has grown too big to hassle such precision. Let the smaller grower walk among his trees and farm by the row. Fussing with one input or another, he can produce 3,500 pounds of nuts an acre. Wonderful, by contrast, shoots for the middle. The scale of production—and the ability to process, market, and sell its own crops—allows Wonderful to be mostly mediocre in the fields and remain highly profitable. No one's going to get fired for bringing home 2,500 pounds of nuts an acre. "These trees are pruned by a machine that hedges one side and then the other," he says. "But the smaller farmer still uses a pruning shears to make his most important cuts. If he knows what he's doing, the shears can make a thousand more pounds an acre."

It's the beginning of September 2016, and battalions of heavy machinery dispatched from the Wonderful equipment yards pound the ground and rattle the trees. No picking of crop agitates the earth like the picking of almonds and pistachios. A plume of dust joins up with other plumes of dust until the sky over the valley turns sickly. By the eighth day of harvest, the sun is gone. Not that long ago, we used to time our sinus infections by the immense cloud of defoliants sprayed on the cotton fields at the end of Indian summer. Now it's the seven-week nut harvest that brings out the inhalers. All this stirring up is a consequence of mechanization. Because a human picker is not needed in the almond and pistachio groves, the nut harvest doesn't spread around money the way it spreads around dust. Wages that used to go to workers stay in the pocket of the nut growers. Maybe not since the wheat barons has the income disparity between farmer and farmworker been greater. Growers a tenth the size of Resnick flee the dust in their Ferraris to their second houses in Carmel.

I follow one of the engines of harvest as it rolls into an orchard like a tank. Giant pincers manned by a single worker grab the tree by the throat and start shaking. For the next two or three seconds, the almonds pour down like hail. The vibration is a stunning piece of violence to behold. It moves in a wave from trunk to limb to nut and back down to earth. The jolt and shudder would tear out the roots of a lesser species. When the clamps let go of the trunk, 8,000 almonds, green outer shells wilted and partly opened, the meat inside a wooden womb, lie scattered on the flat dry earth. Somehow, thirty or forty nuts aren't compelled to drop. The man and his pincers can't be bothered. The rain of almonds has moved on to the next tree. Once each tree has been shaken, the nuts are left on the ground for a few days to dry.

I walk to another part of the orchard and watch phase two. In a swirl of dust, a worker atop a different machine is blowing the almonds from their spot beneath the trees to the middle of the row. The nuts are kept there a few more days—any longer and the ants will attack them—to complete their drying. I then move to the far side of the orchard, where another worker, riding a huge mower, is kicking up an even bigger cloud of dust. He maneuvers down the middle of the row, sweeps up the dried almonds, and throws them into a catcher. The contents of each catcher, 500 pounds of almond meat, are placed on a conveyor twenty feet high and dumped into a big-rig hauler for transport to the Wonderful processing plant.

All told, nine men operating five machines will pick clean this orchard over the next four weeks. They'll take home $11 an hour for their labors. And how will the Resnicks fare? Each tree produces twenty-two pounds of nuts. Typically, each pound sells wholesale for $3.75. That's $83 a tree. By harvest's end, the Resnicks will have put their clamps on 4.4 million almond trees. Nearly $365 million worth of Wonderful almonds will have dropped down from the dry sky.

In the city of trees, I find a paved road with speed bumps that takes me to the harvest of pistachios. The bunches of chartreuse-tipped nuts hanging from antler branches never touch the ground. Two men sit inside separate cabins of a small tractor with pincers on one side and a catcher on the other. One man drives and shakes the tree while the other man makes sure the clusters fall into the butterfly opening of the receiver. The vibration here isn't quite as vehement. As the nuts pour down onto the roof of the catcher, the operator shifts the trough so that it becomes a conveyor belt. The continuous rattle feeds the nuts into a series of bins on the backside of the tractor. There's no waiting around. Unlike the almond, the pistachio is moist and combustible. The nut must be hurried from bin to truck to processing plant to keep it from discoloring. "This is a big crop," the field man tells me.

All told, thirty-six men operating six machines will harvest the orchard in six days. Each tree produces thirty-eight pounds of nuts. Typically, each pound sells wholesale for $4.25. The math works out to $162 a tree. The pistachio trees in Wonderful number 6 million. That's a billion-dollar crop.

The truck driver hits the wide open of Highway 33 and traces the serpentine of the aqueduct. He's headed to the Wonderful plant, thirteen miles north of Lost Hills, to drop off his load. He's carrying 55,000 pounds of crop in two swaggering trailers open to the sun. The load will translate into 18,000 pounds of finished nuts in a matter of days. Whether he realizes it, he's part of the biggest pistachio harvest in history. California growers, in the grip of drought, have produced 900 million pounds of the green nut. That's more than double the crop that Resnick boasted about when I saw him eight years ago. Nearly a third of the harvest—the nuts grown by Wonderful, the nuts grown by hundreds of farmers who belong to the Wonderful brand—will come through these gates.

The new plant, the size of seven super Walmarts and built at a cost of $300 million, rises out of a clearing like an apparition. The eye numbed by the tedium of orchards isn't prepared for the 1.3 million square feet of industrial assault, though the palm trees and roses along the perimeter try for a transition. This is where the pistachios, 400 truckloads a day, 50 days of harvest, come to be weighed, washed, peeled, dried, gassed, sorted, salted, roasted, packaged, and shipped out to the world.

•　　•　　•

No whistle shouts mealtime in the modern-day company town. The graders, sorters, and beeping forklift drivers head to an immaculate café, where the Wonderful Salad—roasted chicken, mixed greens, cilantro, pistachios, and slices of mandarin in a blue-cheese vinaigrette—sells for three dollars. Lynda believes that if they're enticed in the right direction, the 1,300 workers might choose to prepare the same healthy fare at home. Sugar kills, she tells them. It takes a life every six seconds. What spikes blood sugar more than a can of Coke? A flour tortilla. Eat a corn tortilla instead, she urges. She's built a grocery section in the back of the café stocked with grapeseed oil and what she touts are "Whole Foods–quality vegetables and fruits that sell at Walmart prices." Why grapeseed oil, I ask Andy Anzaldo, head of grower relations and a fitness buff, who's taken on the added duties of what might be called Wonderful's minister of health. "Research is showing that grapeseed oil is healthier than corn oil and canola oil and may be better for you than olive oil," he tells me.

Anzaldo's grandfather came from Guadalajara in the 1950s as part of the bracero farmworker program. His father worked as a truck driver, transporting crops to the city. Anzaldo grew up in Bakersfield and attended a Catholic high school where he played football and basketball. For college, he picked California Polytechnic in San Luis Obispo over the hill and majored in agriculture business. The Resnicks brought him aboard in 1999, and now he works alongside Lynda and consults daily with the company chef. Five years ago, they decided to get rid of the nacho chips, french fries, and soft drinks. The workers didn't react well. That's when the Resnicks decided to sell the concept of wellness to their

4,300 employees throughout the valley the same way they sell workplace safety. "We changed the culture of safety, and we think we can do the same with health," Anzaldo says.

The Spanish rice isn't rice but cauliflower made to look like rice. The pizza dough is cauliflower, too. A worker can still order a hamburger, but it's half the size of the old hamburger and costs six dollars—twice what the wild salmon served with creamed leeks and raw asparagus salad costs. Whichever dish they choose, workers are asked not to take a bite until they have considered Lynda's latest concoction: an ounce of apple-cider vinegar cut with ginger, mandarin juice, and turmeric served in small plastic cups like the wine of Mass. Everything about our physical selves, Lynda believes, begins in our guts. To change the microbial life in our digestive tracts and reduce inflammation that leads to disease, we have to reintroduce fermented foods into our diet.

If the workers doubt the benefit of the enzymes from apple-cider vinegar, video banners stream a continuous message of bad food habits to be broken and body-mass indexes to be measured and met. "Rethink Your Drink" is the latest slogan. Coke, Gatorade, and Monster Energy are sky-high in sweeteners, but don't be fooled by that SunnyD, either. "More than half our employees are obese or near obese," Anzaldo tells me. "One out of eight has diabetes. You can't reverse diabetes, but you can control it with a blood sugar level between 6.5 and 8. That's our goal. To manage the disease. Because when we don't manage it, they end up with severe chronic health issues and amputated limbs."

Anzaldo is a man wired for solemn, but he does manage to smile once during lunch, when talking about the 1,150 workers who've earned bonuses of up to $500 for losing a collective 14,000 pounds in two years. That still leaves the majority of the workforce beyond his cajole. "You and I look at this meal," he says. "Wild salmon and all these sides made from scratch. 'Wow. This is only three dollars?' But for a lot of workers, bringing that big fat burrito from home still makes sense."

I had seen what J. G. Boswell had done for the town of Corcoran. The hospital, senior citizens' center, and football stadium all bore the signature of his giving. What the Resnicks were doing for Lost Hills, though, was a level of philanthropy I had never witnessed in the valley. They were hardly the first rich people to use patronage to try to wheedle a citizenry toward their idea of a better life. But this wasn't the Resnick Pavilion at the Los Angeles County Museum of Art. This was Lost Hills, where the people are dependent on the Resnicks from cradle to grave. "There's a lot to commend here," I tell Anzaldo, "but where does persuasion end and coercion begin?"

As a second-generation Mexican American, Anzaldo says he knows the powerful clench of fast food and sugar among his own family. "We are sensitive to that. We can't insist on wellness the way we can insist on plant safety. Being healthy is a choice. Have we gone too far? The feedback we're hearing is 'No.' In fact, some of the workers think that we haven't gone far enough."

The workers aren't around for a quick survey. They've gone back to the nut line. On a Facebook page with postings in Spanish, they offer a glimpse of life "inside pistachio world." They give thanks for a job that provides decent wages and access to a free wellness center next door staffed by a full-time doctor, physician's assistant, registered dietitian, and marriage and family therapist. During paid breaks, they do their fifteen minutes of Zumba, take a walk along a designated path, and munch on the free fruits and veggies put out for them. Mostly, though, they can't wait for the avalanche of nuts to end. "One more bin," a post reads. "So so sleepy," says another. "One more hour and I'm outta this fucking place."

On the way out, the voice in their head, Lynda's voice, goads them to give one more hour to the Wonderful Fitness Center.

Inside, a trainer watches over a line of treadmills, elliptical machines, and stationary bikes. There's a section stacked with weights and a yoga room with mats on a hardwood floor. When the next shift ends, he tells me, the gym will fill up with workers looking to win the cash bonuses from the company's GetFit program. On the whiteboard in front of the weights, the big boys list their totals. They're all chasing Bobby, whose 325-pound bench press, 335-pound squat, and 455-pound dead lift make him the sole member of the 1,000-Pound Club.

·   ·   ·

In the maroon of sundown, I follow the workers back to Lost Hills. Their houses made from railroad boxcars have been painted purple, blue, yellow, and gold. The colors turn brilliant in the light made spectacular by the particles of dust. Down a rutted road, one hundred trailers with foundations dressed in plywood back up against an orchard. Even if they had wheels, they wouldn't be going anywhere. The people here have traveled too far. Some of them have paid $12,000 to buy their trailers and spent thousands more to fix them up. The brick-hard ground can't be bought. They're paying $340 a month for its privilege. As farmworker colonies go, this one isn't as grim as others I've visited. There's no garbage piled high and smoldering, no chickens picking at scratch. The Sureños gang has tagged the front entrance but otherwise has left the inside unmarked. The junk scattered about could be a lot worse. It is the ditch up the road, the one that carries no water, that is filled with old mattresses and spent appliances. Twine strung trailer to trailer hangs with the laundry of fathers, mothers, and children. The space for a family's secrets is only a few feet. Here and there a mulberry tree, its canopy pruned back, breaks up the red-smeared sky.

A woman named Lupe is standing above me on the wooden stairway that climbs to the front door of her trailer. She is small with lively brown eyes and a sweet but confident voice. Her husband, Manuel, will awaken in thirty minutes to prepare for his night shift. Under lights, he prunes, plows, and irrigates the almonds. Lupe and Manuel, like many of the residents, grew up next to each other in a pueblo called San Antonio deep in the state of Guerrero, a mountainous region of dramatic beauty. They were married only a short time when Manuel decided to cross the border almost twenty years ago. He worked as a gardener in Los Angeles and then heard about the almond trees on the other side of the mountain where the living was so much cheaper. He landed a steady job with a big grower and a year later paid a coyote $5,000 to bring Lupe and their baby son to Lost Hills.

She remembers handing the boy to her sister-in-law, who carried phony papers, and watching them cross by bridge into California. Because Lupe had no papers, she followed the coyote for many more miles until they reached a steep pass. Lucky for her that the young man was kind. Before he left her to cross alone, he gave her soda, water, chips, and Cheetos. The baby is now a twenty-year-old student at Bakersfield College. Lupe gave birth to two daughters, U.S. citizens, who are now eleven and six. If she has her way, they will go to college, too. "We tell the children about the fields when they are young so they don't know the fields when they are old," she says. More than a dozen family members have followed Lupe and Manuel to Lost Hills. One cousin arrived only last week. Relatives arranged his passage, paying the coyote the new rate of $12,000. A portion of his wages will be set aside each month to pay down the debt. "We send money home each month to our families left behind," Lupe says. "Then some of the money we save goes to pay the coyote. It takes a lot of work to get ahead." She and Manuel were able to buy their trailer several years ago. He spends much of his off hours fixing it up. He has painted the interior and put down two new patterns of linoleum, one to mark the living room and the other to mark the kitchen. The ceiling, all sheetrock and spackling, remains a work in progress.

Lupe excuses herself to prepare dinner. The bowls on her kitchen table are filled with grapes, berries, bananas, and red and green bell peppers. She washes two kinds of lettuce and cuts up fresh papaya to mix into a salad. I notice she keeps the water running for a long time. I ask her if she is concerned about wasting water, given the drought and the distance the water has traveled—twenty miles from a well in Wasco—and that the cost goes up the more they use. Already, they are paying sixty-nine dollars a month to the local utility district. She tells me the water comes out of the tap yellow and foul smelling, and she doesn't trust it. The family takes showers in it, and she washes their laundry in it, and if she runs the water long enough, she will use it to wash her vegetables and cook her rice and potatoes. But she cannot remember the last time she or Manuel or their children drank it. "It comes out like pee," says her eleven-year-old daughter.

The water is filtered for arsenic, boron, and other salts, and the monthly tests show no violation of state or federal standards. This hasn't convinced the people of Lost Hills, however. Lupe says no one in her family and none of her friends living in the trailer park or on the other side of town drinks the water that comes out of the pipe.

In the kitchen corner, cases of bottled water are stacked halfway up the wall. These are donations from other farmworker families, but they're not for her and Manuel and the kids. Her brother-in-law was killed recently in a car crash along Highway 46. He was headed to the fields at the same time that another farmworker, drunk on beer, was coming home from the fields. The sober man died. What to give a grieving widow and her five children in Lost Hills but drinking water?

In the trailer next door, Lupe's cousin Margarita lives with her husband, Selfo, and their three young children. They were farmers back in San Antonio, growing lettuce, cilantro, and radishes on a small plot of land. Then the drug cartels took over the countryside and planted poppies. One day, gunmen mowed down residents with AK-47s and threw grenades at the church filled with parishioners. "I saw horrible things," Margarita says. "My husband would have been shot dead like the others, but he was lucky. He had left for the cornfields a few minutes before the killings."

That was four years ago. They are still paying off the $27,000 debt to relatives who hired the coyote. The relatives try not to press them, but the arrangement still feels like a form of indentured servitude. Selfo works fifty hours a week as an irrigator. He makes $10.75 an hour. It comes out to $2,000 a month. The rent is $540. The food is more. The gas to and from the orchards costs him $80 a week. They spend $50 a month on bottled water. "There's not much left over," he says. "Our relatives have been patient." He worries because there isn't enough water now to properly irrigate the almonds, pistachios, and pomegranates. He wonders what agriculture will look like in western Kern in ten years.

"A bunch of trees are going dry," he says. "The land is turning to salt. In one orchard, half the trees are dying."

I had traveled the fields of Wonderful from one end of western Kern to the other, looking for dying trees. I had not seen any. "Because of a lack of water?" I ask. "The drought?"

"Yes. It's happening." The bosses won't speak of it, he says. If I want to know more, I need to talk to Lupe's brother, Gustavo, who has worked as an irrigator at Wonderful for five years and knows what the company is planning for the future.

Lupe and I walk to the far side of the trailer park to find Gustavo. He is a single man who rents a bedroom from other family members for $150 a month. Lupe knocks on his door, and he invites us in. The room smells of Vicks VapoRub. A cross of Jesus hangs from the bedpost. "Welcome to San Antonio del Norte," he says. "San Antonio south doesn't exist anymore." He is a small, good-looking man with a patch of black hair under his lip. I ask him how the drought has affected Wonderful. He says his bosses have been instructing him to cut the water each irrigation. There are plans, crazy as it sounds, to take out 10,000 acres of almonds. When the rain returns, some of the ground will be replanted in pistachios, a tree that can better withstand drought. "Wonderful is getting smaller," he says.

The next day, I drive to a spot a few miles beyond the trailer park where the county road dead-ends in a pomegranate orchard, or what used to be a pomegranate orchard before a Caterpillar came crashing through. Every last tree has been torn out of the ground. Thousands of Wonderful acres lay bare. The juice isn't selling like it used to. The POM tanks, I'm told, are backed up with a three-year supply. The Federal Trade Commission found Wonderful guilty of false advertising and ordered the Resnicks to stop claiming that POM cured heart disease and erectile dysfunction. A balancing of books in an office in the city has decided that this orchard and others around it, covered by too little water, can go. Already, Wonderful has bulldozed 8,000 to 10,000 acres of pomegranate trees over the past few years to send more water to its nuts. Across the field, a heavy machine is stacking what's left of the trees into giant mounds. Each mound is fed into an even bigger machine whose teeth pulverize the trees and make sawdust. I park the car and walk across the barren rows. Here and there my boots crunch down on the dried remains of pomegranates that look like small pieces of scat dropped by a coyote. Plastic drip-irrigation lines stick out of the ground at wrong angles. Tender sprouts poke out of the dry soil, and I bend down to feel their prickle. They're baby tumbleweeds that have come home.

IV. The Philanthropist

A giant pistachio nut flashes on the big screen. It cracks open and out pops the head shot of Stewart Resnick in a pistachio green tie. When he materializes onstage, he is wearing narrow black jeans, a black mock turtleneck, and a dark jacket. Damn, if he doesn't look even younger and more fit than the last time I saw him eight years earlier. The Ninth Annual Wonderful Pistachio Conference at the Visalia Convention Center is an invitation-only affair, but I managed to sneak in and grab a seat.

He's getting ready to introduce Lynda, the main speaker, but first he wants to address the federal government's recent recall of Wonderful pistachios. Two strains of salmonella found in their pistachios had caused a multistate outbreak of illnesses. The FDA sent a warning letter, and Wonderful pledged to study the chlorine levels in the bathing tanks. As far as the company can tell, no active salmonella has ever traced back to the plant. Even so, Resnick says, he learned a lesson from the 2004 recall of 13 million pounds of the company's salmonella-tainted almonds: Don't fight the FDA. "When they get on their high horse, you don't want to argue with them."

He launches into a CFO's riff on the pistachio market. Domestic sales are up 42 percent over the past eight years, but foreign sales have stalled. He blames Iran. Since international sanctions were lifted five years earlier, Iran has been crowding the market with its more buttery-tasting pistachios. The Iranians don't irrigate their trees. They rely only on rain, which concentrates the flavorful oils. China, for one, prefers the Iranian pistachio. So do the Israelis, who go to the trouble of repackaging the nuts so it doesn't appear that they're consuming the product of an enemy. Iranian pistachios show up in Tel Aviv as nuts from Turkey.

What market share has been lost in Asia and the Middle East, the company is looking to get back in Mexico with its spicy Latin line of nuts. Thanks to Wonderful's $15 million "Get Crackin'" campaign—the largest media buy in the history of snack nuts— pistachios now rank among the top-ten best-selling salty snack items in the United States "We are no longer processing nuts," he says. "We are creating foods." Nothing keeps prices high like a monopoly. In case the growers are fearing the antitrust cops from the Department of Justice, they needn't. For years, agriculture has been given a wide berth when it comes to monopolistic practices. The net return on the pistachio proves that Wonderful's dominance in the market has benefited every grower in the room. The price for pistachios has climbed from $4.50 a pound to an unbelievable $5.25 a pound. It isn't going down because he won't let it go down.

Then he motions to Lynda, who's standing off to the side of the light-dimmed stage. I've never seen her up close, never watched her in action. She seems a little nervous waiting in the wings. Six hundred pistachio growers in blue jeans isn't her usual crowd. "We saved the best for last," he says. "As you know, our philosophy at Wonderful is doing well by doing good. About five years ago, Lynda started our community-development organization in Lost Hills, and the journey has been an amazing one. We produced a short documentary film. Every time I see it, I'm inspired and proud of what we've been able to accomplish in such a short amount of time. We hope you enjoy *Finding Lost Hills*."

The eleven-minute film opens with a shot of swirling dust. This was Lost Hills before Lynda got involved. "I had no idea what I wanted to do, but I reached a moment in my life where I had to give back in a meaningful way," she tells the camera. "When I started to realize the socioeconomic issues of the Central Valley, I decided to stop writing checks to other charities and bring my business acumen into the project. It took time to gain the respect of the people, and I was afraid. What if I failed? If you're messing with people's lives and it doesn't work, that's serious. . . . It had to work." Tens of millions of dollars spent on philanthropy in Lost Hills wasn't just good for the people, she discovered. It was good for the bottom line. Because the more you invested in your employees and their communities, the more productive they became. The film ends with the laughter of kids playing inside the giant sunburst at the center of the soccer field. "I did not name the town," Lynda says. "But I couldn't have picked a more cinematic name than Lost Hills. Because it's so much fun to say that Lost Hills has been found."

The room full of growers applauds. I applaud, too. Since it is also true that Lost Hills has belonged to the Resnicks for thirty years, one of us might have blurted out, "What took you so long to find it?" As the film runs to credits, I can see that one credit is missing. John Gibler, a freelance journalist, found Lost Hills a year before Lynda. In the summer of 2010, he'd spent several days documenting the deplorable conditions of the modern company town. His account appeared in the *Earth Island Journal*, a small environmental quarterly out of Berkeley. Somehow, it made its way to Lynda. "There is nothing here," one of the townsfolk told Gibler. "This is a forgotten community. And you know why? Because it is a community of all Hispanics."

The piece, I was told, had left Lynda embarrassed and fuming. It must have wounded all the more because she and Stewart thought of themselves as progressive Democrats. Over the years, they had donated large sums of money to political campaigns, and some of it went to Republicans who had pledged to prop up California agriculture. This was how a billionaire who needed more water did politics. At the core, though, the Resnicks were still moved by the duty of social justice, not just as traditional liberals but as secular Jews. Stewart would deny that Gibler's reporting played a part in their philanthropy. "Look, I have no guilt. I've done no big wrong in my life that would cause me to have any. Well, maybe just a little guilt, but that's Jewish." He said the prod for all their giving in Lost Hills happened in Aspen, of all places. In the summer of 2009, he and Lynda attended a dinner lecture by Harvard political philosophy professor Michael Sandel about the moral obligations of wealth. "At the time we were handing out college scholarships in the valley, but Lynda decided it wasn't nearly enough." A year and a half after hearing Sandel—and in the wake of Gibler's story—Lynda kicked into high gear their mission to save Lost Hills and several other farm-worker towns where Wonderful operated its orchards and pro-cessing plants.

They're now building an $80 million charter-school complex in Delano, just down the road from Cesar Chavez High. It looks like no other campus in the valley: a modern, minimalist two-story design that uses paneled wood and fabricated metal, wild colors, and terraced landscaping to create the feel of a high-tech mountain retreat. When all three phases are finished, 1,800 students will be attending the high school, middle school, elementary, and preschool. What Lynda seems to have in mind is a kind of utopian village set amid orchards, not unlike the utopias that were tried by the early dreamers of Southern California. Young men and women from Teach for America will do their two-year stints at the complex and live in village housing. The curriculum is being created by Noemi Donoso, the chief of education for the Chicago public schools before Lynda recruited her to Wonderful. "Lynda isn't just writing checks," Donoso told me. "She's designing the school. She's designing the curriculum."

Lynda is also mapping out a farm-to-food program where students will grow fruits, vegetables, and grains on a plot of village land. A fully equipped teaching kitchen will turn the harvest into school lunches. Already, the high school is filled with hundreds of students bused in from farmworker towns that are among the poorest communities in the West. Among the graduating class are kids headed to Stanford, UC Berkeley, UCLA, Dartmouth, and the state and community college systems. When Lynda learned that half the students receiving thousands of dollars in company scholarships were dropping out of school, she wasn't deterred. She's now providing tutors and counselors in every region of California to boost the graduation rate.

For the bright kids who have no interest in a bachelor's degree, she has designed the Wonderful Agriculture Prep Program to serve an additional 1,000 students. Selling the farm to migrant families has required Lynda to rebrand agriculture. No longer does it have to be a career that brings Mexicans to their hands and knees. Under her "rethink agriculture" program, the kids will be trained in plant science and irrigation technology, marketing and sales.

·   ·   ·

Now Lynda herself stands before us, a single light over her head. She is twinkling from earlobe and finger. Whether it's the glint of a fifteen-carat, yellow canary diamond ring, a twenty-fifth wedding anniversary gift from Stewart, or one of the pomegranate-colored rubies she says are a girl's best friend, it's hard to tell from the back row. She gestures to the young students in the front row, the ones enrolled in the ag-prep classes, and asks them to stand up and take a bow. "They're our future," she says. She is determined that their lives will play out differently from the lives of their parents, but she means no disrespect by this. "It's not easy to hear, but I'm not going to sugarcoat this," she says. "In Kern County, one in two adults and almost one in five children are obese. And it's even worse for the children in Kings County. Fifty-three percent of our employees are obese, and 12 percent of them have diabetes."

The growers start to fidget. It's not the fidget of boredom. There's an unease about the room. This isn't the Lynda posing for photos with Barbra Streisand. This is the Lynda who now endeavors to see farmhands as something more than workers. To the growers, it must feel like a jab in the stomach. They're listening with their heads bent down. Do they sense the shaming about to come? She delivers it in classic Lynda style. "At Wonderful Health and Wellness, we're educating our employees about this health crisis. At the plant, we built our gyms, and we have stretching and walking activities. Being Wonderful means more than growing, harvesting, and distributing the best of the best. It also means giving back."

She walks off the stage with Stewart. He lingers in the crowd long enough to shake hands with a friend from Bel-Air who's planting thousands of acres of pistachios in the worst ground of Tulare Lake. I walk up and reintroduce myself. His face is blank. I remind him of the time we spent together eight years earlier in his Sunset House. His face is still blank. His partner in the mandarins once told me that when Stewart is done with you, he's done with you. He and the Resnicks had fought an ugly legal battle that tore their Cutie brand in two. The partner kept the Cutie name but only after paying the Resnicks tens of millions of dollars. Stewart and Lynda created a new brand, the Halo, from the same variety of mandarin. The Cutie and the Halo are now warring in the fields outside the Visalia Convention Center. Inside, a Wonderful media specialist sees that Resnick needs to be rescued. She deftly places her body between him and me. When I tell her my name, she whispers into his ear. "Ah," he says, "so you're the one who's been snooping around." She grabs him by the wrist, and they make a beeline for the convention hall door.

V. The Secret Pipeline

I catch Highway 99 in rare somnolence. The miles clock by not as road but as story. This is the route my grandfather, one of a legion of fruit tramps, took as he drifted from farm to farm in the 1920s picking crops. He saved up a down payment for a raisin ranch west of Fresno, where my father was born in the worst of the Great Depression. My grandfather lost the farm to vine hoppers is the story he told. My grandmother said it was his leftist politics that ate up that vineyard and the ones that followed. One way or the other, we got rid of our last farm a few years before I was born and moved to the Fresno suburbs.

The men and women who planted, irrigated, sprayed, and picked our crops were phantoms. On our trips to Disneyland, I must have blinkered my eyes heading down 99. I didn't see the tumbleweeds along the roadside and the strip of parched earth that separated what remained of the desert from the perfect rows of irrigated agriculture. I didn't see our creation, much less the figures bent under the canopies of vine that our creation counted on.

This was the same road that took me to Selma, the raisin capital of the world, to pack peaches and plums for Mel Girazian, my father's old friend. I was sixteen, and his packing house was my first job, a baptism into the "money, money, money" world of the men who grew fruit and the men who sold it. The growers would stand in front of the cull line and never stop moaning about how much of their fruit got rejected by Girazian's graders. I learned back then that our farmers thought the whole world was out to screw them.

Maybe this explains why the United Way could declare the valley one of the nation's skinflints, a place where the wealthy farmers donated to the children's hospital or Fresno State athletics but almost never to the communities filled with Mexicans where their crops grew. As a class of people, the farmers and real-estate developers harbor a deep-down contempt for what they have built. They hide from the fact that it relies on the subjugation of peasants from Mexico they themselves have brought here. It exists as one thing they can almost rationalize out in the fields. It becomes something else as soon as they encounter their workers in another guise—as a fellow shopper at Costco or as the parents of the kid who goes to school with their kid. It becomes scorn because they can't allow it to become pity or self-hatred.

I cross the Tulare County line heading south into Bakersfield, and there in front of me, for no eye to miss, stands the Wonderful Citrus complex with its four-story storage building designed in the shape of an almighty box of Halo mandarins. Conceived by Lynda, it cost one fortune to build and a second fortune to light up. I doubt the Resnicks have any idea of the fester that eats at this place, the shame piled on shame.

On this same stretch of 99, I once wrote a story about farm-workers who moonlighted as meth cookers to make ends meet. Bruce Springsteen turned it into a song on his *Ghost of Tom Joad* album. More than one ballad was about the valley, so he came to Fresno. The William Saroyan Theatre was packed that October 1996 night. Halfway through his solo performance, he interrupted his set to tell us a piggy bank had been set up by the exit to donate money to the "hardworking men and women in the fields." When the concert was over, I took my wife and children backstage to meet him. As we sat down to chat, one of his assistants leaned over and whispered into his jewel-studded ear. Springsteen shook his head and smiled a thin, ironic smile. Then he turned and faced me. "Tell me," he asked, though it wasn't entirely a question. "What kind of place is this? Not a single penny was put in that piggy bank."

•   •   •

I cut across Twisselman Road to the pipeline gliding along the aqueduct like a silver snake. I thwack both lines. They thwack back. Yes, they're still delivering water. If I follow them north through Resnick pomegranates, I can find out where the water is coming from. If I follow them south into Resnick almonds, I can see where the water is going. Either way is a trespass. I steer toward the almonds, past a row of worker housing and a main gate. I enter an equipment yard where a Wonderful farmhand is standing next to a tractor. He doesn't wave me off or give chase. He knows what I don't know. This road ends abruptly at the rise of a second fence. Nowhere to turn, I turn back around and roll down my window. He's smiling but speaks only Spanish. He doesn't know what *pipeline* means. But if it's the *tube* that I'm looking to follow, I must drive through the almond grove. A road will pick up and connect me to where the tube is going.

"Why is the tube here?"

"To carry water from someplace far away to another place far away," he says.

I thank him and hurry down the dirt road through the almonds, eyeing the rearview mirror to see if a Resnick truck is following me. I'm driving too fast for the ruts in the road. My head keeps hitting the sunroof. A minute later, I reconnect with the pipeline and pursue its length for a football field. Each section of pipe is forty feet long. I try to calculate how many hundreds of aluminum sections need to be linked seamlessly, or at least watertight, to cover the distance of a mile. Just ahead I can see the last section of pipe throwing a cascade of white water into a main canal belonging to the Lost Hills Water District. I hop out of the car.

Rain for Rent, the pipes say. If Resnick retains every drop, he might squeeze twenty-five acre-feet of water a day out of both pipes. He needs nearly 1,000 acre-feet a day for 165 days—the length of nut-growing season—to hang a good crop across his acres in western Kern. This last-ditch water in Lost Hills won't make everything right. But there's no denying his desperation. It is flowing to a place of dire thirst. For as far as I can see, the water in the canal runs inky through the orchards. Because the road ends here, there is no physical way to follow the canal's flow. I take out my cell phone and swipe across Google Maps. The image of water moves on and on through miles of western Kern. This is one of the ways the Nut King and the Pomegranate Queen are defying the California drought. This is how the land of Wonderful is keeping alive its trees.

I call the manager of the Lost Hills Water District. He used to work for the Resnicks before Stewart put him in charge of the district. He's a decent guy making $216,000 a year who doesn't pretend that he isn't beholden to Wonderful. As the head of a quasi-public agency, he knows he can't completely blow off my questions. He doesn't feign surprise when I tell him about the pipeline, but he dismisses it as a private matter between private parties. It takes my visiting the irrigation district office during a public meeting for him to cough up more details. Yes, the pipeline belongs to Resnick. It's bringing water from the Dudley Ridge Water District in Kings County. He's using it to irrigate his almonds and pistachios in Lost Hills.

I find a former partner of Resnick. He doesn't know about the pipeline. What he knows is that Wonderful is buying up to 50,000 acre-feet of water a year in a series of hidden deals. The sellers include farmers in the Tulare Lake basin who are pumping so much water out of the ground that the levees protecting the town of Corcoran are sinking, not by inches but by feet. During the drought, the Boswell Company has drilled fifty-two holes into the old lake bottom—seven of these wells reaching a depth of 2,500 feet. To fix the subsidence, and keep the town dry in the next flood, residents and the state prison are having to pay $10 million in extra taxes. Altogether, Resnick has purchased 300,000 acre-feet of water from farmers and water districts—at a cost of $200 million—to cover his shortfall during the drought.

I meet up with the Wonderful field man who first tipped me off to the pipeline. He says he doesn't feel sorry for Resnick. He got himself into this jam. "This is a company that runs its resources to the max," he tells me. "When Resnick plants, he plants his trees wall to wall. That's why he's in trouble."

"So he makes a deal for private water?"

"Yep. That's why he built the pipeline. He needs every drop he can get."

"Whose water is it?"

"Don't you know? It's John Vidovich. Billionaire comes to the rescue of billionaire."

"But those two guys hate each other."

"Not anymore. They're drought's best buddies."

.   .   .

John Vidovich will tell you he's the interloper who came over the other mountain, the Coast Range. His father grew grapes, cherries, and apricots in the Santa Clara Valley back when Stanford University still had a reason to be known as the Farm. He sold a chunk of land to the builders of Sunnyvale and decided he could develop the rest himself. His real-estate empire became big enough to bring aboard each of his four children. By the time he died an old man on his tractor in the Cupertino Hills, where he had planted grapes again and was making wine, the transformation of his valley by the silicon chip was complete.

John, his oldest son, had served in the military as an intelligence officer and graduated from Santa Clara law school. He had none of his father's sentimentality. He paved over the last orchard in the Santa Clara Valley with some apartments and then went looking for another valley where he might build his own empire. That's how he came upon the San Joaquin. "There's a lot of people who don't like me," he said after his father's death. "But nobody didn't like my dad."

It was a curious statement but true. The son, five-foot-six and thin, with closely cropped blond hair and blue eyes that fix on you, isn't concerned about ingratiating himself. In a time span even shorter than Resnick's, the sixty-one-year-old Vidovich has bought up more than 100,000 acres of farmland scattered across the valley. He's planting ground that no one has ever planted before. If you study his moves, you can see a method to the acres he is accumulating. Whether it's Fresno or Kings or Tulare or Kern counties, he's grabbing land where the groundwater is plenty or a river runs through it or the aqueduct spills its north-to-south flow. Don't let his boots, blue jeans, and ball cap fool you, the old-timers say. He isn't farming dirt. He's farming water.

In the winter of 2010, Vidovich put up for sale half his draw of state water from the Dudley Ridge Water District. This amounted to 14,000 acre-feet. Everyone knew where it was going. It was going to houses. California had passed a law intended to stop the rising of new towns in the middle of nowhere. Developers now had to identify a source of water before a city or county would green-light their projects. So off the developers went in search of farm water. Resnick himself had sold 5,000 acre-feet to a proposed new town in the farm fields of Madera. Vidovich didn't have to wait long for a buyer to come calling. The Mojave Water Agency in the high desert needed a backup supply to serve its growing communities of Barstow and Apple Valley, Hesperia and Victor-ville. The agency did not balk at the price tag: $5,321 an acre-foot. Vidovich went home with $74 million in his pocket.

The sale got under the skin of valley farmers. It was true that agriculture had been selling state-project water to cities for two decades. But those deals were one water district selling to another water district. This sale made headlines because it was engineered by one farmer—an outsider from the city—for his benefit only. To top it off, the "greedy SOB" (farmers rarely uttered Vidovich's name) intended to keep his 7,000 acres of nut trees in Dudley Ridge. He only needed to find groundwater from another basin to replace the state aqueduct water he had just sold.

Vidovich went on a shopping spree. He bought 20,000 acres in the Tulare Lake basin—land that not even Boswell dared farm. He had no intention of farming it, either. But those 20,000 acres near the town of Pixley came with an endowment: a little spit of earth that produced endless amounts of groundwater. Never mind that this is one of the most over-drafted basins in Califor-nia or that the land is sinking a half-foot a year. Vidovich digs seventeen new wells, several to the depth of 1,400 feet, and pumps groundwater into ditches and canals that move the flow across miles of flat lake bed. Where does the water end up? Right there in the big canal of the Dudley Ridge Water District. He's not only able to irrigate his nut trees with an imported flow of ground-water—40,000 acre-feet in some years. He can mix this private water with his leftover state water and ship it to at least one stranded neighbor who will pay the price.

Who would have thought the two of them in cahoots? Not long before, Vidovich was trying to grab water from Resnick, not give it. He accused Resnick in 2008 of using various shell companies to monopolize control of the Kern Water Bank. A public resource had been privatized for the purpose of growing tens of thousands of acres of nuts, he charged. The matter was headed to court when Vidovich paid a visit to Resnick. His ego had gotten the best of him, he conceded. What if he dropped his lawsuit and the two of them worked together to solve their water problems? That's all fine and good, Resnick replied, but what about the $1 million-plus he'd spent on lawyer's fees? Vidovich wrote out a check for the full amount, then went looking for the water to prop up Resnick's monopoly. He found it.

.   .   .

By car and foot, I trace the silver pipeline as it creeps north through Wonderful pomegranate orchards. One mile, two miles, three miles, four—it keeps going until it reaches another county and back to one of the main canals in the Dudley Ridge Water District. A pump is shooting water out of the canal and into the Rain for Rent pipes. The water is cold, clean, and salty, though not too salty for a desperate man. Or at least that's the way Vidovich puts it when I finally reach him.

"This drought has brought Stewart to his knees. What can I say? We've had our battles in the past, and I don't agree with everything he's doing. But when your neighbor is going to lose his crop, you do what you can to help him."

I tell Vidovich this sounds almost charitable. "How much water are we talking about?"

"I'd rather not get too specific. It isn't a lot of water."

"What's the cost?"

"I'm not going to give you the numbers. Neighbors don't tell on neighbors."

Vidovich has more than one reason to be evasive. Farmers near Pixley already have sued him once for taking too much water out of their ground and moving it. The court settlement allows him to take the water to Dudley Ridge, but it can't go outside Kings County. Yet the Resnick pipeline is doing just that.

"Resnick picks up the water in Dudley Ridge," Vidovich says. "It's his pipe, not mine. Where he takes the water is none of my business."

"He's taking it into his orchards in Kern. That breaks your agreement with those farmers. You can't be exporting ground-water from one basin to another."

"Whatever water he's taking, it's too little, too late."

I try again to pin him down, but he's a man who likes to think of himself as wily. So I ask about the big picture.

"Let's call it what it is," he says. "It's gambling. Stewart gambled and won for many years. He gambled on the price of nuts going up, and he gambled on the water never going dry. He kept planting more and more trees. But he got too big. Too many pistachios. Too many almonds. Too many pomegranates. Like a lot of empires, it comes to an end."

"So what about you?" I ask. "What kind of empire are you trying to build?"

"I'm here to show the farmer that ag's footprint needs to get smaller."

I chew on his answer for a second. The calculation and hubris inside it. The truth a mercenary has landed on. "I get it. You're the one who leads the way on selling agricultural water to the cities.

Fallowing the farm until the footprint gets smaller and smaller. Making hundreds of millions of dollars in the process?"

"It can't be farmed like it was," he says.

VI. The Aftermath

Six hundred and forty acres don't look like 640 acres—a square mile—until they start ripping out the trees. The white flowers have set into buds, and the buds have become baby almonds covered in fuzz. Now it's the Bobcat's turn. The biggest farmer of them all is tearing out 10,000 acres because he doesn't have enough water to cover the nuts to harvest. Since the middle of the drought, the price of almonds has dropped almost by half. In a region of wall-to-wall plantings, one of the walls is crashing down. The way the Bobcat goes full steam, it takes but a few seconds of splendid violence to uproot a tree. The farmer isn't here to smell the cracking open of wood, the ripping open of warm secret earth. No farmer ever is. The sentimental ones stay away. The bloodless ones stay away. On the day the trees fall quietly upon the orchard floor, no one is here but the Mexican on his tractor.

Then the autumn of 2016 arrives with the strangeness of clouds. The rain starts to fall, big, fat, slashing drops that feel like electricity on my open palm. It hardly ceases for the next five months. Drought turning to flood—it is the story of California. The wildfires can't be far behind. The winter goes down as one of the wettest in recorded history. So much snowmelt comes down the mountain that it nearly takes out Oroville Dam. The dam ends up holding and the levees, too. All the new water pours into the delta, and what doesn't go out to sea fills up the aqueduct again. The State Water Project, for the first time in six years, delivers surplus flows. The tule fog sets down again in the valley. The great drought is officially over. California is free to return to its amnesia.

Wonderful has enough water to irrigate its orchards in Lost Hills and park tens of thousands of acre-feet in the water bank. The Resnicks are growing again. From the east side of Tulare County to the west side of Fresno County, they're planting more nuts and Halos. Of the 22,000 acres they ripped during the drought, 18,000 acres are being replanted in pistachios. Along a fan of the Kings River, a raisin farmer in Selma shows me his well that's coughing up sand. He points to the young almond trees that envelop his twenty acres like a siege. "Resnick," he says. "My old well can't compete with his new wells. I'll have to go deeper if I can."

On Sleepy Farm Road outside Paso Robles, the Resnicks were looking to add 380 acres of wine grapes and build a small reservoir with groundwater. One of the neighbors watched in disgust as the bulldozers tore into the hillside. Thousands of California oaks were felled. Only after the media were alerted did Stewart and Lynda claim to have discovered the clear-cutting. Up and down the Central Coast, restaurants are boycotting their wines.

"When we learned of the terrible situation, not to mention our poor reputation within the community, we were ashamed and are sorry," their official statement reads. "We were asleep at the wheel. We are horrified by the lack of regard for both neighbor and nature, and we hope that the community will accept our deepest and most sincere apologies and find it in their hearts to forgive us." They pledge to donate the 380 acres to charity.

I write an e-mail to the Wonderful PR team. A day later, I get a call from Mr. Resnick. It's been more than a year since he gave me the cold shoulder at the pistachio conference. He tells me to meet him in Lost Hills.

He's dressed Italian chin to foot—Loro Piana jeans and Hogan tennis shoes. "I would have worn my Levi's," he says, "but Lynda's here, and she thinks I dress like a bum." We're standing in the sun outside the plant's corporate office, a building whose clean lines and retro furniture wear the imprint of Lynda, too. He's surrounded by a half-dozen of his top men and women, the same ones who've been artfully dodging me for the past three years. They greet me with smiles and handshakes. A van pulls up to the curb, and the door slides open. Resnick has saved the front seat for me. "You're the one who needs to see."

We pull out of the parking lot, past the palm trees and roses, and head up the thin ribbon of Highway 33 into the dust-swirling tunnel of nuts and fruits. The big man with the goatee behind the wheel is Bernard Puget, a Basque sheepman's son who oversees these orchards. As we hop down from the van to inspect the pomegranates on the eve of harvest, Resnick motions to Bernard's belly. In his best Borscht Belt nasal, he takes a jab. "Bernard, what's happened? You get exempted from the company's wellness program?" Bernard has actually lost a few pounds. "I'm down, Stewart," he protests. "I'm down."

The leathery skin on the fruit has turned a nice orange-red. Each bush is saddled with more than a hundred pomegranates the size of softballs and baseballs. The softballs will go to market as whole fruit or as seed pods in a package. The baseballs will be crushed into juice.

"These are loaded," Resnick says. "It sure looks heavier than last year."

Bernard smiles and nods to the others. "He's fishing right now. He thinks I've understated the crop."

Resnick grabs at a pomegranate that might win a blue ribbon at the fair and tries to twist it free. No luck. He yanks and pulls, and it finally comes off, throwing him a foot backward. "You sure this isn't eighteen tons an acre?" he says, goading.

"It's loaded," Bernard says. "But for every good-sized fruit, there's a bunch that never sized up." Resnick is giving him one of his looks. "What? You don't believe me?"

"No, I believe you," Resnick says. "It's going to be what it's going to be. We'll still make money."

We pile back into the van and head up the road. Then it hits me. This isn't any road. This is Twisselman. Bernard, hard to believe, is driving straight toward the aqueduct. The knoll begins to rise. I gaze out the passenger window, looking for the glint of the pipeline. It should be right here, but I don't see it. It's gone. I look back at Resnick. He's oblivious, or so it seems. Bernard's eyes are fixed straight ahead. He's trying to play dumb, but I can see the sliest of grins peeking out from his mustache and goatee.

"It's gone," I say. "How come?"

"We don't need it anymore," he whispers.

·　　·　　·

Back at the plant, Lynda is meeting with Wonderful doctors, nurses, and farmworkers. They're coming up with ideas that might lead to an even bigger drop in the number of employees with diabetes. Stewart tries to interrupt, but he's not the boss in this room. "Thirty-five percent of our prediabetic population has gone into the healthy range," she tells the team. "They're no longer in danger. Now they have to keep that up, right? So how do we do even better next year?"

He guides me to the café, and we grab our lunches from the buffet. He unfolds a twenty-dollar bill from a wad he keeps inside a bent paper clip, and we take a seat in the far corner. For a silent minute, we dig into our bowls. I feel his gaze going past me, his voice turning oddly sentimental.

"When I look around here at what we've built and then look back at my life in New Jersey, I think, 'How did it happen?' For one man and woman to build something like this would be almost impossible today."

One hundred and twenty thousand acres of nuts and fruits and berries in California and still counting. They had survived the drought. Did it teach him any lessons?

"Lessons?" he says, sounding perplexed. "Who knows when a five-year drought is coming? Who anticipates that you can't fill a water bank for six or seven years?"

"Come on," I say. "It's California."

"Sure. But you take some risks in business. And when you've been as lucky as we've been, you start to think you can ride out drought, too."

He did learn one lesson. You can plant only so many acres on ground that has no groundwater. From now on, they'll grow on land that offers a double protection against drought. "State or federal water isn't enough. We want good groundwater, too."

"You mean no more pipelines carrying water in the dead of night?"

"The pipeline . . ." He stammers a bit. "Look, I delegate a lot of things, obviously. I'm sure I knew we had a pipeline in there. But that's not an issue I deal with."

"How much water was it bringing in?"

"I don't even know what it was, to be honest with you."

I take a last bite of cauliflower rice. I know there's a more forceful way to ask the question, but to what end? This was the same distance—geographic, psychic—that allowed him and Lynda to clear-cut the oaks and to kill the independent pistachio commission, to grab a water bank that belonged to the state and to pretend for 30 years that Lost Hills wasn't a place of dire need. It was the same distance that allows them to control more land and water—130 billion gallons a year—than any other man and woman in California and still believe it isn't enough.

"I know I can't do this forever," he says. "I'm eighty years old. Problem is, I feel like I'm fifty. I feel too good to give any of it up."

His oldest son is retired in Seattle. His second son is a psychiatrist. His daughter, who used to own a restaurant, is busy raising her one son. Lynda has a son who works as a musician and a son who suffered a birth trauma and lives in a care facility. The four grandchildren have visited the orchards once or twice. Not a single one of them wants any part of Wonderful.

"Who gets the keys to the kingdom?"

"I don't know. All I know is I don't want to split it up or sell it in some leveraged buyout. I want to know that what we built will continue into the future."

He takes a look at his watch. He's got another meeting to attend. As he walks away, I notice his $400 sneakers. They're dusty with San Joaquin dirt.

I retrace the road I came in on and cross old Tulare Lake, which rose by flood and sank by drought. Four tribes of Yokut lived along its shores. On the shallow bottom, the women fished mussels and clams with their toes. The nets of the Chinese during the Gold Rush caught terrapin that was served as turtle soup in the fanciest restaurants of San Francisco. Then the men of cotton, driven out of the South by the boll weevil, put the five rivers into canals and dried up the lake. They made a new plantation here. Before he died at age eighty-six, J. G. Boswell told me what a fool he and his forebears had been for wasting water, sun, and soil in California to raise fiber, of all things. Cotton still grows on the lake bottom, but less and less each year. Thousands of acres of pistachio trees now await the next flood. Boswell pumps reach 2,500 feet into the earth looking for water to grow crops, looking for water to sell. For now, they're selling to farmers like Resnick who can pay the price.

The extraction of water beneath the lake bottom won't last forever. The state of California has adopted a new law that finally regulates the pumping. When it goes into full effect, in a decade or two, more than a million acres of cropland across the valley will have to be retired. By then, Wonderful, if it still exists, will be a portfolio run by men even farther away than Beverly Hills. The water will be stripped from the land and sold to developers of new towns both here and over the mountain. In my lifetime alone, California has gone from 13 million people to 40 million people. Nothing will stop the houses. The Wheat King begets the Cattle King, and the Cattle King begets the Cotton King, and the Cotton King begets the Nut King and Pomegranate Queen. Like the waters of the lake, the indent of the Resnicks will recede from the land, too. The Yokut had a saying that when the farmer drained the last drops of snowmelt from Tulare Lake, the water would return. It would return as tule fog to remind the white man of his theft. The fog is our history.

The New Yorker

"The Islamic State has been mostly destroyed on the battlefield, but the war is far from over," wrote Ben Taub in December 2018. "Air strikes cannot kill an idea, and so it has fallen to Iraq's fractured security, intelligence, and justice systems to try to finish the task"—and to inflict revenge, as vividly shown in "Shallow Graves." Described by the National Magazine Awards judges as "fearless and resolute," Taub first won recognition from ASME when his reporting from Syria was nominated for the National Magazine Award in 2017; the same year, he received an ASME NEXT Award for Journalists Under 30. For more about Taub, read Esquire senior editor Eric Sullivan's interview with him immediately following the article (Sullivan is also an award-winning journalist; one of the first feature stories he ever edited, "Inside the Iron Closet," by Jeff Sharlet, won the Ellie for Reporting for GQ in 2015).

Ben Taub

Shallow Graves *and* An Interview with Ben Taub by Eric Sullivan

Shallow Graves

A September morning in Baghdad. Traffic halted at checkpoints and roadblocks as bureaucrats filed behind blast walls and the temperature climbed to 115 degrees. At the Central Criminal Court, a guard ran his baton along the bars of a small cell holding dozens of terrorism suspects awaiting trial. They were crammed on a wooden bench and on the floor, a sweaty tangle of limbs and dejected expressions. Many were sick or injured—covered in scabies, their joints twisted, and their bones cracked. Iraqi prisons have a uniform code—different colors for pretrial suspects, convicts, and those on death row—but several who had not yet seen a judge or a lawyer were already dressed as if they had been sentenced to death.

Down the hall, the aroma of Nescafé and cigarettes filled a windowless room, where defense lawyers sat on couches, balancing stacks of paper on their laps. Most were staring at their phones; others sat in silence, arms crossed, eyes closed. In terrorism cases, lawyers are usually denied access to their clients until the hearing begins.

Shortly after ten o'clock, three judges in long black robes shuffled into Courtroom 2 and sat at the bench. Suhail Abdullah

Sahar, a bald, middle-aged man with a thin, jowly face, sat in the center. There were twenty-one cases on his docket that day, sixteen related to terrorism. He quietly read out a name; a security officer shouted it down the hall to one of his colleagues, who shouted it to the guard, who shouted it into the cell. Out came a young man named Ahmed. A security officer led him to a wooden cage in the middle of the courtroom. Judge Sahar accused him of having joined ISIS in Qayyarah, a small town south of Mosul.

"Sir, I swear, I have never been to Qayyarah," Ahmed said.

Sahar was skeptical. "I have a written confession here, with your thumbprint on it," he said.

"Sir, I swear, I gave my thumbprint on a blank paper," Ahmed replied. "And I was tortured by the security services." Sahar listed Ahmed's supposed jihadi associates; Ahmed denied knowing any of them.

"Enough evidence," the prosecutor said. "I ask for a guilty verdict."

Ahmed had no lawyer, and so Sahar called upon an elderly state attorney named Hussein, who was seated in the gallery, to spontaneously craft a defense. Hussein walked over to a lectern, repeated from memory what Ahmed had said, and, without requesting his release, concluded with a plea for "mercy in his sentencing."

Ahmed wept as he was led out of the room. His trial had lasted four and a half minutes.

The next suspect insisted that he had been arrested by mistake—that his name was similar to that of someone in ISIS. A private defense lawyer explained that his client had confessed to ISIS affiliation under torture—he had a medical examination to prove it—but none of the judges appeared to be listening. As the lawyer spoke, they cracked jokes, signed documents, and beckoned their assistants to collect folders from the bench. Sahar yawned. The trial lasted eight minutes.

The third suspect was a twenty-three-year-old from a village near Mosul, charged with ISIS affiliation and arrested while in a displaced-persons camp.

"When did you join ISIS?" Sahar asked.

"I didn't join," the suspect replied.

"Then why did you thumbprint this confession?"

"They blindfolded me and made me do it."

"Enough evidence—I ask for a guilty verdict," the prosecutor said.

The suspect's defense lawyer carefully explained that regional intelligence reports showed that the suspect had been mistaken for someone with a similar name. In terrorism trials, the mere presence of a private defense lawyer can signal the suspect's likely innocence; most lawyers refuse to take on ambiguous cases, out of fear that the security services will harass them for perceived links to the Islamic State. (Last year, Iraqi courts issued arrest warrants for at least fifteen defense lawyers and charged them with ISIS affiliation.) But, as the lawyer spoke, the judges tended to administrative tasks. The trial was over in nine minutes. "I hate ISIS—they blew up my house!" the suspect shouted, in tears, as he was led out of court.

By noon, Sahar had presided over ten trials, involving twenty suspects. The courtroom lost power twice, but Sahar kept going in the dark, skimming documents by the light of his cell phone. The final case before lunch involved three defendants, all badly injured. As they limped into the courtroom, a security officer put three plastic chairs in the cage. The last suspect to appear was a bald, bespectacled man in his midthirties, named Louai; he was hunched over a pair of short wooden crutches and moved as if one of his legs were paralyzed and his vertebrae were no longer aligned. Courtroom 2 was silent, except for the sounds of him struggling toward the cage.

Sahar questioned the other suspects first. One, named Haidar, who wore a back brace, said that he had been mistakenly arrested

for a car-bomb attack in 2014 and that in the course of an interrogation, to make the torture stop, he had started naming ran-
dom people, including Louai. Judge Sahar then called upon
Louai, who rose from his chair and gripped the cage to support
himself. "I went to sell my car in the market," he said. "Then
Haidar called me, and I was ambushed, arrested." He spoke in
an urgent, high-pitched tone, but he stuttered and slurred his
words; during interrogations, he said, officers had beaten him so
badly that he suffered a blood clot in his brain. "They also broke
my back!" he shouted. "They broke my feet and hands! I can
barely walk!"

"Enough evidence—I ask for a guilty verdict," the prosecutor
said. It was the only phrase she uttered in court that morning.

Haidar's lawyer noted that there was no witness and no material evidence and that his request for a medical examination, to
prove that Haidar had been tortured, had been rejected. Louai's
lawyer explained that Louai's confession had been coerced and
made no sense: he had said that he remotely detonated the car
bomb, when, in fact, the police had concluded that it was a suicide attack.

Louai had spent four years in pretrial detention, and, during
the two or three minutes allotted to his defense, the judges had
been talking among themselves. "I haven't seen a judge until
now!" he shouted.

"Take them out," Sahar said. A security officer opened the
cage. It took Louai nearly two minutes to limp to the door. Sahar
took a lunch break, then ordered his execution.

•   •   •

The Islamic State has been mostly destroyed on the battlefield, but
the war is far from over. Air strikes cannot kill an idea, and so it
has fallen to Iraq's fractured security, intelligence, and justice systems to try to finish the task. But, insofar as there is a strategy, it

seems almost perfectly crafted to bring about the opposite of its intent. American and Iraqi military officials spent years planning the campaign to rid Iraq of ISIS, as if the absence of the jihadis would automatically lead Iraq toward the bright democratic future that George W. Bush's administration had envisaged when U.S. forces invaded the country in 2003. But ISIS has always derived much of its dangerous appeal from the corruption and cruelty of the Iraqi state.

For three years, the Islamic State controlled half of Syria and a third of Iraq, a swath of territory approximately the size of Great Britain, which included millions of people. Several members of its senior leadership had been high-level military and intelligence officers in Saddam Hussein's Baathist regime; they combined the structural prowess of a police state with the cosmic certainty of radical jihadism. The group blew up mosques and ancient archeological sites and pursued a campaign of ethnic cleansing through mass murder and sexual slavery. It conscripted local bureaucrats, doctors, and teachers, often on pain of death, and devoted enormous effort to radicalizing a generation of children and inuring them to violence, suffering, and loss. At the height of its success, in 2014, there was a real possibility that ISIS would capture Baghdad, and the Iraqi state would collapse. Now, more than a year after ISIS lost Mosul—its largest source of legitimacy, wealth, and power—hundreds of thousands of civilians are suffering at the hands of their liberators. Anyone with a perceived connection to ISIS, however tenuous or unclear, is being killed or cast out of society.

Not long ago, I met with a senior Iraqi intelligence official who is deeply involved in counterterrorism operations. For three hours, over tea and cigarettes, he described systematic criminality within the security forces, detailing patterns of battlefield executions, murders in detention centers, and cover-ups organized by the state. He spoke as a witness but also as a participant; although he is in a position to have stopped certain abuses, by intervening he would have risked incurring accusations that he is sympathetic to the group he has sought to destroy.

He believes that the Iraqi government's response is as much a tactical blunder as it is a moral one; it plays directly into the jihadis' narrative—that Sunnis, who make up a minority of the Iraqi population, cannot live safely under a government dominated by Shiites. "The reaction is one of vengeance—it is not well thought out," he told me. "We rarely abide by the law."

Thousands of men and boys have been convicted of ISIS affiliation, and hundreds have been hanged. But, according to the senior intelligence official, these cases represent only a small fraction of the total number of detainees. "A few of the suspects are sent to court, but only to maintain the illusion that we have a justice system," he said.

Suspects are tried under a law that makes no distinction between a person who "assists terrorists" and one who commits violent crimes on behalf of an extremist group. The conviction rate is around 98 percent. Family members of the accused rarely show up to watch the hearings, out of fear that they will be detained, too. It's not uncommon for relatives to be rounded up by the security forces and sent to remote desert camps, where they are denied food, medical services, and access to documents. "We're deleting thousands of families from Iraqi society," the official told me. "This is not just revenge on ISIS. This is revenge on Sunnis."

Nine years ago, two CIA officers walked into an Iraqi prison and saw a hallway filled with hooded men, about to be executed for supposed affiliation with al-Qaeda in Iraq, the group that gave birth to ISIS. "We were hammering AQI, but the Iraqi government was just rounding up Sunnis," one of the CIA officers recalled. "And, for a moment, it worked." But, instead of releasing the innocents, the Iraqi government sentenced them to death. "So, of course, they came back," the officer said, of al-Qaeda in Iraq. "What do you expect? You literally killed their dads."

Iraq is now entering one of the most delicate moments in its recent history. To the extent that ISIS functioned as a state, it was entirely predatory. But, by having lost on the battlefield rather than being toppled by its own depravity, the caliphate lives on as a fantasy of Islamic justice and governance that is measured against the corrupt reality of the Iraqi state. What is at stake, in this postconflict period, is whether the Iraqi government can win over the segment of the population for whom ISIS seemed a viable alternative.

.   .   .

On an August night in 2011, eight jihadi commanders were sent across the border from Iraq into Syria by their leader, Abu Bakr al-Baghdadi, to infiltrate Syria's nascent revolution. By late 2012, they had amassed hundreds of followers from dozens of countries and were running training camps near Aleppo. During the next year, ISIS helped the rebels in key battles against the Syrian regime, but as the group became stronger its strategic focus shifted to the formation of a caliphate.

In June 2014, a few hundred ISIS fighters stormed back east across the desert in mud-caked pickup trucks and captured the Iraqi city of Mosul, essentially by mistake. In the preceding months, ISIS had taken over Ramadi, Falluja, and Samarra. But Mosul, with almost two million residents, was the economic center of northern Iraq. The group's plan was to take a few neighborhoods on Mosul's western banks and break into a prison to swell its ranks. Within a week, some 60,000 Iraqi soldiers and federal police officers, many of whom were reluctant to die in defense of a Sunni city, had shed their uniforms and run away.

For Mosul's residents, the announcement of a caliphate from within their city meant that the rest of their lives would be defined by their proximity to ISIS. Some religious minorities, like Christians, could remain in the city, if they paid a religious tax, but

Yazidis and Shiites faced enslavement or slaughter. Half a million civilians fled Mosul. The Islamic State found some support, owing to the abuses that Sunnis had suffered at the hands of the Iraqi government. But most citizens were stuck feigning allegiance to survive, despite the certainty that any compromise with the group would eventually taint them if Mosul were freed.

Some residents spent the next three years waiting out the situation—reading, smoking, counting the days until liberation. For others, interaction with the jihadis was not optional. The Islamic State did not dismantle the Iraqi bureaucracy; it appropriated it, and expanded it. There were departments in charge of almsgiving, the distribution of war spoils, hospitals, and the maintenance and health of rivers. Some institutions operated with greater efficiency and less corruption than before. But, for many bureaucrats, continuing in their duties meant participating in a sectarian criminal enterprise. The role of the estate authorities, for example, shifted from settling everyday land disputes to expropriating and redistributing Shiite property and homes.

For months, the Mosul civil defense—the city's professional firefighters and rescue workers—continued to respond to gas and electrical fires. But soon Iraqi and U.S. forces began conducting sporadic bombing raids, and ISIS informed the rescuers that if they didn't help retrieve wounded jihadis from the rubble they would be killed.

The Iraqi government stopped paying salaries—"If they paid us, ISIS might take the money," a young civil-defense worker whom I'll call Mohammad told me—and so the rescuers risked their lives to save ISIS fighters for free. "Fortunately, coalition planes never hit a civil-defense vehicle," Mohammad said. But, he recalled, "this started to make problems for us, because ISIS thought we were cooperating with the coalition." Mohammad fell under particular scrutiny; he speaks near-fluent English, which he learned by watching American films. In 2015, he quit the civil defense and went into hiding. ISIS fighters set fire to his house and his car.

．　　　．　　　．

The ground campaign to take back Mosul began in earnest in the fall of 2016. Until then, Iraq's factions and militias had little incentive to cooperate. For the Kurds, ISIS's invasion of Mosul had created a power vacuum, which they used to seize oil-rich territory and to try to renegotiate the boundaries of Kurdistan within Iraq. Shiite paramilitary groups, some of which had carried out thousands of attacks against American troops in the previous decade, had mobilized to prevent ISIS from capturing Baghdad, but it was another two years before the Iraqi government integrated them into the armed forces. It was a Faustian bargain; the most powerful militias, which are collectively known as the Hashd al-Sha'abi, are trained, equipped, and funded by Iran's Revolutionary Guard and have a reputation for carrying out the kinds of sectarian abuses that had led many Sunnis to welcome the jihadis in Mosul. "Without the Hashd al-Sha'abi, there would be no security in this country," the senior Iraqi intelligence official told me. "And yet, with them, there is no rule of law. They are above the army, the law, and the sovereignty of Iraq."

The Kurds attacked Mosul from the north and the east. Iraqi security forces approached from the south. American special-operations forces went in, too—officially in a supporting role, but they nevertheless frequently ended up in combat. The U.S.-led coalition decided to leave open the west as a kind of escape valve; this would allow ISIS members to be picked off as they fled into the desert, toward Syria.

What followed was the most intense urban combat since the Second World War. Air strikes pummeled villages and towns in Mosul's periphery, so ISIS contracted its territory, retreating to the city, along with thousands of civilians. "They told us that the Iraqi security forces would kill the men and rape the women," a young woman from the village of Shirqat told me. "We trusted ISIS more than the Iraqi state." Other villagers, who had spent years awaiting liberation, were loaded onto buses at gunpoint by ISIS fighters, and packed into Mosul's frontline neighborhoods, to be used as human shields. In the ensuing months, the jihadis murdered hundreds of people who tried to escape, and hung bodies from electrical pylons.

●　　　●　　　●

By early 2017, Mosul was half free. The city is bisected by the Tigris River. Its east side has wide avenues and low buildings. Backed by coalition airpower, East Mosul was taken mostly by elite Iraqi counterterrorism forces fighting house to house. They took care to minimize civilian casualties and suffered tremendous losses of their own. By the end of the battle for East Mosul, as much as 75 percent of the counterterrorism forces had been injured or killed.

The combat was much worse in West Mosul—especially in the Old City, a densely populated warren of alleyways, tunnels, and souks nestled against the banks of the Tigris. Its streets were too narrow for armored vehicles to pass through, and jihadis could easily slip between roofs and alleys and basements. To an outside force, it was practically impenetrable. The coalition bombed all five of Mosul's bridges and sealed off the western escape valve, while thousands of Iraqi soldiers, federal police officers, and Hashd fighters besieged the Old City.

The Old City was home to Mosul's richest history and poorest residents. Thenoon Younnes Abdullah, a middle-aged father with a bushy mustache, dyed brown, had spent the past couple of decades working as a day laborer, until his body gave out; to provide for his wife, Alaa, and their four children, he resorted to selling bootleg gasoline. Like most of his neighbors, he resented the ISIS fighters, who swaggered through the souks, flush with cash, telling him how to live—especially the foreigners, who barely spoke Arabic and had no connection to Mosul. Some of them had converted to Islam only a few months before coming to Iraq for the jihad. Abdullah's family had lived in the same cluster of houses, on the same block, with the same neighboring families, for as many generations as he could remember.

For three years, the Iraqi Army had told civilians to stay at home and wait for liberation, and Abdullah and his family had listened. Now, as the army encircled the Old City, electricity and water supplies were cut off, and life became impossible. People began to starve. The jihadis were breaking into homes, stealing food, and digging tunnels between basements, to pass undetected. They set up firing positions on people's roofs and stockpiled explosives in living rooms. Anyone who resisted was killed.

The coalition concluded that the Old City could not be captured according to the rules of engagement that had governed the battle in East Mosul, so it loosened its requirements for calling in an air strike. In March, the United States dropped a five-hundred-pound bomb on a roof in the Old City, in an effort to kill two ISIS snipers. The explosion killed a 105 civilians who had been sheltering inside the building. Survivors reported that there were no ISIS fighters in the vicinity at the time of the strike.

One night, when the shelling relented, Abdullah and his family hurried downhill to the banks of the Tigris, carrying inner tubes and two large coolers. None of them knew how to swim. Abdullah helped the kids into the coolers—two in each—and he and Alaa climbed onto the inner tubes, clinging to the children and each other as they floated downstream, to liberated territory.

By early July, ISIS fighters had killed thousands of government troops and police officers, and Iraqi commanders were under enormous pressure to finish the battle. The next few weeks were a bloodbath. ISIS fighters who surrendered were executed on the spot. Iraqi security forces filmed themselves hurling captives off a cliff, then shooting them as they lay dying on the rocks below. Helicopters buzzed the Tigris, bombing people as they tried to swim across. The troops assumed that anyone still living in the Old City sided with the Islamic State. For the rest of the month, corpses bobbed downstream, dressed in civilian clothes. "We killed them all—Daesh, men, women, and children," an Iraqi Army officer told a Middle Eastern news site, using the Arabic acronym for ISIS. As he spoke, his colleagues dragged a suspect through the streets by a rope tied around his neck. "We are doing the same thing as ISIS. People went down to the river to get water, because they were dying of thirst, and we killed them."

When the battle was over, soldiers used construction equipment to shovel rubble into the entrances of ISIS tunnels—ostensibly to suffocate any remaining jihadis, but also to mingle corpses and concrete, thereby obscuring the scale of the atrocities. As late as March of this year, journalists were still finding the bodies of women and children on the riverbanks, blindfolded, with their hands tied behind their backs and bullet holes in their skulls.

.   .   .

A year and a half after Iraq declared victory, the Old City is in ruins. Sunlight gleams through bullet holes in tin garage doors. Massive blocks of concrete dangle from broken roofs. The floors of apartment buildings remain as they fell, in layers, having crushed whatever was between them. The UN estimates that the battle for Mosul has left behind around ten million tons of rubble. Some stone structures have landed at odd angles, to disorienting effect, as if gravity were pulling in every direction. There are burned-out power lines and staircases to nowhere. It is completely silent. Near the site of an old post office, there is a single intact traffic light. It changes every thirty seconds, for no one. Every few feet you catch the smell of desiccated corpses. Also inescapable is the scale of history, obliterated. Many of the buildings were continuously inhabited from the seventh century until the second week of July 2017. To walk through the Old City is to tread on its final generations' graves.

Shortly after the battle ended, Mohammad returned to his job in the civil defense. Every day, locals lined up outside a temporary fire station in West Mosul and asked for help retrieving the bodies of their relatives. "We recorded their names and gave them a date," he recalled. "And when their date came they would come with us to the Old City and show us the house that had been hit by an air strike, and we would dig until we could take out the body."

The coalition has acknowledged a civilian death toll in the low hundreds. But the West Mosul civil defense has retrieved thousands of corpses from the Old City. Last December, the Associated Press obtained a list of nearly ten thousand civilians whose bodies had been registered at the local morgue. Most had been crushed to death by falling concrete; for others, the cause of death had been entered into the morgue's database simply as "blown to pieces." (Thomas Veale, a U.S. Army colonel and a spokesman for the coalition, told the AP that it was "irresponsible" to draw attention to civilian casualties in West Mosul. If not for the coalition's campaign, he said, Iraqis would have suffered years of "needless death and mutilation" at the hands of "terrorists who lack any ethical or moral standards.")

"All of them are civilians," Mohammad said. "When we find unknown bodies, we leave them behind," because there would be no way to apply for a death certificate or to return a corpse to its family for burial. "Sometimes people come here and tell us that they have dead relatives in the Old City, but we know that they are not *from* the Old City," Mohammad said. "They are from Qayyarah or Shirqat," towns where the Islamic State had more support. When that happens, civil-defense workers infer an ISIS link and refuse to retrieve the corpse.

The skeletons in the rubble have not been picked clean by animals or bleached white by the sun. There are fingernails and yellow teeth and dusty clumps of hair. Bone fragments line the roads, amid scraps of fabric and leather and glass. Near the river, I saw a torso dangling loosely from a mess of twisted rebar—swaying hands, fractured skull. Blackened ligaments drooped from the arms. "Daesh," a stranger said to me, smoking a cigarette, pointing at the corpse. He kept moving.

Nearby, I met Thenoon Younnes Abdullah. He waved and carefully wound his way down a three-story pile of rubble—the site of his former home—with his ten-year-old son. The family had returned to salvage whatever they could. Everything of any value had already been looted, but they rescued a broken generator, and tied it to the back of their car.

Abdullah told me that, after the battle, his cousins were the first in his family to return to the Old City; as soon as they opened their door, they were blown apart by IEDs. Months later, when Abdullah arrived, he found his own house in ruins and several dead ISIS fighters inside. He also found Alaa's mother's corpse; she had stayed behind, too frail to run away.

Abdullah led me up the hill of tangled metal and concrete, and we entered his house by ducking under a staircase, through a hole in the bathroom wall. On the floor of the dining room were three stains where fluids had leaked out as the bodies decomposed. Abdullah's brother died across the street, but his body hasn't been found.

It was difficult to move. The floor was littered with debris, but I noticed transistors, ball bearings, and other bomb-making materials scattered about. Then, on my way out, my foot knocked over a concrete block and uncovered an IED. I stopped and noticed two other unexploded bombs a few feet away, as well as four detonators. We climbed back out through the hole in the bathroom wall and came down the hill, past an ISIS corpse in rotting leather sandals.

Reconstruction in the Old City will cost billions of dollars, according to the UN, but, aside from the exorbitant cost, I had the impression that the Iraqi government has been content to leave it in ruins, as a kind of punishment. Abdullah told me that he had seen no evidence of institutional cleanup—only posters from NGOs, warning about the perils of walking in areas filled with unexploded ordnance, which still regularly kills people in the Old City.

Abdullah and his family piled into their car and headed to another part of the city, where they were staying in an abandoned, mostly destroyed building. He navigated by peering through a hole in the windshield, caused by shelling more than a year earlier.

·   ·   ·

The war against the Islamic State displaced a million people in Nineveh Province. Civilians who had fled ISIS at the outset, in 2014, were asked by Kurdish and Iraqi intelligence officers to inform on neighbors who had assisted the group. The names were then entered into databases of terrorism suspects, available to Iraqi security branches, including the Hashd militias. As the war dragged on, the lists became increasingly unreliable. People reported their enemies and wielded the threat of denunciation in personal, tribal, and workplace disputes. "We have thousands of suspects in custody whose names were falsely reported, or are based on incorrect information, and they are treated as ISIS members," the senior Iraqi intelligence official told me. He said that some Hashd fighters ran an extortion racket, demanding thousands of dollars from civilians and adding their names to the terrorism database if they couldn't pay.

To many members of the Iraqi security forces, all civilians who hadn't fled ISIS were suspicious. Some soldiers regarded beards as a marker of affiliation even though the jihadis had punished men who shaved. Others, by contrast, singled out men who had recently shaved or cut their hair, believing that the men were trying to evade detection. Injuries, too, attracted accusations of complicity; how could anyone know whether people who had barely survived shelling and air strikes were targets or merely collateral?

As civilians marched out of Mosul toward camps for the displaced, masked informants stood at checkpoints, pointing out individuals who, they claimed, had worked with the Islamic State. Some of the informants were children, but that didn't matter in court—a suspect would never find out who had denounced him or what was said.

All suspects were supposed to be handed over to the counter-terrorism services for an in-depth security screening. In practice, however, many captives faced vigilante justice in the streets. In October 2016, Iraqi security forces filmed themselves executing a captive in Qayyarah, an hour south of Mosul. They also tied the bodies of several dead ISIS fighters to the back of a Nissan pickup truck and dragged them through Qayyarah's main road, while villagers cheered; children kicked the corpses, and a man stood on one of the bodies, surfing. According to Human Rights Watch, which obtained thirteen videos from the scene, a man from a nearby village came to Qayyarah after hearing that the man who had killed his father and three of his uncles was among the dead fighters. He beheaded the man and cut out his heart, then presented it as a gift to his mother.

Elsewhere in Iraq, security forces filmed themselves punching, kicking, and whipping men in ad hoc detention sites, including school classrooms. They dragged suspects by the hair, stepped on their heads, slammed knees into their faces, and threw furniture at them. They beat people unconscious; they beat people to death. They filmed themselves gunning down captives in open fields and stabbing them in the face with knives. A group of Hashd members struggled to interrogate six foreign fighters who couldn't speak Arabic; in the end, they shot them, doused them in gasoline, and lit them on fire—including two who were still alive. A federal police officer filmed himself beheading captives, including minors, and posted the videos to his Facebook account. He told a Swedish reporter that he had decapitated fifty people so far, all while they were still alive; as he paraded through the streets holding severed heads aloft, other uniformed police officers and soldiers cheered and marched alongside him. All through northern and western Iraq, anti-ISIS forces kept lists of people they wanted to kill. They hung bodies from telephone poles and encouraged civilians to desecrate the corpses of their former jihadi oppressors. The irony was not lost on the killers—they knew that they were mirroring the Islamic State's worst acts.

The Iraqi government has sought to minimize attention to such atrocities. Haider al-Abadi, who served as prime minister between 2014 and October 2018, dismissed them as "individual acts" for which the perpetrators would be held to account. But there have been no meaningful investigations. According to the senior Iraqi intelligence official, "all Hashd violations are carried out with the knowledge and approval of the national-security apparatus, in all governorates." He added that the government has provided official cover for numerous civilian massacres by organizing press conferences and lying about the provenance of mass graves. "The Iraqi government brought in journalists and said, 'Look, ISIS killed these civilians,' when in fact it was the Hashd al-Sha'abi," he said. "The reality is totally different from what ends up in the media. At least ISIS had the courage to not hide its crimes."

Suspects who survived their capture were taken to detention facilities in and around Mosul. Iraqi law stipulates that suspects must be brought before an investigative judge within twenty-four hours of arrest, but many people languished in custody for months. Although there were only around eight thousand ISIS fighters living in Mosul, and far fewer in the surrounding villages, the lists of wanted people grew to some hundred thousand names. Dank, windowless cells held a hundred or more detainees each. Some facilities had no budget for food. Injuries that had been incurred on the battlefield, or during interrogation sessions, grew infected and gangrenous. Amputations were common, and detainees routinely died of suffocation or disease.

"Hundreds of innocent people have been detained because their names are similar to those of wanted people, and the state is doing nothing to solve this," the senior Iraqi intelligence official told me. (Mohammad is thought to be the most common name in the world.) Others are held on the basis of uncontrollable facts of identity: the suspect was a Sunni male of fighting age, from a village where the jihadis enjoyed widespread toleration or support; the suspect was the wife, father, brother, or cousin of a fighter; the suspect was a member of a rural tribe whose leader had pledged fealty to Abu Bakr al-Baghdadi. If someone is found innocent and released, no letter is sent to the entire security establishment to clear his name. "He might be arrested again, and this time not get released," the official said.

In late August, I met a seventeen-year-old ISIS fighter inside a facility in Iraqi Kurdistan that is holding dozens of minors who have been convicted of ISIS-related crimes. His name was Noor, and, along with another teenager, named Ahmad, he volunteered for an interview. In April 2016, when Noor was fourteen, one of his friends recruited him to attend an ISIS training camp. He wouldn't specify what attracted him to the Islamic State, saying only, "If there was something I didn't like about the group, I would not have joined." That October, he was captured by Kurdish forces near the town of Bashiqa, dressed like a member of ISIS, with long sleeves and pants stopping above the ankles, and carrying a Kalashnikov. Noor was the only jihadi in his family—he told me that he had joined ISIS without his parents' knowledge or permission—but, last year, members of a Hashd group arrested his relatives, expropriated their home and property, and sent them to detention camps.

As Noor spoke, Ahmad looked uncomfortable. He said that he wanted to talk but not with Noor in the room. A prison worker escorted Noor back to his cell.

"I've been here for two years and eight months, trapped with all these jihadi kids!" Ahmad said in a rush. "But I'm not ISIS! They picked me up by mistake!" One of his cousins had been recruited, but no one in his immediate family had joined. Nevertheless, when Kurdish forces liberated his town, intelligence officers detained Ahmad and tortured him until he made a false confession. He lifted his shirt to reveal faint lines all over his back, from whipping and beating and a twisted knot of a scar on his upper arm. At this point, Kurdish prison workers said that the interview was over. "I showed the judge that I had been tortured," Ahmad continued. But the judge told him that an unnamed witness had claimed he had carried a gun and sentenced him to five years.

•   •   •

The pace of arrests has recently slowed. In Mosul, there are now only two or three raids per week. Most of them are carried out by an Iraqi SWAT team, with assistance from the United States military, which provides intelligence—names, addresses, sometimes a photograph—as well as vehicles, arms, and air support. In return, American soldiers are given access to detention facilities, to collect the fingerprints and eye scans of high-value targets. Sometimes they take suspects away, returning them days or weeks later, when they've finished their own interrogations.

The most powerful Shiite paramilitary units have a similar relationship with the Iranian Revolutionary Guard. Security and intelligence officers from the Hashd still patrol the ruins of the

Old City, occasionally making arrests. On August 30, a group of them, dressed in plain clothes, detained me in front of the ruins of Thenoon Younnes Abdullah's home and questioned me for three hours. They photographed my face, passport, and Iraqi visa, and the commander, a wide-faced man who goes by Abu Ali, warned that I would be arrested if I returned to the Old City. Then two Hashd intelligence officers grabbed their Kalashnikovs, got into my car, and, with a follow vehicle, escorted me across the bridge to East Mosul. During the drive, the two men showed me cell-phone photos and videos of supposed ISIS fighters they had killed all over Iraq. I asked whether their unit shares intelligence with or receives it from any foreign governments. "We refuse to talk about this," one of them, who was wearing bluejeans and a Gucci baseball cap, said. "Because America is not friendly with Iran."

Pretrial detention can last years, and even if detainees don't die from the conditions they may still never see the inside of a courtroom. Thousands of files have been misplaced within the bureaucracy as detainees have been transferred among sites run by overlapping security agencies—meaning that, on paper, the suspects are missing. "Hundreds more have been killed during interrogations," the senior Iraqi intelligence official told me. Ministry of Health officials, he said, usually classify the cause of death as "unknown" or "heart attack" and then dispose of the corpse.

The process is so corrupt that, according to the official, "only the poor ISIS members go to court. The wealthy ones can buy their way out of the system." Unable to trust their colleagues in other departments not to release ISIS members, some intelligence officers have resorted to murdering high-value detainees.

Not long ago, the senior intelligence official looked on as a group of his subordinates beat a Saudi fighter with iron bars inside an ad hoc detention center near Mosul. The fighter taunted his interrogators, saying that if he recovered he would return to the battlefield and fight them again. They broke his arms and legs, and threw cinder blocks onto his back. "Who knows, exactly, when he died," the official said. "But he wanted to become a martyr, and so the interrogators obliged."

I asked him whether the Iraqi government notifies foreign embassies when its intelligence officers kill their citizens. He said that most European fighters are referred to the judiciary unscathed, because their identities are widely known, and their fates are scrutinized by the international press. "But most of the Arab foreign fighters do not make it to court," he said. "We do not tell their governments what happens to them, and their governments do not ask."

·   ·   ·

In Baghdad, the relentless pace of trials struck me as so incongruous with the lack of evidence, the certainty of convictions, and the severity of sentences that I began to wonder whether judges had access to secret intelligence reports that they weren't sharing in court. One evening, I visited the office of Munir Haddad, a magistrate who presided over the trial of Saddam Hussein. It was a troubled proceeding—defense lawyers were assassinated, and the prime minister pressured judges into issuing a death sentence—but, compared with the ISIS trials, Haddad said, "I believe the process was reasonably transparent. Saddam had lawyers. Only six or seven people were executed. These days, in terrorism courts, at least twenty-five people are sentenced to death every single day."

Haddad lit a cigarette and threw his legs over an elegant wooden chair. Ali Shimari, a handsome young lawyer, sat next to him. Haddad left the bench years ago; he and Shimari now work as a team, defending terrorism suspects whom they believe to be innocent. That morning, Shimari had sat through the same hearings that I had. "Everything that the judge saw, the lawyers saw, too," he said. "There's usually no evidence, just the confession."

I asked Shimari if the arbitrary nature of the trials frustrated him. "What can I do?" he replied, shrugging. "I'm a defense lawyer. I can't tell the judge to pay attention. You can try once or twice, but it has no effect."

Haddad laughed. "We are not in America," he said. "It's not possible to argue with the judge, because if you do he'll just take it out on your client. As a lawyer, you just have to accept the humiliation."

I asked Haddad whether, as a former judge in Iraq's highest-profile tribunal, he believed that judges see their role as meting out a kind of cosmic justice, even if the truth lies beyond the kinds of evidence that can plausibly be collected. "ISIS has so many victims," he said. "There have to be convictions."

Thaer Abd Ali al-Juboori, the spokesman for the Ministry of Justice, told me much the same thing. "Human-rights groups focus on the rights of suspects, but what about the rights of the victims and their families?" he said. "We have undergone thousands of terrorist attacks. There is immense public pressure on the judicial authorities." He continued, "9/11 left three thousand people dead. The whole world obsessed over this attack. We cried for your innocent deaths. But, here in Iraq, we have had a terrorist death toll that has exceeded that by a factor of a hundred. Where is the sympathy that we have shown to the victims of 9/11? This is what Iraqis are upset about. We fight terrorists every day, on behalf of the rest of the world. And no one cares about our suffering."

The amount of time that convicts spend on the waiting list to be hanged fluctuates between months and years because each execution order requires a signature from the president of Iraq. Barham Salih, a progressive Kurd, who was imprisoned and tortured by Saddam Hussein's regime, assumed the presidency in October.

In the past, Salih has distinguished himself through his opposition to capital punishment. In 2002, when he was prime minister of the eastern part of Kurdistan, he refused to sign the death warrant for an unrepentant al-Qaeda sympathizer who had attempted to kill him. "I think this is a fundamental question of what type of society we want," Salih said at the time. "I don't believe that anyone, or the state, should take people's lives." Sixteen years later, it's not clear that any Iraqi presidency could survive such a stance. Throughout the ISIS period, in the aftermath of terrorist attacks, the Iraqi government has carried out mass executions in order to mollify an outraged public. I wrote to Salih's press secretary, Lukman Faily, several times, to ask whether Salih is signing execution orders but did not hear back.

Execution orders are carried out by the Ministry of Justice. In 2009, al-Qaeda operatives detonated a car bomb outside the ministry's headquarters, killing thirty-five employees. Four years later, terrorists attacked the replacement headquarters. "Every time we publicized an execution, we would get attacked," Juboori recalled. Afterward, staffers demanded to be moved to the Green Zone or to have the task of executing convicts referred to a different department. But after a few days they gave up and went back to work. "We have to earn a living," Juboori said. Today, the ministry occasionally publishes the numbers of people executed but leaves out the names; by obscuring the identities, Juboori said, the ministry can accede to the public's demand for results while minimizing the likelihood of retaliatory attacks.

To human-rights groups and foreign officials, the Ministry of Justice's opacity is a source of frustration. "Often we would find out about mass executions by reading about them on the justice minister's Facebook page," a European diplomat who spent much of the past three years in Baghdad told me. "There will be some notification saying that they've killed forty-two terrorists. OK, but who? Of which nationalities?" Juboori denied that this was the case; after a foreign fighter is executed, he said, his colleagues put the body in a refrigerated chamber and inform the relevant embassy.

The Iraqi judiciary has also exposed the willingness of Western liberal democracies to quietly regard due process as a strategic disadvantage. During the battle for Mosul, France deployed elite soldiers to track and kill its own citizens. Some five thousand Europeans joined ISIS, and, of the thousand or more who have returned to their home countries, very few have been charged with crimes, owing to the near-impossibility of collecting court-level evidence in a foreign war zone. European intelligence agencies are overwhelmed; to carry out comprehensive surveillance on a single target requires a team of around thirty people. And so countries that have outlawed capital punishment are tacitly encouraging Iraq to eliminate their jihadi citizens. "If the Iraqi government were just rounding up and killing Iraqis in this way, we could be more vocal" in criticizing it, the European diplomat said. "But we don't have any idea what to do about our own citizens. There is no policy."

$$\cdot \qquad \cdot \qquad \cdot$$

For many terrorism convicts, a stop before the gallows is a spot on Iraqi state television as participants in a reality show called *In the Grip of the Law*. Prisoners explain on camera how they supposedly plotted and committed heinous acts, sometimes visiting the scenes of their crimes. They also renounce terrorism and agree that they deserve to die. One afternoon in September, the host, Ahmad Hassan, welcomed me to the studios of al-Iraqiya, shook my hand, and threatened to sue me if I misquoted him. He recalled an incident in which a foreign journalist had quoted him as saying "jihadis" when he had actually said "ISIS terrorist gangs"; in the days after publication, Iraqi politicians and security officials asked him why he'd used a word that could be perceived in a neutral light.

Just off the set, a director was working on an upcoming episode. A man in an orange jumpsuit was sobbing onscreen. The director spliced in footage from an ISIS video, featuring a mass execution. "This is Mowafaq Ahmad Shihab—he's from a first-class ISIS family," Hassan told me. "Most of his sons worked for the ISIS terrorist gangs." In the ISIS footage, a masked man lifted a pistol to the head of a kneeling hostage. "His son will now carry out an execution of some prisoners," Hassan said, as the footage rolled on. "And what Mowafaq confessed in the investigation is that he was helping his son execute innocent citizens."

He pointed to a figure in the crowd. "Mowafaq is in the background," he said. To my eye, there was practically no resemblance: the man in the ISIS video had a full head of white hair, whereas Mowafaq was mostly bald, and what hair he had was black, except for a bit of gray in his beard. When the show aired, two weeks later, the clip was blurred to obscure the differences. But there was still an inconsistency between the episode and its trailer: the arrows for Mowafaq pointed to two different men.

According to Hassan, the show, which airs on Friday evenings, has millions of viewers. *In the Grip of the Law* is dependent on the involvement of the legal and security-intelligence establishments and glorifies their work. "It's the only program in this country that increases public trust and confidence in the security forces and judicial offices," Mujahid Aboalhail, the head of al-Iraqiya, told me. "It passes the message to the whole world that the fate of these terrorists is in the grip of the law!"

Hassan walked over to the set where he films his opening statements. He took off his jacket and sat behind a large wooden desk—clear, except for a single lamp. Behind him was a map of Baghdad, decorated with images of police reports and mug shots of various suspects. He wore a white shirt with light-blue pin-stripes, a deep-red tie, and an oversized watch; his black hair was slicked back, shining under the stage lights. Hassan put his elbows on the table and scowled—the caricature of a TV detective. There was a bookshelf filled with evidence binders, but they were empty.

"Ask me what you would like to know," Hassan said. I led off with a biographical question. He ignored it, unlocked his phone, and started reading aloud a prepared statement, occasionally stopping in the middle of a phrase in order to catch his breath. "The idea for this program came to me because Iraq suffered many terrorist attacks, lots of vicious acts of bloodshed," he read. "This program doesn't just do interviews. It also shows CCTV, weapons, car bombs, explosives—actual evidence. This has helped maintain pressure against terror groups. It also helps spread awareness to security forces about how terrorist groups operate. It also gives awareness to the citizens to beware terrorist tactics, and helps citizens gain confidence in the security-intelligence establishment." He paused. "Do you want me to talk about how I pick the prisoners?"

"Is that in the statement?" I asked.

"I have written a set of responses to questions I expect you to ask."

Hassan insisted that he merely offers prisoners "a chance to repent" and that they take him up on it because they "feel regret." But the substance and tone of their confessions raise questions. In Mowafaq's episode, he is marched down a sealed-off street in Mosul, handcuffed and blindfolded, and forced to kneel in front of a line of masked members of the security forces. His blindfold is removed; they're holding automatic weapons. It looks like the lead-up to a street execution—the director used a split screen to mirror the ISIS tape—and, as Hassan questions him, it's not at all clear that Mowafaq, who has already been sentenced to death, knows otherwise.

•   •   •

On July 10, 2017, a twenty-five-year-old woman from Shirqat, who goes by Umm Saleh, arrived at a camp for the internally displaced just outside Qayyarah. She had spent the previous week running between buildings in Mosul's Old City, where an air strike on a school had killed her father, her brothers, and one of her sisters. Umm Saleh's husband survived the explosion, but amid the chaos the couple lost track of each other, and so she left Mosul with their three children, carrying the youngest in her arms. Members of the Iraqi security forces robbed and harassed Umm Saleh at every checkpoint. Many of them obscured their faces with balaclavas and masks and had patches on their uniforms of the skull worn by the Punisher, a Marvel Comics antihero who kidnaps, extorts, and murders people in the pursuit of his own conception of jus-tice; the skull is the last thing that his victims see before they die. "If the Americans weren't behind us, we would burn you," a soldier told Umm Saleh. She had left Mosul with some cash and gold but arrived in Qayyarah penniless.

Umm Saleh expected to reunite there with her husband. He hadn't joined ISIS, but his brothers had been conscripted as fight-ers. Because he hadn't denounced them or severed ties, on the way to the displaced-persons camp he was picked out of line dur-ing a security screening and taken away.

One day, a member of the Iraqi security forces visited the camp, promising to look into the cases of detainees for a fee of a thou-sand dollars. Umm Saleh's mother and sister sold all their gold to pay the bribe, and Umm Saleh gave him her husband's name. The soldier took the money and never came back.

At the camp, Umm Saleh was placed in a sector populated by widows of the Islamic State who had also grown up in Shirqat. Because Umm Saleh's husband was mistaken for an ISIS fighter, she is now perceived by camp administrators and guards as the female head of an ISIS family. Her children are growing up fatherless and isolated from the rest of society, unable to attend Iraqi schools. "People look at us differently," another woman in the sector told me. "Even small children in the camp point at my children and say, 'ISIS! ISIS!'" The government refuses to recognize or replace Umm Saleh's infant son's birth certificate because it was issued by the Islamic State; as with tens of thousands of other Iraqi children, his own country has rendered him effectively stateless. The camp is now Umm Saleh's de facto prison; Iraqi security forces stole her identity card at a checkpoint, and without it she cannot leave.

At night, Umm Saleh and the other women in her sector try to avoid the camp toilets, which are unlit, to minimize the chances of being raped by guards. Members of armed groups routinely enter the camp to harass them, rob them, assault them, or burn down their tents. One night, three Hashd fighters raped a young woman named Amani while she was washing inside her tent. "One of them had a shop that I used to visit in Shirqat," she told me. "Another was my neighbor." During the attack, they berated her for her ISIS affiliation.

Amani was abandoned at birth, grew up in an orphanage, and married when she was around fourteen. Two years later, ISIS came to Shirqat. Her husband joined and forced Amani to move with him to Mosul. She was miserable; she hated having to cover her face in public. She became pregnant, and soon afterward her husband went to fight in the Makhoul Mountains, where he met and married another woman. A few months later, he fled with his new bride to Syria and divorced Amani by phone. She deleted his number and escaped from ISIS territory. When she reached Qayyarah, she tried to legally divorce her husband but wasn't able to because her ID had expired and her husband wasn't present. The Iraqi government refuses to issue her a new ID because it considers her an ISIS wife. Without documentation, she has no freedom of movement and is deprived of access to Iraqi civil services. She wants to return to Shirqat, but fears that, even if she made it out of the camp, she would be detained or killed by Hashd fighters or by her former neighbors. "I have not seen happiness at any moment in my life," Amani said, tears streaming down her cheeks.

In another sector, a frail, eighty-two-year-old man named Hellou Hamad, who was also from Shirqat, was lying on a filthy mattress, unable to get up. He had been sent to the camp more than a year ago because three of his sons had joined the Islamic State. "I tried to stop them, but they were bored and single and jobless," he told me. The surrounding tents were populated by his female relatives and their children. Many kids in the camp urinate uncontrollably in the night as a result of the trauma induced by the war; among the women, there are high rates of suicide. "Our houses were burned—we are rejected by our community," Hamad told me. "I am the only man in this block. All the others are in prison or dead."

.   .   .

There are eight camps in the desert near Qayyarah, housing roughly 150,000 people. During the war, most residents were people who had been displaced by the Islamic State. But now the proportion of ISIS-linked families is growing as those who are unaffiliated return to their villages. The largest of the facilities is Airstrip Camp, which I visited twice in late August; between my visits, more than 1,100 ISIS-linked Iraqi men, women, and children arrived in Qayyarah from a camp in eastern Syria. The journey had taken two days, and the Iraqi government had transported them from the border in open trucks, in 115-degree weather, without providing food or water. At least one person died.

At the entrance to Airstrip Camp, down a long, unpaved road, men holding machine guns stood in the shade of a cinderblock hut, near a tattered Iraqi flag. Inside were tents covered in dust—blue canvas turned a deep brown, held to the ground with rope and sandbags caked in mud. Clotheslines and gullies of green sewage separated the tents, and the camp's razor-wire fence had caught thousands of plastic bags, which thrashed noisily in the breeze. Children hauled wheelbarrows and carts filled with water jugs and sacks of grain. On the horizon, a surveillance balloon floated above Qayyarah's air base, from which the U.S. military had staged much of the Mosul campaign.

One of my visits coincided with that of the country head of a major international NGO. "This is set up like a concentration camp," he said, gesturing at the fence. "All the barbed wire, the division of sectors. There are no social spaces. There are no spaces for the children to play. There are no places for people to gather. There's one entrance in and out. And have you seen the guys at the entrance? Most of them are from militias."

Throughout Nineveh Province, camp administrators and workers routinely deprive ISIS-linked families of food, clean water, and medical services. The NGO country director told me that he had traveled more than two hundred miles from Baghdad, "to make sure that our Iraqi staff are not falling into these types of revenge attitudes." He added, "They say, 'These people killed my family, and now I have to help them?'" In some camps, humanitarian workers offer aid in exchange for sex. Many women are pregnant from having been raped by the security forces or from having sex to feed themselves and their children. Although the fighting has ended, "these camps are meant to stay," the NGO director said. "If you are ten years old now, and you have no food, no assistance, and your mother has to prostitute herself to survive, and the whole of Iraqi society blames you because you were close to ISIS—in two, three, four years, what are you going to do? It's clear. The seeds for the next conflict are all here."

At a police compound in West Mosul, I asked a colonel named Mezhar Sedoon whether he thought that the camps are creating more security problems than they are solving. "Some of the mothers in the camp are raising ISIS children, but others have become prostitutes," he said. He laughed. "Money-money, fucky-fucky!" he said in English. "I'd rather they become whores than raise terrorists!"

Some women try to carry out abortions inside their tents. Others give birth and discard the babies in unpopulated parts of the camp. Those who are found alive often end up in the care of Sukaina Mohammad Ali Younnis, an Iraqi government official who is in charge of women's and children's issues in Mosul. Over tea in Erbil, the capital of Iraqi Kurdistan, she showed me hundreds of photographs of children she has found in camps, on the streets, and dead in trash cans. Earlier this year, she saw someone throw a bundle out of a car, and found that it was a baby boy. She showed me a video of herself cradling him in the back of an ambulance as blood bubbled out of his nostrils. He died on the way to the hospital.

Outside the camps, thousands of other children have been abandoned or orphaned by the war. Many of them were born to Yazidi women who had been kidnapped by ISIS and forced into sexual slavery. "After ISIS, the Yazidis accepted the women back into the community, but not their half-ISIS babies," Younnis said. "They force the women to turn over their children to the orphanage. Every day, these women call me, wanting to know how their children are doing."

Hundreds of small children are living in Iraqi prisons. Those whose parents were foreign fighters are often present in the courtroom when their mothers are sentenced to death. Iraqi children whom ISIS trained to become fighters and potential suicide bombers are imprisoned, as if their lives were irredeemable. "They are useless in interrogations—they just cry," the senior Iraqi intelligence official said. "We are holding children as young as twelve in cells with hardcore jihadi fighters."

Thousands of children in Mosul live on the street, searching through the trash for scrap to sell. "After their parents were killed or imprisoned, their relatives refused to take them in," Younnis said. "They are seen as tainted, even if they were too young to absorb the ideology." Many of them hang out in traffic and at checkpoints, choking on dust and diesel, trying to wipe down windshields or sell water and tissues to passing motorists. "They will do anything for fifty dollars," she said. "I go to many government officials, asking to find ways to help these kids, but they all say, 'It's not my area of responsibility.'"

"The camps are a time bomb," Younnis continued. "The fathers are in prison or dead. The mothers are being raped. They will raise the kids accordingly, and their sons will seek revenge. This won't just affect Mosul or Nineveh or Iraq. This will affect the whole world."

.   .   .

One morning in Mosul, I was told that an ardent supporter of ISIS, who goes by Umm Hamad, wanted to speak with me, in the market by the Saddam neighborhood. All three of her sons had been ISIS commanders and were now dead, but she had evaded deportation to the camps. My interpreter and I parked near a vegetable stand, fifty feet from an Iraqi Army checkpoint. There was another checkpoint a couple of hundred feet behind us, and no access to the side streets. For a moment, I wondered if it was a setup. Then two women approached the car, opened the back door, and climbed in.

"I'm still proud of what they did," Umm Hamad said of her sons. She doesn't think of them as having lost—only of having proved that it was possible for a jihadi group to control territory and to govern. Already, since its defeat in Mosul, ISIS has set up checkpoints and carried out abductions and assassinations in several Iraqi provinces. Its leadership has reportedly buried large quantities of weapons and cash in tunnels and sand berms, to be unearthed in the years to come. According to the Pentagon, ISIS is "more capable" now than al-Qaeda in Iraq was at its peak, in 2007, and there are still some thirty thousand fighters operating in Syria and Iraq. Citing the camps, Umm Hamad told me that she expects the Islamic State to return to Mosul. "Not soon, but more powerful than before," she said.

The other woman was Umm Hamad's niece. She was in her twenties and spoke softly and wistfully of the past. "Everyone in my family welcomed the Islamic State, except my youngest brother," she said. "He hated them." Throughout the occupation, she and her other brothers had tried to convince him of the merits of the caliphate, to no avail. Then he was arrested by the Iraqi security forces, under suspicion of ISIS affiliation. He was twelve years old. She has no idea where he is or when he will get out of prison—she knows only that, if the government doesn't kill him, by the time it lets him go it will have taught him that she was right.

An Interview with Ben Taub
by Eric Sullivan

In May 2015, three days after walking the stage to accept his master's degree from Columbia Journalism School, Ben Taub began a trajectory that remains the stuff of fantasy for most j-school grads. He published his first piece in the *New Yorker*. "Journey to Jihad," about a Belgian teen who fled to Syria to join ISIS and the father who set off to find him, was Taub's graduate thesis and his first attempt at a long-form story.

Four years, nine more features—all for the *New Yorker*, where he's now a staff writer—and a small mountain of awards later, Taub won the 2019 National Magazine Award for Reporting, for "Shallow Graves," about the Iraqi government's corrupt, cold-blooded handling of suspected jihadis and their families. He's only twenty-eight.

Although Taub is not the first investigative reporter to reach such heights so quickly—Nellie Bly, a progenitor of the field, broke out in 1877, at twenty-three—he might be the only one who owes his career, at least in part, to a stint on reality television.

In 2012, Taub, then a junior at Princeton University, beat out nearly 100,000 pop-star hopefuls to earn a spot on NBC's *The Voice*. Music had always been a part of his life. His father is a concert pianist and Beethoven scholar; in high school, Taub played the oboe, starred in school musicals, and toured Europe as a vocalist in a jazz orchestra. In college, he considered pursuing acting. The show presented a chance for his big break—until it didn't. Cut in the third episode, he left with a modest stipend and the resolve to seek a career in which, as he puts it, "the stakes were real." With the help of one of his journalism professors, NPR's Deborah Amos, he planned a trip to the Turkish-Syrian border, near ISIS-held territory. The money from *The Voice* helped pay his way.

There, Taub laid the groundwork for what would become his first piece, and he began to explore the themes that run through his body of work: the enduring specter of violent extremism, the trickle-down effects of corrupt governance, the bottlenecking of information caused by a free press that is under threat, and the challenges faced by the people caught in the middle. If Taub has a beat, it is intricate humanitarian crises. He's covered the Syrian regime's systemized use of torture and murder to suppress dissent ("The Assad Files," April 18, 2016); the trafficking routes funneling refugees from western Africa to Europe ("The Desperate Journey of a Trafficked Girl," April 17, 2017); and the geopolitical unrest in Chad ("Lake Chad: The World's Most Complex Humanitarian Disaster," December 4, 2017).

On a Sunday afternoon in early spring, Taub met me on the steps of the Brooklyn Museum. It was exactly one month after the

Ellies, but the award, it seemed, was a remote memory. He was drained; he'd just filed his latest story, about the U.S. military's highest-value detainee at Guantánamo Bay and the guard who befriended him. But once talk turned to Iraq, his demeanor transformed. He spoke with clarity and urgency, as if he were still reporting from the field.

During our conversation, which has been edited for length and clarity, we discussed the moral imperative that drives his work, the challenges of maintaining a social life as a foreign correspondent, and his writing process, which involves sleeping on the floor and heading into the office at three in the morning.

•　　　•　　　•

ERIC SULLIVAN: Why did you decide to write about post-ISIS Iraq?

BEN TAUB: In April 2018, with ISIS in retreat, I wanted to do a sort of autopsy on the territory once held by the caliphate. I was supposed to go to Syria, too, on a U.S. military embed, but it was canceled at the last minute. My contact at Special Operations Command told me that it was because Trump was about to meet Putin in Helsinki, and nobody at the Defense Department had any idea of how that meeting would affect their Syria operations. So I just focused on Iraq.

ERIC SULLIVAN: How did that affect your aims for the piece?

BEN TAUB: The new plan was to frame the story around an Iraqi television show called *In the Grip of the Law*, which airs every Friday night on state television. Its premise is that people who've been convicted of a terrorism charge confess to their crime on camera. They're paraded through the streets of Baghdad or Mosul or wherever and asked to reenact their alleged crime—how they put the detonator in the glove box of the car, that kind of thing. What is not at all clear is whether these confessions have been coerced through torture.

ERIC SULLIVAN: That scene only plays a small role, two-thirds of the way in. The story's scope is vast—11,000 words spread over fourteen sections, with two dozen sources on the record. Why did you pivot away from the show and toward that wide-angle approach?

BEN TAUB: The show's producers turned out to be extremely unreliable. One day they'd promise me access and the next day claim it would be impossible. So there was pretty much nothing to do but report around the show. That process accidentally yielded a more important story, about the scale of the Iraqi government's post-ISIS campaign of revenge.

ERIC SULLIVAN: How long was your trip?

BEN TAUB: Twelve days on the ground, split between Baghdad and Mosul.

ERIC SULLIVAN: You had a fixer?

BEN TAUB: Three, actually—two in Mosul and one in Baghdad.

ERIC SULLIVAN: How did you find them?

BEN TAUB: I talked to journalists from the *Washington Post*, the *New York Times*, and the BBC. Everyone was generous about offering advice on security and logistics, which included recommending fixers. I've always been heartened by the camaraderie among those who report from complicated areas.

ERIC SULLIVAN: What traits do you look for in a fixer?

BEN TAUB: It comes down to the languages they speak, their connections, their rates, their availability, and, perhaps most important, how they handle dangerous situations. For many of my stories, the reporting trip is the first time I've visited the country. I'm not always equipped to assess whether I'm in danger, so I need to trust that they'll detect what I can't.

ERIC SULLIVAN: A good fixer protects you. Are you mindful of protecting your fixer?

BEN TAUB: Yes. If I'd been arrested in Iraq, I might've been held for a couple of hours or days, then deported. But for the fixer it would be a hell of a lot worse. It's my responsibility to make sure I'm not ruining the life of anyone who interacts with me—a fixer, a source—because of the scope of my project or because of my own stupidity. I'm hyperaware of the moral implications of what I'm doing on the ground as an outsider.

ERIC SULLIVAN: Do you ever feel like a parachute journalist? What do you do to mitigate that concern?

BEN TAUB: I write, like, three things a year, so I'm fortunate to have the time to read everything I can before going in and to sit down with people for as long as it takes to understand the situation. In the case of this Guantánamo story I just finished, I read books by former Guantánamo detainees and by people who'd worked there, books about the invasion of Afghanistan. I read probably twenty-five books on national-security law and thousands of pages of government documents.

ERIC SULLIVAN: What was the most surprising thing you witnessed, that no amount of pre-reporting would've prepared you for?

BEN TAUB: I had a pretty good sense of what was going on in the courts before I got there but not of what was happening in the camps, which held women and children who were linked to ISIS fighters. Officially, these camps are for IDPs—internally displaced people—but in practice, they're detention camps. The people held there are not allowed to leave. There's razor wire around the perimeter.

The so-called ISIS families are guarded by militias and suffer tremendous isolation and abuse. Local aid workers often deprive them of food and medical care. I didn't know that until I saw the camps firsthand. And the international NGO workers in those camps, who were trying to make the situation less desperate and less terrible in any tiny way they could, were hesitant to talk about it.

I was warned by war-crimes investigators, government officials, aid workers, and other journalists that if I wrote this story, I might not be allowed to come back to Iraq. I was like, "And if I don't write it, then what the fuck am I here for? And what the fuck are you here for?"

ERIC SULLIVAN: It makes sense that the NGO workers couldn't speak about the conditions in the camp. But why haven't media outlets done more to cover it?

BEN TAUB: A lot of journalists can't say the stuff that I did in the piece because they live in Iraq or the organization for whom they work needs to maintain access in order to function. If you're the Baghdad bureau chief for a media outlet, you have to deal with the consequences of what you publish. It could affect your relationships with Iraqi officials or your visa status.

But I work for a magazine, and I don't write until I'm home. At that point, it's not just a question of having the luxury to write whatever I want. It's my responsibility to tackle the situation fully and vociferously and to say all the things that everyone else wants to but can't. Because I don't have to go back—my livelihood isn't dependent on access to Iraq. So the only morally acceptable thing to do is to write what I know to be true, regardless of whether I burn all my bridges.

ERIC SULLIVAN: Is that how you view your role? To write what others cannot?

BEN TAUB: This is almost crude to say, but I see my job as an effort to trick people into reading 10,000 words on a subject they don't think they care about. I don't mean that in a grandiose way. But I am taking on projects that I think are of great urgency and importance. It's my responsibility to shape the reporting into a readable narrative that people want to get through, even if they don't know about the topic when they start.

ERIC SULLIVAN: Did you fly one-way or round-trip?

BEN TAUB: I usually buy one-way tickets. This was no exception.

ERIC SULLIVAN: How do you know it's time to leave the country you're reporting from?

BEN TAUB: I won't stay any longer than I need to, but I'll stick around until then. This may sound silly, but because I'm very concerned about the situation for local journalists and fixers, I see it as kind of a moral obligation to leave when you're done. Halfway into my trip, I interviewed a senior Iraqi official who ended up playing a big role in the story. After our three-hour conversation, I knew I had enough material to write some version of the piece, but there was more I wanted to do. From that point forward, every day I reevaluated whether I was done.

Less than a week later, Moises Saman, the photographer who shot the story, and I were trying to return to a neighborhood in Mosul. Our fixer reached out to the commander of one of the militia groups in the city. We asked him if we could come back. He said no—that if we came back, he'd arrest us. At that point, it was clear we were done. I got on the next flight out of the country, four hours later.

ERIC SULLIVAN: In the story, you briefly describe how one of those militias detained you. What happened?

BEN TAUB: We were in the Old City of West Mosul, where
ISIS had made its final stand. The neighborhood was
completely flattened. We came upon a family that had
escaped the final slaughter and had returned to rifle
through the rubble of their former home, to salvage
what they could. As they were getting ready to leave, a
pickup truck arrived. The men who got out were dressed
in plainclothes, but they were armed. They told us they
were from the intelligence branch of a Hashd al-Shaabi
paramilitary group that was backed by Iran. They insisted
on seeing our passports and press cards. They texted
photos of our documents up their chain of command then
let us go.

Then, on our way out of the neighborhood, just past
the last checkpoint, the same pickup stopped us again. We
knew then that we were going to have trouble. Twelve
men arrived, including the local commander, and they
held us for about three hours. They went through our
phones and cameras, and eventually they were satisfied
that we weren't ISIS fighters or American spies. Shortly
after they agreed to let us go, two of the men, both
carrying Kalashnikovs, climbed into the backseat of our
car, next to me, and basically said, "You guys are journalists? So do journalism."

ERIC SULLIVAN: "Do journalism."

BEN TAUB: Yeah. They told us to start driving, but not
toward East Mosul, where it was safe. They wanted to
watch us do our jobs in West Mosul. Their pickup followed behind. Moises started taking photos. One of the
men asked why I wasn't doing the same. "I'm a writer," I
told him. "So interview me," he said. The whole thing was
funny in a way. Moises was performing the role of a
photographer, and I was performing the role of an

interviewer, but both of us were counting the seconds until it seemed like we'd given them enough. After fifteen minutes, the men grew bored, got out of our car, and let us leave. But the pickup kept trailing us. We didn't want them to know where we were staying, so we drove for two and a half hours to Kurdistan, where they couldn't follow us.

ERIC SULLIVAN: What was going through your mind while you were detained?

BEN TAUB: There are things that you can control and things that you cannot. I see it as my responsibility to control the safety and logistics that I can, right down to always wearing my seatbelt. But in situations I can't control, like how long they'd hold us there, I strive for a performative calmness. If I act scared or agitated or defensive or too sweet and deferential, it would give them reason to be suspicious. I try to look bored and mildly annoyed, and give them only what they ask for, nothing more.

I also texted my editor, Willing Davidson, to let him know that we'd been detained, along with a pin showing our exact location.

ERIC SULLIVAN: What did he say in response?

BEN TAUB: He was like, "OK. Keep me posted as you can." Willing always has the right reaction. Just as it would've achieved nothing for me be agitated in real time, it would've achieved nothing for him to run around the offices of the *New Yorker* yelling, "Ben's been detained!"

ERIC SULLIVAN: Did the State Department know you were in Iraq?

BEN TAUB: No.

ERIC SULLIVAN: Who did?

BEN TAUB: David [Remnick, editor of the *New Yorker*] and a very small circle of people close to me.

ERIC SULLIVAN: Sounds like a harrowing experience.

BEN TAUB: I can't feel bad for myself for having had a rough time in Iraq, right? It's infinitely worse to be an Iraqi in Iraq than it is to be an American journalist who dithered around the country for twelve days. My relatives aren't getting killed. I'm not getting persecuted. I'm not subjected to the constant fear of awaiting a knock on the door at two in the morning from the security services.

ERIC SULLIVAN: You made it home safely. What did you do next?

BEN TAUB: Once home from reporting, I always transcribe everything, which can take several weeks.

ERIC SULLIVAN: Why transcribe it yourself?

BEN TAUB: Hearing the words, as opposed to reading them, throws me back into the mental space of where I was, right down to little things like birds chirping or a shovel scraping on cement. Those tiny details often end up in the piece.

ERIC SULLIVAN: What comes after transcription?

BEN TAUB: I map out a rough outline.

ERIC SULLIVAN: At what point do you loop your editor into that conversation?

BEN TAUB: As soon as I get back. Willing is a master of structure. He also edits fiction.

ERIC SULLIVAN: Describe your working relationship.

BEN TAUB: I see my role in our relationship in two ways. First, and I think this is a classic editor-writer thing: he is my best friend, but I know I'm not his. And that's fine. Second: I see my job as making each piece easier for Willing to deal with than the last. That's how I know I'm learning. I'll write outlines, and then we'll discuss. But we also have general talks, without any text in front of us, about how something might work structurally. These conversations are essential because when I finally sit down to write, I know I'm not composing drafts based on incoherent structures. If I were to set out on my own, it would be a total disaster.

ERIC SULLIVAN: Why do you say so?

BEN TAUB: I've now done nine pieces, and I'm only just starting to register certain patterns and story arcs. When I was hired by the *New Yorker*, I didn't know how to write anything. That's a preposterous thing to say, but it's true. I'd never written a long-form story, and I didn't know how to do it. Like, at all. The reporting comes relatively intuitively to me; the writing does not. It's a tortured process. It takes weeks and weeks and weeks.

ERIC SULLIVAN: Lead me through it.

BEN TAUB: Well, there are two things. The material I witnessed is much easier to write. The parts where I'm reconstructing a scene are really hard. That's where you have the greatest responsibility, to ensure that you're correct about a larger truth that you didn't witness. Take the Battle of Mosul: I'm trying to boil down a battle I wasn't there for into a couple of paragraphs. And get it accurate—not just the facts but the context, the history. I'll spend a whole day writing one or two paragraphs, adding words and deleting them, then adding more.

ERIC SULLIVAN: What do you think about your writing?

BEN TAUB: It's less bad now. And it's getting less bad with each piece. But I also know I compensate for not having writing come intuitively by working really hard and not having much of a social life.

ERIC SULLIVAN: What do you do for fun?

BEN TAUB: I don't really have a good answer for that. I used to play soccer. I had a girlfriend for a while. Don't anymore. The work is fun.

ERIC SULLIVAN: Where do you write?

BEN TAUB: I find that I write best at the *New Yorker* office [at One World Trade Center, in Lower Manhattan], between three a.m. and ten a.m.

ERIC SULLIVAN: Excuse me?

BEN TAUB: [*Laughs*] I wake up around two a.m., go straight to the office and write till ten, then spend the rest of the day trying to keep up whatever writing pace I'd set in the earliest hours of the morning. Around six p.m., I go home, and I try to fall asleep before nine. I sleep on the hardwood floor because if I am uncomfortable, it's easy to get up when my alarm goes off.

ERIC SULLIVAN: Wow. Is that your everyday routine?

BEN TAUB: Just while I'm writing. And I do it every day— weekdays, weekends, it's all the same—until the story is done.

ERIC SULLIVAN: How did you land on such an extreme schedule?

BEN TAUB: I got frustrated with how I always feel that I'm behind. Sleeping on the floor was a way of feeling that I was doing everything I could.

ERIC SULLIVAN: Why do you feel like you're always behind?

BEN TAUB: Because I know that other people write faster and better than I do. I know I'm never going to be as fast or as good as them, so I push myself to at least try to work harder than they do.

ERIC SULLIVAN: Is that pressure situational? You're at the magazine of record. Your colleagues are among the best writers on the planet.

BEN TAUB: There's that. And there's the fact that I've had a really short tenure in journalism. I graduated from college less than five years ago and from journalism school less than four. I don't have a repertoire of sources and facts to draw upon, so I have to work really hard to build each story from scratch. That's true of anyone starting out. For the first decade, you have to learn a whole set of facts for every assignment. I'm playing catch-up all the time.

ERIC SULLIVAN: Are you concerned about burnout?

BEN TAUB: I'm not sure I'm doing this in the most sustainable fashion, but I am doing what's required to keep up with the caliber of work that my colleagues are producing. The only thing that matters is the work. When I'm writing, I can go weeks, sometime months, without accumulating memories.

I don't want to measure my life only by projects. I want to be able to recall periods of my life in ways that aren't about whether it was a writing month or a travel month or a reading month. I guess what I'm trying to say is that I have not figured out how the life of a foreign correspondent or a magazine writer ought to look. I have no clue. I have some sense of what I like about it and some sense of where I need to find some balance. But I have no sense of how to find that balance.

ERIC SULLIVAN: What else could you do?

BEN TAUB: For a while, I thought I would become a stage actor. I still wonder sometimes whether I should audition for a play. But I never really had much momentum.

ERIC SULLIVAN: Not true! You were a contestant on *The Voice*.

BEN TAUB: So, *The Voice*. It was a fun experience. But I grew unhappy with how the show portrayed people very differently on TV than they were in real life. The producers had this idea of the characters they wanted the contestants to fill. I refused to behave as they had apparently cast me, which was as a caricature of a privileged, Ivy League asshole. I'd much rather get kicked off, with no airtime, than be on TV as someone I'm not. I wanted something where the stakes were real. Six months later, I went to the Syrian border.

ERIC SULLIVAN: Do you miss performing?

BEN TAUB: One of the things I found frustrating onstage was that I hadn't experienced or witnessed the conflicts and the high emotional stakes of the characters I was supposed to portray. A side effect of my journalistic work is that I've now experienced the full range of human emotion. If I were to go back to acting, I wouldn't feel like a fraud.

ERIC SULLIVAN: In the end, maybe your journalism career will have been a means of returning to the stage.

BEN TAUB: [*Laughs*] I wouldn't say no.

Politico

FINALIST—REPORTING

"Even within Myanmar's complex patchwork of ethnic and religious identities, the Rohingya stand apart," writes Nahal Toosi in "The Genocide the U.S. Didn't See Coming." "They are uniquely hated—singled out for their Muslim faith and dark, South Asian features." Since August 2017, more than 680,000 of the 1.1 million Rohingya thought to live in Myanmar have fled to neighboring Bangladesh to escape rape and murder. In this story, Toosi documents not only the brutal treatment of the Rohingya but also the willingness of American policy makers to discount the persistent authoritarianism—and virulent racism—of the government of Myanmar. Before joining Politico *as a reporter, Toosi worked for the Associated Press. Her reporting on Myanmar, like Ben Taub's on Iraq, was supported by a grant from the Pulitzer Center on Crisis Reporting. In the last five years,* Politico *has been nominated for four National Magazine Awards; in 2016 the publication won the Ellie for Feature Photography.*

Nahal Toosi

The Genocide
the U.S. Didn't
See Coming

Cox's Bazar, Bangladesh—The Moynarghona refugee camp, a claustrophobic, chaotic mass of bamboo and tarpaulin shacks, slumps over hillsides stripped bare of vegetation. Scrawny teenage boys in T-shirts and sarongs linger on its edges, staring aimlessly at trucks and rickshaws skidding by. To wander inside the camp is to have your senses assaulted—by the chatter of a thousand half-naked toddlers, the stench of raw sewage, the bitter taste of dust. The heat, which can climb toward 90 degrees during the winter season, only adds to the misery. But the air is stifling mostly because this place, this supposed refuge, has been sucked empty of hope.

Moynarghona is one of several such camps to spring up or expand in southern Bangladesh since August 2017, when hundreds of thousands of Rohingya Muslims began fleeing a military-led crackdown in neighboring Myanmar, also known as Burma. The Rohingya have lived in Myanmar for generations, primarily in the country's Rakhine state, and have long faced severe discrimination from the Buddhist majority, which views them as illegal migrants. But this latest wave of violence is the worst in modern memory. On August 25, after a Rohingya insurgent group killed a dozen members of Myanmar's security forces, the military retaliated with outsize brutality—burning villages, raping women, and slaughtering anyone in the way. Of the 1.1 million Rohingya thought to live in Myanmar prior to last summer, more than 680,000 have fled across the border into Bangladesh, by land and by boat. Thousands of others are believed to have been killed, although just how many remains unknown because Myanmar has restricted access to the conflict zone. U.S. secretary of state Rex Tillerson has called the crisis "ethnic cleansing." More recently, a top United Nations official said it bears "the hallmarks of a genocide."

·   ·   ·

The village of Tula Toli in northern Rakhine state was the scene of some of the worst violence in the days after August 25. Uniformed troops charged the village, shot or hacked the men to death, and raped the women, locked them in houses, and set the houses on fire. Children were not spared: security forces tossed them into the flames or the river bordering the village, several Rohingya who escaped told me. Among the survivors was a young mother, Laila Begum, who ran for the river with her children as the security forces closed in. Begum lost hold of her three-year-old son in the chaos. Then, as she jumped into the water to get away, an assailant tore her eighteen-month-old daughter out of her arms. Back on land, Begum stumbled on the body of a woman whose throat had been slashed. Next to the body sat a dazed little girl covered in blood. Begum grabbed the girl and ran, joining other Rohingya in the exodus to Bangladesh. When I met them in Moynarghona, the round-faced girl, who looked around two years old, called Begum "ma." Begum called the girl Yasmeen.

Begum sat in a dark, dusty hut with clothing hung behind her. Her eyes grew blank and her voice turned soft as she tried to describe what she'd lost. "When I think of my daughter and my son, I don't even want to hear the word 'Myanmar,'" she said. "It was a torturous place for us."

Hundreds of villages were attacked in the weeks after August 25. The assaults could last hours, leaving scores of burned or maimed corpses behind. Multiple Rohingya escapees said they saw the bodies of women whose breasts had been sliced off. Such accounts from survivors are difficult to verify independently, but the stories I heard in the camps match what human-rights groups and the United Nations have discovered: gruesome reports of rape, arson, and murder at the hands of Myanmar's military, other security forces, and Buddhist vigilantes.

It's a moral disaster but also a geopolitical one. The violence against the Rohingya has inflamed ethnic and religious tensions across South and Southeast Asia while also fraying diplomatic ties between Myanmar and the world's Muslim-majority countries. It is straining the resources of Bangladesh, already desperately poor, and deepening the global migration crisis, which has seen a record 65 million people displaced from their homes. There are also fears that Rohingya youth could radicalize and join Islamist terrorist groups, who, even before 2017, were increasingly mentioning the Rohingya in their propaganda.

The violence has also upended what was supposed to be an American success story—the much-fêted opening to an increasingly democratic Myanmar, championed by a U.S. president, Barack Obama, eager to make friends of old enemies willing to change their behavior. For Obama's former advisers, some of whom fought to lift sanctions on Myanmar, it is a slow-rolling disaster that gnaws at their consciences. The country's political transition has meant new rights, freedoms, and opportunities for millions in Myanmar. But for the Rohingya, it has meant despair. "Whenever I close my eyes, I see the people I lost," one twenty-one-year-old Rohingya rape victim said. "I don't see any future."

•　　　•　　　•

Washington, D.C., was having a party.

On September 15, 2016, America's political and business elite gathered at the Four Seasons in Georgetown to honor Aung San Suu Kyi, Myanmar's beloved icon of democracy, on her visit to the U.S. capital. Suu Kyi, a Nobel Peace Prize winner who had spent years under house arrest for resisting Myanmar's military junta, had seen her party win a surprisingly free election in 2015 and was now the country's de facto civilian leader.

The day before the Four Seasons bash, Obama had pledged to do away with the last major economic sanctions on Myanmar—the final big step in a rapprochement that had begun in 2009 and included a significant easing of sanctions in 2012. Sitting next to Suu Kyi in the Oval Office, Obama cited the progress the country had made toward democracy. Scrapping sanctions, he said, "is the right thing to do in order to ensure that the people of Burma see rewards from a new way of doing business and a new government." In her speech the following evening, Suu Kyi urged businesses to invest in Myanmar to help its people as well as its nascent political transition. "We have to prove that democracy works, and what will prove that democracy works is a visible and sustainable improvement in the lives of our people," she said. The mood in the room was giddy: Halfway across the world, democracy was on the march.

But not everyone in the crowd was optimistic. Tom Malinowski, the assistant secretary of state for democracy, human rights, and labor, believed Myanmar's military still controlled too many levers of power to merit clearing sanctions. Malinowski had spent a good deal of time in 2016 pushing back against Obama administration colleagues who wanted the sanctions gone—marking the latest battle in a larger internal struggle over Myanmar policy that had intensified over the previous seven years. On one side was Malinowski's bureau at the State Department, which worried the U.S. opening was moving too fast; on the other was the State Department's Bureau of East Asian and Pacific Affairs, which was happy with the rapid pace of the rapprochement, and Ben Rhodes, the influential Obama aide known for pushing the narrative that America should engage rogue regimes in hopes of changing their behavior. Ultimately, Obama had sided with the Rhodes camp.

The disagreements confused Suu Kyi, who, even after Obama's announcement, was receiving mixed messages about just how far the United States could and would go in eliminating the economic penalties—a situation made all the more perplexing by the complications of sanctions law. Suu Kyi herself hadn't always taken a firm position on sanctions, partly because she worried lifting them would benefit Myanmar's generals, who are major players in the country's economy. When Suu Kyi saw Malinowski at the Four Seasons, she asked for some clarity on the U.S. debate. "She was like, 'What the hell? What's going on here? What's the reality?'" Malinowski recalled. "I said, 'Look, at this point there's not much more I can say. So whatever it is that you want us to do, you need to make that clear to the White House.'"

Suddenly, Scot Marciel, the U.S. ambassador to Myanmar, interrupted the conversation, apparently worried that Malinowski was assuring Suu Kyi some sanctions could stay in place. Marciel, a proponent of clearing as many sanctions as possible, tried to cut off the discussion, telling Suu Kyi that it was too late to reverse the president's decision, according to Malinowski's recollection. (Marciel confirmed he was there but declined to share details other than to say, "At that point, the president had already made his decision and announcement on lifting of sanctions.") It was a heated moment, enough so that others in the room noticed before things calmed down.

In the end, Obama fulfilled his pledge. In the final months of 2016, as he prepared to make way for Donald Trump, Obama went about as far as he legally could to scrap economic sanctions on Myanmar in hopes of spurring an economic and democratic flowering.

Malinowski and his allies at State weren't alone in doubting Obama's decision. As the administration rolled back sanctions in late 2016, Myanmar security forces began murdering Rohingya in a vicious campaign that displaced tens of thousands—and human -rights activists were appalled. They worried that Obama was so determined to fortify his legacy of outreach to adversaries that he was ignoring how far from a true democracy Myanmar still was and how splintered a nation it remained. Some feared that the 2016 violence was a harbinger of far worse to come for the Rohingya.

The activists sent letters, arranged grassroots campaigns, and communicated their concerns in meetings with Obama aides. "We kept warning them that with each sanction they lifted, it emboldened the military to commit more human rights abuses," said Jennifer Quigley, an official with Human Rights First who has extensive Myanmar experience. "And the Rohingya were exceptionally vulnerable, to the point where we warned they could face a genocide."

Today, as those fears are coming true, Obama-era officials on all sides of the debate have been looking back on the decisions they made, asking themselves if they could have done anything more to prevent Myanmar's bloody purge. Among the dozens of officials and analysts I spoke to, there's no real consensus as to what, if anything, went wrong. But there is a sense that Obama-administration officials were overly optimistic about what democracy could mean for all the people of Myanmar—that they didn't understand the special peril Rohingya Muslims faced in a country with such complicated ethnic and religious dynamics. And all said they worry about what will happen to the Rohingya under the presidency of Trump, who has been openly hostile toward Muslims and downplayed human rights in his dealings with other countries.

"I don't think anyone would have predicted you could push out 700,000 people," said Derek Mitchell, who was U.S. ambassador to Myanmar for most of Obama's second term. "We never felt that there was an imminent danger that required us to forgo a diplomatic-engagement approach for a more hostile policy. We didn't want to get rid of everything over an issue that we didn't know would actually blow up this bad."

.   .   .

The dire circumstances of 1.1 million Rohingya might not have been a deal-breaker when it came to U.S. engagement with Myanmar. But the fate of one woman was.

Suu Kyi, a slender, elegant politician often called simply "the Lady," is the daughter of Aung San, a beloved nationalist leader who played a key role in negotiating what was then Burma's independence from Britain in the late 1940s before he was assassinated. In 1962, while Suu Kyi was based in India with her diplomat mother, a military coup overthrew the Burmese government and ushered in a long period of oppression. The junta silenced dissent and pursued a mix of isolationism, nationalism, and socialism that deepened the country's poverty. The military leaders also engaged in a brutal civil war against an array of armed ethnic groups that displaced hundreds of thousands of people. Eventually, the junta changed Burma's name to Myanmar, partly as a break from its colonial past, and embarked on bizarre projects like carving a new capital out of the jungle deep in the country's interior.

In 1988, Suu Kyi—by then living in Britain with her husband, whom she had met while studying at Oxford University, and their two children—returned to Myanmar to care for her ailing mother. Within months, the high-profile daughter of Aung San had become a leader in the country's prodemocracy movement, helping establish a new political party, the National League for Democracy, and demanding more rights and freedoms through massive demonstrations. In July 1989, the junta put Suu Kyi under house arrest. The next year, with Suu Kyi still detained, the NLD won resoundingly in a general election, but the military refused to give up power.

Suu Kyi's peaceful resistance to the government, which kept her under some form of arrest for fifteen of twenty-one years, made her an international hero and endeared her to Western leaders. U.S. officials, who began increasingly using sanctions to penalize the junta for its antidemocratic actions, based much of their policy toward Myanmar on how Suu Kyi and her party were treated. For example, in 2003, after an alleged junta-backed attack on Suu Kyi's motorcade, followed by her rearrest, Congress passed new sanctions. Then-U.S. president George W. Bush called the punishment "a clear signal to Burma's ruling junta that it must release Nobel Peace Laureate Aung San Suu Kyi, along with all other political prisoners, and move down the path toward democracy."

Many scholars argue, however, that Myanmar's central challenge—and the key to understanding it—is not about democracy but whether the country can overcome its mind-boggling number of ethnic and religious conflicts. For decades, the central government and military, both dominated by the country's largest ethnic group, the Bamar (or Burman), have battled an array of militias—sometimes thousands strong, often in uniform—fighting for the rights of the country's various ethnic groups. Much of the fighting occurs along Myanmar's borders with China and Thailand, resource-rich areas where some ethnic groups, such as the Kachin and the Kayin, control significant territory.

But even within Myanmar's complex patchwork of ethnic and religious identities, the Rohingya stand apart. They are uniquely hated—singled out for their Muslim faith and dark, South Asian features. Many people in Myanmar view the country, which is nearly 90 percent Buddhist, as a critical bastion for Buddhism in a region where Islam has been spreading for centuries. And they see the Rohingya as malevolent interlopers out to upend those demographics—suspicions fueled by the perception that the Rohingya have unusually high birthrates. Myanmar's leaders do not count the Rohingya among the nation's 135 officially recognized ethnic groups. Most refuse even to use the term "Rohingya"; to do so would give legitimacy to a people most Burmese insist are illegal migrants from what is now Bangladesh. But the more pressure they've faced, the more the Rohingya have clung to the label.

The exact origins of the name, and the people, are disputed. The Rohingya say many in their community can trace their roots in Myanmar back centuries to when Rakhine, a long strip of land on Myanmar's western coast, was an independent kingdom. Other Rohingya ancestors are said to have migrated there during the colonial days, when the British encouraged migrants from British India to move to Burma. Muslims were at times favored by the British, earning resentment from Buddhists. World War II also exacerbated communal tensions in Rakhine state, as Muslims largely sided with the British while many Buddhists sided with the Japanese.

After the 1962 military coup, the junta launched a long campaign of oppression against the Rohingya that escalated at times into violent military crackdowns, with hundreds of thousands of Rohingya fleeing to Bangladesh. A 1982 law effectively stripped the Rohingya of their citizenship, and further laws and regulations restricted the group's ability to marry and have children. Today, after years of junta and Buddhist propaganda, the Rohingya are loathed by most people in the country. In impoverished Rakhine state, the Rohingya also are frequent targets of their neighbors the Rakhine Buddhists, another ethnic minority that faces discrimination from the Bamar. Some Rakhine Buddhists aspire to expel all Rohingya Muslims from their state and gain more independence from the central government.

Many Rohingya have been persecuted for so long that they have no memory of anything else. When I traveled through the camps in Bangladesh, I met a woman named Gulfaraz, who estimated her age as eighty-five. Gulfaraz was among the Rohingya who fled to Bangladesh in the late 1970s during a crackdown the Myanmar military called "Operation Dragon King." She eventually returned to Myanmar. In the violence in 2017, she saw several of her relatives shot dead in her village by security forces who shouted: "You're Bengalis! Go back to your own country! Leave this place!"

"I've thought of myself as Rohingya since I was a child," she said on Christmas Day. "I feel burning pain when I think about my family. But I fear if I go back, even to look for their bodies, I will be killed."

. . .

By the early 2000s, Myanmar's generals seemed ready for a change. After decades of totalitarian rule, they adopted a road map to what they called a "disciplined democracy." And in 2008, they held a flawed referendum on a constitution that, while still keeping the military entrenched in power—including giving its representatives 25 percent of parliamentary seats—allowed for partial civilian rule.

The changes in Myanmar dovetailed with the arrival of an American president intrigued by the possibility of bringing rogue regimes in from the cold and determined to prove that engaging dictators was a more effective way to promote democracy than spurning them. Obama said as much in his first inaugural address, promising authoritarian leaders such as Myanmar's generals that America would "extend a hand if you are willing to unclench your fist." He was also determined to shift the focus of U.S. foreign policy from the Middle East to the Asia-Pacific, a vast region he viewed as the future of geopolitics. The need to manage the rise of China, long Myanmar's chief patron, and reduce the nuclear threat from North Korea—which was believed to have provided missile and other defense know-how to Myanmar—added hard-headed reasons to try to midwife a democratic transformation.

"This is a country of, like, 56 million people, 55.9 million of whom had nothing to do with the government. So, there was the sense that, if there's a possibility to effect real change, we should be in the game and not on the sidelines," recalled Colin Willett, who dealt extensively with Myanmar while on the National Security Council and at the State Department. "The president's attitude was: better to try and fail than not try."

In 2009, under Secretary of State Hillary Clinton, the State Department led a review of Myanmar policy that concluded that diplomatic engagement should deepen but sanctions should stay in place. In November 2010, Suu Kyi and her party boycotted Myanmar's general elections, which Western powers declared a sham. But days after the vote, Suu Kyi was released from house arrest to great global fanfare. And upon taking power in March 2011, the country's new president, former general Thein Sein, began introducing reforms at a pace that astonished even hardened skeptics. Media censorship was eased, a new labor law permitted unions and strikes, and restrictions on the internet were largely lifted. Myanmar also began releasing political prisoners, thanks to a major push by the human rights bureau at the State Department. Ultimately, around 1,500 political prisoners were released.

Things were changing so rapidly that the Obama administration could barely keep up. The U.S. approach to Myanmar was initially based on a concept called "action for action," meaning that Myanmar would have to take a positive step for the United States to respond in kind. A "matrix" was even drawn up charting out matching actions, sources involved said. But the chart was quickly outdated because Myanmar officials moved faster than the Americans expected. "There was a real sense, too, that we had a window and that it wouldn't stay open forever," Willett said.

"The Burmese, you'd meet with them, and it was just shocking how eager they were to do things differently. They'd talk to you, they'd discuss the way things could be changed. They just were like 'OK, I'm going to tell you everything I know.'"

Clinton visited Myanmar in late 2011, the first U.S. secretary of state to do so in more than fifty years. She and Suu Kyi, two of the world's most famous women, wore white as they met for dinner, then hugged and held hands the next day before reporters at the Nobel laureate's lakeside home. When parliamentary by-elections were held in April 2012, Suu Kyi and her National League for Democracy won most of the seats. In the days that followed, the United States took its diplomatic engagement with Myanmar to a new level. Clinton announced the administration would begin easing sanctions on Myanmar's access to U.S. investment and financial services, and that it would reopen a USAID mission in the country. The administration also named Mitchell, who had been serving as a special envoy to Myanmar, as U.S. ambassador—the first person to hold the post since 1990, the year the junta refused to recognize the NLD's historic election win. As the months wore on in 2012, the administration made another momentous decision: Obama would visit Myanmar that November.

•   •   •

The heady talk of progress glazed over serious policy struggles behind the scenes as the Obama administration debated just how far to go in peeling back economic sanctions. U.S. officials across the board remained suspicious of the Myanmar military's true motives. But, according to people involved in the 2012 discussions, officials in the East Asia bureau at the State Department pushed for quicker, broader sanctions relief while those in the State Department's Bureau of Democracy, Human Rights, and

Labor, along with many outside rights activists and some U.S. lawmakers, urged a more cautious approach.

Those who wanted fast and wide sanctions relief argued that economic advances could boost democratic institutions, including Suu Kyi's political party, by proving that political reforms could lead to prosperity among ordinary people. Plus, advocates of easing sanctions noted, the longstanding U.S. penalties hadn't really hurt their intended target, the junta; Myanmar's generals were well off in an otherwise poor country. Some military leaders had indicated to U.S. officials that they wanted to open up their country to the West not because they cared about the sanctions' effect on their own fortunes but because Myanmar was economically trailing its neighbors. They also resented that China was throwing its weight around and saw the United States as a potential balancing force. "What they said was, 'We want to take Burma from being impoverished up to the level of a Malaysia or even a Singapore. To do that we need American businesses, not Chinese,'" said Daniel Russel, the senior director for Asian affairs at the National Security Council in 2012 who later went on to lead the State Department's East Asia bureau.

American businesses eager to explore a near-virgin market, despite Myanmar's exceptional poverty and limited infrastructure, were also pressuring the administration to open up the country to U.S. investment. As sanctions were eventually eased, Coca-Cola jumped in with its sugary drinks, and General Electric started exploring the Myanmar health-care market. (Still, U.S. business investment in Myanmar today lags well behind several other countries.)

Those wary of easing sanctions in 2012 had their own arguments. Many understood the desire to reward Myanmar for its reforms, but they felt the administration was offering too much economic relief too fast. They worried that the White House, which loved to use the phrase "Burma's democratic transition," was blind to just how far from a genuine democracy the country really was. The military did not answer to the civilian leadership, controlled vast portions of the government, and gave no sign it planned to exit the political arena. This group acknowledged that sanctions offered little leverage in Myanmar, but, they argued, why give up even that limited leverage? "It was the diplomatic equivalent of burning money," said John Sifton of Human Rights Watch. "The Burmese junta ran the country for a half a century. They'd completely infected every sector. There needed to be a sword hanging over their head to keep them motivated." Plus, easing the sanctions would send a symbolic signal that all was well in Myanmar, when it really wasn't, the pro-sanctions advocates maintained.

Willett, who was on the National Security Council at the time, remembers one emotional roundtable with several NGOs in mid-2012 at which Obama administration officials discussed easing the sanctions. Human-rights activists present pointed out that Myanmar's military was still brutalizing ethnic minorities; at the time, the armed forces were pursuing an offensive against the Kachin after the collapse of a seventeen-year cease-fire. "People were crying. People were just so upset with us," Willett said. In one private encounter with an activist not long afterward, things got personal. "I've never been called a baby killer before," Willett recalled. "I was really kind of shaken by the whole thing."

The result of the wrangling was a set of compromises. For instance, the move to ease U.S. financial and investment restrictions on Myanmar did not permit new investment with the country's armed forces. It also was coupled with an Obama executive order that gave the Treasury secretary authority to sanction people in Myanmar who undermined democratic reforms or abused human rights. State Department human-rights officials also successfully fought to require U.S. companies newly investing more than $500,000 in Myanmar to issue reports detailing how they addressed labor, environmental, and various social challenges there. Those same officials lost out, though, when they tried to bar U.S. oil and gas companies from taking advantage of the eased investment rules.

U.S. officials weren't thinking much about the Rohingya in early 2012. They knew the group existed and was under pressure, but, sources indicated to me, they didn't consider the possibility that the Rohingya were so despised that they would be excluded from the benefits of change. They assumed that Myanmar's pledges to reconcile with armed ethnic groups would also cover the Rohingya.

That's not because they were never warned otherwise. In March 2012, as the administration's debate over sanctions heated up, U Kyaw Min, a prominent member of the Rohingya community who had been freed after years as a political prisoner, met with a State Department official. Kyaw Min viewed Myanmar's desire to improve ties with the United States as a special opportunity to negotiate more security for his people—and to signal that the U.S. was watching out for them. He worried about what could happen without that protection.

When I recently saw him in Yangon, Myanmar's largest city, Kyaw Min told me that during that meeting he'd conveyed a straightforward request: Don't relax sanctions on Myanmar unless the Rohingya are given back their citizenship. His request went nowhere.

·   ·   ·

During the second half of 2012, as life improved for many of the people of Myanmar, the Rohingya's already tenuous standing took an ugly hit.

In June, a few months before Obama would make his first visit to the country, tensions between the Rohingya and the Rakhine Buddhists exploded after three Muslim men were blamed for the rape and murder of a Buddhist woman. Villagers and vigilantes from both sides staged riots and fought each other, but as time went on, according to human rights groups, security forces stood aside or even joined in when the Buddhists attacked Muslims. In July, as Obama made the sanctions easing official, Thein Sein suggested that not only did Myanmar not want the Rohingya, but that they should be resettled in any third country "willing to take them." A second wave of violence that year became more organized and more directed at the Rohingya. According to Human Rights Watch, on October 23, thousands of Rakhine Buddhist men "armed with machetes, swords, homemade guns, Molotov cocktails, and other weapons descended upon and attacked Muslim villages in nine townships throughout the state. State security forces either failed to intervene or participated directly in the violence."

In other countries emerging from dictatorship, lifting the government's heavy hand has led to dramatic explosions of ethnic violence. In Iraq after the 2003 U.S. invasion, it was Sunni versus Shia Muslims, with minority Christians a target, too. In Indonesia, as pressure grew on the dictator Suharto to step down in 1998, ethnic Chinese minorities became the target of riots. "When transitioning to democracy, political actors want to be popular, so they'll inflame certain passions," noted Thomas Carothers, a leading authority on political transitions.

In Myanmar, one of the loudest anti-Rohingya voices was that of Ashin Wirathu, a monk dubbed by critics the "Buddhist bin Laden." Wirathu took advantage of the increased freedom of speech and access to social media, delivering anti-Muslim sermons at rallies and warning that the Rohingya were trying to Islamify Myanmar. "We are being raped in every town, being sexually harassed in every town, being ganged up on and bullied in every town," Wirathu was quoted as telling the *Guardian*, claiming: "In every town, there is a crude and savage Muslim majority."

In Washington, U.S. officials watched the 2012 violence with varying degrees of alarm. One U.S. official recalled arguments over whether to call the fighting "communal"—blaming all sides and thus striking a more neutral tone—or, as the violence increasingly appeared to be one-sided, "anti-Muslim." There was also uncertainty about how to deal with the rise of voices like Wirathu's. "We had a lot of conversations about how to counter that kind of speech and putting pressure on the government to crack down on the incitement," Willett said. "But when you are at the same time advocating free speech and expansion of media, it's kind of a difficult line to walk, you know?"

Myanmar's leaders responded to the 2012 violence in Rakhine state by creating a series of camps for displaced persons. To this day, some 120,000 Rohingya are confined to those facilities, which UN officials describe as so squalid that parts of them are "literally cesspools."

"The conditions in the Rohingya camps were awful. People were living in mud. You saw people with diseases who clearly needed medical attention," said Dan Baer, a former deputy assistant secretary in the State Department's human-rights bureau who visited Rakhine state in September 2012 to better understand the violence. Baer was struck in particular by the dehumanizing way the Rakhine Buddhists discussed the Rohingya and how many said they would never again live alongside people who were once their neighbors. He worried that if the viral hatred wasn't addressed, more violence lay ahead: "What we saw was a powder keg ready to go off."

As they urged their counterparts in Myanmar to stop the mistreatment, the Americans began to grasp another reality: The Rohingya simply had no popular support in the country—in fact, persecuting them was popular. Most shocking was the attitude of some of the prodemocracy activists the United States had backed for so many years. Suu Kyi, for example, viewed the Rohingya as political poison, and she wouldn't utter their name—at least not in public—for fear of damaging her base of support. Others in her sphere—many of whom, like Suu Kyi herself, hail from Myanmar's ethnic Bamar majority—could be outright racist when discussing the Rohingya.

"It's hard to explain this," a former State Department official said, "but if you go inside Burma and ask almost anyone you meet about the . . . Rohingya, and they feel they're not being recorded or whatever, they will say almost all the same thing: that they're terrorists, that they're dirty, that they don't belong to our country. It is shocking."

But the spasms of violence in 2012 did not lead Obama to scrap his November visit; there were just too many positive changes in Myanmar, which had become exhibit A in the administration's case for engaging adversaries. Some in the administration took to calling Myanmar "Oburma," a recognition of how important it was to the president. Even the ethnic strife seemed manageable, with Myanmar officials taking just enough steps to ease U.S. concerns. For instance, at the urging of Samantha Power, a National Security Council official and genocide scholar who later became Obama's ambassador to the United Nations, Thein Sein agreed to what became known as the "eleven commitments," a set of benchmarks related to Rakhine state and other human-rights and democracy-related challenges in Myanmar.

As the commitments were unveiled during Obama's much-ballyhooed six-hour visit in November 2012, Thein Sein's gesture raised hopes that the rapprochement was worth pursuing. Fresh off his reelection, Obama, the first sitting U.S. president to visit Myanmar, praised its democratic reforms and called for more. "Reforms launched from the top of society must meet the aspirations of citizens who form its foundation," he said in remarks at the University of Yangon. "The flickers of progress that we have seen must not be extinguished."

To his credit, Obama also named the group that must not be named. "There is no excuse for violence against innocent people," he said. "And the Rohingya hold themselves—hold within themselves the same dignity as you do, and I do."

·　　·　　·

Obama may have tried to raise sympathy for the Rohingya, but their daily life grew steadily worse during his second term as president.

Security forces would often pick up Rohingya men on the flimsiest of pretexts, torturing them and demanding bribes for their release, several people in the Bangladesh camps said. Men could be whisked away for having a cell phone without permission, not informing authorities they'd purchased a goat, or simply being somewhere without prior approval. The more educated men, or economically successful ones, seemed to be in extra danger of such state-sponsored abductions. To avoid the hassle of an encounter with the security forces, many Rohingya tried to move around at night. They also tried to avoid their Buddhist neighbors, who frequently aided the security forces in the oppression.

The security forces often accused Rohingya men of being "terrorist" members of the Arakan Rohingya Salvation Army, the insurgent group behind the August 2017 attacks that triggered the military retaliation. Mohammad Idrees, thirty, said he was detained twice and told to confess to nonexistent ARSA ties. "They tied me up and beat the soles of my feet. They threw hot water on me," he said, tears welling in his eyes. "It didn't matter what I answered. They beat me either way."

Armed Rohingya groups have come and gone over the years, though not with the longevity and scale of some of Myanmar's other armed ethnic groups. ARSA seems to be the latest iteration— a rebel band that emerged in recent years as discrimination against the Rohingya intensified. The group remains weak, with limited access to weapons—"a dozen guys with swords" is how one U.S. official put it. Even so, Myanmar's leaders, both civilian and military, say they are alarmed by ARSA's emergence. The Rohingya I met said soldiers would routinely raid their homes, searching for weapons and confiscating even small kitchen knives. Many Rohingya are angry with ARSA for sparking the latest military crackdown. But some predict that, if their conditions worsen, more will join the group. "It's not right to use violence, but we have no choice. We are helpless," said Abdul Mannan, an imam at a mosque in one camp.

In 2014, the Myanmar government refused to let people register as "Rohingya" in the country's first nationwide census in three decades. In 2015, an international crisis emerged as thousands of Rohingya trying to flee the oppression were stranded at sea when nearby nations refused to accept them. That same year, Myanmar passed a series of so-called race and religion protection laws that targeted certain Muslim religious and cultural practices, including polygamy. To top it off, the government blocked the Rohingya from voting in the 2015 elections, even though they'd been allowed to cast ballots five years earlier. The decision, activists said, effectively stripped Myanmar's Rohingya of their last political right.

During Obama's second term, as Myanmar was supposedly transitioning to democracy under the watchful eye of the United States, a growing number of researchers started using the terms "ethnic cleansing" and "genocide" to describe the Rohingya's plight—both because of the physical violence they suffered as well as the legal and political repression they faced. By 2015, the British-based International State Crime Initiative declared that the Rohingya were facing the "final stages" of genocide. The Obama administration and other Western powers avoided using similar labels; declaring a genocide in theory comes with legal obligations to intervene. Meanwhile, the United States pressed ahead with the rapprochement.

It was also during Obama's second term that Ben Rhodes took a greater role in the Myanmar portfolio. Rhodes, whose title of deputy national security adviser for strategic communications belied his vast influence with the president, was the administration's fiercest advocate of engagement with rogue regimes— not just with Myanmar but also with Cuba and Iran. He made détente with Myanmar a personal mission, overseeing the administration's messaging and negotiating policy with other officials involved. By 2016, Rhodes was arguing that Obama should remove the remaining economic sanctions on the country. "The people sanctioned in Burma were the richest people in Burma," Rhodes said. "The sanctions, in our assessment, were punishing ordinary Burmese."

So in that final year of Obama's presidency, administration officials and rights activists found themselves in a more intense replay of the 2012 sanctions debate—pitting Rhodes and the Bureau of East Asian and Pacific Affairs against State Department human-rights officials and outside rights campaigners. This time, the stakes were higher: Obama was considering lifting economic sanctions on military-linked entities and terminating the nearly two-decade-old U.S. declaration of a "national emergency" with respect to Myanmar. That "national emergency" declaration was the legal basis on which many of the sanctions were crafted and implemented. By the time of the Four Seasons party, after Obama had indicated he would take both those steps, feelings on both sides were more than a little sore. (Thanks in part to Congress, some notable restrictions on the U.S. relationship with Myanmar remained in place, including an arms embargo and limits on military-to-military ties.)

On October 9, 2016—just two days after Obama revoked the "national emergency" order—Rohingya insurgents attacked several Myanmar border posts, killing at least nine guards. As Obama went ahead with unraveling sanctions, Myanmar's security forces went after the Rohingya. After an initial crackdown that displaced at least 87,000 people, the armed forces started showing up in villages to raid homes practically every day, Rohingya in the Bangladesh camps said. During their patrols, the security forces would sometimes grab "the more beautiful girls," some of the women said, and take them to a nearby school for an hour or two to rape them. Other times, they'd gather many of the village women in one place, separate the prettier ones, and strip them of their scarves so that they could better see their figures. One woman I met grabbed her own breasts and pulled up her shirt to describe the way the Myanmar security forces would grope them.

There was no fighting back.

"We didn't say a word," said Arifa Begum, forty-six. "They'd slit our throats."

.   .   .

More than a year later, as a new wave of violence has sent hundreds of thousands of Rohingya pouring into Bangladesh, former Obama administration officials have been e-mailing one another and agonizing over what more—if anything—they could have done to prevent the current crisis. Did they pay enough attention to this one group? Were they blinded by the positive changes in Myanmar and naive about the impact on the Rohingya? Was it a mistake to lift the sanctions?

Critics of U.S. policy, many of them human-rights activists and some former administration officials, blamed Rhodes, and by extension Obama, for not pushing hard enough to protect the Rohingya. Rhodes was so invested in his narrative about engaging adversaries, these critics charged, that he failed to fully appreciate the Rohingya's plight. Some former and current U.S.

officials I spoke to said they found it difficult to point out problems with the "Oburma" legacy, especially in Obama's second term. "It was really hard to issue statements that suggested not all was well with the U.S. relationship with Myanmar, even when it came to the Rohingya," one U.S. official involved in the process said. "Everything had to sound positive."

Other U.S. officials and outside analysts insisted the administration was right not to hinge its Myanmar policy on the fate of one ethnic group. After all, Myanmar had, and has, lots of problems. This was a country that was home to drug trafficking, child soldiers, forced labor and a decades-long civil war with various armed ethnic groups. With everything else happening in the relationship—above all, the emerging outlines of a democracy— protecting the Rohingya couldn't necessarily be the sole or even top priority.

In my talk with Rhodes, he took exception to any assertion that protecting a vulnerable population wasn't at the top of his list. "That's offensive to me," Rhodes said. He described the Rohingya as an important topic in conversations that he, Obama and other administration officials held with Myanmar's leaders. "I raised the Rohingya issue more with the Burmese government than any other," he said. "We were making it a front-and-center part of this relationship, and working really hard to prevent this from happening. It wasn't about putting a trophy on the wall. It was about making life better for the people of Myanmar."

Rhodes argued that the Rohingya problem was simply so sensitive, and hatred of the group so powerful, that threatening to keep or add sanctions based on how the minority was treated would not have moved Myanmar's generals. When U.S. officials raised the topic with their Myanmar counterparts, Rhodes and others said, they would often be met with dead-end answers along the lines of, "It's complicated." Continued U.S. engagement through Obama's second term, on the other hand, kept things from getting even worse for the Rohingya, Rhodes argued, and it's the only real solution moving forward. Under Obama, "the pressure basically averted further deterioration without solving the problem," he said. "Sometimes that's all you can accomplish. Sometimes it takes a significant amount of pressure and engagement just to preserve a bad status quo."

Mitchell said he, too, made the Rohingya a special priority during his time as U.S. ambassador. He gathered diplomats from other countries to jointly speak out against violence in Rakhine. He traveled to Rakhine state multiple times, met with Rohingya representatives and urged Myanmar's leaders to accept the Muslim minority into the fabric of the country. "I was having constant conversations about that issue with the government, saying 'You need to have a road map, get in front of this, you have to deal with these questions of citizenship,'" Mitchell recalled. "To be honest, we would see some of the right things being said, the right things being done, but they never quite did enough over the years. . . . They would say 'Give us time and space.'"

Sometimes, Mitchell said, Myanmar officials would indicate they wanted to do something to help the Rohingya, such as jump-start a citizenship restoration process. But such initiatives would get derailed by disputes over whether to use the word "Rohingya." "At a certain point, I just felt like maybe they were playing for time, they were playing me," Mitchell said. But he agreed with Rhodes that the hatred of the Rohingya is so strong in Myanmar that even if the United States had left economic sanctions in place purely because of that group's issues, nothing would have changed. "They don't care about that," Mitchell said. "They feel this is their sovereignty, that these people are not Burmese and are out to get them."

Besides, even some of the most ardent human-rights observers in the administration failed to foresee the worst. Malinowski, who joined the State Department from Human Rights Watch in Obama's second term, noted that his arguments against lifting the sanctions in 2016 were more about keeping pressure on the military to reduce its role in governance: "I was not thinking, 'Oh my God, they are going to ethnically cleanse all of the Rohingya from the country.'"

.   .   .

I asked several current and former U.S. officials whether the Obama administration would have stopped the rapprochement with Myanmar had Suu Kyi been taken back into custody or the NLD been outlawed. They all said, basically, yes. "We would not have done the engagement," Rhodes said.

But now that one of the world's most recognizable icons of democracy is running Myanmar's civilian government, she has said little about the violence in Rakhine. She won't say the word "Rohingya," and she's largely avoided criticizing the military for its brutal campaign. Her stance has wrecked her image abroad. Other Nobel laureates have excoriated her, and there are calls that she be stripped of her Peace Prize.

Current and former U.S. officials who know the seventy-two-year-old Suu Kyi hesitate to describe her as a racist. But there is a growing belief among them that Suu Kyi is at her core a Bamar nationalist with a significant appreciation for the armed forces—after all, her father was a military man. "She may be talking about democracy, but she's authoritarian in her manner," said the former State Department official. (Suu Kyi didn't respond to an interview request.)

Suu Kyi's defenders in Washington and Myanmar note she has made some effort on behalf of the Rohingya—including supporting the creation of a commission led by former UN secretary-general Kofi Annan on how to help the people of Rakhine state. But they also argue that, even if she wanted to do more, she has no control over the military—and to loudly defend a hated group might constitute political suicide. The military's domestic popularity has risen because of its campaign against the Rohingya, leading to speculation that Senior General Min Aung Hlaing, the commander in chief of Myanmar's armed forces, will ride that support to the presidency in the next election.

Nationalist or no, Suu Kyi and her party represent the democratic aspirations of tens of millions of people. Would it be worth giving that up to protect one besieged minority? This dilemma is one reason Suu Kyi's supporters in Myanmar are exceedingly cautious about how they discuss the Rohingya. Some question the media accounts and suggest the refugees are making up stories about the raping, maiming, and murdering. When I spoke to Aung Lynn, Myanmar's ambassador to the United States, he dismissed claims of ethnic cleansing and said the international community had yet to provide credible evidence. Ko Jimmy, a democracy activist and former political prisoner I met in Yangon, worried that international pressure on Suu Kyi's government over the troubles in Rakhine could scuttle the country's political transition. "Still, we are struggling for democratization in our country," he said. "Still, we are struggling against the military group."

That's probably why Suu Kyi retains notable support in Washington. Even former and current U.S. officials deeply disappointed in her attitude toward the Rohingya see no alternative but to keep working with her and her party to stay on the path of democratization. Senate Majority Leader Mitch McConnell, a longtime advocate for democracy in Myanmar and fan of Suu Kyi, has expressed his continued support in recent months despite the bloodshed in Rakhine state. "Publicly condemning Aung San Suu Kyi, the best hope for democratic reform in Burma, is simply not constructive," the Republican senator said in September.

In the dusty camps in Bangladesh, support for Suu Kyi is nearly nonexistent. Rohingya refugees said they'd hoped that once she and her party won the elections in 2015, their lives would improve, that she would speak out on their behalf. They were disappointed.

"Aung San Suu Kyi never did anything good for us," said Gulfaraz, the eighty-five-year-old.

When Kyaw Min warned the United States six years ago not to lift sanctions unless his people's citizenship was restored, he feared the disaster playing out today. Sitting with him in Yangon, I pointed out that the majority of people in Myanmar are living a freer life. Does it make sense, I asked, to forgo the rights of one small group, the 1.1 million Rohingya, to bring the benefits of democracy and economic investment to some 55 million other people?

Without hesitation, Kyaw Min said no. "Democracy," he said, "does not mean that minorities can be exploited for the majority's satisfaction."

$\bullet \qquad \bullet \qquad \bullet$

For Rhodes, it's hard enough hearing about the atrocities befalling the Rohingya. Just as frustrating is what he sees as the Trump administration's failure to respond in a meaningful way. "I understand the impulse to make this about the Obama administration," Rhodes chided me. "But we're not in power now."

There's no question the worst wave of violence took place well into Trump's tenure. His administration was slow to react, and it has sent mixed messages as the months have worn on. Nikki Haley, the U.S. ambassador to the United Nations, was one of the first U.S. officials to warn the Myanmar military against attacking civilians. But in mid-October, after hundreds of thousands of Rohingya had already streamed into Bangladesh, her office released a statement in which she urged "all sides" to end the violence—as if the villagers fleeing their homes were as culpable as the security forces attacking them. In early November, NBC News reported that Tillerson had understood the gravity of the situation only after reading news reports and realizing the violence was much more serious than what his own East Asia bureau had told him.

Tillerson visited Myanmar in mid-November, urging the government there to allow a credible investigation into the alleged atrocities. A week later, he formally declared the violence against the Rohingya to be "ethnic cleansing," and since then, the State Department announced it was imposing sanctions on a top Myanmar general accused of overseeing many of the abuses. Some members of Congress also have prepared legislation to impose sanctions on Myanmar military officials—but it's not clear how far those proposals will get given resistance from McConnell.

As for Trump, he has yet to say much about the Rohingya tragedy publicly, although the White House said he raises it with counterparts in private settings. In remarks to a gathering of Asian leaders in November, Trump said the United States "supports efforts to end the violence" and to "ensure accountability for atrocities committed." Some Trump critics have even wondered whether Myanmar's military leaders read Trump's inflammatory rhetoric about Muslims and refugees as a sign that he would not care if they cracked down on the Rohingya. Regardless of the reason, few in the region are counting on Washington for leadership. China, which has economic interests in Rakhine state, has already tried to fill the vacuum, laying out a broad three-stage strategy to resolve the crisis: a cease-fire; a workable agreement between Myanmar and Bangladesh on how to deal with the refugees; and a long-term plan to alleviate poverty in Rakhine state.

.   .   .

For the Rohingya, a solution feels out of reach. Many have tried to stick it out in northern Rakhine state. But it's hard to get food or engage in any sort of livelihood in the area, so Rohingya are still trickling into Bangladesh. Abul Kalam, a sixty-year-old farmhand and fisherman who reached Bangladesh on Christmas Eve, told me that the killing wasn't over. It's just quieter. "The military has stopped killing by gun," he said, shaking his head. "Now they use thick sticks and beat people to death. It's brutal."

Bangladesh and Myanmar have struck a deal on repatriating the Rohingya, but its implementation has been delayed, and almost no one I talked to takes it seriously. One Bangladeshi official said that, realistically, most of the Rohingya refugees will be staying in camps in Bangladesh for the foreseeable future. It's an extraordinarily heavy lift for Bangladesh, an impoverished, densely populated country prone to natural disasters.

Diphtheria and measles have spread in the camps, and some fear more diseases lurk in waiting. The conditions are likely to get worse during monsoon season. Yet I couldn't find a single Rohingya who wanted to return to Myanmar anytime soon. The refugees insisted they wouldn't go back until they are given citizenship and their rights are guaranteed.

I asked whether there was anything the United States could do, but few Rohingya knew much about America. Some said that the United States was "strong" and they hoped that strength would translate to benevolence. Few had heard of Trump. Obama was a more familiar name—some Rohingya called him the American "raja," or king. But with the challenges the Rohingya face each day, the international debate over their fate seemed worlds away.

"I don't care about politics overseas," one Rohingya woman said. "I'm just trying to make sure my family and I survive."

National Geographic

FINALIST—PUBLIC INTEREST

The headlines in the June 2018 issue of National Geographic *are stark: "For Animals, Plastic Is Turning the Ocean Into a Minefield"; "We Know Plastic Is Harming Marine Life. What About Us?"; "Planet or Plastic?" Part of* National Geographic's *"multi-year effort to raise awareness about the global plastic waste crisis," the issue used photography, infographics, and maps, complemented online by multimedia tools, to explore the dimensions of the problem that Laura Parker meticulously describes in "We Made It. We Depend on It. We're Drowning in It. Plastic." Yet this is not a problem without a solution, as* National Geographic *showed by challenging readers to sign a "Planet or Plastic?" pledge "to keep single-use plastic out of our environment." Parker is a staff writer at* National Geographic *who characterizes herself as "an easy mark for a homeless cat." Her story was part of the package that earned* National Geographic *its eighth National Magazine Award for General Excellence.*

Laura Parker

We Made It. We Depend on It. We're Drowning in It. Plastic

If plastic had been invented when the Pilgrims sailed from Plymouth, England, to North America—and the *Mayflower* had been stocked with bottled water and plastic-wrapped snacks—their plastic trash would likely still be around, four centuries later.

If the Pilgrims had been like many people today and simply tossed their empty bottles and wrappers over the side, Atlantic waves and sunlight would have worn all that plastic into tiny bits. And those bits might still be floating around the world's oceans today, sponging up toxins to add to the ones already in them, waiting to be eaten by some hapless fish or oyster, and ultimately perhaps by one of us.

We should give thanks that the Pilgrims didn't have plastic, I thought recently as I rode a train to Plymouth along England's south coast. I was on my way to see a man who would help me make sense of the whole mess we've made with plastic, especially in the ocean.

Because plastic wasn't invented until the late nineteenth century, and production really only took off around 1950, we have a mere 9.2 billion tons of the stuff to deal with. Of that, more than 6.9 billion tons have become waste. And of that waste, a staggering

6.3 billion tons never made it to a recycling bin—a figure that stunned the scientists who crunched the numbers in 2017.

No one knows how much unrecycled plastic waste ends up in the ocean, Earth's last sink. In 2015, Jenna Jambeck, a University of Georgia engineering professor, caught everyone's attention with a rough estimate: between 5.3 million and 14 million tons each year just from coastal regions. Most of it isn't thrown off ships, she and her colleagues say, but is dumped carelessly on land or in rivers, mostly in Asia. It's then blown or washed into the sea. Imagine five plastic grocery bags stuffed with plastic trash, Jambeck says, sitting on every foot of coastline around the world—that would correspond to about 8.8 million tons, her middle-of-the-road estimate of what the ocean gets from us annually. It's unclear how long it will take for that plastic to completely biodegrade into its constituent molecules. Estimates range from 450 years to never.

Meanwhile, ocean plastic is estimated to kill millions of marine animals every year. Nearly 700 species, including endangered ones, are known to have been affected by it. Some are harmed visibly—strangled by abandoned fishing nets or discarded six-pack rings. Many more are probably harmed invisibly. Marine species of all sizes, from zooplankton to whales, now eat microplastics, the bits smaller than one-fifth of an inch across. On Hawaii's Big Island, on a beach that seemingly should have been pristine—no paved road leads to it—I walked ankle-deep through microplastics. They crunched like Rice Krispies under my feet. After that, I could understand why some people see ocean plastic as a looming catastrophe, worth mentioning in the same breath as climate change. At a global summit in Nairobi last December, the head of the United Nations Environment Programme spoke of an "ocean Armageddon."

And yet there's a key difference: Ocean plastic is not as complicated as climate change. There are no ocean trash deniers, at least so far. To do something about it, we don't have to remake our planet's entire energy system.

"This isn't a problem where we don't know what the solution is," says Ted Siegler, a Vermont resource economist who has spent more than twenty-five years working with developing nations on garbage. "We know how to pick up garbage. Anyone can do it. We know how to dispose of it. We know how to recycle." It's a matter of building the necessary institutions and systems, he says—ideally before the ocean turns, irretrievably and for centuries to come, into a thin soup of plastic.

· · ·

In Plymouth, under the gray gloom of an English autumn, Richard Thompson waited in a yellow slicker outside Plymouth University's Coxside Marine Station, at the edge of the harbor. A lean man of fifty-four, with a smooth pate rimmed with gray hair, Thompson was headed for an ordinary career as a marine ecologist in 1993—he was working on a Ph.D. on limpets and microalgae that grow on coastal rocks—when he participated in his first beach cleanup, on the Isle of Man. While other volunteers zoomed in on the plastic bottles and bags and nets, Thompson focused on the small stuff, the tiny particles that lay underfoot, ignored, at the high tide line. At first he wasn't even sure they were plastic. He had to consult forensic chemists to confirm it.

There was a real mystery to be solved back then, at least in academic circles: Scientists wondered why they weren't finding even more plastic in the sea. World production has increased exponentially—from 2.3 million tons in 1950, it grew to 162 million in 1993 and to 448 million by 2015—but the amount of plastic drifting on the ocean and washing up on beaches, alarming as it was, didn't seem to be rising as fast. "That begs the question:

Where is it?" Thompson said. "We can't establish harm to the environment unless we know where it is."

In the years since his first beach cleanup, Thompson has helped provide the beginnings of an answer: The missing plastic is getting broken into pieces so small they're hard to see. In a 2004 paper, Thompson coined the term "microplastics" for these small bits, predicting—accurately, as it turned out—that they had "potential for large-scale accumulation" in the ocean.

When we met in Plymouth last fall, Thompson and two of his students had just completed a study that indicated it's not just waves and sunlight that break down plastic. In lab tests, they'd watched amphipods of the species *Orchestia gammarellus*—tiny shrimplike crustaceans that are common in European coastal waters—devour pieces of plastic bags and determined they could shred a single bag into 1.75 million microscopic fragments. The little creatures chewed through plastic especially fast, Thompson's team found, when it was coated with the microbial slime that is their normal food. They spat out or eventually excreted the plastic bits.

Microplastics have been found everywhere in the ocean that people have looked, from sediments on the deepest seafloor to ice floating in the Arctic—which, as it melts over the next decade, could release more than a trillion bits of plastic into the water, according to one estimate. On some beaches on the Big Island of Hawaii, as much as 15 percent of the sand is actually grains of microplastic. Kamilo Point Beach, the one I walked on, catches plastic from the North Pacific gyre, the trashiest of five swirling current systems that transport garbage around the ocean basins and concentrate it in great patches. At Kamilo Point the beach is piled with laundry baskets, bottles, and containers with labels in Chinese, Japanese, Korean, English, and occasionally, Russian. On Henderson Island, an uninhabited coral island in the South Pacific, researchers have found an astonishing volume of plastic from South America, Asia, New Zealand, Russia, and as far away as Scotland.

As Thompson and I talked about all this, a day boat called the *Dolphin* was carrying us through a light chop in the Sound, off Plymouth. Thompson reeled out a fine-mesh net called a manta trawl, usually used for studying plankton. We were close to the spot where, a few years earlier, other researchers had collected 504 fish of 10 species and given them to Thompson. Dissecting the fish, he was surprised to find microplastics in the guts of more than one-third of them. The finding made international headlines.

After we'd steamed along for a while, Thompson reeled the manta trawl back in. There was a smattering of colored plastic confetti at the bottom. Thompson himself doesn't worry much about microplastics in his fish and chips—there's little evidence yet that they pass from the gut of a fish into the flesh we actually eat. He worries more about the things that none of us can see— the chemicals added to plastics to give them desirable properties, such as malleability, and the even tinier nanoplastics that microplastics presumably degrade into. Those might pass into the tissues of fish and humans.

"We do know the concentrations of chemicals at the time of manufacture in some cases are very high," Thompson said. "We don't know how much additive is left in the plastic by the time it becomes bite-size to a fish.

"Nobody has found nanoparticles in the environment—they're below the level of detection for analytical equipment. People think they are out there. They have the potential to be sequestered in tissue, and that could be a game changer."

Thompson is careful not to get ahead of the science on his subject. He's far from an alarmist—but he's also convinced that plastic trash in the ocean is far more than an aesthetic problem. "I don't think we should be waiting for a key finding of whether or not fish are hazardous to eat," he said. "We have enough evidence to act."

.   .   .

How did we get here? When did the dark side of the miracle of plastic first show itself? It's a question that can be asked about many of the marvels of our technological world. Since helping the Allies win World War II—think of nylon parachutes or lightweight airplane parts—plastics have transformed all our lives as few other inventions have, mostly for the better. They've eased travel into space and revolutionized medicine. They lighten every car and jumbo jet today, saving fuel—and pollution. In the form of clingy, light-as-air wraps, they extend the life of fresh food. In airbags, incubators, helmets, or simply by delivering clean drinking water to poor people in those now demonized disposable bottles, plastics save lives daily.

In one of their early applications, they saved wildlife. In the mid-1800s, piano keys, billiard balls, combs, and all manner of trinkets were made of a scarce natural material: elephant ivory. With the elephant population at risk and ivory expensive and scarce, a billiards company in New York City offered a $10,000 reward to anyone who could come up with an alternative.

As Susan Freinkel tells the tale in her book, *Plastic: A Toxic Love Story*, an amateur inventor named John Wesley Hyatt took up the challenge. His new material, celluloid, was made of cellulose, the polymer found in all plants. Hyatt's company boasted that it would eliminate the need "to ransack the Earth in pursuit of substances which are constantly growing scarcer." Besides sparing at least some elephants, celluloid also helped change billiards from solely an aristocratic pastime to one that working people play in bars.

That's a trivial example of a profound revolution ushered in by plastic—an era of material abundance. The revolution accelerated in the early twentieth century, once plastics began to be made from the same stuff that was giving us abundant, cheap energy: petroleum. Oil companies had waste gases like ethylene coming out the stacks of their refineries. Chemists discovered they could use those gases as building blocks, or monomers, to create all sorts of novel polymers—polyethylene terephthalate, for example, or PET—instead of working only with polymers that already existed in nature. A world of possibilities opened up. Anything and everything could be made of plastic, and so it was, because plastics were cheap.

They were so cheap, we began to make things we never intended to keep. In 1955 *Life* magazine celebrated the liberation of the American housewife from drudgery. Under the headline "Throwaway Living," a photograph showed a family flinging plates, cups, and cutlery into the air. The items would take forty hours to clean, the text noted—"except that no housewife need bother." When did plastics start to show their dark side? You might say it was when the junk in that photo hit the ground.

Six decades later, roughly 40 percent of the now more than 448 million tons of plastic produced every year is disposable, much of it used as packaging intended to be discarded within minutes after purchase. Production has grown at such a break-neck pace that virtually half the plastic ever manufactured has been made in the past fifteen years. Last year the Coca-Cola Company, perhaps the world's largest producer of plastic bottles, acknowledged for the first time just how many it makes: 128 billion a year. Nestlé, PepsiCo, and others also churn out torrents of bottles.

The growth of plastic production has far outstripped the ability of waste management to keep up: That's why the oceans are under assault. "It's not surprising that we broke the system," Jambeck says. "That kind of increase would break any system not prepared for it." In 2013 a group of scientists issued a new assessment of throwaway living. Writing in *Nature* magazine, they declared that disposable plastic should be classified not as a housewife's friend but as a hazardous material.

In recent years the surge in production has been driven largely by the expanded use of disposable plastic packaging in the growing economies of Asia—where garbage collection systems may be underdeveloped or nonexistent. In 2010, according to an estimate by Jambeck, half the world's mismanaged plastic waste was generated by just five Asian countries: China, Indonesia, the Philippines, Vietnam, and Sri Lanka.

"Let's say you recycle 100 percent in all of North America and Europe," says Ramani Narayan, a chemical engineering professor at Michigan State University who also works in his native India. "You still would not make a dent on the plastics released into the oceans. If you want to do something about this, you have to go there, to these countries, and deal with the mismanaged waste."

•   •   •

The Pasig River once flowed majestically through downtown Manila, capital of the Philippines, and emptied into pristine Manila Bay. It was a treasured waterway and civic point of pride. It's now listed among the top ten rivers in the world that convey plastic waste to the sea. As many as 72,000 tons flow downstream each year, mostly during the monsoon. In 1990 the Pasig was declared biologically dead.

The Pasig River Rehabilitation Commission, established in 1999, is working to clean up the river, with some signs of success. Jose Antonio Goitia, the commission's executive director, says he is optimistic that the Pasig could be restored someday, although he acknowledges he has no easy way of doing that. "Maybe the best thing to do is ban plastic bags," he says.

The remaining challenges are clearly visible every day. The river is fed by fifty-one tributaries, some of them overflowing with plastic waste from squatter settlements that cantilever precariously over creek banks. A tributary near Chinatown, where rickety shanties are wedged between modern buildings, is so choked with plastic debris you can walk across it, forgoing the footbridge. Manila Bay's beaches, once recreational respites for greater Manila's 13 million residents, are littered with garbage, much of it plastic. Last fall Break Free from Plastic, a coalition including Greenpeace and other groups, cleaned a beach on Freedom Island, which is advertised as an ecotourism district; volunteers picked up 54,260 pieces of plastic, from shoes to food containers. By the time I visited a few weeks later, the beach was littered again with bottles, wrappers, and shopping bags.

The scene in Manila is typical of large, overcrowded urban centers across Asia. The Philippines is a densely populated nation of 105 million people that is still struggling with the most basic public-health issues, including waterborne diseases such as typhoid and bacterial diarrhea. It's no surprise that it has trouble managing the explosion of plastic garbage. Manila has a metropolitan garbage collection system that stretches across seventeen separate local governments—a source of chaos and inefficiency. In 2004 the region was already running out of land to safely dump garbage. The shortage of landfill space, and thus the crisis, continues today.

A small part of the slack is taken up by Manila's informal recycling industry, which consists of thousands of waste pickers. Armando Siena, thirty-four, is one of them. He and his wife, Angie, thirty-one, have lived their entire lives surrounded by trash. They were born on Smokey Mountain, an internationally notorious dump that was officially closed in the 1990s. They now live with their three children near Manila's waterfront in a one-room flat lit by a single bulb, furnished with a pair of plastic chairs, and lacking plumbing, bedding, or refrigeration. The flat is in a garbage-filled slum named Aroma, next to another slum named Happyland.

Every day Siena rides a rickety bicycle beyond Aroma's boundaries, scanning the streets for recyclable rubbish that he can stuff into his sidecar. Plastic soup containers are high-value finds, paying twenty pesos (thirty-eight cents) a kilogram. Siena sorts and sells his load to a junk shop owned by his uncle, who trucks the waste to recycling plants on the outskirts of Manila.

Waste pickers like Siena are part of the solution, some activists argue; they just need a living wage. In the Baseco waterfront slum in Manila, a tiny recycling shop operated by the Plastic Bank of Vancouver, British Columbia, pays a premium for bottles and hard plastic collected by waste pickers. It then sells that plastic at a higher price to multinationals, which market their recycled products as socially responsible.

Siegler, the Vermont economist, has worked in enough countries and run enough numbers to be skeptical of such schemes. "There is not enough value in plastics to make that work," he says. "It's cheaper to fund a solid-waste-management system than to subsidize collecting plastic."

The waste that clogs Manila's beaches and waterways reinforces Siegler's point. Much of it consists of sachets—tear-off packets that once held a single serving of shampoo, toothpaste, coffee, condiments, or other products. They are sold by the millions to poor people like Siena and his family, who can't afford to buy more than one serving at a time. Sachets blow around Manila like leaves falling from trees. They're not recyclable, so no waste picker will retrieve them. Crispian Lao, a member of the National Solid Waste Management Commission, says, "This segment of packaging is growing, and it has become a real challenge for solid-waste management."

When Greenpeace cleaned the Freedom Island beach, it posted a tally of the brand names of the sachets its volunteers had collected. Nestlé ranked first, Unilever second. Litterbugs aren't the only ones at fault, says Greenpeace's Abigail Aguilar: "We believe that the ones producing and promoting the use of single-use plastics have a major role in the whole problem." A Unilever spokeswoman in Manila told me the company is developing a recyclable sachet.

·   ·   ·

After Malaysia Airlines Flight 370 disappeared from radar screens in March 2014 while on its way from Kuala Lumpur to Beijing, the search for it extended from Indonesia to the southern Indian Ocean. It captivated a global audience for weeks. No sign of the wreckage appeared. On several occasions, when satellite images revealed collections of objects floating on the sea surface, hopes soared that they would turn out to be aircraft parts. They weren't. It was all trash—pieces of broken shipping containers, abandoned fishing gear, and, of course, plastic shopping bags.

Kathleen Dohan, a scientist and the president of Earth and Space Research in Seattle, saw opportunity in the horror: The images from space were pushing a problem into view that had long been neglected. "This is the first time the whole world is watching," she told me at the time. "It's a good time for people to understand that our oceans are garbage dumps." Dohan sensed a tipping point in public awareness—and the events since suggest she may have been right.

The most heartening thing about the plastic-waste problem is the recent explosion of attention to it and even of serious if scattered efforts to address it. A partial list of the good news since 2014 would include, in no particular order: Kenya joined a growing list of nations that have banned plastic bags, imposing steep fines and jail time on violators. France said it would ban plastic plates and cups by 2020. Bans on plastic microbeads in cosmetics (they're exfoliants) take effect this year in the United States, Canada, the United Kingdom, and four other countries. The industry is phasing them out.

Corporations are responding to public opinion. Coca-Cola, which also produces Dasani water, announced a goal to "collect and recycle the equivalent of" 100 percent of its packaging by 2030. It and other multinationals, including PepsiCo, Amcor, and Unilever, have pledged to convert to 100 percent reusable, recyclable, or compostable packaging by 2025. And Johnson & Johnson is switching from plastic back to paper stems on its cotton swabs.

Individuals are making a difference too. Ellen MacArthur, a British yachtswoman, has created a foundation to promote the vision of a "circular economy," in which all materials, including plastics, are designed to be reused or recycled, not dumped. Actor Adrian Grenier has lent his celebrity to the campaign against the plastic drinking straw. And Boyan Slat, twenty-three, from the Netherlands, is charging ahead with his teenage vow to clean up the largest garbage patch in the North Pacific. His organization has raised more than $30 million to construct an ocean-sweeping machine that is still under development.

All of these measures help at some level—even beach cleanups, futile as they sometimes seem. A beach cleanup hooked Richard Thompson on the plastic problem a quarter century ago. But the real solution, he now thinks, is to stop plastic from entering the ocean in the first place—and then to rethink our whole approach to the amazing stuff. "We've done a lot of work making sure plastic does its job, but very little amount of work on what happens to that product at the end of its lifetime," he says. "I'm not saying plastics are the enemy, but there is a lot the industry can do to help solve the problem."

There are two fundamental ways industry can help, if it wants or is forced to. First, along with academic scientists such as Jambeck, it can design new plastics and new plastic products that are either biodegradable or more recyclable. New materials and more recycling, along with simply avoiding unnecessary uses of the stuff, are the long-term solutions to the plastic-waste problem. But the fastest way to make a big difference, Siegler says, is low tech. It's more garbage trucks and landfills.

"Everyone wants a sexy answer," he says. "The reality is, we need to just collect the trash. Most countries that I work in, you can't even get it off the street. We need garbage trucks and help institutionalizing the fact that this waste needs to be collected on a regular basis and landfilled, recycled, or burned so that it doesn't end up going all over the place."

That's the second way industry could help: It could pony up. Siegler has proposed a worldwide tax of a penny on every pound of plastic resin manufactured. The tax would raise roughly six billion dollars a year that could be used to finance garbage collection systems in developing nations. The idea never caught on. In the fall of 2017, though, a group of scientists revived the concept of a global fund. The group called for an international agreement patterned after the Paris climate accord.

At the Nairobi meeting in December, 193 nations, including the United States, actually passed one. The United Nations Clean Seas agreement doesn't impose a tax on plastic. It's nonbinding and toothless. It's really just a declaration of a good intention—the intention to end ocean plastic pollution. In that way it's less like the Paris Agreement and more like the Rio de Janeiro treaty, in which the world pledged to combat dangerous climate change—back in 1992. Norway's environment minister, Vidar Helgesen, called this new agreement a strong first step.

The Atlantic

FINALIST—COLUMNS AND COMMENTARY

In these three columns for The Atlantic, *Caitlin Flanagan explores the intersection of gender and power in modern-day America, at least in part by recalling the easily (by some) forgotten world of pre-#MeToo America and her own experience of it. Why, asked Donald J. Trump after he appointed Brett Kavanaugh to the Supreme Court, didn't Kavanaugh's accuser tell anyone that he assaulted her when they were students in high school? Because, writes Flanagan, "Christine Blasey Ford was not a fifteen-year-old girl in the present; she was a fifteen-year-old girl in the past." Flanagan is one of the most honored writers in the history of the National Magazine Awards. Her work for* The Atlantic *has received seven nominations: in Feature Writing in 2018, Essays in 2005, and Reviews and Criticism in 2002, 2003, 2004, and 2008, when she won the award in the category.*

Caitlin Flanagan

The First Porn President *and* I Believe Her *and* The Abandoned World of 1982

The First Porn President

"I can now retire from politics," he said—the king of cool, the ironist in chief—"after having had 'Happy Birthday' sung to me in such a sweet, wholesome way": JFK, speaking to the vast audience at Madison Square Garden as Marilyn Monroe tottered away on her high heels, in her flesh-colored dress, leaving behind the hot trail of her sexual desire glowing in the darkness. In less than two years, they would both be dead, but that moment will live forever, reminding us always of our first and only *Playboy* president. The "playboy," as the publication invited its reader to think of himself, was urbane, sophisticated—able to handle a wide variety of amorous women, from the Miss Porter's sophisticate with her expensive underwear and afternoon passions to the Hollywood showgirl whose naked photographs had been published against her wishes in that very magazine. In reality, of course, the *Playboy* reader was just as likely to be a henpecked masturbator, trying to find a few minutes away from the old ball-and-chain while he gazed at a shaking image held in one ever-tightening fist.

But that homely truth was beside the point. It was the way he thought of himself when the pages were shaking that really mattered, and what *Playboy* said was this: You know how to handle all of these beautiful girls, they are here for your pleasure, and they will only add to your legend.

Bill Clinton was our first frat-boy president. He could cheerfully reach into an enthusiastic intern's pants and then, without washing his hands, pick up the phone and conduct the nation's business. He was careless, self-confident, a winner. He would deny, deny, deny, but when there was no plausible version of reality that could still include a denial, he handed out a few breadcrumbs of contrition: "I misled people, including even my wife." Although Clinton was always called shameless, he wasn't—not really. He was humbled and embarrassed by many of the things that he brought on himself through his mistreatment of women.

Down the ladder we go until we reach the bottom rung: Donald Trump. He is miles away from *Playboy* and its endless offerings of clean, healthy girls who were high-school cheerleaders and education majors and whose prettiness was as central as their sexiness. He's not an undisciplined golden boy whose private behavior, if exposed, could destroy his image. He is the first truly shameless president, the first porn president, and that is why it is Stormy Daniels—more than the FBI or the IRS or the string of women who have claimed sexual harassment or abuse by him—who just might take him down. Daniels and Trump built their careers in different industries. She is entirely self-made; he is not. But the business approach she has taken to her porn career is similar to the one he has taken in his real-estate and political enterprises, and although the asymmetry of their respective powers—the aging sex worker and the president of the United States—might seem insurmountable, in many respects they are equally matched.

•   •   •

Hef is dead. The Playboy mansion was sold to the Twinkie king, Daren Metropoulos, who is the co-owner of Hostess, purveyor of lunchbox treats to good little girls and boys. The magazine itself has lost its way, overcome by the porn revolution and unable to find safe ground for its gauzy, almost romantic images. In 2015, it made the bold decision to discover how many people really do buy it for the articles and stopped publishing nude photos altogether—taking it from a slow death spiral to a suicidal plunge—before it spread out a safety net and began publishing the pictures again. "I'll be the first to admit that the way in which the magazine portrayed nudity was dated," Hef's son Cooper tweeted.

What was so dated? Not just the restraint of *Playboy*'s images—a problem for the magazine since the pre-internet advent of *Penthouse* and *Hustler*, with their para-gynecological explorations of the female reproductive tract—but its insistence that Playmates have not just a backstory but one that emphasized a certain kind of "niceness," the famous "girl next door" quality of its models. Anyone with enough money can hire a sex worker, even a famous one. But what kind of man has the power to undress another man's well-cared-for daughter, to unleash the hidden sexual eagerness of all the beautiful, spurning girls who walk the high-school corridors of this country, emerging into respectable professions before being snapped up by wealthy doctors and lawyers and becoming the soccer moms of tomorrow? Only a playboy. In its heyday, the magazine offered not just sexual pleasure but matchless status to the men who imagined squiring these verified sex kittens to parties and bedrooms. That is why the brand has long held an irresistible appeal for Donald Trump, who actually appeared on a cover of the magazine in 1990, alongside twenty-one-year-old Brandi Brant. (Like many *Playboy* cover girls, she was a live wire, ultimately getting sentenced to six years in prison for cocaine trafficking. It was the Playmate inside that issue—Deborah Driggs, Miss March—who typified the ideal:

cheerleader; figure skater; homecoming queen at Saddleback College in Mission Viejo, California.)

It is from this world of middle-class, young female respectability—as it was calibrated, circa 1966—that Karen McDougal emerged. In late March, McDougal appeared in a long, broken-hearted CNN interview with Anderson Cooper, in which she seemed to have been briefly cleaved from the princess telephone on which one French-manicured hand has been resting since 2006, willing it to ring, hoping to hear one more time from the man who stole her heart and took her to bed but refused to commit himself to her.

If Karen McDougal had not existed, *Playboy* would have had to invent her. She so encapsulates the magazine's ideal that she could have been created from Hugh Hefner's rib and a handful of fairy dust. In only one respect does her biography differ from that of the dream girl: she is the child of divorce. But what can a publisher do when it is forced to merchandise the biographies of actual women and when the basic facts of their lives are so stubbornly uniform? McDougal makes up for this imperfection by having not one, not two, but three protective older brothers, their names a tom-tom of protective "all-American" maleness: Bob, Dave, and Jeff. Raised in Michigan, she was a high-school cheerleader, member of the color guard, and volleyball player, who was known, in the corridors and locker rooms of River Valley High, as "Barbie" and who was surely bound for respectability as it was measured in 1980s Michigan. Off she went to Big Rapids, to study elementary education, emerging two years later as a teacher of pre-K (kindergarten itself being too much of a fallen world for this radiantly innocent but rapidly ripening creature), and then, it begins: the chance encounter with a swimsuit competition, an exciting win, and the career as glamour, promotional, and swimwear model.

All of these are not euphemisms, exactly, but they were powerful signifiers to the *Playboy* reader: she had been recognized as a perfect physical specimen and had been rewarded for it in the farm leagues, but while she may have been circling close to the venues where nudity is required, there is very good chance—or at least it was plausible for the consumer to believe—that these *Playboy* photos were her first experience with the form. Playmate photos of previously obscure women offer the appeal that "audition" videos of women in porn offer: the moment of crossing over, the introduction to the world of serving men. Time passed and she became not just the December 1997 Playmate of the Month but a Playmate of the Year and then the runner-up to the "Playmate of the 1990s." And then, in 2006, she tugged on her bunny costume to appear at the Mansion in a party scene for *Celebrity Apprentice.* By then Hef's ever-present bathrobe suggested less a swinging lifestyle than an assisted-living wing; by then, the complex had gone a bit to seed, the grotto pools reeking of chlorine, the Jacuzzis needing a skim. And it was there she met Donald Trump, the beginning of what she described to Cooper—beautiful eyes occasionally filling with tears, embarrassing questions causing her to look down at her lap—as a great love affair between two good people who were deeply attracted to one another.

The CNN interview revealed a stunningly pretty woman, one day shy of her forty-seventh birthday, wearing a tasteful blue dress and simple jewelry. She looked like a rich man's wife, the kind of L.A. mom who picks up her kids in a Range Rover and ferries them home to a $10 million house for tutoring, soccer drills, and a Whole Foods dinner. She described her months with Trump the way that kind of woman would describe her romance with the investment banker or law partner she married: She loved that he was "an interesting person; he's brilliant"; she was attracted to his good looks and "great posture." She loved how much fun they had together, how "we would talk about anything and everything from what kind of food do you like to how's your family?" He was "respectful"; he was romantic; he called her "Baby" and "Beautiful Karen." He told her that he loved her. Sure, she cried her eyes out in the back of the limo after he tried to pay her the first time they'd been "intimate." ("I'm not that kind of girl," she said, deeply hurt. "You're really special," he said, before sending her home with a driver.)

Yes, it had been an ugly surprise to discover that during one of their romantic getaways, to a July 2006 golf tournament in Lake Tahoe, he'd also apparently been having sex with other women, including Stormy Daniels. McDougal's eyes welled up with big, *All My Children*–style tears of guilt and apology when Cooper confronted her with the fact that she had conducted this affair while her lover's wife was busy with their newborn son. When she finally called it off—a prelude, she said, to becoming "a different kind of girl" and getting "involved in my church"—McDougal told Trump that her mother would be disappointed in her, but she never stopped loving him. She may have worked in the world of soft-core sex, but she was also a hardcore Republican, who revealed on CNN that she had voted enthusiastically for her old beau.

But if McDougal was crushed by the breakup, she got over it quickly. Her eyes glinted as she told the story of how she'd managed to sell her story for $150,000 to AMI, the parent company of the *National Enquirer*, and how it had been a fantastic deal. It offered her the chance to "rebrand" herself in a new career, as the author of occasional fitness columns in three of the conglomerate's other titles: *Star*, *OK*, and *Radar Online*. Far from feeling victimized by a "catch and kill" scheme by AMI, she had loved the organization's plan—which they had not hidden from her, but openly explained before she signed the contract—not to run the story about her affair. It would allow her to maintain the kind of "wholesome" image that is apparently demanded by consumers of fitness advice in *OK* magazine. Indeed, her only complaint—despite her welling eyes—was that AMI hadn't published enough of her columns. In the end, she was small time, a bunny, looking for a creative way to face the challenges of being "an older model."

.   .   .

On the other hand: Stormy Daniels, who was never for one second in love with Donald Trump, who was not an admirer of his posture or his good looks or his brilliance. "Ugh," she thought the first time she saw him on his bed waiting for her, "here we go." She had not been raised with Bob, Dave, and Jeff to protect her. She had grown up hard, in Baton Rouge, Louisiana, and everything she has, she earned.

Stormy Daniels was not given a million dollars in seed money from a rich father, but in many other respects she is like Trump. She sees human sexuality as rife for transaction, she has no shame, and she's tough. She, too, cultivates a passion of the leisure class (he golfs; she owns and rides horses competitively) and she shares his vision for imposing her name on a vast landscape. For Trump, this means blighting skylines with ugly buildings, each of them crowned with his big eighties logo, that arrangement of gilded letters that stands for the worst of the decade. She seeks to control a vast region of online pornography by writing and directing and starring in films that fuse the storytelling and prop-filled premises of the seventies long form with the contortionist extremes and necessary visual tropes of the contemporary short form. Like Trump, she understands that to be a winner you must be your own brand and that if you spend your life as a Miss December, you will never really come out ahead: it's your name you want on the building—or the Pornhub channel—not your employer's.

Like Trump, Daniels knows that the range of acceptable public and private behavior is ever widening in this country, and like him she was once a surprise candidate on the Republican ticket, exploring a run for U.S. senator from Louisiana in 2009. (His campaign slogan: "Make America Great Again." Hers a more forthright: "Screwing People Honestly.") She, too, has been married three times, and she, too, has a deeply loved daughter, who has justified all of the struggle. The oldest American story there is: the sins of one generation paying for the genteel pursuits of the next.

When she was interviewed by Anderson Cooper on *60 Minutes* (and even here she was a winner over McDougal: the Tiffany network for the porn star, basic cable for the bunny), she seemed entirely different from the quivering playmate. Daniels is almost ten years younger, but she looked strained and tired, with circles under her eyes. She was not tearful; she was not remorseful; she did not call sexual intercourse "being intimate." Her complaints were simple, believable, and—as far as Trump is concerned—potentially grave. She had sex with him one time and had kept up a phone-line flirtation on the off-chance that he would make good on his offer to try to get her on *Celebrity Apprentice*. When it was clear it wouldn't happen, she dropped him.

"Were you attracted to him?" Anderson asked.

"No," she replied, forthrightly but without rancor.

"Not at all?"

"No."

"I thought of it as a business deal," she said of the relationship. Two weeks before the election in 2016, she made another business deal: signing a nondisclosure agreement for $130,000, brokered by Trump's personal lawyer, Michael Cohen. This agreement has caused her tremendous difficulties, but it is Trump who may ultimately be its greatest victim. According to Trevor Potter, a former chairman of the Federal Election Commission who also appeared on *60 Minutes*, the money may very well constitute "a coordinated, illegal, 'in-kind' contribution by Cohen for the purpose of influencing the election." In the end, the person who may bring down Donald Trump just might not be a hapless James Comey or a slow-moving Robert Mueller. It could in fact be the star of *Nymphos* and *Snatched,* the woman who started stripping at seventeen and learned very quickly that if you want to get rich serving the needs of men, you want to control the means of production.

Stormy Daniels is angry; she's not backing down; and the facts, as she presents them, could constitute a crime. She objects to any characterization of herself as an opportunist, despite her current "Make America Horny Again" tour. "Tell me one person who would turn down a job offer making more than they've been making, doing the same thing that they've always done," she said to Anderson Cooper. She is one more worker in the great service economy of a post-global America, and—unlike so many others in her general situation—she is making it work for her.

In the end, Trump, McDougal, and Daniels are three Republicans who are happy to build, inhabit, and impose upon all of us a heartless world, untroubled by the one consistently compelling notion that the GOP used to offer: that the American institution most worthy of respect was the family, the home, the shelter of one another. To the three of them, a wife—even one who had recently delivered a new baby—was not deserving of any special consideration or protection or even of decency in its broadest possible definition. But McDougal is the odd one out, clinging as she does to her cloying simulacrum of "wholesomeness," trying to will herself into a world in which Donald Trump would build her a golden cage, treat her kindly, and call her "Beautiful Karen" for all the rest of her days. He's not a playboy or, really, much of a husband. He's a porn president, where every intimate interaction is for sale if the money is right and where the underlying truth of each deal is that at the end of it somebody is going to get screwed. This time—maybe, maybe—it could be him.

I Believe Her

"Dear Caitlin," an inscription in my twelfth-grade yearbook begins. "I'm really *very* sorry that our friendship plummeted straight downhill after the first few months of school. Really, the blame rests totally on my shoulders. To tell you the truth, I've wanted to say this all year. I know you'll succeed *because* you're very smart and I regard you with the utmost respect . . . Take care—love always."

He was headed to a prestigious college. I was headed to a small, obscure liberal-arts college, which was a tremendous achievement, not just because I was a terrible student but also because I had nearly killed myself as a response to what he apologized for in my yearbook. He had tried to rape me during a date that I was very excited to have been asked on, and his attempt was so serious—and he was so powerful—that for a few minutes, I was truly fighting him off.

I had grown up in Berkeley, but just before my senior year of high school, my father took a job on Long Island. Berkeley, California, in 1978 was about as much like Suffolk County, New York, in 1978 as the moon is like the black sky around it. I didn't know a single person. I desperately missed my friends—although I only found out years later, my father was confiscating all of their letters to me. He thought they were a bad influence and that I should make a clean break. I felt completely alone.

I had already been depressed; severe depression was the only healthy response to growing up in my family. But the move was terrible. I couldn't figure out how to make friends; the high school was a John Hughes movie before there were John Hughes movies. But then a good-looking senior offered to drive me home one day. I was excited—I'd had my eye on him, and in the promise of this ride home I saw the solution to all of my problems: my sadness, my loneliness, my inability to figure out how to go to the parties the other kids were always talking about in the hallways and before class started.

He drove me home, looked around my empty house for a bit, and then suggested we drive to the beach. It was in his car, in the deserted parking lot of that beach, that he tried to rape me, although neither of us would have used that word for it. It was only in college that I heard the term *date rape*. The way dates between high-school students in the 1970s were understood was the way that dates had been understood since the 1920s. The idea was that anything bad that happened was the girl's fault. She had agreed to go off in a car with a boy alone; she was taking her chances. Boys would be boys, and it was up to girls to manage their coercive, importuning sexuality. But this was not coercive: This was a very strong kid, an athlete, trying to pin down a girl who weighed 116 pounds and was part of the pre–Title IX generation. We struggled against each other, and then—suddenly—he stopped. He started the car and drove me home in silence.

I told no one. In my mind, it was not an example of male aggression used against a girl to extract sex from her. In my mind, it was an example of how undesirable I was. It was proof that I was not the kind of girl you took to parties or the kind of girl you wanted to get to know. I was the kind of girl you took to a deserted parking lot and tried to make give you sex. Telling someone would not be revealing what he had done; it would be revealing how deserving I was of that kind of treatment.

My depression quickly escalated to a point where, if I'd been evaluated by a psychiatrist, I would probably have been institutionalized as a danger to myself. I had plans for how I was going to kill myself. I managed to make a few friends, who introduced me to acid, which was no help with the depression. I sat in classes in a blank state, except for English. ("To the girl about whom I will someday say, 'I knew her when,'" my English teacher wrote in that yearbook, words that stunned me when I first read them, and that I've never forgotten.)

But then, at the beginning of the second semester, my fortunes turned, and another boy asked me out. Another drive home, another trip to a beach parking lot—you'd think I would have learned, but from the minute we got in the car, I knew this was different. We bought a bottle of wine and sat in his car drinking it and talking, and by the time he drove me back home, I felt rescued.

·   ·   ·

I have been entirely agnostic about Brett Kavanaugh's Supreme Court nomination. Republican presidents nominate conservative judges, and Democratic presidents nominate liberal judges. This guy sounded like he was entirely qualified for the job. When Dianne Feinstein made her announcement about the super-secret mystery letter by the anonymous woman that she had sent to the FBI, I thought it was a Hail Mary pass aimed at scotching the nomination, the kind of distasteful tactic that makes people hate politics.

But on Sunday morning, sitting in the Santa Monica Elks Lodge, watching a friend get inducted into the Santa Monica High School Hall of Fame, I took advantage of a lull in the program to scroll through my news feed and quickly found the *Washington Post* report that broke the news about Christine Blasey Ford, the woman who wrote the letter. I read about two different psychologists noting that Ford had told them about her distress over the incident long before Kavanaugh was nominated. I read about the polygraph test. *She's telling the truth*, I said to myself, in a way that was neither outraged nor political, just matter-of-fact. The event she described is completely believable, but the psychologists' notes sealed the deal. Maybe some new piece of evidence will come to light to change my mind, but with the facts on the ground as we now have them, I believe her.

When I came home from Santa Monica, a friend dropped by the house. I asked him whether he'd heard the news about Kavanaugh, and he said, "Yeah—but are we really going to hold something he did when he was seventeen against him?"

Teenagers make mistakes, some of them serious. One measure of a kid's character is what he or she does afterward. Take another look at the note at the top of this essay. I can't remember why I would have asked him to sign my yearbook. He was in my new boyfriend's circle of friends, so maybe he was at the same parties and events I went to. Reading the note now, as a fifty-six-year-old woman, I think it's an astonishing thing for an eighteen-year-old kid to have written; it took courage and self-reflection. But that was not his only apology.

Two years after the yearbook was signed, when I was a far more confident person and when I was in the midst of transferring from the obscure college to a great university, I had a summer job at a department store. One morning, while ringing up a sale, I saw in my peripheral vision that someone was approaching the register. When I finished the sale, he was gone. A few minutes later, I saw him coming back; it was the boy who'd tried to rape me. He had tears in his eyes, and he seemed almost overwrought. And right there—in the A&S department store in the Smith Haven Mall—he apologized profusely.

"It's okay, it's okay," I kept saying to him. "I forgive you, don't worry." It was a weird ambush of intense guilt and apology, and it was the wrong place and time—but the thing was, I really did forgive him. My life had moved on, and things were better. It felt good to get the apology and—as it always does—even better to forgive him. He'd done a terrible thing, but he'd done what he could to make it right. I held nothing against him, and I still don't.

But if Ford's story is true, Brett Kavanaugh never apologized. He never tried to make amends, never took responsibility for what he did. In my case, the near-rape—as awful as it was at the time and in its immediate aftermath—didn't cause any lasting damage. But by Ford's account, Kavanaugh's acts did cause lasting damage, and he has done nothing at all to try to make that right. And that is why the mistake of a seventeen-year-old kid still matters. The least we should do is put this confirmation on hold until we can learn more about what happened. If it's not true, Kavanaugh should be confirmed without a cloud of suspicion. If it is true, we'll have to decide whether you get to attack a girl, show no remorse, and eventually become a Supreme Court justice. My own inclination is: No.

The Abandoned World of 1982

We are invited now to consider the late adolescence and early young manhood of Judge Brett Kavanaugh. It seems to be a trajectory that follows a classic pattern, familiar to us from literature as well as from its pale reflection, life. Call it a very modified version of the Prince Hal–to–Henry V flight plan: from wastrel youth with low companions to hero capable of leading men into battle. Call it something older than that: *When I was a child I spake as a child, I understood as a child, I thought as a child. But when I became a man, I put away childish things.*

It is the judge who has claimed this narrative for himself, choosing august occasions to tell esteemed audiences about his glamorous, rebellious youth. During a 2015 speech at Catholic University's Columbus School of Law, he reflected that three of its graduates had been classmates of his in high school. "Fortunately," he said, "we've had a good saying that we've held firm to to this day, as the dean was reminding me before the talk, which is, 'What happens at Georgetown Prep stays at Georgetown Prep.' That's been a good thing for all of us, I think." In a 2014 speech to the students of Yale Law School, he fondly remembered "falling out of [a] bus onto the front steps of the Yale Law School at about 4:45 a.m." It seems almost that he doesn't even want us to regard his youthful self as Prince Hal but as Falstaff.

Begin at the beginning, or close enough: the ninety-three acres of Georgetown Prep, a Beltway school where Kavanaugh's education was in the hand of the Jesuits and where academics were rigorous, sports were king, fealty to school and fellows was absolute, and a culture of heavy drinking fit right in with that of the other private academies. In his twelfth-grade yearbook, Kavanaugh described himself as the treasurer of the "Keg City Club—100 Kegs or Bust." These schools were known, then and now, for a parent-sponsored, seven-day bender called "Beach Week" that has made more than one six-figure head of school bash his or her head against the wall. Kavanaugh seems to have reveled in it: according to his yearbook, he also belonged to "Beach Week Ralph Club" and "Rehoboth Police Fan Club." (What kindness did the officers extend to club members? And were they as generous with town visitors who were not the white sons and daughters of wealthy men? Unspecified.)

There was also—as there always is in top Catholic schools that wish to be considered on the same intellectual and social plane as the great Protestant schools—a constant, grinding, and not misplaced sense of inferiority among many of the students. I e-mailed a friend—close to my age and to Kavanaugh's—who grew up in a posh D.C. family and attended the unremittingly soigné National Cathedral School—and asked her to tell me about the reputation of the Georgetown Prep of her youth. In seconds, she fired back the words: "always bad—frat boys, catholic, republican golf Bethesda." The judgment, so immolating that even the commas had burned up by the end of it, is the chip on the shoulder of the Georgetown Prep boy. A friend who was a teacher at a top D.C. prep school at the time offered a more forensically crushing assessment of the institution: "St. Albans Lite. Upper-Classy Catholic kids, but most of the Kennedys and Shrivers and such preferred St. Albans." These slight humiliations make the boys fiercer on the playing field, more eager to succeed, and—let my Catholic-school girlhood and memories of my own "brother school" inform this sentiment—determined to cultivate a certain toughness in the face of it. A Catholic-school prep boy might not be a menacing character in the mean corridors of a D.C. public school, but put him against a St. Alban's boy, and my money's on the Catholic.

Let the committee now be introduced to the person and character of Mark Judge, a close pal of the high-school Kavanaugh, who grew up to be a successful conservative writer and filmmaker, who has struggled mightily with alcoholism and other addictions, and who was, to young Brett Kavanaugh, a Rabelaisian figure, the soul of all merriment and the devotee of vomitous excess. On his twelfth-grade yearbook page, Judge included a quotation: "Certain women should be struck regularly, like gongs." If you want to get a sense of the tenor of a boys' school in the mid-1980s, look no further than the fact that no one—no Jesuit priest or yearbook adviser or teacher—thought this was an inappropriate thing to have printed in a book published by the school. This may be an example of the freedom of expression that made the pre-PC days so halcyon, but it is definitely an example of the fact that in a boys' school in the eighties, sexual frustration was combined with a casual misogyny—if not of deed then of word—that the authorities were in no way concerned about. Judge grew up to write a roman à clef about his wild days at Georgetown Prep, in which he revealed himself to be a stone-cold partier and a horrible creator of pseudonyms: We encounter one "Bart O'Kavanaugh" who has puked and passed out in a car, the victim of heavy drinking.

Life at the top is a constant series of zero-sum games, and Kavanaugh handily won the next one, getting admitted to the Yale University class of 1987. He was clubbable enough, pledging the college's newly reconstituted chapter of Delta Kappa Epsilon and thereby participating in the great 1980s return to fraternity life. In Joan Didion's 1970 essay "On the Morning After the Sixties," she recalls spending a day in 1953 lying on the leather couch in a fraternity house, listening to a man playing the piano. She had been invited to an alumni lunch at the house, and her date had gone off to the football game, but she had decided to stay behind, reading. The point of the anecdote is to suggest to the reader the recently abandoned world from which she had emerged: "That such an afternoon would now seem implausible in every detail—the very notion of having had a 'date' for a football luncheon now seems to me so exotic as to be almost czarist—suggests the extent to which that abstract called 'the revolution' has already taken place, the degree to which the world in which so many of us grew up no longer exists."

In the 1980s, however—thank Ron and Nancy, thank the stock market, thank the thousand flowers blooming in the investment banks that were luring so many male Ivy Leaguers to build their fortunes—that world reasserted itself. As *A Century and a Half of DKE* describes the period: "In the early eighties, the pendulum of American ideals began to sway to the right once again. College students developed a new sense of values and appreciation for tradition as the country finally recovered from the chaos of the sixties. Fraternities in general began to thrive once more."

In fact, as I've written before, fraternities took the chaos of the sixties—drugs, sexual liberation, communal living that allowed for a high degree of squalor—and combined it with the chaos of the fraternity, including brutal hazing, the sexual conquest of women that often crossed into illegality, and a self-conscious embrace of collegiate machismo of the sophomoric kind. The system soon racked up so many ruinously expensive lawsuits that it eventually created a complex and inflexible risk-management protocol, which at least indemnified the national organizations. But until then, the 1980s were a time of essentially unsupervised, extreme, and often violent behavior.

Yale's DKE chapter in Kavanaugh's college years did not have a house, the necessary element for most crimes of fraternity life. Its public face was the public face of all fraternities—the self-consciously upper-class events and the silly spectacles meant to goose campus pieties. A photograph published by the *Yale Daily*

News in 1985, when Kavanaugh was a sophomore—he is not in the photograph—depicts a moment from a DKE initiation, in which pledges carry a flag made of bras and panties. To one Yale woman, a junior, who wrote a letter to the campus newspaper, the flag looked like "scalps that warriors attach to their belts, relics that advertise their conquest and ward off the enemy as they swing in the breeze." Then, as now, fraternities provided a big white ass pressed against the glass windows of campus feminism, and in a sense the two are dependent on each other for their ongoing vitality.

The next big test for Kavanaugh? Application and admission to Yale Law School and the opportunity to distinguish himself as an excellent student of the law. It seems that at some point soon after graduation, he started to become the kind of man he wanted to be—certainly, his proudly told tales of youthful insouciance end there. He earned two prestigious clerkships. (One of them was with former Ninth Circuit judge Alex Kozinski, who recently retired after nine female law clerks made allegations of sexual harassment against him. He was accused, among other things, of showing them internet pornography in his chambers; Kozinski explained to the press that he "had a broad sense of humor and a candid way of speaking to both male and female law clerks alike.")

Kavanaugh soon combined his developing gravitas with his frat-boy inclinations by helping to draft America's only publicly funded work of extended pornography, the Starr report. ("At one point, the President inserted a cigar into Ms. Lewinsky's vagina, then put the cigar in his mouth and said: "It tastes good."). He became a partner at Kirkland & Ellis, made bank, married, and began what he would like us to understand as his life's great work, the intensive coaching of his daughter's Catholic-school basketball team, where he is beloved by the players. Perhaps he is salving the primal wound of not making the Yale basketball team as a freshman and having to spend his collegiate years—another humiliation—playing JV and writing about the Bulldogs for the

Yale Daily News. Or maybe he's decided to make an eleventh-hour investment in girl power, getting the little girls of Blessed Sacrament to crash the boards like they mean it.

Now he hovers on the edge of having all of this, every bit of it, paid off in a spectacular way by being confirmed to the Supreme Court, or—his defenders insist—of becoming another Robert Bork, the victim of an angry feminism that will casually take a man down on the basis of nothing but its own fantasies. For reasons having to do with my long history reporting on fraternities, I am on an e-mail chain with several members of DKE—none from Yale—who are a couple of decades older than Kavanaugh. Here's a representative sample of how they're taking the confirmation process: "As I told one of my correspondents, Φ of ΔKE Brother Brett Michael Kavanaugh, Yale '87, LAW '90, appears to be in a #MeToo fem-jam down Wah-hee-tawn way."

.　　.　　.

If Christine Blasey Ford—at this writing, the most well known of the women accusing Kavanaugh of assault—is to be believed, she experienced a violent sex crime and then told absolutely no one about it for decades, a prospect that many people find incredible and that President Donald Trump weaponized against her, tweeting: "I have no doubt that, if the attack on Dr. Ford was as bad as she says, charges would have been immediately filed with local Law Enforcement Authorities by either her or her loving parents. I ask that she bring those filings forward so that we can learn date, time, and place."

Why wouldn't a fifteen-year-old girl tell anyone, not even her "loving parents"? Because Ford did not grow up in today's girl culture. Christie Blasey was a fifteen-year-old girl in 1982.

As it happens, 1982 was a seminal year in the history of the way American girls would come to be raised and educated and in how millions of them would come to regard their life. It was the year Carol Gilligan published her book *In a Different Voice* and *Ms.* magazine published an article called "Date Rape: A Campus Epidemic?" A decade later, the ideas expressed in these two works exploded into the mass consciousness, the former in Mary Pipher's problematic, blockbuster 1994 book, *Reviving Ophelia*, and the latter in a 1991 *Time* magazine cover story called "Date Rape."

Setting aside all arguments—and they are legion—about the manifold and grave problems with Gilligan's research and also about the deep injustices that have taken place on American college campuses as a response to the theory of date rape, the fact is that both her research and the theory changed everything for girls in this country. Today, a girl who experienced what Ford says happened to her would find countless resources on the internet to help her, would have been explicitly told by teachers and administrators that there were people she could (and should) talk to if anyone tried to force sex on her, would be immersed in all the elements of popular culture—songs, movies, teen fiction, blogs—explaining to her that what happened was a profound wrong and that it was not her fault.

But Christine Blasey Ford was not a fifteen-year-old girl in the present; she was a fifteen-year-old girl in the past. Unless she was an extremely precocious, niche reader who was tearing her way through the arcane works of the radical feminist Susan Brownmiller, she would literally never have *heard* the term "date rape"—neither would her friends, parents, teachers, or school administrators. Cheerful teen movies aimed at the high-school audience—John Hughes films among them—accurately reflected commonly held American attitudes about the male need for sex and the comic nature of the extremes a normal, suburban male would go to extract it from girls, often against their clearly stated wishes.

None of these facts, of course, locates Brett Kavanaugh and Christine Blasey Ford in a bedroom in 1982. None of it is enough to disqualify him from the confirmation that now hangs in the balance. But, for what it's worth—probably nothing—more and more outside observers are starting to believe Ford. And more and more of Kavanaugh's supporters are starting to move to the quiet position that he might have attacked her but that he should not pay a price for it: Banish Falstaff, and banish all the world.

In the midst of it all (the Georgetown Prep way, the frat-boy tradition, the Irish problem—who knows) seems to lie an ocean of alcohol. If there is one common assessment of the D.C. private schools in the 1980s, it is that they were centers of titanic amounts of drinking.

A friend of mine, a recovering alcoholic with several decades of sobriety, said of Kavanaugh, "I can't tell if he's a blackout drinker or a convenient forgetter."

And maybe Christine Blasey Ford is an inconvenient rememberer.

The New Yorker

FINALIST—ESSAYS
AND CRITICISM

In "Misjudged," Jill Lepore provides a careful appraisal of Ruth Bader Ginsberg's career not only as a jurist but also as a wife, mother, scholar, advocate, and now pop-culture icon—though as Lepore writes, "It is no kindness to flatten her into a paper doll and sell her as partisan merch." This is one of three articles by Lepore nominated for the National Magazine Award for Essays and Criticism. In the others, Lepore examines Mary Shelley's Frankenstein and the career of Rachel Carson, now remembered chiefly—and, argues Lepore, wrongly—for her last book, Silent Spring. Lepore is a staff writer at he New Yorker and a professor of history at Harvard University. Her latest book, This America: The Case for the Nation—which Lepore describes as "a call for a new Americanism, as tough-minded and openhearted as the nation at its best"—was published earlier this year.

Jill Lepore

Misjudged

R uth Bader Ginsburg blinked behind giant, round eyeglasses. It was the first day of her confirmation hearings, in July of 1993, the year after the Year of the Woman, and Joe Biden, the chairman of the Senate Judiciary Committee, was very pleased to see her. Keen to do penance for the debacle of the Clarence Thomas hearings, just two years before—the year before the Year of the Woman—when an all-male committee, chaired by Biden, failed to credit what Anita Hill had to say about George H. W. Bush's Supreme Court nominee, he could hardly have been friendlier to Bill Clinton's nominee, a much respected and widely admired sixty-year-old appellate judge. She sat with the stillness of a watchful bird. "Judge Ginsburg, welcome," Biden said, heartily. "And, believe me, you are welcome here this morning."

He had more reasons, too, to beam at Ginsburg. Only weeks earlier, Clinton had withdrawn his nomination of Lani Guinier as assistant attorney general, an abandonment that had followed the very new president's unsuccessful nominations of two female attorneys general, Kimba Wood and Zoë Baird. Clinton and Biden needed a successful, high-profile female appointment, one without a discussion of pubic hair or video porn or nannies. On the way to work on the first day of the Ginsburg hearings, Biden had read the *New York Times* on the train and found that there was no mention of Ginsburg on page 1 or page 2 or page 3, which, he told Ginsburg, "was the most wonderful thing that has happened to me since I have been chairman of this committee." He flashed his movie-star grin.

During that first session, scheduled for two and a half hours, the committee members—sixteen men and two lately added women—did nearly all the talking, delivering opening statements. Not until the outset of the second session did Biden sidle up to a question. "The Constitution has to be read by justices in light of its broadest and most fundamental commitments, commitments to liberty, commitments to individual dignity, equality of opportunity," he said, putting on his glasses, and taking them off again. Ginsburg blinked and stared and waited.

Biden's question concerned a recent speech, the Madison Lecture, in which Ginsburg had said that in making decisions concerning rights not listed in the Constitution judges should be "moderate and restrained" and avoid stepping "boldly in front of the political process," as he reminded her. "But, Judge," Biden said, "in your work as an advocate in the seventies you spoke with a different voice. In the seventies, you pressed for immediate extension of the fullest constitutional protection for women under the Fourteenth Amendment, and you said the Court should grant such protection notwithstanding what the rest of society, including the legislative branch, thought about the matter. . . . Can you square those for me or point out their consistency to me?"

What Biden was getting at has been mostly lost in the years since, years during which Ruth Bader Ginsburg, a distinguished justice, has become a pop-culture feminist icon, a comic-book superhero. In the past year alone, the woman known to her fans as the Notorious RBG has been the subject of a *Saturday Night Live* skit; a fawning documentary; an upcoming bio-pic, *On the Basis of Sex* (from a screenplay written by Ginsburg's nephew); a CNN podcast, *RBG Beyond Notorious*; and a new biography, *Ruth*

Bader Ginsburg: A Life (Knopf), by Jane Sherron De Hart, an emeritus history professor at the University of California, Santa Barbara.

Such lavish biographical attention to a living Supreme Court Justice is unusual and new, even if that change is easy to lose sight of amid the recent intense scrutiny of the high-school and college years of the Trump nominee, Brett Kavanaugh, who has been accused of sexual assault. (He has denied the allegations.) Unlike candidates for political office, most sitting justices have preferred to remain, if not anonymous, largely unknown. The position is unelected, the appointment is for life, and the justices are not supposed to place themselves in the public eye, for fear of making themselves beholden to public opinion: arguably, the less attention to their personal lives the better. Before the past, tumultuous decade, few, if any, Justices who hadn't previously held an elected office had been the subject of a full-dress biography while still serving on the Court.

Writing a biography of a sitting justice introduces all kinds of problems of perspective, authority, and obligation. Ginsburg has not yet deposited her papers in any archive and, having refused calls to resign under Obama's watch, says that she has no plans to retire. De Hart, who began the project fifteen years ago, relied on published material, public records, and, extensively, interviews. Her publisher describes the book as "written with the cooperation of Ruth Bader Ginsburg." It would have been impossible to write the book without that cooperation, but it comes at no small cost.

Making De Hart's problems worse is Ginsburg's unprecedented judicial celebrity. On Matt Groening's animated series *Futurama*, Ginsburg appeared as an artificially preserved head, and although Antonin Scalia's severed head made a cameo or two as well, it was the Ginsburg character's catchphrase—"You Ruth Bader believe it!"—that ended up on T-shirts and coffee mugs and is the thing your teenager says to you at the dinner table. This winter, Ginsburg, eighty-five, did her daily workout with Stephen Colbert on *The Late Show*. "I'm a huge fan!" Colbert said. Thurgood Marshall never lifted weights with Johnny Carson. This summer, three goats were brought to Montpelier to eat the poison ivy spreading throughout the Vermont state capital: they are named Ruth, Bader, and Ginsburg. To my knowledge, no flock of sheep were ever named Oliver, Wendell, and Holmes.

God bless Ruth Bader Ginsburg, goats, bobbleheads, and all. But trivialization—RBG's workout tips! her favorite lace collars!—is not tribute. Female heroes are in short supply not because women aren't brave but because female bravery is demeaned, no kind more than intellectual courage. *Isn't she cute*? Ginsburg was and remains a scholar, an advocate, and a judge of formidable sophistication, complexity, and, not least, contradiction and limitation. It is no kindness to flatten her into a paper doll and sell her as partisan merch.

Doing so also obscures a certain irony. Ginsburg often waxes nostalgic about her confirmation hearings, as she did this September, when, regretting the partisan furor over Brett Kavanaugh— even before Christine Blasey Ford came forward—she said, "The way it was was right; the way it is is wrong." The second of those statements is undeniably and painfully true, but the first flattens the past. What Biden was getting at, in 1993, was what the president himself had said, dismissing the idea of nominating Ginsburg when it was first suggested to him. "The women," Clinton said, "are against her."

.   .   .

Ruth Bader was born in Brooklyn in 1933. At thirteen, she wrote a newspaper editorial, a tribute to the Charter of the United Nations. Her mother, an admirer of Eleanor Roosevelt, died when she was seventeen. Bader went to Cornell, where she liked to say that she learned how to write from Vladimir Nabokov. At Cornell, she also met Martin Ginsburg and fell in love. They married in 1954 and had a baby, Jane, in 1955. Brilliant and fiercely independent, Ginsburg was devoted to Marty, to Jane, and to the law. At Harvard Law School, which first admitted women in 1950, she was one of only nine women in a class of some five hundred. In one of the first scenes in *On the Basis of Sex*, Erwin Griswold, the dean of the law school, asks each of those nine women, during a dinner party at his house, why she is occupying a place that could have gone to a man. In the film, Ginsburg, played by Felicity Jones, gives the dean an answer to which he can have no objection: "My husband, Marty, is in the second-year class. I'm at Harvard to learn about his work. So that I might be a more patient and understanding wife." This, which is more or less what Ginsburg actually said, was a necessary lie. It was possible for a woman to attend law school—barely—but it was not possible for her to admit her ambition.

In 1957, Marty was diagnosed with testicular cancer. During his illness and treatment—surgery followed by radiation—Ruth not only cared for him and for the baby but also covered all of his classes and helped him with his papers. She kept up an almost inhuman schedule, often working through the night. After Marty graduated, he took a job in New York, and Ruth transferred to Columbia. She graduated first in her class. "That's my mommy," four-year-old Jane said, when Ginsburg crossed the stage to accept her diploma.

Looking for work, Ginsburg confronted the limits of the profession's willingness to take female lawyers seriously. Felix Frankfurter, the first Supreme Court justice to hire an African American clerk, in 1948, refused to hire a woman, even after he was reassured that Ginsburg never wore pants. Stymied, Ginsburg went to Sweden to undertake a comparative study of Swedish and American law. On her return, in 1963, she accepted a position at Rutgers, teaching civil procedure. A year and a half later, when she found herself pregnant—given her husband's medical history, this blessing was unexpected—Ginsburg delayed informing the university, for fear of losing her position.

Ginsburg, in other words, had plenty of experience of what would now be called—because she called it this—discrimination on the basis of sex. In 1969, Ginsburg was promoted to full professor and her son, James, entered nursery school, rites of passage that freed her to explore a new interest: she began volunteering for the ACLU. Working with and eventually heading the ACLU's Women's Rights Project, Ginsburg pursued a series of cases designed to convince the Supreme Court, first, that there is such a thing as sex discrimination and, second, that it violates the Constitution.

Influenced by the pioneering constitutional analysis of Pauli Murray and Dorothy Kenyon, Ginsburg borrowed, too, from the strategy of Thurgood Marshall, who, as head of the NAACP's Legal and Educational Defense Fund beginning in 1940, had pursued his agenda step by step, case by case, over fourteen years, all the way to *Brown v. Board*, decided in 1954. Erwin Griswold, notwithstanding his resentment of women law students, eventually dubbed Ginsburg "the Thurgood Marshall of gender equality law."

She prepared herself for litigation by teaching courses on women and the law, a subject that had rarely been taught. An undisputed leader of an emerging field, she soon left Rutgers. ("Columbia Snares a Prize in the Quest for Women Professors," the *Times* reported.) Unlike Marshall, who was very often on the front lines of civil unrest and political protest, Ginsburg worked full time as a law-school professor, which placed constraints on her time and kept her at some remove from protests taking place on the streets. And, as De Hart observes, several crucial features distinguish their strategies. Marshall relied on the equal-protection clause—"No State shall . . . deny to any person within its jurisdiction the equal protection of the laws"—of the Fourteenth Amendment, which was adopted after the Civil War in order to stop the former Confederate states from denying former slaves equal rights. Ginsburg also invoked the equal-protection clause, but was left to argue only by analogy, suggesting that discrimination on the basis of sex is the same sort of thing. Finally, while there were plenty of rifts within the civil-rights movement, Marshall never had to battle African Americans opposed to the very notion of equality under the law; Ginsburg, by contrast, faced a phalanx of conservative women, led by Phyllis Schlafly, who objected to equal rights altogether.

In one of the earliest of Ginsburg's antidiscrimination cases, *Reed v. Reed* (1971), she established that an Idaho law that gave preference to men over women in the administration of estates violated the equal-protection clause. Ginsburg called her victory in *Reed* "a small, guarded step." She next hoped to bring to the Supreme Court a case called *Struck v. Secretary of Defense*. When Captain Susan Struck became pregnant, she decided to have the baby, but air force policy meant that she would lose her job unless she had an abortion. Ginsburg prepared to argue Struck's case on equal-protection grounds: since no air force policy barred men from having children, the government was discriminating against Struck on the basis of sex. In choosing a case that would advance a desperately needed argument about reproductive autonomy, Ginsburg had cleverly selected one in which the litigant had chosen to have a baby, rather than to end a pregnancy, so that the Court's attention would be focused on the equality claims of women (and not on the politics of abortion). But the air force changed its policy and, in 1972, at the urging of then solicitor general Erwin Griswold, the case was dismissed, a decision that had profound consequences: the following year, the Court ruled on *Roe v. Wade* instead, and struck down antiabortion legislation not on the ground of equal protection but on the ground of a much weaker constitutional doctrine, the right to privacy.

If *Struck* was Ginsburg's next, carefully placed stepping stone across a wide river, *Roe* was a rickety wooden plank thrown down across the water and—Ginsburg thought—likely to rot. In a lecture she delivered in 1984, she noted the political significance of the fact that the Court had treated sex discrimination as a matter of equal protection but reproductive autonomy as a matter of privacy. When the Court overturned laws on the basis of sex discrimination, no great controversy ensued, she observed, but *Roe v. Wade* remained "a storm center." She went on, "*Roe v. Wade* sparked public opposition and academic criticism, in part, I believe, because the Court ventured too far in the change it ordered and presented an incomplete justification for its action."

There are more what-ifs than there are stars in the sky. But *Roe* helped conservatives defeat the Equal Rights Amendment, which had passed Congress and appeared well on its way to ratification until Schlafly warned, starting in 1974, that the "ERA means abortion." Following Ginsburg's logic, it's impossible not to wonder whether, if the Court had heard *Struck* instead of *Roe*, the ERA would have passed, after which reproductive rights would have been recognized by the courts as a matter of equal protection. And the nation would not have become so divided. If, if.

Asked by the ACLU to take on litigation relating to the defense of *Roe*, Ginsburg declined. Instead, she continued to pursue antidiscrimination cases and first appeared before the Supreme Court in *Frontiero v. Richardson*, in 1973, advocating for Sharron Frontiero, an air force lieutenant who had been denied benefits for her husband which were granted to men for their wives. "I ask no favor for my sex," Ginsburg told the nine men on the bench, quoting the nineteenth-century women's-rights advocate Sarah Grimké. "All I ask of our brethren is that they take their feet off our necks." Ginsburg won, though the Court's holding was narrow. As she proceeded to try to widen that holding, she continued teaching at Columbia and writing law-review articles. In 1979, after Jimmy Carter signed legislation expanding the federal judiciary, Ginsburg began pursuing a judgeship.

Carter was determined to appoint women and asked Sarah Weddington, the lawyer who had argued *Roe*, to help him find them. By 1970, only three in a hundred lawyers and fewer than two hundred of the nation's ten thousand judges were women. In 1971, Chief Justice Warren Burger, on hearing that Richard Nixon was considering nominating a woman to the Court, drafted a letter of resignation. "Feminist Picked for U.S. Court of Appeals Here," the *Washington Post* announced in December of 1979, even before Carter had officially named Ginsburg to the D.C. circuit.

Strom Thurmond, whose office dismissed the nominee as a "one-issue woman," cast the lone vote against her nomination in the Senate Judiciary Committee, and she took a seat on the notoriously fractious D.C. court. There she became known as a consensus builder who adhered closely to precedent, wrote narrowly tailored decisions, and refused to join intemperately written opinions. A 1987 study showed that she voted more often with Republican appointees than with Democratic appointees. In *Dronenburg v. Zech* (1984), she voted against rehearing a case involving a sailor's allegation that the navy had discriminated against him by discharging him for homosexual conduct. She generally agreed with conservatives in opposing expanded regulation of corporate conduct. She insisted on the importance of not getting ahead of the law. In *Women's Equity Action League v. Cavazos* (1990), she dismissed a two-decades-old suit, arguing that the litigant groups' claim that federal agencies had failed to comply with their own antidiscrimination statutes "lacks the requisite green light from the legislative branch."

Of the fifty-seven people she hired as law clerks, interns, or secretaries during her time on the D.C. bench, not one was African American. Ginsburg was asked about this when she appeared before the Senate Judiciary Committee, and she promised, "If you confirm me for this job, my attractiveness to black candidates is going to improve." But in her quarter century on the Supreme Court she has hired only one African American clerk (a record that, distressingly, does not distinguish her from most of the bench). And, as both judge and justice, she has frequently sided with conservatives on questions concerning criminal-justice reform. In *Samson v. California* (2006), she joined an opinion, written by Clarence Thomas, upholding warrantless searches of people on parole; in *Davis v. Ayala* (2015), she declined to join an opinion condemning solitary confinement.

De Hart describes Ginsburg's thirteen years on the circuit court as something like a decontamination chamber, in which Ginsburg was rinsed and scrubbed of the hazard of her thirteen years as an advocate for women's rights. By 1993, she had been sufficiently depolarized to be appointed to the Supreme Court.

．　　．　　．

On March 9, 1993, seven weeks after Bill Clinton's inauguration, Ginsburg delivered the James Madison Lecture on Constitutional Law, at New York University. She took as her subject the importance of collegiality in decision making and moderation in style. The lecture can be read as an indictment not just of judicial excess but of the changing character of American political discourse. She inveighed against "too frequent resort to separate opinions and the immoderate tone of statements." Ginsburg had no use for grandstanding or the cheeky remark or even the snippy footnote. She offered a list of phrases used by dissenters who disparaged majority opinions by calling them "outrageous," or "inexplicable" or "Orwellian" or a "blow against the People." As an example of the sort of screeds she wished federal judges would stop writing, she cited a dissent that began this way: "Running headlong from the questions briefed and argued before us, my colleagues seek refuge in a theory as novel as it is questionable."

One measure of how politics has descended into acrimony since then is that the Notorious RBG is now celebrated for just this kind of blistering, contemptuous dissent, as if spitting had become a virtue. Consider a recent *Bustle.com* feature, "4 Epic Ginsburg Dissents That Prove She's a Badass," or the signature line of Kate McKinnon's RBG: "That's a Ginsburn!" In fact, there really aren't many Ginsburns to be found in the records of the Supreme Court. Ginsburg has indeed produced forcefully written dissents, especially as the Court has moved to the right, but they are not themselves immoderate. Instead, they scold her colleagues for their immoderacy, as when, in 2013, objecting to the majority's decision to overturn much of the 1965 Voting Rights Act, she complained, "The Court's opinion can hardly be described as an exemplar of restrained and moderate decision making."

Early in 1993, less than two weeks after Ginsburg delivered her Madison Lecture, Justice Byron White notified President Clinton of his intention to retire. The White House counsel, Bernard Nussbaum, gave the president a list of some forty possible nominees. No Democratic President had appointed a Supreme Court Justice since Lyndon Johnson named Thurgood Marshall, in 1967. Clinton, as in so many things, proved indecisive; he was also distracted and still staffing his Justice Department. He conferred with senators, but relied on seventy-five (unnamed) D.C. lawyers for advice. He contemplated Mario Cuomo and George J. Mitchell, the Senate Majority Leader. Most presidential selection processes—in the days before Trump's *Survivor*-style public charades—took place secretly and quickly. Clinton's process was open and interminable. The longer he took to make his decision the more interest groups were able to influence the process, not least because the White House invited them in. Over eighty-seven days and nights, Clinton asked all sorts of people their opinions. Kim Gandy, the executive vice-president of NOW, told the historian Richard Davis that her conduit to the president was the press: "We were frequently asked, 'What do you think about Bruce Babbitt for the Supreme Court?' and 'What do you think about Breyer?'" He just couldn't make up his mind.

Janet Reno, Clinton's very new attorney general, urged him to name a woman. But Ginsburg, for all that she had done to advance women's rights during the 1970s, was apparently not on the lists sent to the White House by women's groups. In her Madison Lecture, Ginsburg cited *Roe* to illustrate a crucial problem in judicial decision making—"doctrinal limbs too swiftly shaped, experience teaches, may prove unstable." It would have been better, she thought, if the Court had decided *Struck* instead. Saying this took courage. In 1993, Operation Rescue ("If you believe abortion is murder, act like it's murder") was protesting outside abortion clinics. Other feminists disagreed with the reasoning behind *Roe*—just as some feminists today lament the tactics of the #MeToo movement—but calling *Roe* into question in public when abortion clinics were being bombed seemed beyond the pale. Many also found Ginsburg's counterfactual implausible. "Coulda, woulda, shoulda," NOW's president, Patricia Ireland, said; prolife activists "don't care about the legal theory—they care about stopping abortion and controlling women's lives."

And so when Clinton, eager to please, entertained names proposed by women's groups, he learned that some of them refused to support Ginsburg, because they were worried that she might be willing to overturn *Roe* (which is not what she had written, but one gathers that the Madison Lecture was more often invoked than read). At one point, Clinton asked Senator Daniel Patrick Moynihan to suggest a woman. "Ruth Bader Ginsburg," Moynihan answered. "The women are against her" was the president's reply. Moynihan called Martin Ginsburg and said, "You best take care of it."

Ginsburg, a prominent and well-connected tax lawyer, was already running a behind-the-scenes campaign, without his wife's knowledge. In February 1993, he'd organized a breakfast meeting with the president of a leading women's group in D.C. to seek her support for his plan to get his wife nominated as solicitor general. He did not succeed. He had the same experience at a meeting in New York. In April and May, he courted the press and solicited at least thirty-four letters of support, largely from the legal academy, where Ginsburg, an excellent scholar, was widely admired. Fourteen members of the faculty of NYU Law School—people who had been in the room when Ginsburg delivered the Madison Lecture—wrote a joint letter to say that they were "distressed that her remarks at NYU have been misconstrued as anti-choice and anti-women."

All spring, the Ginsburg family kept up the campaign, which involved bringing the lack of support among women's groups out into the open, so that it could be countered. The Brookings Institution fellow Stephen Hess, a cousin of Ginsburg's, warned reporters, including the *New York Times* columnist Anthony Lewis, that feminists were opposed to Ginsburg, and mailed them copies of the Madison Lecture. "I do not know Judge Ginsburg," Lewis wrote in his column on May 10. "I do not support or oppose her as a possible choice for the Supreme Court. I just find the knee-jerk arguments invoked against her—and against others who have been mentioned—depressing."

Nine days later, the heads of the National Women's Law Center, the Women's Legal Defense Fund, and NOW's Legal Defense and Education Fund (on whose board Ginsburg had served) sent Nussbaum a remarkable joint statement: "It has been reported that the women's movement would oppose the nomination of Judge Ruth Bader Ginsburg to the Supreme Court. We want to be certain there is no confusion about where our organizations stand: at this stage in the process, we have not taken any position in favor or in opposition to any candidate." It was hardly a ringing endorsement. Nussbaum faxed a copy of the letter to Marty Ginsburg, who later recalled, "I saw it as a pearl beyond price," since it would allow him to expose and embarrass the authors. He sent copies of the letter to members of the press. Eventually, key women's groups, which had been unwilling to oppose Ginsburg publicly, ceased opposing her privately, especially after May 29, when Clinton hired David Gergen as a senior adviser. Women's groups believed that Gergen was steering Clinton toward Bruce Babbitt and Stephen Breyer. "One minute there were all these female nominees," Kim Gandy said. "And then, as soon as David Gergen gets there, suddenly all the nominees look like David Gergen."

Summoned to the White House on Sunday, June 13, Ginsburg met with the president for ninety minutes. He made his decision later that day, and, after watching a Chicago Bulls game that went into three overtimes, called her nearly at midnight. The *Wall Street Journal* posited a rule: "When Bill Clinton is doing the picking, it's better to be last than first." The *Washington Post* applauded Clinton for valuing "reputation rather than celebrity." The next day, in the Rose Garden, Clinton announced his nomination, and Ginsburg delivered a moving acceptance speech. Her daughter had written in her high-school yearbook in 1973, under "Ambition": "To see her mother appointed to the Supreme Court. If necessary, Jane will appoint her." Ginsburg told the crowd, "Jane is so pleased, Mr. President, that you did it instead."

When Ginsburg finished, Brit Hume, then at ABC News, asked a question:

> The withdrawal of the Guinier nomination, sir, and your apparent focus on Judge Breyer, and your turn, late it seems, to Judge Ginsburg, may have created an impression, perhaps unfair, of a certain zig-zag quality in the decision-making process here. I wonder, sir, if you could kind of walk us through it, perhaps disabuse us of any notion we might have along those lines. Thank you.

If you watch the footage today, the question comes across as gentlemanly, even Edwardian. But Clinton turned beet red and said: "I have long since given up the thought that I could disabuse some of you of turning any substantive decision into anything but political process. How you could ask a question like that after the statement she just made is beyond me."

And then he took no more questions.

.   .   .

It was a month later, riding the train into the capital, that Biden was thrilled to discover no mention of Ginsburg's nomination hearings on the front pages of the *Times*. She was an excellent nominee. "My approach, I believe, is neither liberal nor conservative," Ginsburg told the committee. The Senate voted to confirm her ninety-six to three, with one abstention. But the idea that her appointment was uncontroversial is almost entirely a myth.

Few Justices have been better prepared to appear before the Senate Judiciary Committee than Ginsburg, who had made an academic study of the history of the process. As she had related in a law-review article, it was in many respects surprising that the executive would play so great a role in shaping the judiciary. At the Constitutional Convention in 1787, the Senate was initially granted the exclusive power to appoint Supreme Court Justices; that measure, proposed on June 13, was accepted without objection. A proposal made on July 18 for the president to name Justices and for the Senate to provide advice and consent was defeated. Only on September 7, ten days before the final draft, did the Convention revisit this question and adopt the proposed sharing of power.

In 1988, taking stock of two hundred years of Supreme Court nominations, Ginsburg observed that more than a hundred men and one woman had served on the Court, and the Senate had rejected twenty-eight, of whom only five had been blocked in the twentieth century. No nominee was questioned before the Senate Judiciary Committee until 1925, when Harlan Stone made a brief appearance to answer questions specifically about the Teapot Dome scandal. The next nominee to appear before the committee was Felix Frankfurter, in 1939, who announced:

"While I believe that a nominee's record should be thoroughly scrutinized by this committee . . . I should think it not only bad taste but inconsistent with the duties of the office for which I have been nominated for me to attempt to supplement my past record by present declarations. That is all I have to say."

He relented, but largely for the purpose of denying that he was a communist. Only since 1955 have nominees routinely appeared before the committee. All followed some version of the Frankfurter rule, placing strict limits on what they would discuss, until Robert Bork, who said, on the first day of his confirmation hearings, "I welcome this opportunity to come before the committee and answer whatever questions the members might have." He quickly clarified that, although he said he was happy to discuss his "judicial philosophy," he would demur on specific cases—a distinction, as Ginsburg observed, that "blurred as the questions and answers wore on," not least because Bork, Nixon's former solicitor general and the last man standing after the Saturday Night Massacre in 1973, seemed delighted by the attention.

Bork's confirmation hearings were both the last episode of the Watergate scandal and the first episode of a new and enduring scandal, the blurring of the legislative and judicial branches of the federal government. Bork's nomination elicited paid television advertisements, as if he were running for an elected office. Since then, the distance between the judiciary and the political process has almost entirely eroded. With Merrick Garland, Senate Republicans, acting with breathtaking heedlessness, abandoned the constitutional principle that a Supreme Court nomination is meant to be insulated from public opinion, Mitch McConnell arguing that the American people, not the sitting American president, would name the next Supreme Court Justice. "I wish I could wave a magic wand and have it go back to the way it was," Ginsburg said in September, after the first Kavanaugh hearings. Partisanship has corrupted the confirmation process. The legitimacy of the Court has declined. Women have yet to gain the equal protection of the law. And there is no wand.

·　　·　　·

In the summer of 1993, when Biden finally sidled up to his question, he was asking Ginsburg to explain the distance between her 1973 Frontiero brief and her 1993 Madison Lecture. How could she at one point say that the Court can move ahead of public opinion and at another point say that it shouldn't? The transcript reads:

> THE CHAIRMAN: Can you square those for me or point out
>   their consistency to me?
> JUDGE GINSBURG: Yes.
> THE CHAIRMAN: That is a good answer. Now we will go on
>   to the next question. [*Laughter*]

Biden pressed; Ginsburg evaded. "I saw my role in those days as an advocate," she said, talking about Reed and those stepping stones.

"Judge, I don't mean to cut you off," Biden said. "I am trying to square, though, your—I understand your position as an advocate. Then you became an appellate-court judge, and you gave a lecture this year called the Madison Lecture. . . ."

Biden found her charming. And she *was* charming, and she was smart, and she was much better prepared than he was. He could not nail her down. Ginsburg answered with a precision that was characteristic of her briefs, of her oral arguments, and of her opinions from the federal appellate court but also with a self-control honed by decades of experience arguing with people who underestimated her.

"My time is up, Judge," Biden eventually said, wearily. "You have been very instructive about how things have moved, but you still haven't—and I will come back to it—squared for me the issue of whether or not the Court can or should move ahead of society." Ginsburg offered a short sermon about reticence: "We cherish living in a democracy, and we also know that this Constitution did not create a tricameral system. Judges must be mindful of what their place is in this system and must always remember that we live in a democracy that can be destroyed if judges take it upon themselves to rule as Platonic guardians."

She never answered Biden's question. Instead, she established her own rule: the Ginsburg precedent, a rule of restraint. But there are very few rules left anymore, and even less restraint.

The New Yorker

WINNER—COLUMNS AND
COMMENTARY

*In these columns published online
at newyorker.com, Doreen St. Félix
traces the inescapable legacy of
racism ("Our awe at the notion of
a raceless future only betrays the
truths of our present," she writes
in "The National Geographic
Twins and the Falsehood of Our
Post-Racial Future"); celebrates the
role of Meghan Markle's mother,
Doria Ragland, at her daughter's
wedding; and ascribes to Brett
Kavanaugh "the conservative's
embrace of bluster and petulance
as rhetorical tools" during his
testimony before the Senate
Judiciary Committee. The National
Magazine Awards judges praised
St. Félix for her sense of history
and described these columns as
"measured, sensitive and sharp."
St. Félix joined the* New Yorker *as
a staff writer in 2017. The same
year, she was nominated for the
National Magazine Award for
Columns and Commentary for
her work for MTV News. She was
twenty-six years old when these*
New Yorker *columns were written.*

Doreen St. Félix

The National Geographic Twins and the Falsehood of Our Post-Racial Future *and* The Profound Presence of Doria Ragland *and* The Ford-Kavanaugh Hearing Will Be Remembered as a Grotesque Display of Patriarchal Resentment

The National Geographic Twins and the Falsehood of Our Post-Racial Future

On Monday, *National Geographic* opened its April issue with a somber letter from the editor, Susan Goldberg, presented with the even more somber headline "For Decades, Our Coverage Was Racist. To Rise Above Our Past, We Must Acknowledge It." "The Race Issue," which marks the fiftieth anniversary of the assassination of Dr. Martin Luther King Jr., inaugurates the magazine's yearlong "Diversity in America" series. In the letter, Goldberg—who is the first woman and the first Jewish person in the top post since the magazine's founding, in 1888—informs her readers that John Edwin Mason, a historian of photography and of the African continent, having studied the magazine's archive, found that, through failures of omission, overwrought inclusions, a melodramatic tone, and other editorial choices, *National Geographic* had mismanaged its reportage on nonwhite cultures. As Goldberg summarized, "until the 1970s *National Geographic* all but ignored people of color who lived in the United States. . . . Meanwhile it pictured 'natives' elsewhere as exotics, famously and frequently unclothed, happy hunters, noble savages—every type of cliché."

The magazine's admission is rare and vindicates readers who, like me, have always had a visceral reaction to *National Geographic*'s covers and ethos. A recent project at the *Times* was similarly refreshing—offering obituaries for the indefatigable journalist Ida B. Wells, the writer Sylvia Plath, and thirteen other women who hadn't been memorialized in the paper at the time of their deaths. The *Times,* which calls its project "Overlooked," uses oddly passive language in presenting its past missteps: its archives offer "a stark lesson in how society valued various achievements and achievers," the copy reads. Mason uses more pointed language: "*National Geographic* comes into existence at the height of colonialism . . . and *National Geographic* was reflecting that view of the world."

Do institutions serve primarily as reflections, or might they also be authorities from which Western views of the world originate? As Tobi Haslett writes in "Unseen: Unpublished Black History from the New York Times Photo Archives," his review of a similar project produced by the *Times*, "The newspaper graciously provides us with the very images it had so imperiously overlooked, as the whole endeavor calmly reasserts the grip of the media on the public imagination."

On Monday, *National Geographic* announced its new era of racial lucidity with a cover photograph of the English eleven-year-olds Marcia and Millie Biggs, apparently symbols of our postracial future. Their matching dresses and long, flowing hair emphasize what can be determined from their faces: that these girls are sisters—fraternal twins. "They both have my nose," their father, Michael Biggs, says in the story. "Marcia had light brown hair and fair skin like her English-born mother," the article states; "Millie had black hair and brown skin like her father, who's of Jamaican descent." A statistical geneticist clarifies that it is not a rarity for one child to resemble one parent and vice versa; the issue's abstract says that "race is a human invention" and that skin color has misguidedly been used as a "proxy" for race. And yet the magazine cover undermines all of these correctives. "Black and White," it reads, under the portrait of the twins. "These twin sisters make us rethink everything we know about race." The online promotion is even more contradictory: "These Twins, One Black and One White, Will Make You Rethink Race." The framing inspires the kind of coarse racial quantifying from which the issue is ostensibly trying to escape. Linking to the article on social media, several people observed that both sisters "look" black.

The sisters first went viral in 2007, in the *Daily Mail*, where they were also described as belonging to separate races and were called "million to one" biological anomalies. In the *National Geographic* coverage, we learn that what sounded like a statistic in the *Daily Mail* is, in fact, just something that the girls' adoring mother, Amanda Wanklin, likes to say. It is telling that both of the girls' parents think of their daughters this way, as do their peers in Birmingham. A more interesting and more accurate angle for an article might have made the human perception of race the point of their story, examining the long shadow of pseudoscientific classification, the legacy of passing, and the oppressiveness of phenotype. The paradox of race—a social myth with real repercussions—can never be overexplained. Instead, the *National Geographic* article, a perfect demonstration of good intentions gone awry, has the girls talking about how they are stared at but have thankfully never endured racist abuse. As Mason is quoted in the accompanying editorial, "It's possible to say that a magazine can open people's eyes at the same time it closes them."

Certain people will always be collected and displayed—in magazines, in museums, in imaginations. Sometimes, these people aren't even real. In 1993, *Time* published "The New Face of America," a computer-generated woman with light-brown skin created from "a mix of several races." For its 125th-anniversary issue, in 2013, *National Geographic* profiled multiracial people to illustrate the "changing face of America." In recent years, the multiracial person, who breaks the rules of the caste system, has become the subject of liberal, cross-racial desire, vaunted as diviners of social progress, or of apocalypse. Barack Obama is the most famous member of the newly consolidated Loving Generation, as it is termed in a new docu-series from Topic; one only has to look at the excitement around Meghan Markle or the dozens of accounts on Instagram and Facebook devoted to fawning over mixed-race "swirl babies" to see the fixation develop. But, for centuries, a significant portion of colonized populations have qualified as multiracial, even if their genes do not manifest in the look of light skin, hazel or blue eyes, and hair that grows in perfect ringlets. It follows that multiraciality ought not to be the vessel for social hope. Our awe at the notion of a raceless future only betrays the truths of our present.

The Profound Presence of Doria Ragland

The day of the royal wedding, we could not keep our eyes off her. What was she thinking, as she sat in the pews of the five-hundred-year-old chapel, enveloped in history and irony? I mean the mother of the bride, Doria Ragland. A millennium of world-shifting encounters—of violence and of romance and of acts in between—produced this scene: the sixty-one-year-old Ragland, an American who teaches yoga and does social work in Culver City, California, sitting in the opposite and equivalent seat to Queen Elizabeth II. They'd agreed on green, the color of beginnings—Ragland in churchy, pastel Oscar de la Renta, the Queen in electric-lime Stewart Parvin. One is a descendant of the enslaved, a child of the Great Migration and Jim Crow and seventies New Age spirituality; the other, the heir to and keeper of empire. Blood had long ago decided what life would be like for both.

But love barges in and finds a way. Love brings together Prince Harry and Meghan Markle, whose train of identifiers—biracial, actress, Angeleno, divorcée, feminist, former lifestyle blogger—complete the Mad Libs of the new American vogue. Love brings together their families: the House of Windsor and a one-woman house. Genuine attraction seemed to pulse between them, as

Harry, biting his lip, giddily whispered to his bride, "You look amazing." Markle's doe eyes glinted. Nearby, Ragland radiated with what looked like maternal pride. Certainly it was more complex than just that.

Ragland isn't an actress like her daughter, but she said many things with her face. Photographs of her and Markle pressed close to one another in the Rolls-Royce on the way to the chapel show the mother trying on a regent's wave, smiling warmly but tentatively. Inside, she executed her duties with grace. Her locs had been swept beneath her pillbox hat; the shine of her tiny nose ring gleamed like the shine in her eyes. There was not much emoting in the crowd of royal fascinators, although many screwed their faces as Bishop Michael Bruce Curry, the first black head of the Episcopal Church, thundered in his sermon about the possibility of a "new world." But one could perceive Ragland softly reeling beneath her composure. Her lips trembled as her daughter walked down the aisle. She cried gently. When Curry spoke about the example of Martin Luther King Jr. and the power of radical, social love, she nodded unreservedly; when the East London choir roused the room with Ben E. King's "Stand By Me," she swayed. Sometimes the cameras would catch Ragland as if she were in a trance, lost in some intimate thought.

What we know of the relationship between mother and daughter has an "us against the world" feel to it. After her parents divorced, when she was six, Markle spent weekdays with her mother. Ragland doted on her only child, calling her "Flower." When Markle became wealthy, she paid for her mother to attend graduate school; in a Mother's Day post on her blog, she swooned with reverence over Ragland's resilience. There's no "Imitation of Life" drama here, in which the mixed-race daughter shuns her darker-skinned mother. Markle clearly delights in what she euphemizes as her mother's "free spirit." But they are different women. Markle makes it a point to call herself biracial. She vaguely invokes the "wounds" of American history but is careful not to frame herself as a race hero. The skin of the mother is honey brown, but the daughter has been cast as ethnically ambiguous. In essays, Markle recalls that, as a child, strangers in the Valley mistook her mother for her nanny. In front of billions, Markle entered one of the oldest halls of whiteness, with the flowers of former colonies sewn onto her veil, and blended in. Ragland stood out.

It is true that Markle and her groom beautifully threaded black rituals throughout the ceremony. But claims about the wedding's "wokeness" are a little jarring. This was a royal marriage set against the backdrop of the government threatening to deport Britons of the Windrush generation. Was that melancholy in Ragland's eyes? A worry about whether her daughter would be truly accepted in the family and what she may have to do to usher in that acceptance? Did she recall the Christmas luncheon that Markle attended in December, at which Princess Michael of Kent wore a blackamoor brooch clipped to her jacket? Markle had longtime friends in her party, but Ragland was the sole representative of her family. Ragland's mother, Jeannette, who reportedly watched Markle as a child while Doria worked, died in 2000. Through her presence, Ragland implied a lineage of black women—and represented the fraught lineage of a nation.

It should not be lost on anyone that, despite the pitiful shenanigans of her ex-husband, Thomas Markle, and the gossiping of her ex-stepchildren, Ragland flew to Heathrow to do what black women do: straighten the mess up. One vision of the black mother depends on this kind of self-effacing altruism. The public has fallen for Ragland. On Twitter, people speculate that Lady Diana Spencer, whose legend of social rebellion is especially idolized by black women, would have adored her. At an afternoon tea on Friday, Ragland "charmed" the Queen, and she has quit her job at the mental-health clinic to avoid the paparazzi. The big interview will likely come via Oprah, who, swaggering into the castle on Saturday in pink, called attention to her own supremacy. But how

Ragland will participate in the cult of her daughter's marriage is yet to be seen. There is new pressure on the duke and duchess of Sussex—who take their titles after the first and only duke of Sussex, who supported abolition—to liven up the monarchy's reputation. The hunger for a cordial kind of racial harmonizing is strong. I know Markle feels that burden, and I know that Ragland does, too.

The Ford-Kavanaugh Hearing Will Be Remembered as a Grotesque Display of Patriarchal Resentment

Judge Brett Kavanaugh is almost certainly going to be appointed the next member of the Supreme Court of the United States. Whatever Christine Blasey Ford said in her testimony before the Senate Judiciary Committee on Thursday, and whatever Kavanaugh said in his, and however credible and convincing either one seemed, none of it was going to affect this virtual inevitability. The Republicans, if they stick together, have the necessary votes. A veneer of civility made it seem as if the senators were questioning Ford and Kavanaugh to get to the truth of whether Kavanaugh, as a drunk teenager, attended a party where he pinned Ford to a bed and sexually assaulted her, thirty-six years ago. But that's not what the hearing was designed to explore. At the time of this writing, composed in the eighth hour of the grotesque historic activity happening in the Capitol Hill chamber, it should be as plain as day that what we witnessed was the patriarchy testing how far its politics of resentment can go. And there is no limit.

Dressed in a blue suit, taking the oath with nervous solemnity, Ford gave us a bristling sense of déjà vu. "Why suffer through the annihilation if it's not going to matter?" Ford had told the *Washington Post* when she first went public with her allegations. With the word "annihilation" she conjured the specter of Anita Hill, who, in her testimony against Clarence Thomas, in 1991, was basically berated over an exhausting two-day period and diagnosed, by the senators interrogating her, with "erotomania" and a case of man-eating professionalism. Ford's experience—shaped by the optics of the #MeToo moment, by her whiteness and country-club roots—was different. The Republicans on the committee, likely coached by some consultant, did not overtly smear Ford. Some pretended, condescendingly, to extend her empathy. Senator Orrin Hatch, who once claimed that Hill had lifted parts of her harassment allegations against Thomas from *The Exorcist*, called Ford "pleasing," an "attractive" witness. Instead of questioning her directly, the Republicans hired Rachel Mitchell, a female prosecutor specializing in sex crimes, to serve as their proxy. Mitchell's fitful, sometimes aimless questioning did the ugly work of softening the Republican assault on Ford's testimony. Ford, in any case, was phenomenal, a "witness and expert" in one, and it seemed, for a moment following her testimony, that the nation might be unable to deny her credibility.

Then Kavanaugh came in, like an eclipse. He made a show of being unprepared. Echoing Clarence Thomas, he claimed that he did not watch his accuser's hearing. (Earlier, it was reported that he did.) "I wrote this last night," he said, of his opening statement. "No one has seen this draft." Alternating between weeping and yelling, he exemplified the conservative's embrace of bluster and petulance as rhetorical tools. Going on about his harmless love of beer, spinning unbelievably chaste interpretations of what was, by all other accounts, his youthful habit of blatant debauchery, he was as Trumpian as Trump himself, louder than the loudest on Fox News. He evaded questions; he said that the allegations brought against him were "revenge" on behalf of the Clintons; he said, menacingly, that "what goes around comes around." When

Senator Amy Klobuchar calmly asked if he had ever gotten black-out drunk, he retorted, "Have you?" (He later apologized to her.)

There was, in this performance, not even a hint of the sagacity one expects from a potential Supreme Court Justice. More than presenting a convincing rebuttal to Ford's extremely credible account, Kavanaugh—and Hatch and Lindsey Graham—seemed to be exterminating, live, for an American audience, the faint notion that a massively successful white man could have his birth-right questioned or his character held to the most basic type of scrutiny. In the course of Kavanaugh's hearing, Mitchell basically disappeared. Republican senators apologized to the judge, incessantly, for what he had suffered. There was talk of his reputation being torpedoed and his life being destroyed. This is the nature of the conspiracy against white male power—the forces threatening it will always somehow be thwarted at the last minute.

The Hill-Thomas hearings persist in the American consciousness as a watershed moment for partisanship, for male entitlement, for testimony on sexual misconduct, for intraracial tension and interracial affiliation. The Ford-Kavanaugh hearing will be remembered for their entrenchment of the worst impulses from that earlier ordeal. What took place on Thursday confirms that male indignation will be coddled and the gospel of male success elevated. It confirms that there is no fair arena for women's speech. Mechanisms of accountability will be made irrelevant. Some people walked away from 1991 enraged. The next year was said to be the Year of the Woman. Our next year, like this one, will be the Year of the Man.

Esquire

"In 2001, when I was twenty-four
and living in Sheepshead Bay,
Brooklyn, I'd shot a fellow drug
dealer to defend my turf," writes
John J. Lennon. "[S]ix years into my
sentence—twenty-eight-to-life—
I was shanked six times by his
friend in retaliation. Ambulanced
to an outside hospital with a
punctured lung, I didn't snitch.
In this upside-down kingdom,
my backstory gave me cred."
That "upside-down kingdom" is
the New York state prison system,
and "This Place Is Crazy" is both
the story of Lennon's redemption—
"Enrolled in a privately funded
college program, I take night
courses and will soon earn a
bachelor's in behavioral science"—
and an investigation of the
mental-health crisis that besets
prisons nationwide. The National
Magazine Awards judges described
Lennon's prose as "muscular and
empathetic." A contributing writer
at the Marshall Project, he will be
eligible for parole in 2029.

John J. Lennon

This Place
Is Crazy

J oe Cardo was out hunting for half-smoked cigarettes. From my perch at the white-boys' table of the A Block yard, I watched his eyes scan the patched grass and cracked pavement. *Shuffle, stoop, shuffle, stoop.* It was evening rec period, May 2015. A warm front had settled over Attica Correctional Facility in upstate New York, and prisoners were taking advantage. Days earlier, on the ground where Joe now stood, a Crip had been shanked in the heart and dropped dead like someone hit his off button.

I called out to Joe. He snapped up his head and lumbered over. I introduced myself and asked if he'd answer a few questions. "John thinks he's a reporter," said Dave (not his real name), pointing at me. I placed a pouch of tobacco on the concrete table. (Wood, corrections officers learned the hard way, too easily concealed weapons.) Joe's eyes went wide. He was thirty-four, white and slight—five-seven, 165 pounds—with a scraggly beard and a two-car-garage hairline. "Oh, man," he said. "Is that for me?" "Yeah," I said.

"Then I'll answer whatever you want."

Weather permitting, the yard was where we spent most of our free time: Hour-long sessions, three times a day, morning, afternoon, and evening. A CO observed from a cage at the yard's center; a few more COs walked laps, watching us watch them; another, armed with an AR-15, stood guard in a thirty-foot watchtower. No more than six prisoners were allowed at any one of the tables that lined the perimeter. Each was claimed. There was ours—the white-boys' table, populated by a gritty group of high school burnouts, old in age but not in maturity, covered in faded tattoos of skulls and empty phrases like death before dishonor. The Puerto Ricans sat next to us; the Dominicans and the Jamaicans were nearby. The Bloods, the Rat Hunters, and the Latin Kings had tables, too.

My first question for Joe was whether he was a sex offender. A prisoner's place in the pecking order is calculated in part by the transgression that got him here. Those whose crimes are committed against others in the life—gangsters, murderers, drug dealers—tend to land highest. Those whose crimes affect inno-cent civilians—burglars, perverts, assaulters—are somewhere in the middle. Sex offenders, especially pedophiles, are at the very bottom; talking to them can destroy one's reputation by associa-tion. If Joe was in for rape or child pornography, our conversa-tion would need to end immediately.

He wasn't. In clipped sentences, he described how, in Octo-ber 2014, with a BB gun in his hand and a knitted ski mask pulled over his head, he tried to rob a Smokers Choice in Oneonta, New York. "I shouted to the girl behind the counter, 'Give me the money, bitch!'" As he spoke, his eyes flickered between sadness and fear. "She looked me up and down and shouted back, 'No!' Out of nowhere, this three-hundred-pound guy tackled me."

As Joe spoke, Dave, whose all-American good looks had been whittled by years of heroin use—bad teeth, track-mark scars snaking across weathered skin—was rolling his eyes. I figured he'd bounce to the next thing if I continued to ignore him; he had the attention span of an excited puppy. But when Joe said, "I was *glad* when the police came," Dave burst into laughter, and I couldn't stop from joining. In prison, even humor is corrupted.

Joe said he was sentenced to two years. Attempted robbery in the second degree carries a minimum of three and a half years;

the judge must've allowed him to plea to a lesser charge and given a "skid bid"—a short sentence. For most, that would mean time served in one of the state's thirty medium-security facilities. But Attica is maximum-security, arguably New York's toughest. Its notoriety mostly stems from a 1971 uprising that erupted over long-simmering complaints by prisoners of mistreatment. They took control of the prison, killing one CO and three prisoners in the process; five days into the standoff, under Governor Nelson Rockefeller's orders, state police stormed the fortress, killing thirty-nine, including ten hostages. The whiff of distrust between COs, mostly white, and prisoners, mostly not, still lingers. "Why'd they send you *here?*" I asked.

"Bro," Dave cut in, "he's a bugout." Prisonspeak for someone with mental illness.

"What's your diagnosis?" I asked.

"Schizoaffective disorder," Joe said, a form of schizophrenia. He asked what I was in for. "Murder," I replied. In 2001, when I was twenty-four and living in Sheepshead Bay, Brooklyn, I'd shot a fellow drug dealer to defend my turf; six years into my sentence—twenty-eight-to-life—I was shanked six times by his friend in retaliation. Ambulanced to an outside hospital with a punctured lung, I didn't snitch. In this upside-down kingdom, my backstory gave me cred.

"Oh, man—you don't *look* like a murderer," Joe said as if this were the first time he noticed the hard cases who surrounded him. "Bugout" was the label Joe carried, just as "murderer" was mine. Here, where bugs were considered bottom-feeders, I wouldn't want to switch places.

•   •   •

Nearly 20 percent of the 52,000 prisoners in New York's prison system—10,000 in all—have mental illness. The Department of Corrections and Community Supervision (DOCCS), which runs the state's correctional facilities and supervises its parolees, is not alone: nearly 400,000 of 2.2 million prisoners nationwide have a psychiatric diagnosis. Compare that with the 38,000 thousand patients that the country's state-run psych hospitals can accommodate. The math is as easy as it is shocking: Ten out of every eleven psychiatric patients housed by the government are behind bars.

The financial toll is enormous: Treating prisoners with mental illness costs twice as much as providing community-based care. State prisons spend an estimated $5 billion each year to imprison nonviolent offenders with a disorder. As the National Alliance on Mental Illness says, "In a mental-health crisis, people are more likely to encounter police than get medical help." Jails and prisons have become our de facto asylums.

I didn't need such figures and reports. In 1998, my brother Eugene, thirty-two and ten years older than me, was diagnosed with bipolar disorder. Though our family had known for a while something was wrong, we'd chalked it up to his crack addiction. But it was the other way around: he used drugs to mask an unraveling mind. He'd lost his job as an electrician at a hospital in the Bronx; he'd been evicted from one apartment after the next; friends spotted him wandering the streets, shoeless, strumming a guitar and ranting Bible verses. He was at the mercy of psych wards, shelters, and jail. If there was a safety net, he'd slipped through it.

Eugene was actually my half brother, fathered—along with his brother and sister—by a strict, old-school Italian on Long Island our mother married when she was eighteen. They divorced a decade later, and he got custody. Mom moved to Manhattan in 1976 and married an Irish bartender; a year after I came along, he split. (I never met him, and later learned he'd committed suicide.) She landed a four-bedroom apartment in the Sheepshead Bay Houses, a housing project in South Brooklyn, where my siblings visited us on the weekends. My first memories of Eugene are of him arguing with Mom. The issue was always the same: He resented her for leaving them behind.

Though he drifted in and out of my childhood, we remained close. When I was ten, Mom married a third time, to a longshoreman with an apartment in Hell's Kitchen. As a teen, I started hanging out with the neighborhood's street-corner gangsters. I became one, doing time in juvenile halls and the adolescent unit at Rikers Island.

When I was eighteen, Eugene and I briefly lived together in an SRO. I was selling crack, and Eugene was smoking it. By then, his mental illness had started to breach. He'd been to Rikers a couple times himself—drug possession, shoplifting—serving the occasional ninety-day stint. There, he didn't receive psychiatric care, despite his diagnoses. He was just another bugout thrown in with the general population, left to fend for himself.

·   ·   ·

In 2015, after Joe was sentenced, he was sent to one of the state's four prisoner-distribution warehouses, or "reception centers," as they're known. Like everyone else entering the system, he received a mental-health exam. On a scale of six through one—six meaning no psychosis and one indicating a serious diagnosis—Joe was level one. That meant he would be placed at one of the state's fifteen prisons supposedly equipped to treat mental illness, all but three of which are maximum-security. The medium-security spots Joe might've been placed if he didn't require special care resemble grassy, dorm-dotted college campuses, except fenced. Instead, he ended up behind the wall at Attica.

Seeing Joe searching for butts brought up the same question that bothered me about Eugene: How could a guy like him end up not in treatment but behind bars? Over the next several months, I spoke with prison-reform advocates and read reports. What I learned is as tragic as it is absurd: By locking up those with psychiatric diagnoses, we've boomeranged back to the way things were done in antebellum America. In 1843, during a presentation to Massachusetts legislators on the deplorable conditions she'd seen in penitentiaries across the state, reformer Dorothea Dix called out the problem the government faced. "Prisons are not constructed in view of being converted into county hospitals," she wrote, "and almshouses are not founded as receptacles for the insane. And yet, in the face of justice and common sense, wardens are by law compelled to receive, and masters of almshouses not to refuse, insane and idiotic subjects in all stages of mental disease and privation."

The aim of the modern penitentiary, the first of which had opened in Philadelphia a little over a decade before, was penitence, not caretaking. Dix's solution—institutions dedicated to the treatment of mental disorders—revolutionized psychiatric care. By 1880, when the United States released its first demographic study of mental illness, forty thousand patients had been moved out of jails and prisons; only four hundred people with a disorder remained locked up.

But by the mid-twentieth century, most of these institutions were rotten with abuse. Thanks to a growing public awareness of such conditions and the release of the first antipsychotic drugs, the government concluded that Dix's model no longer worked. Mental illness, it was decided, should be treated through community-based services aimed toward rehabilitation.

Thus kicked off the era of deinstitutionalization. Asylums closed. In 1955, government-run mental hospitals housed 560,000 patients; by 1980, that number had dropped by nearly 80 percent. That year, Mark David Chapman, whose schizophrenia went largely untreated, shot the musician whose name I share. He spent three decades of his life sentence at Attica, where we lived under the same roof until his recent transfer.

In 1981, Ronald Reagan—who also was shot by a man with an undertreated psychotic disorder—called for the repeal of a massive bill signed by Jimmy Carter that would have expanded federal community mental-health programs. As psych-hospital beds disappeared and the support systems that were meant to replace them lost funding, hundreds of thousands of people with mental illness were caught in a cycle of homelessness, emergency hospitalizations, and lockup.

At the same time, mass incarceration was under way. In 1950, there were 265,000 prisoners in the United States; today, that number has shot up by nearly a factor of ten. A 2006 Department of Justice report stated that 24 percent of those in jail and 15 percent of those in state prisons "had at least one symptom of a psychotic disorder," numbers that rival estimates at the time Dix began her crusade. Even Donald Trump has expressed concern. In the wake of the school shooting in Parkland, Florida, this past February, the president told state and local officials, "We're going to be talking seriously about opening mental-health institutions again."

·　　·　　·

"I wasn't always like this, you know," Joe said one late-summer evening in the A Block yard. He grew up in Oneonta, a dead-end city four hours northwest of New York City. While his mother worked a string of clerical jobs, her parents helped raise Joe and his older sister, Maria. Their father lived nearby, but they weren't allowed to see him.

In its early stages, schizoaffective disorder can seem like the behavior of a troublemaker. Joe dropped out of school in ninth grade and never got his GED. He began living a sort of low-fat criminal lifestyle—shoplifting and selling weed, mostly to friends—and notched a few misdemeanors along the way. Maria was the first family member who suspected Joe's quirks were symptoms of something more than the antics of a bad egg. But her mother dismissed her concern, Maria told me. Around the time of his mother's death, from lung cancer in 2005, Joe's mind began unraveling.

One morning, he woke up believing that a creature had caused him to lose nearly fifty pounds overnight. It was his first full-fledged psychotic episode. In the months and years that followed, his symptoms worsened: A mole on his arm contained a hidden message; he thought he could shoot white energy orbs out of his palms; he showed anyone who'd listen a grainy video on his flip phone, footage, he claimed, of UFOs, angels, and demons.

Nevertheless, he scraped by. Around 2009, at Maria's prompting, he saw a county psychiatrist. He was diagnosed with schizoaffective disorder and began taking a motley regimen of medications. He also began receiving a monthly disability check.

Then, in 2014, broke, evicted, and nearly blacked out on Klonopin, he pulled a ski mask over his face, palmed a BB gun, and entered a Smokers Choice. Seven months and one plea bargain later, Joe was just another Attica bugout.

•   •   •

Built in 1931 on a thousand-acre plot forty miles east of Niagara Falls, Attica houses twenty-two hundred prisoners behind its thirty-foot walls. I spent time on each of its five cellblocks, and A Block was without question the worst. Its residents were considered true degenerates; its yard was nicknamed "Afghanistan" for the near-daily violence that broke out on its dusty ground. It tended to be where guys were placed after getting out of the Special Housing Unit, otherwise known as the Box, otherwise known as solitary. After a verbal altercation with a CO on the honor block where I'd lived for about two years, I was sent here, too. By some sadistic luck of the draw, so was Joe.

One afternoon in the A Block yard, I asked him about his treatment. He said his pharma plan was similar to the one he had on the outside: Risperdal, an antipsychotic; Depakote, a mood stabilizer; and Buspar, an antianxiety pill he'd sometimes store in his cheek when the nurse checked his mouth and, once back in his cell, crush and sniff. That way, it hit harder. He also saw a counselor. This was not talk therapy with a Freudian shrink; it was a once-a-month check-in to make sure he wasn't going off the rails. The therapist was employed by the Office of Mental Health. OMH was created to run the state's handful of remaining psychiatric hospitals; since 1976, it has also overseen mental-health care in all of New York's correctional facilities. Its in-prison employees are literal guests in DOCCS's home, resulting in an unfortunate if predictable power dynamic. "There's inherent conflict between what the mental-health staff should be doing, which is engaging and empowering patients," says Jack Beck, a director of the Correctional Association of New York, a nonprofit that monitors the state's prisons, "and that which Corrections does: disempowerment and control, and in a very punitive way."

OMH oversees several programs, but its flagship is known as the Intermediate Care Program, in which prisoners live together and receive twenty hours of therapeutic programming each week. According to the latest available data, OMH has beds for around twelve hundred prisoners, less than a quarter of the fifty-six hundred statewide who test on the mental-health exam as levels one or two—the most serious cases.

Joe wasn't one of them, not at first. He was part of the general population, just like me. When I asked him why, he wasn't sure. His clinical records, which Joe provided to *Esquire*, don't clear things up. Special programming was first floated to him as an option three weeks after arriving at Attica. Then, and throughout his incarceration, despite clinicians' assurances otherwise, he voiced concern that receiving mental-health care would lengthen his sentence. Regardless, as the note from his first therapy session states, "He reports being very interested" in such programming and that a referral would be made. But in the notes from a session nearly two months later, Joe's therapist wrote, " He reports he has not been met with" by "ICP or TRICP staff yet and would like programming." The therapist's response: "He was encouraged to be patient."

Meanwhile, Joe struggled to adjust to prison etiquette. His daily slew of medications exhausted him, making it a challenge to follow the simplest procedures. To go to the mess hall for meals or the yard for recreation, you had to be "on your bars"—standing by your cell door—at a certain time each morning and make the request with a CO breezing by. Joe often overslept and missed his opportunity.

Small amenities made the day-to-day tolerable, if you could afford them. Personal clothing was allowed in and around your cell—a few T-shirts, sweatshirts, sweaters, sweats, a couple pairs of shoes. Each cell connected to basic cable. Televisions were available for purchase at the commissary, which we were allowed to visit biweekly. Electronics were made with clear plastic to minimize hiding spaces. My radio, television, and typewriter: all clear.

The commissary also sold food. I'd buy tins of oysters, clams, tuna; oatmeal, instant rice, black beans, spaghetti, tomato sauce, onions, garlic, and herbs. I built a makeshift stove by removing the coil from a hot pot and placing it on top of an empty, turned-over tin can; I bought a metal sauce pot from a prisoner for five packs of Newports. We weren't supposed to have this mini-kitchen setup, but it was tolerated if you were on good terms with the COs. I cooked my own meals, wore my own clothes—Ralph Lauren shirts, Calvin Klein underwear, Timberland chukka boots—and watched my favorite shows on the television in my cell. In one corner, I kept a stack of magazines, including this one, and some books on writing—Lopate, Zinsser, Pinker, Strunk and White. Pictures were taped to the wall: my then-lady blowing kisses at the camera; my mother, smiling, on a Florida beach, her windblown hair framing her face, her hand curled by Parkinson's.

Joe couldn't afford his own TV, and his only clothes were the standard-issue state greens. He ate in the mess hall, a cavernous, chaotic space where the risk of being picked on left him exposed. Getting there was a tense journey, mostly spent waiting for gates to open and shut and for other prisoners to shuffle by, no talking allowed. And the food—beef goulash, say, or chicken tetrazzini, delivered to the kitchen in industrial plastic bags—was awful. (The meals prepped for guys with dietary restrictions—vegetarian, kosher—were often better; you'll never find as many black Jews as you will in prison, so the joke goes.) Joe had no books or magazine subscriptions, no pictures on his wall, no mother.

In September 2015, three and a half months after arriving at Attica and a full ten weeks after he expressed interest, Joe was enrolled in ICP. But the program meant to improve his life behind bars didn't work out that way.

· · ·

My brother Eugene was capable enough to live on his own but never for very long. One evening in 1998, during a manic episode, he trashed his Sheepshead Bay apartment. By the time my mother and I arrived, the police thought he might jump off the fifth-floor balcony. I convinced them to stay put and let me go inside instead.

I found Eugene in the kitchen, shirtless, bald, his eyebrows gone, with a cross shaved into his chest. I pleaded with him to surrender. "Balombo," he said—his nickname for me since childhood—"I bless you, my son," then threw water in my face. As he turned to set down the glass, I tackled him. Police forced him into a straitjacket and took him to the psychiatric ward at Coney Island Hospital, where he'd become a regular.

Around that time, he bought a bag of heroin from one of my foot soldiers. When I found out, I was livid, and Eugene was already hooked. Soon after, he was arrested for possession and sent to Rikers. He begged Mom to bail him out. She called me and, through choked sobs, said she couldn't. She thought he was safer locked up than on the street.

Eugene called me. He said he'd been beaten up by a few guys inside who'd recognized him as my brother. In an instant, I connected the dots: I'd been selling to a woman who smuggled the gear to her husband, a prisoner at Rikers. A couple of weeks earlier, I'd been making a delivery when a stranger walked through her front door, and I pulled out my 9mm. It turned out to be her father. Shaken, I refused to continue selling to her. I gathered that her husband had attacked my brother to retaliate. "I don't know what happened, but you did something to these people," Eugene said over the jailhouse phone. "You gotta get me out of here." I bailed him out that night.

.   .   .

Enrolled in Attica's Intermediate Care Program, Joe continued to decline. He replaced regular showers with "bird baths," splashing water on himself from the sink in his cell. He didn't go to the prison barber, nor did he shave. His stringy hair grew long and matted. He still saw UFOs and shot light orbs at will.

He was assigned a new therapist and, after just four sessions, a third. According to clinical records, Joe rarely went to ICP's programs. He chalked up his poor attendance to exhaustion, wrote one therapist. But notes from the same session suggest another explanation: "Mr. Cardo . . . is concerned about his programming and how this may affect his CR"—conditional release, the date he would, with good behavior, be set free. He was never able to shake the fear that his psychosis would keep him behind bars. Or perhaps he didn't go because he feared other ICP residents. "He indicated that he . . . is being teased by other inmates," reads a note from March 2016. "One inmate, he said, choked him in the

ICP bullpen." There's no indication in his OMH records that the alleged attack was investigated.

Joe spent most of his time alone in his cell, listening to the radio. Meals were brought to the cells of ICP residents, so he no longer had to make the journey to the mess hall. The CO who took down the names of prisoners heading out for recreation walked the floor slowly, and Joe was able to be on his bars in time. This small gesture, this simple decency, was the thing he liked best about being on the unit.

I'd catch up with him during rec period. One day, as Joe searched the ground for butts, the Puerto Ricans at the next table gave me a signal: a raised brow, a lift of the chin in the direction of a mounting beef.

It was silence, then action. Just as a dozen prisoners broke out into a brawl—a blur of fists, feet, and weapons dug out of the ground just moments before—I called Joe to our table. Guys with shanks thrust forward and back; guys with razor blades made circular whips at others' faces. A CO shouted over the loudspeaker, "Fighters, drop your weapons! Get on the ground!" The tower guard trained his AR-15 on the crowd. "Everyone else: Get on the wall!" Dozens of COs spilled into the yard with batons drawn, barking orders. The fighters dropped to their stomachs. The rest of us scrambled to the perimeter, zigzagging in case bullets began to fly.

Joe ended up next to me on the wall as we waited. We eventually saw a bright light approaching in the sky, bringing with it a familiar sound: A helicopter descended behind the outside wall of the cellblock. One of the fighters needed to be airlifted. Joe hung his head between his outstretched arms, his palms fanned out against the wall. He turned to me, tears welling in his eyes. "Oh, man," he said. "This place is *crazy*."

·　　·　　·

By 2001, my drug operation was coming to an end. At its peak, I'd netted $7,500 in a good week. I had a fancy car with a customized stash compartment in place of the passenger-side airbag. I sported a Cartier watch with diamonds ringing the bezel. But I'd been arrested on a gun charge and jumped bail, and a warrant was out. Plus, I'd done something much worse.

The man I murdered was a dealer, too, who I knew from the projects. Then twenty-five, a year older than me, he'd already beaten a murder rap. He'd been shaking down one of my street dealers, which I couldn't let stand. One night, I invited him to join me on my rounds. I'd rented a car and had placed an assault rifle in the trunk. In East Williamsburg, noticing that he was distracted by his phone, I pulled over on a deserted street, grabbed the gun, and shot him. It was over in three seconds. I put his body in the trunk and sped home on side streets. A couple days later, an associate and I put the body in a laundry bag affixed to cinder blocks and threw him off a pier into Sheepshead Bay. Two and a half months later, he washed ashore. By then, I was already in Rikers, picked up on the outstanding warrant, and found out via a *New York Daily News* clip that another prisoner passed along. I later learned from a Gambino capo that weighing the body down wasn't enough, that to keep him under I would've had to puncture his lungs, let the air out.

At first, I felt a selfish sort of regret: facing a few years was one thing, but now I was looking at life. The remorse came years later. Fellow prisoners tend to romanticize my crime—*it's gangster to kill a gangster!* Yes, he was a wild guy. But so was I. They'd be saying the same thing if somebody had taken *me* out. And what does that say about my worth?

Just as true as it is that I was once a dopey twenty-four-year-old dealer, I'm also, sixteen years later, a prison journalist. I'm a murderer, but I'm a lot of other things. The man I killed was a lot of other things, too: a son, a brother, an uncle. I hurt his family deeply. I'm sorry.

Once I began serving my twenty-eight-to-life, I called Eugene a half-dozen times a year. He also knew the man I killed, and when he found out what I'd done, he didn't throw religion in my face, not this time. "How could you do that, John?" was all he said. Still, he visited me, sporadically, each time less lucid than the last. In 2008, during a bad visit, he was anxious and distracted; all he could talk about was when he'd get to smoke his next cigarette, then he left early. That turned out to be the last time I saw him.

In December 2011, Eugene's body was discovered in an SRO in Times Square. He'd overdosed on pills and heroin. He'd been dead for days. No one knew he was gone until the neighbors noticed the smell.

•　　•　　•

On June 29, 2016, Joe was free. He'd been at Attica for one year and two months. Four hundred twenty-one days. Ten thousand one hundred and four hours.

For someone with psychosis, the challenges of transitioning back into society are nearly insurmountable. There is a strong correlation between mental illness and a raised risk of recidivism: one recent study found that parolees with a psychiatric diagnosis are 36 percent more likely to violate parole. And a number of studies suggest what common sense dictates: reentry programs tailored for people with mental illness help reduce that recidivism, particularly ones built around multidisciplinary teams—mental-health providers, substance-use specialists, social workers.

Last year, *Esquire* helped me track Joe down. Two months before he was released, his discharge planning began, a coordinated effort between DOCCS and OMH that's meant to serve the needs of someone who, like Joe, has serious mental illness. He was set up with a parole officer, a case manager, public housing, paperwork to apply for benefits such as Supplemental Security Income, appointments with a psychiatrist and a therapist.

Once out, Joe moved back to Oneonta. In his first few days of freedom, he said, he marveled at watching television, drinking fresh coffee, smoking as many cigarettes as he wanted. His first meal was at McDonald's.

He lived for a while in a sober-living halfway home, then at an SRO, until he was forced to leave after a dispute with two residents. Since February of last year, he's lived in a one-bedroom apartment in a building that the city recently declared unsafe. He sometimes calls his sister Maria to tell her about strange men snooping around his mailbox or whispering about him on the street. His application to restore his SSI benefits was denied for reasons that remain unclear. As of press time, an appeal is still pending.

As for me, in November 2016 I moved to Sing Sing, thirty miles up the Hudson River from New York City. Enrolled in a privately funded college program, I take night courses and will soon earn a bachelor's in behavioral science. As an assignment, I work alongside OMH staff on the facility's ICP. Every morning, I coax residents to get up, wash up, and walk down the hill to the program building. Through its huge windows facing west, the worst-off prisoners watch trains screaming down riverside tracks, leading to somewhere else.

In a recent group session on life skills, the head psychologist asked me why I chose to be here. She talked about countertransference: how working alongside these men may kick up my own issues. I told the room about Eugene, about Joe, about how I saw parts of them in the men who sat before me. I opened up about my shame for having been a bad brother and a bad man. I said that this work made me feel, if not good, then better. The tears that followed, though unexpected, were long overdue.

Joe's parole ended in April, so he and I are now allowed to talk. He's usually at home, alone, doing nothing. "Chilling," he calls it. He loves watching horror movies and made me promise to mention a hidden message halfway through 1973's *The Exorcist*.

"When the priest sprinkles holy water on Regan and she speaks backwards," Joe tells me, "you have to listen closely. She says, 'Maria, Joey, Luigia'—that's my sister, me, and our grandmother!" He still produces light orbs. Just the other day, he shot new footage of paranormal activity on his phone. He hopes it will finally prove to the world he's okay.

The Marshall Project with *Vice*

FINALIST—COLUMNS
AND COMMENTARY

This is one of three articles that earned the Marshall Project *its first nomination for the National Magazine Award for Columns and Commentary. Like the other two pieces—"Death Row's First Ever Talent Show," by George T. Wilkerson, and "What It's Like to Be a Cutter in Prison," by Deidre McDonald—"Getting Out of Prison Meant Leaving Dear Friends Behind" was published as part of a series called "Life Inside." The series, said the National Magazine Awards judges, "delivers powerful, poignant accounts of crime and punishment in America" from the perspective of those who know the system best: the incarcerated. After nearly fifteen years in prison, Robert Wright is now a research assistant at the Center for Justice at Columbia University. The nonprofit* Marshall Project *covers issues relating to criminal justice. The organization won the National Magazine Award for General Excellence in 2017, and this year, the award for news and opinion websites.*

Robert Wright

Getting Out of Prison Meant Leaving Dear Friends Behind

I have spent countless nights like this, lying awake, anticipating life, trying to escape imprisonment through my mind's eye. I imagine the things I will do once I'm free. Flashes of me laughing with family and friends at a cookout or enjoying the company of a beautiful woman play out in my mind like a silent movie.

I remember the images, so different from these, that swam through my mind on my first night in prison. Hopelessness describes it best. Sorrow, self-pity, and regret stood in the way of my future, along with the steel bars that caged me in. I could not wrap my head around the fact that the next sixteen years of my life would be spent in a cell so small that I could lie on my bunk and touch the toilet, sink, and desk without getting up. I was buried alive. Alive but not living.

Suddenly, the door of my cell opens, and an officer says, "Wright, are you ready?" As I rise from my bunk, I am thinking, *Is he fucking serious?* I've been ready since the day the jury foreman read "guilty" off a little index card at my trial.

I grab my mattress, as inmates are made to do, along with a few personal belongings—photo albums, holiday cards, and personal letters—and walk out of my cell. I turn around, mentally bidding farewell to the tomb in which I spent the last nine years of my life. I've only told a few people I was going home. How can I look into the eyes of a man who will probably spend the rest of his life in captivity and tell him that my exodus has come? We were comrades in sorrow. What united us was pain. What now could I say to this friend to convince him we are still in this fight together?

As I walk down the gallery saying goodbye to faces that are as familiar as my own family's, I'm filled with mixed emotions. I am ecstatic, afraid, and guilt-ridden. The guilt comes from all those I will leave behind. All who suffered with me for so many years. We leaned on each other. We found reasons to laugh while in agony. As I pass them, it strikes me how much these men in their cages resemble dogs in a kennel awaiting their fate. Looking at me with eyes that tell how painful their story is. Wishing to be saved, hoping someone will answer their prayers.

I stop in front of the cell of one of my oldest friends. He looks at me and turns away, wishing me well without looking into my eyes. I give him information on how to get in touch with me. When I go to hand him the piece of paper, I can see he has tears in eyes that he is desperately trying to prevent from falling in my presence. He was sentenced to forty to life. Never in the ten years that I have known him have I ever seen him in a moment of weakness. And now it is my departure that is the cause of his vulnerability. We hug through the bars that separate us and exchange I love yous. I walk away knowing he was watching the image of me in the mirror he stuck outside his bars become smaller and smaller, until it would be the last he ever sees of me.

I wish they would have released me in the middle of the night while everyone was asleep. I almost feel the need to explain myself to them. I want to shout, "I'm still one of you!" But they would never believe me because it would be a lie. While they are missing their families, I will be with mine. Their view of the world will be blocked by the bars that lock them in at night, while my new view will be endless no matter which direction I turn my head. And for some reason, I feel the need to apologize for it.

The officer escorting me is becoming impatient as I stop every few steps to say goodbye to someone else. A couple of officers walking by wish me good luck. I'm humored at the thought of luck being the determining factor in my success. I'm also a little insulted. You do not survive trauma and chalk it up to luck. No, I won't dare shortchange myself in that way. I've been crushed like so many of the men I am leaving behind. To overcome that takes defiance and courage, not luck.

"Come on Wright, don't you wanna get outta here?" the officer says as he waits for me at the center gate that leads to the processing room. I ignore him while struggling to keep the mattress on my shoulder. I begin to have a déjà vu moment. Every facility I entered over the years required me to carry a mattress to the cell in which I would be housed. Suddenly I become upset. Even on the day that the state has determined that I have repaid my debt to it, I'm still treated with the same contempt as when I walked into this place. I drop the mattress and keep walking, now only carrying the few belongings I refuse to leave behind.

The officer escorting me looks confused. I continue walking as he begins calling my name. I pay him no mind. I'm a free man now. I have come too far, overcome so much. The mattress represented the chains that cuffed my wrist so tight that they ached for days. It symbolized every strip search in which I had to bend over and was told to "spread 'em." In that moment every dehumanizing second of my incarceration was removed from my flesh.

Being processed out takes over two hours. My anxiety and excitement about taking my first breath of freedom keeps getting interrupted by inmates who just want to say their goodbyes. The truth is, I think they just want an opportunity to touch the closest thing to freedom most of them will ever come into contact with. They are living through me. Placing themselves in my shoes for the moment they so desperately yearn for.

After the formalities of telling the processing officer my birth date and other information that verifies my identity, I am allowed to put on the clothes that my family sent a week earlier. This is the first time I have worn street clothes in fifteen years. It feels weird. Before my incarceration, I wore my clothes very big and baggy, as was the style at the time. Now all the jeans fit very tight. I stare at one of the porters for assurance that I look cool. He nods his head in approval and says, "That's what they wearing out there." I'm not convinced, but other inmates agree.

There is another inmate being released alongside me. Because his family has not sent any clothes for him, he is given court clothes by the facility. This consists of an oversized white dress shirt and a pair of tan slacks that are too small. Very little is said between the two of us as we wait for the officer to drive us to the train station. There is too much going on inside our minds to entertain any chitchat.

After what seems like another hour, we are ushered into a prison van—only this time I am not shackled. Still, all the times I was transported in a van just like this from one facility to the next cross my mind. I feel chills. *Maybe they aren't really letting me go. Maybe this is a trick.*

Just as my mind begins to get the best of me, I see this slender woman in a wool hat standing in front of the entrance to the train station. As the van slows down I recognize the beautiful brown face. I frantically start pulling on the door handle, but it won't budge. The officer gets out and slides open the van door. He says something as I hurry past him into the waiting embrace of my mother.

Finally, I can breathe.

New York Times Magazine

WINNER—ESSAYS
AND CRITICISM

Graduate of the University of Maryland and Yale Law School. Published poet and member of the bar. Husband. Father. Prisoner of the past. At the age of sixteen, Reginald Dwayne Betts pleaded guilty to carjacking, attempted robbery, and a weapons charge and was sentenced to nine years behind bars. When he got out, he was eight months short of his twenty-fifth birthday. "I left prison convinced that the third of my life lost to maximum security wouldn't haunt me," Betts writes. "I was wrong." "Getting Out" is not only his story—from convicted felon to legal scholar—but also a study of the ways our nation continues to punish men and women long after they leave prison. The Ellies judges credited Betts's "brilliance and determination—above all, the honesty and generosity of his work" for their decision to give the New York Times Magazine *its second National Magazine Award for Essays and Criticism in the last three years.*

Reginald Dwayne Betts

Getting Out

One afternoon in the fall of 2016, I sat in a windowless visiting room at the Manson Youth Institution in Cheshire, Conn. A recent graduate of Yale Law School, I was a certified legal intern on a fellowship in the New Haven public defender's office. J., a lanky eighteen-year-old brown-skinned kid sitting across from me was my first client. He didn't talk. Instead he stared at me as if I were the police. Sanford O. Bruce III, my supervising attorney, listened as I explained to J. (one of his initials) what we knew of the charges against him. A young man with whom J. attended high school had claimed that J. and another kid he didn't know had threatened him with a pistol, then robbed him of his cell phone and a couple of hundred dollars. Officers arrested J. minutes later, but the other suspect, who supposedly held the gun, was never found.

The prosecutor thought he should serve time in prison. I let J. know this and described what would happen next: a series of court dates, a bond-reduction motion, plea-bargain offers. After remaining silent for nearly forty minutes, he leaned forward in the blue plastic chair, cutting me off, and asked, "Aren't you the one who did time in prison?" With a single question, this kid reminded me of what a law degree, even one from Yale, could not do—make my own criminal history vanish.

On December 7, 1996, a month and two days after my sixteenth birthday, I climbed with four other people into a beat-up ink-colored sedan in Prince George's County, Md. During that year, I'd read the Evelyn Wood guide to speed reading and J. California Cooper's novel *The Wake of the Wind*. My Advanced Placement U.S. history teacher at Suitland High School had nicknamed me Smoky after he spied me rolling a blunt before his first-period class. I hadn't won a fight since second grade. Had been suspended half a dozen times—once for setting off a stink bomb but every other time for what teachers called being disruptive but was really just talking too much. People knew me for finding four-leaf clovers, doing back flips, and making too many jokes. I didn't know who I was.

The driver, who was in his early twenties, was a stranger to me. I half-knew his cousin. I'd brought my friend Marcus, who had played on the junior-varsity basketball team with me, to the cousin's house to get high. In the passenger seat, another face I'd just met said a robbery would pad our pockets. Weed, ignorance, and a desire for a come-up, wanting just a few more dollars than we had, made us believe him. We ended up on I-95 at night, headed to the Springfield Mall in Fairfax County, Va. The driver gave me his pistol—because I'd asked for it. I stared at it, my life about to be riven.

He told me not to take the gun's safety off, for any reason. An accidental gunshot could get us all killed or sent to prison for life. At the mall, I first approached two people headed toward a parked car. My arm stretched toward the ground, the pistol dangling in my hand. One of them turned and saw me. Before I knew it, two women jumped in their car and disappeared. Minutes later, I approached one of the few cars in the lot. I saw a man asleep. I tapped twice on the window with the pistol's barrel, demanded that he get out of the car and turn over his keys and his wallet. Marcus and I drove away in the stolen vehicle. The next day, before the end of the Sunday church service Marcus's mother attended, the police had us in handcuffs, caught at a different Virginia mall shopping with another man's credit card.

After meeting with J., I sat in my office with his file, a thin sheaf of no more than a dozen pages. I pulled out my own criminal record. One hundred-odd pages spilled from the accordion folder. I stared at the documents scattered across my desk: my neat cursive on the handwritten confession; a faded yellow summons demanding my mother appear in court, as if my crime belonged to her; the sentencing order consigning me to prison. The prison scrubs that J. wore, the jail cell that held him, the early mornings when deputies would take him shackled and cuffed to court, connected us. I wanted him to believe that the worst of what might happen could be overcome. But I wasn't sure if that was true.

Some ten months later, I would receive a letter from the Connecticut Bar Examining Committee. The committee, it said, would not recommend me for admission to the bar. Under Connecticut law, felons are presumed to lack the character and fitness required to practice law unless they can prove otherwise. I might eventually be allowed to practice law, or, I realized with a cold, dull clarity, I might not.

One time in prison, I watched a man crack the jaw of another man with a padlock rolled up in a sock. Everyone knew the victim as the man who made wine by letting bread, fruit, and jelly ferment in a black trash bag. He brought happiness and escape to the men there. When he was struck, blood squirted from his nose and mouth. He seemed startled that such pain had found him, astonished that he had been hurt in that way. But me, I'd known what to expect before the disappointing news from the bar examiners arrived. And still, the letter left me weeping.

.   .   .

Months after pleading guilty to carjacking, attempted robbery, and a firearm charge, I sat shackled and cuffed in the Fairfax

County Courthouse, waiting for my sentencing. I faced a maximum of life plus thirteen years. My mother, two aunts, and one uncle, along with two family friends, sat in the audience, anxious. The man whose car I'd stolen quietly looked on. Back then, I would have said we hadn't injured him, but the truth is that PTSD is a real injury, and the pistol I waved in his face may stay with him still.

My mother didn't testify. Bronchitis had taken her voice, but I knew heartbreak had left her unable to speak my name without crying. I couldn't forget how devastated she looked when I told her what I'd done. Three witnesses—my Aunt Pandora and the two family friends—spoke on my behalf. Their testimony was punctuated with the talk that troubles courtrooms where young black men are sentenced to prison: "He was having difficulties making that adjustment of not having a father in the household."

Before sentencing me, Judge F. Bruce Bach asked if I wanted to address the court. After apologizing to my mother, to my family, to the man I robbed, I told the court that I hadn't committed the crime because my father had no hand in raising me. I said that it wasn't my mother's fault. But, so afraid of what might happen, I could barely articulate my regret. I couldn't explain how a confluence of bad decisions and opportunity led me to become the caricature of a black boy in America. The mandatory-minimum sentencing law demanded that the judge give me three years for the gun; he could have sent me to serve that time in a juvenile facility. Instead, he sentenced me to nine years in adult prison. My sentencing hearing began at 12:10 p.m.; twenty-eight minutes later, deputies walked me, shackled and cuffed, back to my cell in the county jail.

Later, leaning against a cinder-block wall, hoping to disappear, I called my Aunt Pandora. "You heard the story of Terrence Johnson?" she asked me. He was someone she'd known about from her high school days. Then she told me he was sent to prison as a sixteen-year-old and after serving more than a decade became a law student at the University of the District of Columbia. She probably imagined that this story would comfort me, but my surviving prison was too hypothetical for his success to matter then. This is how I think my clients saw things, too. Their problems were wildly complicated, and my success looked to them like Willy Wonka's golden ticket.

A little while after my aunt told me Johnson's story, I saw on the news that he, barely two years out of prison, had committed suicide during a botched bank-robbery attempt. *That* I noticed. Afterward, I carried his story in my head. On some days, it was an anchor; on others, a caution.

Several months later, after I was transferred from the Fairfax County jail to Virginia's Southampton Correctional Center, I met Markeese Turnage. Markeese—Keese—was my cellmate on the first floor of Building C2. We were both seventeen but had been charged as adults. He was tall and skinny and generous, with an encyclopedic knowledge of Tupac. When some fools from Richmond wanted to rob me, they asked him to leave our cell door unlocked so that they could steal what I owned—a little food from the commissary, a few books. He refused.

Without saying it, we decided to trust each other, even in that unsettling place, surrounded by razor wire. We were like Conrad's secret sharers. If you'd looked into our cell at night, seeing the two of us exchanging our stories, me on the top bunk looking down, him sitting up slightly turned toward me, you might have imagined we were a single child, talking in whispers to his shadow. We pieced together the scraps of our identities in those conversations. I was my mother's only child; he, already a father, his namesake born the year he was convicted.

Keese stole cars. He turned a rusted screwdriver into a skeleton key to the movable city. He got caught, and after, as is typical in most lockups, he was allowed to call his family. Whatever was said during that call crushed Keese. Later, while handcuffed, he grabbed an officer's gun and tried to turn it on himself. The gun never discharged. Officers claimed he tried to kill one of them. Keese was seventeen when he was convicted of attempted capital murder with a gun and grand larceny auto; he was given fifty-three years in prison.

Together we wrote a letter to the ACLU. We were so naïve, we couldn't imagine they would decline to help a kid facing death in prison. This was 1998. Three years earlier, John DiIulio, a political scientist, published his essay "The Coming of the Super-Predators" in the *Weekly Standard*. DiIulio predicted that there would be 30,000 more juvenile robbers, murderers, and rapists on the streets by the year 2000. That DiIulio was no oracle didn't matter. The Republican Party made prosecuting children as adults part of its national platform. Some Democrats embraced this idea as well. Hillary Clinton infamously said of juveniles in gangs, "They are often the kinds of kids that are called 'superpredators.' No conscience, no empathy, we can talk about why they ended up that way, but first we have to bring them to heel." Still, each day made it plain that we were children in an adult prison, and we hoped the ACLU would fight for Keese; instead, they mailed him a form letter declining to provide any assistance.

By my twenty-fourth birthday, I had called five prisons home. One, Red Onion State Prison, was a high-security facility patrolled by armed guards and built in a mountaintop crater on an abandoned coal mine. I went to the hole five times, including thirty days for cursing and ten for being punched in the eye. I sat on a cell floor and read Ernest J. Gaines's *A Lesson Before Dying*, from start to finish; cried while reading Edwidge Danticat's *Krik? Krak!*. I read every book written by Richard Wright, all of Steinbeck, and most of Alice Walker. I discovered the poetry of Robert Hayden, Lucille Clifton, Wanda Coleman, and Agha Shahid Ali, and wrote 1,000 bad poems. I completed a paralegal course and became a bootleg jailhouse lawyer. I taught myself Spanish to speak the language of men I met from seven countries whom I'll most likely never see again. And once, I turned my back on a man being stabbed. I'd seen and heard enough to understand how prison ruins everyone: prisoners, guards, family, the ground it's built on. I left prison convinced that the third of my life lost to maximum security wouldn't haunt me. I was wrong.

.　　　.　　　.

On March 4, 2005, eight months before my twenty-fifth birthday, I arrived at my mother's home with the funk of prison, the lye soap, still clinging to my skin like a felony conviction. Twenty-four hours before that moment, I'd been at Coffeewood Correctional Facility on a weight-pile bench-pressing 295 pounds surrounded by men serving decades. My mother hugged me, then held me at arms' length to see my face. I returned a man with a scruffy beard who spoke too loudly. Though she had visited me often, I could see her taking in the disappeared years, as she tried to find the boy who left so long ago in the body of the man before her.

My mother's townhouse looked vacant. "I wanted to surprise you," she told me. Remnants of the life I'd left threatened to burst from boxes on the floor, waiting to be moved into a single-family home she had just purchased—a place with a backyard that needed a son to mow it. A place where people whose children don't go to prison lived. My mother worked at the Federal Deposit Insurance Corporation. She was also a reservist in the navy who served active duty in Iraq after September 11. She saved for around twenty-five years to buy the single-family home that awaited me on my release from prison.

That first night home, Marcus picked me up from my mom's house. We hadn't been free together since more than a dozen officers had pointed their guns at our heads in a parking lot near the Pentagon City mall where we were caught. Marcus now worked at Duron Paints, a store on Fourteenth and Clifton in Northwest Washington, half a block from Ben's Chili Bowl. Duron's employment application included the question, "Have you been convicted of a felony over the past seven years?" Our crimes were almost a decade old. Marcus checked no. Still needing to explain his thin employment history, he reinvented himself as a recent college student who had nearly earned an associate degree. He never mentioned that he received the college credits while incarcerated at the Brunswick Correctional Center. I came home lacking even that. Living in one jail and five prisons, I was never offered a single opportunity to further my formal education. I came home with far more sense than I had the night a pistol nearly ruined my life, but not a single thing I could put on a résumé.

Marcus hooked me up with an interview at Duron. The interviewer, a black man in his thirties, asked me questions about my life. Everything I said that morning was a lie—I talked about moving to Virginia to be with my grandmother, about pursuing a career as a writer. I knew the truth wouldn't get me employed: twenty-four years old, eight years in prison, no job experience. I walked out of my interview with an entry-level job. But most people with criminal records cannot sidestep their felony convictions. A month later, two black men entered Duron job hunting. They confessed their stints in a Washington jail to the manager. When they left, applications in hand, someone made a joke about ex-cons. Laughter followed. I knew they'd never be hired.

According to the *Oxford English Dictionary*, the word "felon" once meant a vile or wicked person, a villain, wretch, or monster, and was sometimes applied to the devil or an evil spirit. No wonder once the word is associated with your name, everything becomes more difficult. Unlike Duron Paints, most employers ask applicants if they have *ever* been convicted of a crime. This question, known as the box, condemns many with criminal records to joblessness. In 1998, Hawaii passed the first legislation barring public and private employers from asking about an applicant's criminal history before a conditional employment offer. Five years later, All of Us or None, a project created by people with criminal records, started what became known as the ban-the-box campaign. Since then more than thirty states and the federal government have enacted varying fair-hiring practices through legislation and executive orders. Under some, criminal-history inquiries must wait until a job offer is made; others preclude denying employment solely based on the existence of a criminal record; eleven states mandate the removal of criminal-history questions by private employers.

Still, discrimination persists. In a July 2018 report, "Out of Prison and Out of Work," the Prison Policy Initiative, a criminal-justice public-policy think tank in Northampton, Mass., wrote that formerly incarcerated people are unemployed at a rate "higher than the total U.S. unemployment rate during any historical period, including the Great Depression." In recent years, the NAACP Legal Defense Fund joined a class-action lawsuit against Target claiming that, by preventing "applicants with arrest or irrelevant conviction records from obtaining employment opportunities," the company had discriminated against African American and Latino applicants. This past April, Target settled for $3.74 million.

State and federal licensing regulations often block people from entering certain professions before they ever touch an application. The American Bar Association has documented more than 25,000 state restrictions on occupational licenses. A felony conviction restricts access to professions as disparate as teaching, purchasing precious stones and metals, becoming a private investigator, or operating a funeral home. Many careers—for example, fire-fighting, athletic training, and dentistry—can be threatened by even a misdemeanor conviction.

Whether you can vote after a felony conviction depends on where you live. Some states permanently disenfranchise felons; others require that they complete their prison sentence and any term of probation or parole; only Maine and Vermont let all citizens vote, imprisoned or not. In Virginia, felons cannot vote without having their rights restored by the governor; in Maryland, at the time I returned, I had to wait until I'd gotten off probation. Today in Maryland, a person can vote the day he or she walks out of prison.

By the time Marcus was out of prison for eight years, he had started a tech company called Flikshop. Through its app, Flikshop allows people to mail cell-phone photos as postcards to people in prison, transforming how loved ones communicate with one another. But when he applied to rent an apartment from a private-property developer, the fact that he was a small-business owner with excellent credit didn't outweigh the felonies we shared. People in public housing fare worse. Brian Gilmore, a Michigan State law professor who was a tenant attorney in Washington during the late 1990s, says that after Congress passed President Bill Clinton's 1996 Housing Opportunity Program Extension Act, which made it easier for public housing agencies to evict tenants for drug use or criminal convictions, he frequently represented clients who were removed from public housing under the new policy. By 2002, the Supreme Court had taken it a step further, ruling in the case *Department of Housing and Urban Development v. Rucker* that public housing authorities could evict tenants for the drug-related activity of household members or guests, even if the tenant had no knowledge of the criminal activity. Though not mandatory, these policies are still in effect today.

The Personal Responsibility and Work Opportunity Reconciliation Act and Higher Education Amendments, two other Clinton-era policies passed in 1996 and 1998, respectively, made it more difficult for people with felony drug convictions to receive food stamps, public assistance, and college financial aid. President Barack Obama relaxed some of the restrictions on accessing Pell grants, and only a handful of states continue to enforce the bans on food stamps and public assistance. These policies become another punishment, disastrous for people coming out of prison, struggling to remember how to be part of society—one that seems to want them to fail.

.   .   .

In May 2005, two months after I was released from prison, I walked into an adviser's office at the University of Maryland. I told him I wanted to start college as soon as I could, that week if possible. He stared, as if I'd lost my mind, as if he were waiting for the punch line. "Young man, we've chosen the class of 2009." I didn't understand. "Oh, that's cool, I want to start now, not 2009." I'd left prison with enough money for bus fare and a fast-food meal—but without the knowledge of how to enroll in college. It had taken me nine trips to the DMV to get my license, each time learning that a different thing was needed: proof of residence, Social Security card, birth certificate. I'd just learned to search for things on the internet and had barely set up an e-mail account.

I told the adviser the story that I wanted to erase: carjacking at sixteen, prison, recent release. Outside his office, the university spread out into a vast landscape of green. He suggested that I enroll at Prince George's Community College. After a semester, or maybe a year, he said, I'd be ready to transfer to Maryland.

A week later, my Aunt Pandora took me to a gospel concert at Bowie State University. Karibu, an independent African American bookstore with multiple locations in the area, had a table set up outside the concert hall with stacks of books, many familiar to me from my prison reading: *The Destruction of Black Civilization*, by Chancellor Williams; *Under a Soprano Sky*, by Sonia Sanchez; *The Miseducation of the Negro*, by Carter Godson Woodson. I talked to Yao Glover, the bookseller, for an hour about literature. "Where'd you go to school?" he asked. It was the first time outside prison that someone thought me college-educated. I didn't have an answer, and so I told the truth: "Man, I just got out of prison." Yao turned out to be one of Karibu's owners. Days later, the manager at the Bowie location called and asked if I'd be interested in an opening there. By summer's end, I had enrolled full time in Prince George's Community College and had a full-time gig at Karibu selling black literature to strangers.

On September 19, 2005, I rushed from an eight a.m. class to open the bookstore. "Good morning, welcome to Karibu," I said, instinctively, when the bell announced the day's first customer. Terese Roberson smiled. She wore blue jeans, a black T-shirt, and black New Balance sneakers. Also a student at the community college, she had come to the store to buy Mario Azevedo's *Africana Studies* for her African American studies course. We talked for a good minute. I read her an elegy that I'd written for a friend murdered in high school. I was afraid to ask her out. For six months, I thought about her without once seeing her face in the halls of the college. Then, during the next semester's final-exam period, I remember running into her three times in a week. The third time, I persuaded her to have lunch with me.

After our first couple of dates, I began wondering if I owed Terese the story of my time in prison. I'd come home believing that keeping quiet about what I experienced was best. Nearly every password I created back then reflected that thinking: 1Silence, NeedSilence, WantSilence, as if muteness could save me. But by the time we went out, I'd become accustomed to confessing that I carjacked a man. Often, with potential employers, with schools, my criminal record would come up early and derail future conversations. With Terese things were different. Maybe because I didn't act as if the penitentiary had swallowed a third of my life. She looked at me as if she knew the telling pained me. And I think, maybe, my sadness was part of the reason she answered the next time I called.

Two years later, Terese and I prepared to graduate from Prince George's Community College. I'd cross the stage as an Honors Academy scholar, a program that provided its members seamless transfer to several local universities, including Howard, the historically black university in Washington. I was completing an application, expecting to be a Howard Bison, until I got to this question: "Have you ever been adjudicated guilty or convicted of a misdemeanor, felony, or other crime?" The question made me stop. I feared that my enrollment was already in jeopardy. A few weeks later, Dr. Melinda Frederick, then the coordinator of the Honors Academy, and I went to Howard to sign my enrollment papers. An admissions officer paused when we told her about my felonies. She told us that in the past, Howard had at times declined to admit students who had criminal records. "But don't worry," she said. "We'll get back to you shortly." They never did. Recently, more than a decade later, I called to find out what happened. Howard says its records list my application as incomplete. When I asked if there were a policy to decline admissions to people with criminal records, a university spokeswoman said that applications by people with criminal records are evaluated on a case-by-case basis.

I applied to the University of Maryland and was admitted with a full-tuition academic scholarship. Terese, pregnant with our first son, Micah Michael-Zamir, was accepted at Towson State University. After my two years at Maryland, I was chosen by a group of deans and administrators to give our graduation's student commencement address. Before more than 15,000 people— classmates, professors, friends, and family members—I told the audience that I had served eight years and three months in prison. I made my criminal record, even in the middle of an accomplishment, visible—brutally permanent. A tattoo. That's how I saw it. And if I was going to be scarred, I wanted to reveal it myself.

●　　　●　　　●

Before my thirtieth birthday, I'd earned a bachelor's degree and an MFA in poetry; published *A Question of Freedom*, a memoir about my time in prison; published a collection of poetry, *Shahid Reads His Own Palm*; and still knew my state number by heart. I applied for just about every teaching gig at colleges and private schools in the Washington area without getting a single interview. Peers without records—and some without publications—were getting jobs, or at least interviews. My first job in prison, washing dishes, sweeping and mopping floors in the kitchen, paid twenty-three cents an hour. Some days I felt I had a better chance of getting that job back than teaching poetry at a nearby school. I stretched my job search to all of the United States. Terese, completing her master's degree in occupational therapy, was pregnant with our second son, Miles Thelonious, who was born on October 10, 2011. And I was gravid with fear: unemployed and too embarrassed to admit to Terese that I worried I'd never be gainfully employed, able to pay the rent or purchase diapers.

Then one day in March 2011, the director of Harvard's Radcliffe Institute for Advanced Study left a phone message offering me a Radcliffe fellowship to finish working on the collection of poems that would become *Bastards of the Reagan Era*," published in 2015. I listened to the message five times, elated and disbelieving. Applying for the fellowship had been a Hail Mary. And then we were moving to Massachusetts, 300 miles away from the only family we knew, a little boy barely potty-trained in tow and another on the way.

About a year later, apprehensive about trying and failing to get a teaching job, I decided to apply to law school. I figured that at least for three years, my student loan bill wouldn't be due each month. The first sentence of my personal statement read, "The part of my life that has been most influential in my drive to go to law school is also the greatest obstacle to my being admitted to law school and becoming an attorney."

By April 2013, I'd been accepted to law schools at Yale, Harvard, Columbia, the University of Michigan, Georgetown, the

University of Pennsylvania, Northwestern, and Boston College, told yes by one school for every year I'd been in prison. Before I was admitted to Northwestern, Clifford Zimmerman, then dean of students, called me. He asked me to tell him something that wasn't on my résumé. We talked about the book club for six-to-seventeen-year-old black boys, YoungMenRead, that I started while at Karibu Books; about my sons; about Terese. We talked about the character and fitness challenges I might confront later. He didn't ask about prison, though he did give me the names of lawyers in three states who might assist me when it came time to be admitted to the bar. Even before I began law school, I knew what was ahead of me.

I enrolled at Yale Law School just shy of my thirty-third birthday. During admitted-students weekend, the dean, Robert Post, gave my 1L class a speech. In our number, he said, was a Cordon Bleu chef, military officers, a poet—me. He didn't say that among us was a person formerly incarcerated, a felon, an ex-con—he said "poet." I imagined that I'd begun to outpace the worst of my past. Until one day Supreme Court Justice Sonia Sotomayor came to Yale for a public conversation with the former *New York Times* legal correspondent Linda Greenhouse. During the discussion, Greenhouse asked why the term "undocumented immigrant" was more accurate than "illegal alien." Justice Sotomayor replied that "many of these people are people I know, and they are no different than the people I grew up with or who share my life. And they are human beings with a serious legal problem—but the word 'illegal alien' made them sound like those other kinds of criminals. And I think people then paint those individuals as something less than worthy human beings." My classmates applauded. I sank into the chair, unable to stretch my legs, like a man constrained by shackles—understanding that for many people, I was one of "those other kinds of criminals."

A few weeks after the Sotomayor event, Micah's kindergarten teacher told me that one of his classmates, having overheard a conversation between his parents, had told Micah that I'd stolen a car and went to jail. He and Miles, who was two, were at a local private school. Terese and I had grappled with what to tell their teachers about my past. We opted for silence, maybe without ever really agreeing on it. Micah's teacher told me that he had cried and was visibly upset—but he was now OK. And I couldn't help wondering what "now OK" meant.

That afternoon, when Micah came home, we sat at the dining room table to talk. Prison has always been the distance between the world and me, but that distance didn't matter until I realized it also became the distance between me and my sons. Terese and I had never discussed *when* we might tell them—yet we expected to dictate that when. But we hadn't. Everything Micah had known about me had collapsed into a word: *jail.* I didn't know if I was OK but was certain that he couldn't be. *Micah, this is what happened.* And I explained, though not everything. Instead of a pistol and a man being told to "get the [expletive] out" of the car and then prison and the rest, it was just: I stole a car and went to jail. He asked me how long. When I told him eight years, I could see in his eyes that he was struggling with what it meant for me to have been in prison longer than he'd been alive. Eight years. "But don't bad people go to jail, Daddy?" Micah's voice sounded like the air whistling out of a balloon. I was a first-year law student, explaining how prison, how crime, was never just about being bad. I also recognized that conversations about criminal-justice reform and the new Jim Crow were convenient ways to avoid admitting I'd pulled a gun on a man without a good reason. I wondered if there was room for me to escape being characterized as bad by the six-year-old boy who first made me feel free.

•　　•　　•

The morning of law-school commencement in May 2016, my classmates and I gathered with thousands of students in the center of Yale's campus. It was just over nineteen years to the date of my sentencing. I carried the law-school flag, leading the graduates from that yard to the college's Old Campus. We walked the old colonial streets, crossing Elm, making a left turn onto High Street. From somewhere in the crowd, my cousin Reds watched, seeing me lead the procession in a Yale blue gown with a purple hood draped across my back. Arrested at age fourteen, he had recently been released after fifteen years in prison, about two decades before his original sentence was set to finish. His early release was unexpected, mercy from a judge whose reasons I cannot begin to divine.

But what do you do with a second chance that no one prepared you for? No prison officials would have thought it their responsibility to teach Reds anything more than standing for count. When he came home at age twenty-nine, tattoos adorned his body, and he had long dreadlocks that he sheared to appear more employable. He had participated in the job-training programs suggested by his probation officer. He had learned to write a résumé, though fifteen years of prison gives little to seduce an employer. Nothing worked. During the next two years, he would be denied dozens of jobs. Job applications became a wall preventing him from ever speaking to a person with the authority to hire him, from having the opportunity to explain that he was more than his crime and time in prison. He teetered on the verge of homelessness. I watched and didn't do nearly enough.

What Reds needed most—time to both fail and grow—no one was willing to offer him. I was graduating from one of the best law schools in the world. Still, I was worried that despite my degree, I'd be prevented from practicing law. And so our situations were similar and dissimilar; though it seems peculiar to suggest that graduating with a Yale law degree leaves anyone, no matter how many felonies he has, in a situation as desperate as Reds's.

• • •

When I was given J.'s case, a few months after my graduation, he had been incarcerated for a month. J. was already eighteen, and the charges he faced were serious enough that a long prison sentence was a possibility. The only information I had about J.'s case was a video of police officers interviewing him; another one of officers interviewing the victim, a kid my client's age, and his mother; and a few charging documents. I watched the video of the officers' interviewing my client; J. leaned his plastic chair against a wall, his arms tucked into his sweatshirt, the room freezing. For an hour, he said nothing. In the interview with the kid who'd been robbed and his mother, with each detail of the supposed crime, she would say: "I told you about hanging around those devils. I told you about hanging around those devils." Later, the officers brought out a photo of my client. Is this him? they asked. "Let me see that picture," the mother said. After a pause, her voice dropped: "He could be my son."

I understood what she meant. The way it was easy for a bad decision to transform any of the black boys around us from students into victims or criminal defendants. And because I'd been there—and because J. was my first client—keeping him out of prison and without a felony record had become my lodestar. But the facts were overwhelmingly against J. Mitigating evidence was the only thing that might persuade the judge and prosecutor that J. should get a break. I talked to J.'s mother, his teachers, the administrators at his school. They all told me he was charming and thoughtful, intelligent, though he rarely took the time to do his work and was often near trouble. But mostly I spent hours on the phone with the victim's mother. By the end, she, too, was telling me that prison wasn't where J. belonged.

After months of conversation, the prosecutor's stance toward J. softened. What began as a plea bargain for a sentence to be determined by the judge—a maximum of five years with the right to argue for a sentence of as little as six months—became an offer of time served plus three years of probation, in return for a guilty plea to a felony. He avoided a prison cell. We thought of it as a win. But I knew from experience what it meant to walk out of that courtroom with a felony conviction.

On the morning of May 5, 2017, the Connecticut bar examiners released the results of the bar exam. Exactly 50 percent of those who took the test that day passed. When I checked the website, the names were listed in alphabetical order. The sixth entry from the top was Reginald Dwayne Betts. I stared at the name that I share with my father and took a deep breath. He never visited me in prison. I didn't invite him to my wedding. He had missed four college graduations. And still, I thought of him first, our name a reminder of how success never erases history. Reginald Dwayne Betts, still connected to 251534, my state number. For so many years that number was more important than that name, and it might still be.

About three months later, the letter came from the Connecticut Bar Examining Committee telling me that the committee needed more time to decide if I had the character and fitness required of a lawyer. The committee would continue reviewing my application. They might contact my references, ask me to appear at an investigative hearing, look into my life before and after my incarceration.

Character and fitness, loosely defined qualities, are required of attorneys in every state. States take various approaches to determining if someone with a criminal record meets that standard and will become a licensed attorney. For those convicted of felonies in Florida, the governor must restore your civil rights by petition, a years-long process, before you can sit for the bar exam. In Washington State, bar examiners must determine that a person has the appropriate character and fitness to practice law before they may sit for the bar exam. In Mississippi, for most felons, there is no record of rehabilitation; no stretch of time spent outside prison; no letter written by any defense attorney, prosecutor, or judge; no prayer that will persuade the bar examiner to confer a law license on you. Texas, Kansas, and Missouri require that five years pass after a felon finishes his prison sentence or probation time before he or she can apply for bar admission.

Willie Dow, a local New Haven attorney, agreed to represent me. Soon after, Michael Wishnie, a Yale Law professor, volunteered to serve as co-counsel. We put together a packet of more than 200 letters from friends, colleagues, and professors attesting to my character. The support was humbling, but it also felt strange to create an elaborate record to prove that I was worthy of doing a job that I was qualified to do. Once the packet was collected, Willie sent it to the Connecticut bar examiners, and we waited. I knew that if the committee declined to admit me to the bar, I would have to wait two years to reapply for admission, at which point I would probably have to take the bar exam again and also pay the $800 fee again. I knew that what I did as a sixteen-year-old in Virginia would forever be a hellhound on my trail, but I hoped that I had outpaced my scapegrace. The committee's July letter let me know: not yet; maybe, not ever.

.   .   .

When I despaired, I thought about Benjamin Franklin Rayborn. J. Edgar Hoover, the former director of the FBI, said that Rayborn was "the most notorious bank robber since World War II." Upon his arrest, his local paper, the *Courier-Journal* of Louisville, Ky., on December 18, 1949, called Rayborn "the trigger-happy fellow with the cold, blue eyes." Before Rayborn turned thirty, he had been sentenced to life in Kentucky for a string of bank robberies; sentenced to thirty years in federal prison for being caught in a hotel room full of machine guns; led a riot against prison conditions in Kentucky; and been transferred to Alcatraz, then one of the most violent prisons in America, as punishment for his role in the riot. But by 1956, Rayborn had fashioned himself into a legal mind astute enough to successfully challenge several federal convictions and get ten years knocked off his federal prison sentence. His next legal feat was more astonishing. Once he seemed primed for an early release, Kentucky sought to have him extradited back to state prison to serve the rest of his life sentence. Rayborn again filed suit, arguing that Kentucky, by voluntarily transferring him to Alcatraz, had relinquished any jurisdictional claims it had to his body. A judge agreed. Finally free, Rayborn, according to an acquaintance, sought a job as an accountant at General Electric. After achieving a perfect score on an exam given by the company, he was asked where he had studied accounting. Alcatraz, he told them. That disqualified him. He went on to rob another bank and returned to federal prison.

In 1966, John Cleary, the first executive director of the Federal Defenders of San Diego, met Benjamin Franklin Rayborn in prison in Atlanta. Cleary, impressed by Rayborn's habeas corpus filings on behalf of other prisoners, helped him get grant money to be paid as a jailhouse lawyer. After his second release from prison, Cleary tapped Rayborn to work with the federal defenders. He called Rayborn a one-man appellate division. From 1971 until his death in 2004, Rayborn was the chief legal research associate. In his role, he wrote hundreds of appeal briefs and had his handprint on thousands of others. For three decades, one of the most brilliant legal minds, with a photographic memory and decades of doing time, ran the appellate division of the federal defenders. All told, he spent more than twenty years incarcerated and more than three decades on the job. Cleary called him among the top 1 percent of attorneys in the country, and he had never earned a law degree or been licensed to practice law.

There are others. Frankie Guzman, found guilty at age fifteen of armed robbery in a juvenile court, was admitted to the California Bar and is now director of the California Youth Justice Initiative at the National Center for Youth Law. Noah Kilroy, Christopher Poulos, and Shon Hopwood have also traded in inmate numbers for bar numbers. Kilroy served time for drug charges in Florida. He works as a prosecutor for the city of Providence and has started his own criminal-defense practice. Poulos went from doing federal time for drug trafficking to working in President Obama's White House for the Office of National Drug Control Policy; he's now director of the Washington Statewide Re-entry Council.

Hopwood might be the Rayborn of the group. While serving a twelve-year sentence for bank robbery, he became a jailhouse lawyer and managed to get two cases in front of the United States Supreme Court. Now a professor at Georgetown Law, Hopwood recently represented Tarra Simmons before the Washington Supreme Court. The three years Simmons served in prison for drug charges almost kept her from becoming an attorney. The Washington Bar Examining Committee, citing character and fitness issues, wouldn't permit her to take the bar exam. Arguing before the same body that admitted him, Hopwood helped make Simmons's own legal career possible.

Hopwood, Simmons, Poulos, Guzman, and Kilroy are all licensed attorneys embodying the history of thousands of men and women standing for count. Their stories reminded me of my long-ago cellmate Keese, and I wondered what might be possible for him if he were set free. More than twenty years after a Richmond judge sentenced him to over five decades in prison, and with my own future as a lawyer uncertain at best, I managed to find three attorneys in Washington who agreed to rumble for Keese the way he had been ready to rumble for me. Maybe we all pursued law to save someone left behind; maybe we pursued it to save ourselves.

·　　·　　·

Prison taught me how to wait. I learned to break up a nine-year sentence into a million moments of waiting: waiting for rec, for chow, for count time, waiting for mail call, for visits, waiting to walk in the world without thinking constantly about danger, waiting for freedom. Waiting to hear back from the bar committee felt similar—once again, I was just waiting for mail. When the letter came, it began: "Dear Mr. Betts: The Connecticut Bar Examining Committee is pleased to advise you . . . that you have been recommended for admission to the Connecticut Bar."

On Nov. 3, 2017, two days before my thirty-seventh birthday, my mother, along with my Aunt Pandora and Uncle Darren, who had driven more than 300 miles to watch it all, walked into the New Haven Superior Court on 235 Church Street. They deposited keys, watches, belts, and cell phones into a gray bucket before walking through a metal detector. Minutes later, Terese, Micah, Miles, and I followed them through the same gantlet. Most black families walking into this courthouse are headed into a disaster. But that day, my folks joined my friends and colleagues in a small fourth-floor courtroom to celebrate.

Inside, the deep, rich mahogany pews called to mind the Fairfax County courtroom where I learned I'd do time. Looking around, I thought about the squalor and violence of the prison cells. Minutes later, I stood before Judge Omar Williams with my friend and supervising attorney Sanford O. Bruce III, who goes by Trey. The swearing-in, for most, is simply a ritual; in courtrooms across the country, judges administer the oath to countless new attorneys each time bar results are released. But this was different. I stood alone before the judge, with just a lawyer to the right of me, as I'd done so many years before.

Trey asked the court to approve my admission to the Connecticut Bar. "You've fought long and hard with the sword to get here today," Judge Williams said, "and today you're presented with the shield." Nearly three years before that day, as a second-year law student at Yale, I walked into the office that Trey and Judge Williams, then a public defender, shared. I told Trey that I had a record and asked if it would be a problem for me to work in the Criminal Justice Clinic. He told me that if there was anyone who should be working in the clinic, it was someone like me, who from experience understood what the clinic's clients were going through.

Reciting the oath to become a member of the court took a fraction of the time that it took me to be sentenced. I wondered if becoming an attorney would fill the hole in my mother's heart that my becoming a felon created. The courtroom was where she lost her son; maybe it would be where she got him back, too.

I could see my mother wiping her eyes, but smiling this time. Someone clapped. My Uncle Darren had his phone out, recording. Terese, who had been there long before any of this was a possibility, was beaming, her arms wrapped around Micah and Miles. Everyone there knew that I once walked out of a courtroom headed to prison, except my younger son, Miles, who was six. Terese and I hadn't decided when we would let Miles know. But we hoped that it would be on our terms and not because of a classmate or an overheard conversation.

After the fifteen-minute ceremony, I turned to everyone, without thinking, and began speaking as my uncle kept recording: "The last time my mom saw me in court, I was sentenced to nine years in prison." I wanted to say something about the journey. I'd already revealed too much. Miles, sitting beside his brother, paused and looked up. I could tell something confused him. He had questions in his eyes. He stared, listening, as I confessed the thing that I'd been holding back. What man wants to tell his child he's done time in prison? But I had. And, in that single breath, I'd given him this: an image of his father as both a convict and an attorney.

New York

WINNER—LEISURE INTERESTS

In its twenty-year history, the Best American Magazine Writing series has rarely included examples of service journalism, focusing instead on feature stories, essays, and political commentary. Yet service is central to the mission of most magazines and a growing number of websites. Which is not to suggest that the inclusion of "How to Be an Artist" is intended as a form of atonement. That would be another mistake because this story exemplifies magazine writing at its idiosyncratic best, and no wonder—Jerry Saltz is the winner of both the 2015 National Magazine Award for Columns and Commentary and the 2018 Pulitzer Prize for Criticism. The thirty-three rules propounded here are "all you need to know to make a life for yourself in art," writes Saltz. "Or 34, if you count 'Always be nice, generous, and open with others and take good care of your teeth.' And No. 35: 'Fake it till you make it.'"

Jerry Saltz

How to Be an Artist

A rt is for anyone. It's just not for everyone. I know this viscerally, as a would-be artist who burned out. I wrote about that last year, and ever since, I've been beset— every lecture I give, every gallery I pop my head into, somebody is asking me for advice. What they're really asking is "How can I be an artist?"

When, last month, Banksy jerry-rigged a frame to shred a painting just when it was auctioned, I could almost hear the whispers: "Is that art?" This fall, the biggest museum event in New York is the Whitney's retrospective of Andy Warhol—the paradigmatic self-made, make-anything-art-and-yourself-famous artist. Today, we are all Andy's children, especially in the age of Instagram, which has trained everyone to think visually and to look at our regular lives as fodder for aesthetic output.

How do you get from there to making real art, great art? There's no special way; everyone has their own path. Yet, over the years, I've found myself giving the same bits of advice. Most of them were simply gleaned from looking at art, then looking some more. Others from listening to artists talk about their work and their struggles. (Everyone's a narcissist.) I've even stolen a couple from my wife.

There are 33 rules—and they really are all you need to know to make a life for yourself in art. Or 34, if you count "Always be nice, generous, and open with others and take good care of your teeth." And No. 35: "Fake it till you make it."

Step One: You Are a Total Amateur

Five lessons before you even get started.

Lesson 1: Don't Be Embarrassed

I get it. Making art can be humiliating, terrifying, leave you feeling foul, exposed, like getting naked in front of someone else for the first time. You often reveal things about yourself that others may find appalling, weird, boring, or stupid. People may think you're abnormal or a hack. Fine. When I work, I feel sick to my stomach with thoughts like *None of this is any good. It makes no sense. But art doesn't have to make sense. It doesn't even need to be good.* So don't worry about being smart and let go of being "good."

Lesson 2: "Tell your own story and you will be interesting."—Louise Bourgeois

Amen, Louise. Don't be reined in by other people's definitions of skill or beauty or be boxed in by what is supposedly high or low. Don't stay in your own lane. Drawing within the lines is for babies; making things add up and be right is for accountants. Proficiency and dexterity are only as good as what you do with them. *But also remember that just because it's your story, that doesn't mean you're entitled to an audience.* You have to earn that. Don't try to do it with a big single project. Take baby steps. And be happy with baby steps.

Lesson 3: Feel Free to Imitate

We all start as copycats, people who make pastiches of other people's work. Fine! Do that. However, when you do this, focus, start to feel the sense of possibility in making all these things your own—even when the ideas, tools, and moves come from other artists. Whenever you make anything, think of yourself as entering a gigantic stadium filled with ideas, avenues, ways, means, and materials. And possibilities. Make these things yours. *This is your house now.*

Lesson 4: Art Is Not About Understanding. Or Mastery.

It is about doing and experience.

No one asks what Mozart means. Or an Indian raga or the little tripping dance of Fred Astaire and Ginger Rogers to "Cheek to Cheek" in *Top Hat. Forget about making things that are understood.* I don't know what Abba means, but I love it. Imagination is your creed; sentimentality and lack of feeling your foe. All art comes from love—love of doing something.

Lesson 5: Work, Work, Work

Sister Corita Kent said, "The only rule is work. If you work, it will lead to something. It's the people who do all of the work all the time who eventually catch onto things."

I have tried every way in the world to stop work-block or fear of working, of failure. There is only one method that works: work. And keep working.

Every artist and writer I know claims to work in their sleep. I do all the time. Jasper Johns famously said, "One night I dreamed that I painted a large American flag, and the next morning I got up and I went out and bought the materials to begin it." How many times have you been given a whole career in your dreams and not heeded it? It doesn't matter how scared you are; everyone is scared. *Work.* Work is the only thing that takes the curse of fear away.

Step Two: How to Actually Begin

An instruction manual for the studio.

Lesson 6: Start with a Pencil

Don't worry about drawing. Just make marks. Tell yourself you're simply diagramming, playing, experimenting, seeing what looks like what. *If you can write, you already know how to draw*; you already have a form of your own, a style of making letters and numbers and special doodles. These are forms of drawing, too. While you're making marks and drawing, pay attention to all the physical feedback you're getting from your hand, wrist, arm, ears, your sense of smell and touch. How long can your mark go before you seem to need to lift the pencil and make a different mark? Make those marks shorter or longer. Change the ways you make them at all, wrap your fingers in fabric to change your touch, try your other hand to see what it does. All these things are telling you something. Get very quiet inside yourself and pay attention to everything you're experiencing. *Don't think* good *or* bad. *Think* useful, pleasurable, strange. Hide secrets in your work. Dance with these experiences, collaborate with them. They're the leader; you follow. Soon you'll be making up steps too, doing visual calypsos all your own—ungainly, awkward, or not. Who cares? You'll be dancing to the music of art.

Carry a sketchbook with you at all times. Cover a one-by-one-foot piece of paper with marks. But don't just fill the whole page border to border, edge to edge. (Way too easy.) Think about what shapes, forms, structures, configurations, details, sweeps, build-ups, dispersals, and compositions appeal to you.

Now do this on another surface, any surface, to know what kind of material appeals to you. Draw on rock, metal, foam-core, coffee cups, labels, the sidewalk, walls, plants, fabric, wood, whatever. Just make marks; decorate these surfaces. Don't worry about doing more. *All art is a form of decoration.* Now ask someone what ideas they get when they look at what you've made. They've just told you more about what you've already done. If the other person sees it in your work, it's there.

Next, draw the square foot in front of you. This can be tight, loose, abstract, realistic. It's a way to see how you see objects, textures, surfaces, shapes, light, dark, atmosphere, and patterns. It tells you what you missed seeing. *This will be your first masterpiece.* Now draw the same square foot from the other side. You are already becoming a much better seeing machine and you don't even know it.

Lesson 7: Develop Forms of Practice

For instance, on the subway, while waiting or sitting around, practice drawing your own hands. Lots of hands on the same page, hands over other hands. Other people's hands, if you want to. You can draw other parts of your body that you can see, too. But you have to look and then describe with your pencil or pen what you see. *Don't make it up!* Mirrors are fine, even if you want to draw only where your cheek turns into your mouth. Play with different scales, make things bigger, smaller, twisted.

EXERCISE: FORGET BEING A GENIUS AND
DEVELOP SOME SKILLS
I think all artists should:

- Build a clay pot.
- Sew pieces of fabric together.
- Prune a tree.
- Make a wooden bowl on a lathe, by carving.

- Make a lithograph, etching, or woodblock print.
- Make one hokey Dalí-like painting or mini Kusama light installation to get this out of your system.

You are now in possession of ancient secret knowledge.

Lesson 8: Now, Redefine Skill

Artistic skill has nothing to do with technical proficiency, mimetic exactitude, or so-called good drawing. *For every great artist, there is a different definition of skill.* Take drawing classes, if you wish; learn to draw "like the masters." You still have to do it in an original way. Pollock could not draw realistically, but he made flicking paint at a canvas from above, for a time, the most prized skill in the art world. You can do the same—*your skill will be whatever it is you're doing differently.*

Lesson 9: "Embed thought in material."—Roberta Smith

What does this mean? *An object should express ideas*; art should contain emotions. And these ideas and feelings should be easy to understand—complex or not.

These days, an artist might exhibit an all-brown painting with a long wall text informing us that the artist took the canvas to Kosovo near the site of a 1990s Serbian massacre and rubbed dirt on the canvas for two hours while blindfolded to commemorate the killing. Recently, while I was looking at boring black-and-white photographs of clouds in the sky, a gallerist sidled up to me and seriously opined, "These are pictures of clouds over Ferguson, Missouri, in protest of police violence." I started yelling, "*No! These are just dumb pictures of clouds and have nothing to do with anything.*"

There is a different way. In the winter of 1917, Marcel Duchamp, age twenty-nine, bought a urinal at J. L. Mott Iron Works on Fifth Avenue, turned it on its side, signed it "R. Mutt 1917," titled it *Fountain*, and submitted it to the nonjuried Society of Independent Artists exhibition.

Fountain is an aesthetic equivalent of the Word made flesh, an object that is also an idea—that anything can be an artwork. Today it is called the most influential artwork of the twentieth century.

This project of embedding thought in material to change our conception of the world isn't only a new development. When we see cave paintings, we are seeing one of the most advanced and complex visual operating systems ever devised by our species. The makers of the work wanted to portray in the real world something they had in their head and make that information readable to others. It has lasted tens of thousands of years. With that in mind . . .

EXERCISE: BUILD A LIFE TOTEM

Using any material on any surface, make or draw or render a four-foot-tall totem pole of your life. From this totem, we should be able to know something about you other than what you look like or how many siblings you have. Include anything you want: words, letters, maps, photos, objects, signs. This should take no longer than a week. After a week, it's finished. Period. Now show it to someone who does not know you well. Tell them only, "This is a totem pole of my life till now." That's all. It doesn't matter if they like it. Ask them to tell you what it means about your life. No clues. Listen to what they tell you.

Lesson 10: Find Your Own Voice

Then exaggerate it.

If someone says your work looks like someone else's and you should stop making it, I say *don't stop doing it*. Do it again. Do it 100 times or 1,000 times. Then ask an artist friend whom you trust if your work still looks too much like the other person's art. If it still looks too much like the other person's, try another path.

Imagine the horror Philip Guston must have felt when he followed his own voice and went from being a first-string Abstract Expressionist in the 1950s to painting clunky, cartoony figures smoking cigars, driving around in convertibles, and wearing KKK hoods! He was all but shunned for this. He followed his voice anyway. This work is now some of the most revered from the entire period. In your downtime . . .

EXERCISE: AN ARCHAEOLOGY

Make an index, family tree, chart, or diagram of your interests. All of them, everything: visual, physical, spiritual, sexual. Leisure time, hobbies, foods, buildings, airports, everything. Every book, movie, website, etc. The totality of this self-exposure may be daunting, scary. But your voice is here. This will become a resource and record to return to and add to for the rest of your life.

Lesson 11: Listen to the Crazy Voices in Your Head

I have my own sort of *School of Athens* in my head. A team of rivals, friends, famous people, influences dead and alive. They're all looking over my shoulder as I work; none of them are mean. All make observations, recommendations, etc. *I use music a lot.* I think, *Okay, let's begin this piece with a real pow! Like Beethoven.* Or the Barbara Kruger in my head says, *Make this sentence short, punchy, declarative, aggressive.* Led Zeppelin chimes in with, *Try a hairy experiment here; let it all show.* All the Sienese paintings I've ever seen beg me, *Make it beautiful.* D. H. Lawrence is pounding on the table, Alexander Pope is making me get a grip, Wallace Stevens listens to my language and recommends words, Whitman pushes me on, my inner Melville gets grandiose, and Proust drives me to make longer and longer sentences till they almost break, and my editor cuts these into eighths or edits them down to one. (Writers need editors. No exceptions.) *These voices will always be there for when things get tough.*

Lesson 12: Know What You Hate

It is probably you.

EXERCISE: MAKE A LIST OF ART

Make a list of three artists whose work you despise. Make a list of five things about each artist that you do not like; be as specific as possible. Often there's something about what these artists do that you share. Really think about this.

Lesson 13: Scavenge

Life is your syllabus: Gather from everywhere.

Andy Warhol said, "I always like to work on . . . things that were discarded, that everybody knew were no good." He also understood that "department stores will become museums," meaning that optical information can come from everywhere, even from a Celestial Seasonings package.

Originality did not conveniently die just in time for you and your generation to insist it no longer exists. *You just have to find it.* You can do this by looking for overlooked periods of art history, disliked and discredited styles, and forgotten ideas, images, and objects. Then work them into your own art 100 times or 1,000 times.

Step Three: Learn How to Think Like an Artist

This is the fun part.

Lesson 14: Compare Cats and Dogs

Okay, this sounds ridiculous, but call your dog and it comes right over to you, placing its head in your lap, slobbering, wagging its tail: *a miraculous direct communication with another species.* Now call your cat. It might look up, twitch a bit, perhaps go over to the couch, rub against it, circle once, and lie down again. What am I saying?

In seeing how the cat reacted, you are seeing something very close to how artists communicate.

The cat is not interested in direct communication. The cat places a third thing between you and it and relates to you through this third thing. Cats communicate abstractly, indirectly. As Carol Bove says, "You don't just walk up to beauty and kiss her on the mouth!" *Artists are cats. (And they can't be herded.)*

Lesson 15: Understand That Art Is Not Just for Looking At

Art does something.

In the past hundred years or so, art has been reduced to being mainly something we look at in clean, white, well-lit art galleries and museums. Art has been limited this way, made a passive thing: another tourist attraction to see, take a picture in front of, and move on from.

But for almost its entire history, art has been a verb, something that does things to or for you, that makes things happen. Holy relics in churches all over the world are said to heal. *Art has been carried into war; made to protect us, curse a neighbor, kill someone; been an aid in getting pregnant or preventing pregnancy.* There are huge, beautiful, multicolored, intricately structured Navajo sand paintings used in ceremonies to ask the gods for assistance. The eyes painted on Egyptian sarcophagi are not there for us to see; they are there so the interred person can watch. The paintings inside the tombs were meant to be seen only by beings in the afterlife.

Have you ever cried in front of a work of art? *Write down six things about it that made you cry. Tack the list to your studio wall. Those are magical abracadabras for you.*

Lesson 16: Learn the Difference Between Subject Matter and Content

One of the most crucial lessons there is!

The subject matter of Francis Bacon's 1953 *Study After Velázquez's Portrait of Pope Innocent X* is a pope, a seated male in a transparent sort of box. That's it. The content might be a rebellion or an indictment of religion. It might be claustrophobia or hysteria or the madness of religion or civilization.

The subject matter of Michelangelo's *David* is a standing man with a sling. The content might be grace, beauty—he was just seventeen, if you know what I mean—pensiveness, physical awareness, timelessness, eternal things, a form of perfection, vulnerability. This content is High Renaissance. Bernini's *David,* made 120 years later, is Baroque—all action and drama.

When you look at art, *make subject matter the first thing you see—and then stop seeing it.*

Try to find the *content* in a painting by Robert Ryman, who has been making almost-all-white work since the 1950s. Ask what Ryman's (or any artist's) ideas are and what his relationship to paint is, to surface, to internal scale (meaning what size brushstrokes were used in the work), to color. What is white to Ryman? Note the date: 1960. Why would he make this painting then? Would this have looked like other art at the time? How would it have been different? Ask yourself what else was being made then. How is the work hung on the wall? Is it in a frame? Is the stretcher or surface thick, thin, close to the wall? How is this like or unlike other almost-monochrome works by Ellsworth Kelly, Barnett Newman, Agnes Martin, or Ad Reinhardt? *Is the surface sensual or intellectual?* Does the painter want you to see the work all at once or in parts? Are some parts more important than others? Is every part of the surface supposed to be equally important? *What are the artist's ideas about craft and skill?* Do you think this artist likes painting or is trying to paint against it? Is this anti-art? What is Ryman's relationship to materials, tools, mark making? How do you think he made the work? How might it be original or innovative? Why should this be in a museum? Why should it not be in a museum? Would you want to live with it? Why or why not? Why do you imagine the painting is this size? Now try a Frida Kahlo.

Lesson 17: See as Much as You Can

Critics see by standing back, getting close, stepping up and back; looking at a whole show, comparing one work to another; considering the artist's past work, assessing developments, repetitions, regressions, failures, lack of originality; etc.

Artists see very differently: They get very close to a work; they inspect every detail, its textures, materials, makeup; they touch it, look at the edges and around the back of the object.

What are the artists doing? They will say, "Seeing how it is made." I would say, "*Stealing.*"

You can steal from anything. You should! You better! Bad art teaches you as much as good art. Maybe more! *Great art is often the enemy of the good; it doesn't leave you enough room to steal.*

Lesson 18: All Art Is Identity Art!

This is because it is made by *somebody.*

And don't worry about being "political" enough: Kazimir Malevich painted squares during World War I; Mark Rothko made fuzzy squares during World War II; Agnes Martin drew grids on canvas during the Vietnam War. All art is a confession, more or less oblique.

Artists who claim that art is supposed to be good for us need also to see that there are as many ways of art being "good for us" as there are works of art.

Lesson 19: All Art Was Once Contemporary Art

Never forget this, that all art was made by artists for and in reaction to their time. It will make you less cynical and closed off and more understanding and open to everything you ever see. *Please do this!* It applies to all of us.

Step Four: Enter the Art World

A guide to the snake pit.

Lesson 20: Accept That You Will Likely Be Poor

Even though all we see of the art world these days are astronomical prices, glitz, glamour, and junkie-like behavior, remember that only 1 percent of 1 percent of 1 percent of all artists become rich off their artwork. You may feel overlooked, underrecognized, and underpaid. Too bad. Stop feeling sorry for yourself; that's not why you're doing this.

Lesson 21: Define Success

But be careful. Typical answers are money, happiness, freedom, "doing what I want," having a community of artists, having people see what I do.

But . . . if you marry a rich person and have lots of money, would you be satisfied with just the money? Also, Subway sells a lot of sandwiches, but that doesn't make them good.

What about being "happy"? Don't be silly! A lot of successful people are unhappy. And a lot of happy people aren't successful. I'm "successful," and I'm confused, terrified, insecure, and foul all the time. Success and happiness live on different sides of the tracks.

Do you want the real definition of success? The best definition of success is time—the time to do your work.

How will you make time if you don't have money? You will work full time for a long time. You will be depressed because of this for a long time—resentful, frustrated, envious. I'm sorry, that's the way it is.

But you're a sneaky, resourceful artist! Soon you figure out a way to work only four days a week; you start to be a little less depressed. But then on Sunday night, you're depressed again, back on your ride-to-nowhere job that's still taking up too much of your time.

But you are really sneaky and resourceful; this is a life-and-death matter to you. Eventually—and this comes for fully 80 percent of the artists I have ever known—*you scam a way to work an only-three-days-a-week job.* You may work in a gallery; for an artist or a museum; as a teacher, an art critic, an art handler, a bookkeeper, a proofreader, whatever.

Now you aren't depressed anymore: You have time to make your work and hang out more; you are now the first measure of successful. Now get to work. Or quit being an artist.

Lesson 22: It Takes Only a Few People to Make a Career

Exactly how many? Let's count.

Dealers? You need only one dealer—someone who believes in you, supports you emotionally, pays you promptly, doesn't play too many mind games; who'll be honest with you about your crappy or great art, who does as much as possible to spread your work out there and try to make money from it, too. This dealer doesn't have to be in New York.

Collectors? You need only five or six collectors who will buy your work from time to time and over the years, who really get what you're up to, who are willing to go through the ups and downs, who don't say, "Make them like *this.*" Each of these six collectors might talk to six other collectors about your work. Even if you have only six collectors, that's enough for you to make enough money to have enough time to make your work.

Critics? It would be nice to have two or as many as three critics who seem to get what you're doing. It would be best if these critics were of your generation, not geezers like me.

Curators? It would be nice to have one or two curators of your generation or a little older who would put you in shows from time to time.

That's it! Twelve people. *Surely your crappy art can fake out twelve stupid people!* I've seen it done with only three or four supporters. I've seen it done with one!

In 1957, gallery owner Leo Castelli discovered Jasper Johns while visiting Robert Rauschenberg's studio. Castelli immediately offered Johns his first solo show. It was there that Alfred Barr, the founding director of New York's Museum of Modern Art, purchased three works. Additional works were bought by Philip Johnson and Burton and Emily Hall Tremaine. Before the show even went up, executive editor Thomas Hess put a Johns on the cover of *ARTnews*.

In 1993, Elizabeth Peyton's New York breakthrough was staged by dealer Gavin Brown in Room 828 of the Chelsea Hotel. Visitors asked for the key to the room at the front desk. They went upstairs, unlocked the door, and entered a small studio apartment facing Twenty-Third Street. There they saw twenty-one small-to-medium-size black-and-white charcoal-and-ink drawings of dandies, Napoleon, Queen Elizabeth II, Ludwig II, and others. Any of the works could have been stolen; none were. Since then, Peyton has had museum shows all over the world; her works sell for close to a million dollars. According to the hotel ledger, only thirty-eight people saw the show after the opening. It doesn't take much.

I can't sugarcoat this next part: Some people are better connected than others. They get to twelve faster. The art world is full of these privileged people. You can hate them. I do. It is unfair and unjust and still in operation around women and artists of color especially, not to mention artists over forty. This needs to change and be changed. By all of us.

Lesson 23: Learn to Write

When it comes to artist statements, Keep it simple, stupid.

Don't use art jargon; write in your own voice, write how you talk. Don't try to write smart. Keep your statement direct, clear, to the point. Don't oppose big concepts like "nature" and "culture." Don't use words like *interrogate, reconceptualize, deconstruct, symbolize, transcendental, mystical, commodity culture, liminal space,* or *haptic.* Don't quote Foucault, Deleuze, Derrida. Those guys are great. But don't quote them. Come up with your own theory. People who claim to hate or have no theory: That's your theory, you idiots!

Important things are hard to write about. That's the way it is. Deal with it. And if it's pretentious to say, don't say it.

EXERCISE: ARTIST'S STATEMENT
Write a simple 100-to-150-word statement about your work; give it to someone who doesn't know your work. Have them tell you what they think your work looks like. Note the differences.

Two Tips:
(A) Don't make writing a big deal. Just write, you big baby! You already know how to write.
(B) Never just say, "You tell me what it is." That's pompous bullshit. When it comes to your work, you're the best authority there is.

Step Five: Survive the Art World

Psychic strategies for dealing with the ugliness (inside and out).

Lesson 24: Artists Must Be Vampires

Stay up late every night with other artists around your age. *Show up.* Go to openings, events, parties, wherever there are more than two of your kind.

Artists must commune with their own kind all the time. There are no exceptions to this rule, even if you live "out in the woods." Preferably commune in person, but online is more than fine. It doesn't matter where you live: big city, small city, little town. You will fight and love together; you will develop new languages together and give each other comfort, conversation, and the strength to carry on. This is how you will change the world—and your art.

To protect yourselves, *form small gangs.* Protect one another no matter what; this gang will allow all of you to go out into and take over parts of the world. Argue, sleep with, love, hate, get sick of your fellow gang members. Whatever happens, you need one another—for now. Protect the weakest artist in your gang, because *there are people in the gang who think you're the weak one.*

Lesson 25: Learn to Deal with Rejection

In 1956, "after careful consideration," the Museum of Modern Art rejected a shoe drawing by Warhol that he had given to the museum. Monet was rejected for years from the Paris Salon exhibitions. *The work of Manet and Courbet was rejected as scandalous, sensationalist, ugly.* Manet's paintings were said to exhibit "inconceivable vulgarity." Manet didn't want to show with Cézanne because he thought *he* was vulgar.

Stephen King's most renowned and first book, Carrie, was rejected thirty times. King threw the first pages of the book out. His wife went through the trash, rescued them, and persuaded him to keep writing.

The Beatles were rejected by Decca Records, which believed "guitar groups are on the way out," and "the Beatles have no future in show business."

But don't just ignore criticism. Instead, keep your rejection letters; paste them to your wall. They are goads, things to prove wrong. *You may be Ahab about these bad reviews, but don't get taken down by them; they don't define you.*

Much trickier: Accept that every criticism can have a grain of truth to it, something you did that allowed this person to say what was said. You might be ahead of your time, but the person couldn't see it. Or maybe you're doing something that isn't up to snuff, that allowed them not to appreciate your work, or you haven't found a way to make your work speak to the people you want it to speak to. That's all on you.

In general, you must be open to critique but also develop an elephant skin. And remember that nothing anyone says to you about your work can be worse than the things you've already thought and said to yourself a hundred times.

I always tell anyone criticizing me, "You could be right." It has a nice double edge that the person often never feels and that gives pleasure.

Lesson 26: Make an Enemy of Envy

Today!

Envy looks at others but blinds you.

It will eat you alive as an artist; you live in the service of it, always on the edge of a funk, dwelling on past slights, watching everything, always seeing what other people have, scanning for other artists who are mentioned instead of you. Envy erodes your inner mind, leaves less room for development and, most important, for honest self-criticism. Your imagination is taken up by what others have, rather than what you need to be doing in your own work to get what you want. From this fortress, everything that doesn't happen to you is blamed on something or someone else. You fancy yourself a modern van Gogh, a passed-over genius the world isn't ready for. You relinquish agency and responsibility. Your feelings of lack define you, make you sour, bitter, not loving, and mean.

Poor you. Too bad that all those other "bad artists" are getting shows and you're not. Too bad they're getting the articles, money, and love! Too bad they have a trust fund, went to better schools, married someone rich, are better looking, have thinner ankles, are more social, have better connections, or use their connections, networking skills, and education. *Too bad you're shy.*

A secret: Almost everyone in the art world is almost equally as bashful and skittish about putting themselves out there. I'm unable to attend seated dinners. We all do the best we can. But "poor me" isn't a way to make your work better, and you're out of the game if you don't show up. *So grow a pair of whatever and get back to work!*

Lesson 27: Having a Family Is Fine

There is an unwritten rule—especially for women in the art world—that having children is "bad for your career." This is idiotic.

Probably 90 percent of all artists have had children. These artists have mostly been men, and it wasn't bad for their careers. Of course, women were tasked almost exclusively with domesticity and child-rearing over the centuries, not permitted in schools and academies, not even allowed to draw the nude, let alone apprentice to or learn from artists. That is over.

Having children is not "bad" for your career. Having children means having less time or money or space. So what? Most children raised within the art world have amazing lives.

As artist Laurel Nakadate has observed, *being a parent is already very much like being an artist.* It means always lugging things around, living in chaos, doing things that are mysterious or impossible or scary. As with art, children can drive you crazy all day, make you wish all this could go away. Then in a single second, at any point, you are redeemed with a moment of intense, transformative love.

Step Six: Attain Galactic Brain

Jerry's cosmic epigrams.

Lesson 28: What You Don't Like Is as Important as What You Do Like

Don't say, "I hate figurative painting." You never know when you will see a so-called figurative painting that catches your attention. So don't be an art-world undertaker pronouncing mediums dead! "Painting is dead," "The novel is dead," "The author is dead," "Photography is dead," "History is dead." *Nothing is dead!*

Lesson 29: Art Is a Form of Knowing Yourself

Art is not optional, not decorative landscaping in front of the castle of civilization. It is no more or less important than philosophy, religion, economics, or psychology.

Lesson 30: "Artists do not own the meaning of their work."—Roberta Smith

Remember: anyone may use your art—any art—in any way that works for them. You may say your work is about diaspora, but others might see in it climate change or a nature study. *Cool.*

Lesson 31: All Art Is Subjective

What does this mean? We have consensus that certain artists are good, but you may look at a Rembrandt and find yourself thinking . . . *It's pretty brown.* That's fine! It doesn't mean you're dumb.

It does mean that while there is one text for *Hamlet,* every person who sees the play sees a different *Hamlet.* Moreover, every time *you* see *Hamlet,* it is different. This is the case with almost all good art. It is always changing, and every time you see it anew, you think, *How could I have missed that before? Now I finally see!* Until the next time it rearranges your thinking.

This brings you into one of art's metaphysical quasar chambers: Art is a static, nonchanging thing that is never the same.

Lesson 32: You Must Prize Vulnerability

Radical vulnerability.

What's that? It's following your work into its darkest corners and strangest manifestations, revealing things about yourself that you don't want to reveal until your work requires you to do this, and never failing in only mediocre or generic ways. We all contradict ourselves. We contain multitudes. You must be willing to fail flamboyantly, do things that seem silly and that might get you judged as a bad person.

Can you?

Lesson 33: Be Delusional

At three a.m., demons speak to all of us. I am old, and they still speak to me every night. And every day.

They tell you you're not good enough, didn't go to the right schools, are stupid, don't know how to draw, don't have enough money, aren't original; that what you do doesn't matter, and who cares, and you don't even know art history, and can't schmooze, and have a bad neck. They tell you that you're faking it, that other people see through you, that you're lazy, that you don't know what you're doing, and that you're just doing this to get attention or money.

I have one solution to turn away these demons: After beating yourself up for half an hour or so, stop and say out loud, "Yeah, but I'm a fucking genius."

You are, now. Art is for anyone, it just isn't for everyone. These rules are your tools. Now use them to go change the world. *Get to work!*

5280

The city of New York is usually thought of as magazine central, but there are dozens of places across the country where local magazines flourish. Denver is one of those cities, and 5280 is its magazine (Denver is that many feet above sea level). Founded in 1993, 5280 had received eight nominations for National Magazine Awards since 2005 but had never won—until this year. The team behind this story— Kasey Cordell and Lindsey B. Koehler—was already familiar to the National Magazine Awards judges: Koehler's work had been nominated twice before, and a story by Cordell, "The 5280 Guide to Four Corners," was nominated just last year. So it was no surprise when the judges decided that " 'The Art of Dying Well' was exactly what a personal-service package should be—well reported, well written, well designed, with practical advice on a subject of importance" and gave the National Magazine Award for Personal Service to 5280.

Kasey Cordell and
Lindsey B. Koehler

The Art of
Dying Well

Merely Mortals

This is a story about death.

About how we in the United States—and maybe to a slightly lesser degree, here in Colorado and the West—tend to separate ourselves, emotionally and physically, from both the ugliness and the beauty of our inevitable ends. We don't like to think about dying. We don't like to deal with dying. And we certainly don't like to talk about dying. Maybe that's because acknowledging that human bodies are ephemeral short-circuits American brains groomed to (illogically) hope for a different outcome. Perhaps it's also because the moment death becomes part of the public discourse, as it has in the Centennial State over the past several years, things can get uncomfortably personal and wildly contentious.

When Coloradans (with an assist from Compassion & Choices, a national nonprofit committed to expanding end-of-life options) got Proposition 106, aka the Colorado End-of-Life Options Act, on the ballot in 2016, there was plenty of pushback—from the Archdiocese of Denver, advocacy groups for the disabled, hospice directors, hospital administrators, and more physicians than one might think. But on November 8, 64.9 percent of voters OK'd the access-to-medical-aid-in-dying measure, making Colorado the fifth jurisdiction to approve the practice. (Oregon,

California, Montana, Washington, Hawaii, Vermont, and Washington, D.C., have or are planning to enact similar laws.) Not everyone was happy, but if there's one thing both opponents and supporters of the legislation can (mostly) agree on, it's that the surrounding debate at least got people thinking about a very important part of life: death.

"As a society, we don't do a great job of talking about being mortal," says Dr. Dan Handel, a palliative medicine physician and the director of the medical-aid-in-dying service at Denver Health. "My secret hope is that this [new law] prompts talks about all options with dying." We want to help get those conversations started. In the following pages, we explore everything from how to access the rights afforded in the Colorado End-of-Life Options Act to how we should reshape the ways we think about, plan for, and manage death. Why? "We're all going to die," says Dr. Cory Carroll, a Fort Collins family practice physician. "But in America, we have no idea what death is." Our goal is to help you plan for a good death—whatever that means to you.

Death's Having a Moment

Colorado's end-of-life options legislation isn't the only way in which Coloradans are taking charge of their own deaths. Some Centennial Staters have begun contemplating their ends with the help of death doulas.

—Meghan Rabbitt

As the nation's baby boomers age, our country is approaching a new milestone: more gravestones. Over the next few decades, deaths in America are projected to hit a historic high—more than 3.6 million by 2037, which is one million more RIPs than in 2015, according to the U.S. Census Bureau. Here in Colorado, home to Boulder's Conscious Dying Institute, there are a growing number of "death doulas" trained to help us cross over on our own terms.

Death doulas offer planning and emotional support to the dying and their loved ones, and since 2013, the Conscious Dying Institute has trained more than 750. Unlike doctors, nurses, hospice workers, and other palliative-care practitioners who treat the dying, death doulas don't play a medical role. In much the same way that birth doulas help pregnant women develop and stick to birth plans, death doulas help their clients come up with arrangements for how they want to exit this life. That might mean talking about what projects feel important to finish (like writing that book) or helping someone make amends with estranged family members or friends or determining how much medication someone wants administered at the end. "When people are dying, they want to be heard," says Nicole Matarazzo, a Boulder-based death doula. "If a doula is present, she'll be able to fully show up for the person who's dying—and model that presence for family members."

Over the past year, the Conscious Dying Institute has seen a noticeable jump in the number of Coloradans using its directory of doulas and inquiring about training. When she started working in end-of-life care in 1998, founder Tarron Estes says no one had heard of death doulas. Now she's getting roughly twenty-five calls a week. "More people are getting comfortable talking about death," Estes says. "In cities like Denver, there's a willingness to talk about topics that are taboo in other areas of the country." Medical aid in dying is, of course, a prime example.

That embrace of the end might be just another part of what is becoming known as the "death-positive movement." More than 314,000 people have downloaded a free starter packet from the Conversation Project, a nonprofit that gets people talking about their end-of-life wishes. And more than 6,700 "death cafes," where people gather to talk about death over tea and cake, have popped up around the nation, including several in Colorado. Ready to make a date with death? The Denver Metro Death Cafe's next meeting is on October 20.

Knocking on a Death Doula's Door

WHAT TO LOOK FOR IN AN END-OF-LIFE GUIDE.

1. *Ask to see a certificate of education and research the organization that provided the doula's training.* Look for curricula that involve at least some in-person instruction. For example, the Conscious Dying Institute's eight-day, on-site training portion includes lectures, writing exercises, demonstrations, and partner practices. It's also split into a three-day session and a five-day session, with a ten-week internship requirement between each on-site phase.

2. *Compare fees.* Death doulas in Colorado charge about $25 to $125 an hour and may offer a sliding scale based on their clients' financial means.

3. *Pay attention to the doula's listening skills.* The last thing you want as you prepare to cross over is someone who hasn't been hearing you all along.

Ink Your Legacy

If a good death includes making sure your family is cared for, one of the greatest favors you can do for your loved ones is to provide a clear path to all of your worldly possessions. Putting in the time—and paperwork—to plan for the dissemination of all your stuff can save your family months of headaches, heartaches, and contentious probate battles. Not sure what kind of estate planning documents you need? We spoke with Kevin Millard, a Denver-based estate planning attorney, to help you get started.

If you don't care about who gets your stuff . . .

Great; then you probably don't need a will. If you don't have a will, your stuff—cars, jewelry, artwork, etc.—goes to your closest relative(s) under what are known as "intestate succession laws" (the laws that govern how your stuff is divided after your death). The state maintains very specific equations for different scenarios. For instance, if you die with a spouse and children from a previous relationship, your spouse gets the first $150,000 of your intestate property plus half of the remaining balance, and the descendants get everything else. Or, if you die with a spouse and living parents, your partner gets the first $300,000 of your intestate property and three-quarters of anything over that. Your parents get the rest.

If you do care about who gets your stuff and some of your "stuff" is minor children . . .

At the very least, you need a guardian appointment document to determine who will care for your children after your death. Physical custody is different from managing any money you might have set aside for your children. You can name one person to manage the money and another to actually care for your children. Also, if your selected guardian doesn't live where you do, he or she gets to decide whether or not your kids have to move.

If your most valuable stuff is not really "stuff" at all, but more like life insurance policies, 401(k) plans, bank accounts, etc. . . .

Then you've probably already designated who gets what by appointing a beneficiary for those things. Anything with a beneficiary—life insurance policies, payable-upon-death bank accounts, retirement plans, or property held in joint tenancy (e.g., your house)—does not get distributed according to intestate succession laws (the laws that govern how your stuff is divided after your death if you don't have a will). It goes to the listed beneficiary. However, you might want to consider also designating a durable financial power of attorney to manage all of your accounts in the event you become incapacitated before you die. Ditto for a medical power of attorney.

If your stuff is worth millions . . .

In addition to a will, you should consider a trust. This can protect your estate from being included in lawsuits if you're sued, and it can also ease some of the estate tax burden on your heirs. But if you're worth millions, then you probably already have people on retainer who've told you this.

If your stuff isn't worth millions . . .

You need a will if you want to make life easier for your heirs. (In Colorado, any estate valued at more than $65,000 must go through probate court—a process that takes many months to finalize because you cannot close an estate here until six months after a death certificate has been issued, which can take several days or even weeks.) The general rule in Colorado is that a will must be signed by two witnesses to be valid. If you go through the trouble of having it notarized, it becomes a self-proving will, which means the court doesn't have to track down the witnesses to certify its validity. You can also handwrite and sign your will; that's known as a holographic will and does not require witnesses—but it does come with a lot of hand cramps.

My Father's Final Gift

> When it came to preparing for the end of his life, my father planned for the worst, knowing that would be best for me.
> —Jerilyn Forsythe

It was June in Arizona, and it was hot inside my dad's kitchen. The whole place smelled musty, the way old cabins do, and I watched as a swath of sunlight coming through the window illuminated lazy plumes of dust. My thoughts felt as clouded and untethered as the drifting specks. I had flown in from Denver the day before and driven more than 100 miles from Phoenix to collect some of my father's things and bring them to the hospital, where he lay in a medically induced coma.

It had all happened so fast. I'd received a midnight call from a neurosurgeon in Phoenix—the same one who had done a fairly routine surgery to mend a break in my dad's cervical spine a few weeks earlier. Somehow, the physician said, my father had accidentally undone the surgery, leaving two screws and a metal plate floating in his neck. The doctor explained that he had operated emergently on my dad, who would be under a heavy fentanyl drip—and a halo—until he stabilized.

Although my parents had been divorced since I was two years old, my mother was there to help me that afternoon in Dad's cabin. Between coaching me through decisions like which of his T-shirts to pack and whether or not I should bring his reading glasses, she happened upon a navy blue three-ring binder, with a cover page that read "Last Will and Testament, Power of Attorney & Living Will for Larry Forsythe," in his bedroom.

He had never told me about the binder, but my name graced nearly every page within it. On a durable financial power of attorney. On a durable medical power of attorney. On a living will. And on his last will and testament. My typically nonconformist dad had prepared a collection of legal files that would become my bible in the ensuing months.

During the roughly sixteen weeks he was hospitalized, I would reread, reference, fax, scan, copy, and e-mail those documents—particularly the powers of attorney—countless times. I also thought, on nearly as many occasions, how fortunate I was that my dad, who probably struggled to pay for a law firm to draw up the papers, had done so just a year before he was unexpectedly admitted to the hospital. Without his wishes committed to paper,

I know I would not have been able to fully and confidently make decisions on his behalf. But, navy blue binder in hand, I was empowered to speak with authority to doctors, nurses, bank executives, and even the cable company, which would not have stopped the monthly payments that were dwindling his already heartbreakingly low bank account had I not been designated his financial power of attorney.

I always thought that having a sick or dying loved one meant hospital visits and flowers and tears—all of which is true—but I spent far more time on the phone with medical professionals, financial institutions, and social workers than I did crying. I imagine all of that strife would have been magnified dramatically had we not found that binder.

My dad died a year ago this month. His passing brought more challenges for me, but for a long time after, I silently thanked him for having the foresight to visit that estate-planning law firm, for considering what I'd go through when he was no longer here. It was one of the last—and best—gifts he ever gave me.

Process Oriented

Navigating the myriad steps to legally access medical-aid-in-dying drugs can be an arduous undertaking already. Some obstacles, though, are making it even more frustrating for terminally ill patients and their families.

Step No. 1: Determine Eligibility

For a person to be eligible to receive care under the law, he or she must be eighteen years or older; a resident of Colorado; terminally ill with six months or less to live; acting voluntarily; mentally capable of making medical decisions; and physically able to self-administer and ingest the lethal medications. All of these requirements must be documented by the patient and confirmed by the patient's physician, who must agree to prescribe the medication.

PROCEDURAL GLITCH
Because the law allows individual physicians to opt out of prescribing medical-aid-in-dying drugs for any reason and because some hospital systems and hospices have—in a potentially illegal move—decided not to allow their doctors to prescribe the meds, it is sometimes difficult for patients to find physicians willing to assist them.

Step No. 2: Present Oral and Written Requests

An individual must ask his or her physician for access to a medical-aid-in-dying prescription a total of three times. Two of the requests must be oral, in person, and separated by fifteen days. The third must be written and comply with the conditions set in the law (signed and dated by the patient; signed by two witnesses who attest that the patient is mentally capable of making medical decisions, acting voluntarily, and not being coerced by anyone).

PROCEDURAL GLITCH
Although mandatory waiting periods are required in all jurisdictions with medical-aid-in-dying laws, these requirements are especially challenging for patients in small towns or rural areas, where there might not be a doctor willing to participate for a hundred miles. For terminally ill patients, making two long road trips to present oral requests can be next to impossible.

Step No. 3: Get a Referral to a Consulting Physician

The law requires that once a patient's attending physician has received the appropriate requests and determined the patient has a terminal illness with a prognosis of less than six months to live, the doctor must refer the patient to another physician, who must agree with the diagnosis and prognosis as well as confirm that the patient is mentally capable, acting voluntarily, and not being coerced.

PROCEDURAL GLITCH
Once again, difficulties with finding a willing physician can cause lengthy wait times.

Step No. 4: Fill the Prescription at a Pharmacy

Colorado's medical-aid-in-dying law doesn't stipulate which drug a physician must prescribe. There are multiple options, which your doctor should discuss with you. Depending on your insurance coverage (Medicare, Medicaid, and many insurance companies do not cover the drugs), as well as which hospital system your doctor works in, getting the medication can be as simple as filling a script for anything else.

PROCEDURAL GLITCH
Not every hospital system will allow its on-site pharmacies to fill the prescriptions—HealthOne, for example, doesn't. Corporate pharmacies, like Walgreens, and grocery-store-based pharmacies often will not fill or do not have the capability to fill the prescriptions. What's more, Colorado pharmacists are able to opt out of filling the prescription for moral or religious reasons. That leaves doctors and patients in search of places to obtain the drugs once all of the other requirements have been fulfilled.

Step No. 5: Self-Administer the Medications

Although the time and place are mostly up to the patient, if he or she does decide to take the life-ending drugs, he or she must be physically able to do so independent of anyone else. Physical capability is something patients must consider, especially if their conditions are progressing quickly and could ultimately render them incapable of, for example, swallowing the medications.

PROCEDURAL GLITCH

Depending on the drug that is prescribed and the pharmacy that fills it, patients or their families are sometimes put in the position of having to prepare the medication before it can be administered. Breaking open one hundred tiny pill capsules and pouring the powder into a liquid can be taxing even under less stressful circumstances.

Step No. 6: Wait for the End

In most cases, medical-aid-in-dying patients fall asleep within minutes of drinking the medication and die within one to three hours. The law encourages doctors to tell their patients to have someone present when they ingest the lethal drugs.

PROCEDURAL GLITCH

Although most doctors who prescribe the medication do not participate in the death, it is worth asking your physician or your hospice care organization in advance about what to do in the minutes immediately after your loved one has died at home, as 78.6 percent of Coloradans who received prescriptions for life-ending meds under the law and subsequently died (whether they ingested the drugs or not) did in 2017. Someone with the correct credentials will need to pronounce death and fill out the form necessary for a death certificate (cause of death is the underlying terminal illness, not death by suicide) before a funeral home can pick up the body.

Alternative Endings

An Oregon nonprofit is Colorado's best aid-in-dying resource.

Although Oregon's Compassion & Choices is best known here as the organization that helped push Proposition 106 onto Colorado's November 2016 ballot, the nation's oldest end-of-life-options nonprofit didn't abandon the Centennial State after the initiative passed. "First, we help states enact the laws," says Compassion & Choices' Kat West, "then we stick around to help with implementation and make sure it's successful."

In Colorado, the rollout has been fairly fluid. Perfect? Certainly not. Fortunately, Compassion & Choices has been trying to smooth some of the wrinkles in the system. The biggest help so far might be its website. The nonprofit keeps its online content updated with everything a Coloradan needs to know about the state's End-of-Life Options Act. Of particular note: the Find Care tool, which lists clinics and health systems that have adopted supportive policies, since finding participating physicians, hospitals, and pharmacies is still challenging. "Patients don't have the time or energy to figure this out on their own," West says. "We do it for them."

Hospice Hurdles

Why some local hospices aren't as involved in Colorado's aid-in-dying process as you'd expect.

Despite what you might have heard, hospice is not a place where one goes to be euthanized. "That misconception is out there," says Nate Lamkin, president of Pathways hospice in Northern Colorado. "We don't want to perpetuate the thought that we're in the business of putting people down. That's not what we do." That long-standing myth of hospice care is, in part, why many Colorado hospices have declined—potentially in violation of state law—to fully participate in the End-of-Life Options Act.

By and large, the mission of hospice—which is not necessarily a place, but a palliative approach to managing life-limiting illness—has always been to relieve patient suffering and to enhance quality of life without hastening or postponing death, Lamkin explains. "This law kind of goes in opposition to that ethos," he says. To that end, like many other hospices, Pathways has taken a stance of neutrality: Pathways physicians cannot prescribe the life-ending medication, but the staff will support their patients—by attending deaths, by helping with documentation—who choose the option. "We are not participating by not prescribing," Lamkin says. "But it is the law of the land, and we fully support those who choose medical aid in dying."

Pathways is not alone in its abridged participation. Other large Front Range hospice-care providers, like the Denver Hospice, have also either taken an arm's-length stance on the practice or opted out entirely. End-of-life options advocacy nonprofit Compassion & Choices regards this as willful noncompliance, which could leave hospice providers exposed to legal action, especially considering that 92.9 percent of Colorado's patients who died following the reception of a prescription for aid-in-dying meds in 2017 were using hospice care to ameliorate symptoms and make their deaths as comfortable as possible. But, says Compassion & Choices spokesperson Jessie Koerner, when hospices abstain from fully supporting medical aid in dying, it strips away Coloradans' rights—rights to which the terminally ill are legally entitled.

Filling More Than Just Prescriptions

After spending years at a chain pharmacy, Denverite Dan Scales opened his own shop in Uptown so he could better serve his customers. *5280* spoke with him about being one of the few pharmacists in Colorado meeting the needs of medical-aid-in-dying patients.

5280: Of the roughly seventy medical-aid-in-dying prescriptions written in Colorado in 2017, Scales Pharmacy filled approximately twenty-two of them. Why so many?

DAN SCALES: As a pharmacist, you have no obligation to fill a script that's against your moral code. So there are many pharmacists who won't fill the drugs. Also, many chain pharmacies—like Walgreens—don't mix compounds, which means they can't make the drug cocktail a lot of physicians prescribe. That leaves independent pharmacies like ours.

5280: You don't have any objections to the state's End-of-Life Options Act?

DAN SCALES: I really believe we kinda drop the ball at the end of life. We do a poor job of allowing people to pass with dignity. I won't lie, though: After filling the first couple of prescriptions, I did feel like I helped kill that person. I needed a drink. But talking with the families after helps.

5280: You follow up with your patients' families?

DAN SCALES: Yes. We ask them to call us after their loved one has passed. We want to know how it went, how the drugs worked, how long it took, was everything peaceful? I'd say about 30 percent call us to offer feedback. It helps us know how to better help the next person. You have to understand, this is not a normal prescription; we talk with these people a lot before we even hand them the drugs. We get to know them.

5280: If you could change one thing about the process, what would it be?

DAN SCALES: It's frustrating that there's not more pharmacy participation in our state. We're having to mail medications to the Western Slope because people can't find the services they need.

Final Destination

She couldn't travel with him this time, but a Lakewood woman supported her husband's decision to go anyway.

They met online, way back in the fuzzy dial-up days of 1999. J and Susan (Names have been altered to protect the family's privacy.) weren't old, exactly, but at fifty and forty-nine, respectively, they had both previously been married. They quickly learned they had a lot in common. They were both introverts. Each had an interest in photography. And they loved to travel, especially to far-flung places, like Antarctica. After about two years of dating, they got married in a courthouse in Denver. For the next seventeen years, they saw the world together and were, Susan says, "a really great team."

The team's toughest test began in fall 2017. Susan says she should've known something was wrong when she asked J if he wanted to go on an Asia-Pacific cruise and he balked. Upon reflection, Susan realized J likely hadn't been feeling well. "That hesitation was a clue," she says. The diagnosis, which came in January 2018, was a devastating one: stage three-plus esophageal cancer. It was, as Susan puts it, "a cancer with no happy ending."

It would also be, Susan knew, a terribly difficult situation for J to manage. He had never been able to stand not being healthy; she was certain he wouldn't tolerate being truly sick. And esophageal cancer makes one very, very sick. The tumors make swallowing food difficult, if not impossible. As a result, some sufferers lose weight at an uncontrollable clip. They can also experience chest pain and nasty bouts of acid reflux. J knew he was dying—and that he didn't want to go on living if he could no longer shower or go to the bathroom alone or be reasonably mobile. He broached the topic of medical aid in dying with Susan in February. "Honestly, I had already thought about it," she says, "so I told him I thought it was a great idea."

As a Kaiser Permanente Colorado patient, J had access to—and full coverage for—the life-ending drugs. The process, Susan says, was lengthy but seamless. J got a prescription for secobarbital and predose meds; they arrived by courier to their house in April. Having the drugs in hand gave J some peace. He wasn't quite ready, but he knew he was in control of his own death. He would know it was time when he began to feel like his throat would be too tight to swallow the drugs—or when he became unable to care for himself.

That time came in late June. He was weakening, and he knew it. Having decided on a date, J had one last steak dinner with his family on the night before his death. "He was actually able to get a few bites down," Susan says. "He was also able to have a nice, not-too-teary goodbye with his stepchildren. It was wonderful."

Although she was immeasurably sad when she woke the next day, Susan says seeing the relief on J's face that morning reinforced for her why medical-aid-in-dying laws are so important. She knew it was unequivocally the right decision for him—a solo trip into the unknown, but he was ready for it. At noon on June 25, J sat down on the couch and drank the secobarbital mixed with orange juice. "Then he hugged me," Susan says, "and he said, 'It's working' and fell asleep one minute later. It was really perfect. He did not suffer. It was all just like he wanted it."

Drug Stories

A numerical look at medical-aid-in-dying meds.

$3,000 to $5,000: Cost for a lethal dose of Seconal (secobarbital), one of the drugs doctors can prescribe. The price for the same amount of medication was less than $200 in 2009; the drugmaker has increased the cost dramatically since then. Many insurance companies will not cover the life-ending medication.

4: Drugs that pharmacists compound to make a lower-priced alternative to Seconal. The mixture of diazepam, morphine, digoxin, and propranolol, which is reportedly just as effective as Seconal, costs closer to $500 (predose medications included).

5: Ounces of solution (drugs in powder form that are dissolved in a liquid) a medical-aid-in-dying patient must ingest within about five to ten minutes.

2: Predose medications—haloperidol to calm nerves and decrease nausea and metoclopramide to act as an antivomiting agent—patients usually take about an hour before ingesting the fatal drugs.

10 to 20: Minutes it typically takes after the meds are ingested for a patient to fall asleep; death generally follows within one to three hours.

Uncomfortable Silence

Just because roughly 65 percent of voters approved Colorado's End-of-Life Options Act in 2016 doesn't mean Centennial Staters are completely at ease with the idea of the big sleep. Just ask these health care professionals and death-industry veterans.

> "In a perfect world, I think one should be with family at the end. There are benefits of sitting with a dying person. Compassion means 'to suffer with.' Sometimes that suffering isn't physical; it's emotional. A lot of healing can happen at the end."
>
> —Dr. Michelle Stanford, pediatrician, Centennial

> "If people's existential needs and pain are addressed—things they need to talk to their doctors and family about—natural death can be a beautiful thing. It doesn't have to be scary. In American society, we don't talk about death and dying. It's because we fear it. We are afraid of the anticipated pain, of having to be cared for. In other cultures, there is more family

support and there is no thought of being a burden. This is a part of life, part of what should naturally happen."

—Dr. Thomas Perille, internal medicine, Denver

"Doctors don't die like our patients do. We restrict health care at the end of our lives. My colleagues don't do the intensive care unit and prolonged death. We, as doctors, are not doing a good job helping patients with this part of their lives. Dying in a hospital is the worst thing ever. There is an amazing difference dying at home around friends and family."

—Dr. Cory Carroll, family practice physician, Fort Collins

"Most people are unprepared for what needs to happen when a death occurs. Those who choose to lean toward the pain with meaningful ritual or ceremony are the ones I see months later who are moving through this process toward healing. The ones who think that grief is something that occurs between our ears are the ones who struggle the most. Sadly, we live in a society and a culture where grieving and the authentic expression of emotion is sometimes looked down upon."

—John Horan, president and CEO of Horan & McConaty
Funeral Service, Denver

"We only die once, so let's do it right. When death happens, whether it's our own or a loved one or someone we know, it's not just their death that we're acknowledging, but it's life that we are all acknowledging. I think it's helpful and healthy to honor death because in doing so, we are helping to celebrate life."

—Brian Henderson, funeral celebrant, Denver

63: Percentage of Americans, eighteen years or older, who die in hospitals and other institutional settings, like long-term care facilities and hospices. In 1949, however, statistics show that only 49.5 percent of deaths occurred in institutions. Because death in the home has become more uncommon, experts say, few Americans have direct experience with the dying process and that separation has, in part, led us to fear, misunderstand, and essentially ignore the end of life as an important stage of life itself.

Sources: Centers for Disease Control and Prevention; American Psychological Association

What Remains

While there are myriad ways to die, in Colorado there are only a few methods by which your body can (legally) be disposed: entombment, burial, cremation, or removal from the state. We spoke with Centennial State funeral homes and cemeteries to understand the options. Just remember: Colorado law says the written wishes of the deceased must be followed, so discuss what you want with your family ahead of time so they aren't surprised.

Burial

Typical cost: From about $5,000 for a casket and full funeral service, plus about $5,000 for cemetery fees (plot, headstone, etc.)

What you need to know: In Colorado, a funeral home cannot move forward with a burial (or cremation or transportation across state lines) until a death certificate is on file with the county and state, which normally takes a few days. The funeral home will need information like social security numbers and the deceased's mother's maiden name to begin the process. Further, state law requires that if a body is not going to be buried or cremated within twenty-four hours, it must be either embalmed (using chemicals as a preservative) or refrigerated, so make sure your loved ones know what you prefer. Your family can opt to have your body prepared at a funeral home and then brought home for a viewing or service, though. Finally, federal law mandates that your family be given pricing details about caskets, cemetery fees, and the like before they make a decision, so they are prepared for the costs.

Cremation

Typical cost: From about $600 for transportation, refrigeration, and cremation; additional fees for urns, memorials, or funeral services

What you need to know: Choosing cremation does not preclude having a funeral; many people opt to have funeral services and then have the body cremated. (In this case, you'll still need a casket, but you can rent one instead of purchasing it.) Once you've gone the ashes-to-ashes route, you can't be scattered willy-nilly on federal land, in part because straight cremains are not healthy for plants. For example, your family will need to apply for a free permit—which stipulates how and where ashes can be spread—if you'd like to have your cremains placed inside Rocky Mountain National Park. The most popular national park in Colorado got more than 180 such requests last year.

Green Burial

Typical cost: From about $1,500.

What you need to know: Only one Colorado cemetery (Crestone Cemetery) and handful of funeral homes (like Fort Collins's Goes Funeral Care & Crematory) have applied for and been certified by the Green Burial Council. That doesn't mean there aren't various shades of "green" burial available throughout Colorado, though, at places such as Littleton's Seven Stones Chatfield–Botanical Garden Cemetery and Lafayette's the Natural Funeral. Among the greener ways to go: avoid embalming (so the harmful chemicals don't seep into the ground upon decomposition); opt for a simple shroud or biodegradable casket; have your grave be dug by hand, instead of with machinery, which comes with a carbon footprint; or select a cemetery or cremation garden that uses environmentally friendlier plants for landscaping (for example, Seven Stones uses rhizomatous tall fescue for its meadow, which requires less water to maintain).

Smithsonian

FINALIST—FEATURE
WRITING

*This story is about the lionfish:
"With its bold stripes and
extravagant fins, its regal bearing
and magisterial stillness, every
lionfish is a hand-lacquered
eleventh-century Japanese fan,"
writes Jeff MacGregor. "It is a diva,
a glamourpuss, a showoff." The
bad news? "The lionfish has Florida
in a noose, and from Mobile,
Alabama, to Cape Hatteras, North
Carolina, the lionfish is a blight, a
plague, an epidemic." The good
news? "Lionfish is delicious." This
story is also about spear fishing,
Whole Foods, mermaids sporting
forty-pound silicone tails, and
280-word sentences that unreel
with dazzling clarity. A writer at
large at* Smithsonian, *MacGregor
is the author of "Sunday Money:
Speed! Lust! Madness! Death!
A Hot Lap Around America with
Nascar." A frequent National
Magazine Awards finalist,*
Smithsonian *received its first
nomination in Feature Writing,
the most competitive of all Ellies
categories, for "Taming the
Lionfish."*

Jeff MacGregor

Taming the Lionfish

Friday

We were somewhere around Pensacola Pass, on the edge of the Gulf of Mexico, when the over-the-counter drugs failed to take hold.

Just after sunrise the seas are running two or four or six feet and at the mouth of the Gulf where the bay opens up and the tide meets the wind from the east and the west and the north and the south is a washing machine of razorback crests and sub-basement troughs, waves running horizon to horizon, some as big as houses, whitecaps peeling off the long rollers, the water every blue and every green, the rise and fall of our little boat a series of silences, groans, engine noises and cymbal crashes as we pitch and roll and the whole boatload of gear works itself loose from the fittings, the tanks and the spears and the wet suits and the vests and the fins and the buckets and the coolers and computers and the compasses and regulators and the backups to the back-ups to the backups, every dive system three times redundant now soaked and streaming, bobbing in the bilges, and the waves coming over the side, the top, the stern, the bow, all of us pitching and yawing and rolling and moaning and swearing and all that gear floating at our ankles with the bags of white cheddar pop-corn and the wasabi and the Red Vines, all of us grabbing for the gunwales or the rails or each other, Captain Andy at the wheel calm as a vicar, Barry with his feet planted, singing at the top of his lungs, "Welcome back, my friends, to the show that never ends," and the planetary surge of 500 quadrillion gallons of angry water pouring through the tiny nautilus of my inner ear on its way to my stomach. I lean over the side and throw up again. Doubled over the transom, John casually does likewise. The motion-sickness tablets do nothing.

We all laugh.

We're here to hunt lionfish.

.　　　.　　　.

Before we get to the marine biology, this has to be said: The lionfish is one of the most beautiful animals alive. With its bold stripes and extravagant fins, its regal bearing and magisterial stillness, every lionfish is a hand-lacquered eleventh-century Japanese fan. It is a diva, a glamourpuss, a showoff. If you ran a hedge fund in Greenwich or Geneva or Tokyo, the first fish you'd buy for that 100,000-gallon aquarium in your lobby would be a lionfish. It is in every respect spectacular. And in this hemisphere it is an eco-killer, a destroyer of worlds.

Four-hundred-twenty-two words of marine biology boiler-plate, a NOAA cribsheet, and a warning:

> In the southeast U.S. and Caribbean coastal waters the lion-fish is an invasive species. It competes for food and space with overfished native populations. Scientists fear lionfish will kill off helpful locals such as algae-eating parrotfish, allowing sea-weed to overtake coral reefs already stressed by rising water temperatures and bleaching. Lionfish kill off other small cleaner-fish, too, which increases the risk of infection and dis-ease among sport fish and cash fishery populations. In U.S. waters, lionfish stocks continue to grow and increase in range.

> Lionfish have no known predators here and reproduce all year long; a mature female lionfish releases roughly two million eggs a year, which are then widely dispersed by ocean currents.

Two million eggs a year.

Scientific Name: *Pterois volitans* (red lionfish)

Unscientific, badass nickname: devil firefish

Identification: Lionfish have distinctive brown and white or maroon and white stripes covering the head and body. Tentacles protrude above the eyes and below the mouth. They have fanlike pectoral fins and long dorsal spines. An adult lionfish can grow as large as eighteen inches.

Native Range: The South Pacific and Indian oceans, where natural predators, including grouper, keep their population in check.

Habitat: Lionfish are found in the tropics, in warm water, and in most marine habitats. Lionfish have been found in or on hard-bottom ocean floor, mangrove, sea grass, coral and artificial reefs at depths from 1 to 1,000 feet.

Nonnative Range: Since the 1980s, lionfish have been reported in growing numbers along the southeastern United States coast from Texas to North Carolina. Juvenile lionfish have been collected in waters as far north as Long Island, New York.

Lionfish are eating machines. They are active hunters that ambush their prey by using their outstretched pectoral fins to corner them. If lionfish are unable to adapt to declines in their prey, their population might decrease. In the short term, however, they will turn to cannibalism.

Warning! Lionfish spines deliver a venomous sting that can last for days and cause extreme pain. Also sweating, respiratory distress, and even paralysis. Lionfish venom glands are located in the spines on the top and the sides and the bottom of the fish. They can sting you even after the fish is dead. The venom is a neurotoxin. Once the spine punctures the skin, the venom enters the wound through grooves in the spine. If stung, seek medical attention immediately.

The guys on the dock will tell you that the sting of a lionfish is like "getting hit hard by a hammer, then injecting the bruise with hot sauce." Wear gloves.

How they got here no one really knows. Like giant shoulder pads and the music of Frank Stallone, some things about the 1980s remain inexplicable. The arrival in American waters of the lionfish is one of these mysteries. There are a couple of recurring stories, but they don't really add up to a truth. The first is that some home aquarium owner emptied a few of them into the ocean one night—the narrative equivalent of the New York City alligator-down-the-toilet story. Another story suggests a big resort hotel in the Caribbean mishandled the filtration setup on its giant destination aquarium and pumped them out into the sea. Or that a breeding pair escaped during Hurricane Andrew. Maybe they arrived here in the water ballast of big cargo ships from the Pacific.

Now they're everywhere. Like locust. That's the bad news. The lionfish has Florida in a noose, and from Mobile, Alabama, to Cape Hatteras, North Carolina, the lionfish is a blight, a plague, an epidemic. A perfect evolutionary machine for eating and ruin, every lionfish is the lace-collared cutthroat in your underwater Elizabethan costume drama.

The good news? Lionfish is delicious.

·　　·　　·

All this I learned at the Smithsonian Marine Station in Fort Pierce, Florida. They have a team of molecular scientists and marine biologists there, and benthic ecologists and visiting zoologists and doctoral candidates and postdocs and technicians and reef experts. They have a research laboratory and a public aquarium where a couple of times a day you can watch a little lionfish get fed. This is out on Seaway Drive, and on a hot spring morning the light here is like the aftermath of a blast. In fact, when you drive from here to Pensacola, all of Florida feels like a trick of the light. Overbright or too dark, at once too soft and too sharp, underwater or above it, you're never sure what you're seeing. At noon the asphalt shimmers and the sand dazzles, and at midnight the stars swim in an ink-black heaven above the cypress and the slash pine. Is that a Disney castle rising in the distant murk, or just a jet of swamp gas? From Daytona to the Everglades to the Keys, from Universal Studios to the Fountain of Youth, Florida is a fever dream, an unreliable narrator. Florida is a fiction. It is an impossible place.

.   .   .

And that's how we all wound up in this little boat at the Lionfish World Championship. One of dozens of lionfish rodeos or derbies or hunts around the state, events like this are the first line of defense against the lionfish takeover. The premise is simple: Whoever spears the most lionfish wins. Sponsored by Coast Watch Alliance and the Florida Fish and Wildlife Conservation Commission, Reef Rangers, the Gulf Coast Lionfish Coalition, and about a dozen others, over the last few years this tournament has cleaned thousands of lionfish out of the local ecosystem. In 2016 alone it brought in more than 8,000 fish—in a weekend. I'm here to watch one of five or six teams kill every lionfish it sees.

Even before dawn the marina is loud with gulls and banging halyards and happy obscenity. As the sun rises so does the wind, and wary talk of what a wild, e-ticket ride the day's going to be. Before any of us steps aboard, the little boat is already filled with gear, and we're still lashing coolers to the deck. There isn't a spare inch anywhere. But off we go.

Capt. Andy Ross is a fidget spinner of a man, quiet, apparently motionless, but going a thousand miles an hour. He is fit and tanned and of some glorious sunworn indeterminate middle age. He is one of the tournament founders, too, and master and commander of the *Niuhi*, a twenty-five-foot catamaran dive boat with a small deckhouse and cabin and twin Yamaha 150s to push us out into the Gulf. Generally soft-spoken, from time to time while I'm redistributing my breakfast over the portside gunwale, he calls out to me with a small sideways smile, "Sporty today!"

Why yes, Cap'n, yes it is.

On the other hand, Barry Shively, the mate and dive master, never stops talking. Never stops. Never stops singing or storytelling. He is a dynamo, what grandma would have called a real live wire. He dives and spearfishes mostly for fun. His day job is repairing MRI and CT scanners and other nuclear imaging equipment. He is exactly the kind of charming knucklehead savant you need on a day like today. I was able to sit upright long enough to ask him to describe the early days of the lionfish siege in this part of the Gulf.

"So, we first started seeing them showing up here probably four or five years ago. The first year we seen like one or two. And we'd alert FWC and they were like, 'Well where'd you see it? Let's get some maps going.' Then the science started and every time we came in they wanted to know. . . . I mean they were meeting us at the dock asking questions. So, concern was growing, and we didn't realize it was going to bloom like this. The next year, it quadrupled. And then the year after that, it was 100-fold more than the prior year. It's been an explosion and they have just taken over."

John McCain, smiling a wide smile and vomiting calmly across from me, is a sales manager from Dive Rite, a manufacturer of scuba equipment. Next to him is Carl Molitor, an underwater photographer, calm as the Buddha and somehow eating a breakfast of yogurt and fruit. Next to Carl is Allie ElHage, who has been trying very hard to light a cigarette in the wind for the last few minutes. He invented and makes and sells the Zookeeper, a length of wide, clear PVC pipe with a plastic flange at one end and a Kevlar bag at the other, into which one stuffs one's speared lionfish. He is smiling, too, and when he leans back and tips his face to the sun he is a picture of absolute happiness. Alex Page, salon owner and paralegal and recreational slayer of lionfish, sits on the midships gear locker with the peaceful mien of a man on his third morning at the spa. Everyone on this little boat but me is a lionfish serial killer.

The last thing you see of Pensacola as you motor out into the Gulf are the checkerboard water towers at the Naval Air Station. That's what the town is famous for, naval aviators. Fighter jocks. And for prizefighter Roy Jones Jr. Otherwise, the travel posters are filled with beaches, seafood, board shorts, and T-shirts and flip-flops. It's the panhandle Eden.

Here's how it works, even on a day as rough as this. You and your buddies head out past the horizon, about eighteen miles. You'll locate by GPS and by chart and by fish-finder an underwater structure likely to harbor a population of lionfish. Some of these structures are known to every charter captain everywhere, and some are jealously guarded secrets. There aren't many coral reefs in the northern Gulf—it's mostly a hard sand bottom down there—so these underwater features are almost entirely man-made. Picture a pyramid of I-beams six or eight feet high, or a sphere the same size. The state sinks them to promote habitat for sport fishing. Most of them, anyway. There are some shipwrecks down there, too, and some "habitat" sunk by enterprising locals in less enlightened times, like rusted school bus bodies and little hillocks of old appliances.

As a charter captain, Andy is a great example of a grass-roots response to an environmental problem. He was taking folks out spearfishing for snapper and triggerfish and he was seeing more and more lionfish crowding them out of the habitats.

"It just seemed like a light suddenly came on. I had written in to someone at one of the local chambers of commerce, I think we've got a big problem here. We need to probably address it and I wasn't sure how to go about doing that. The Perdido Key Chamber of Commerce said, 'Well, we've got some funds available for special projects. Why don't we at least raise some awareness?' I go, 'That's a great idea. How do we go about doing it?' Let's put together a tournament. It was a little rough at first, but we managed to pull off four or five small tournaments the first year that we had some funding. That just got the whole ball rolling pretty fast."

With the water coming over the bow, you're not going to anchor, you're going to circle while your divers head down in twos and threes. The water out here is between 90 and 120 feet deep, so the divers breathe nitrox from their tanks, a cocktail of nitrogen and oxygen that allows them to make safer trips up and down and stay a little longer on the bottom. Program all that into your dive computer, and it gives back a precise dive profile: how long it takes to descend, how long you can stay, and how fast you can resurface. These are quick "bounce" dives, about ten minutes descending, ten minutes on the bottom, ten minutes back. And these are all very experienced divers. But even for them, it's a bruising proposition trying to pull on gear while being flung from corner to corner, falling, colliding, tripping, swearing. Did I mention they're all carrying spears? You hunt lionfish with what amounts to a modest trident, powered by a short length of surgical tubing.

That's OK, fellas, I'll wait here.

"Are we parked?" the divers yell.

"Yep," says Andy, and the guys wobble the regulators into their mouths and roll backward into the water with a splash.

And that's how we spend the day. Two or three of us always on board and two or three of us almost continually over the side hunting lionfish. Crocs and Kevlar gloves and weapons-grade sunglasses slosh around the bilge. We circle the divers' bubbles until they're ready for pickup. A lot of the exchanges at the stern ladder go like this,

"How many did you get?"

"Twenty-five or thirty."

"How many did you leave?"

"None."

Then empty the Zookeepers into the cooler, get the lionfish on ice and head for the next spot. Andy peers into the fish-finder; Barry tells another story; Allie lights another cigarette. It's all jawboning and affectionate insult and classic rock on the loud-speaker, "Radar Love" and PG-13 punch lines. Barry hauls the jumbo sandwiches out at midday and the Italian dressing and the peanut butter crackers and I excuse myself to go below. The boys are bringing up fish a dozen or two at a time. At one point, Alex brings up more than a hundred fish himself. This is why we came. He is a giant killer.

"Be afraid, lionfish, be very afraid," says Barry.

The rest of the day is a montage of iridescent water and Tintoretto sky, wisecracks and tattoos and lionfish. The coolers slowly fill, and by late afternoon we're surfing back to the pass. The wind is up and the trip home rolls like a motocross track. "I'm tired, man," says Allie to no one in particular.

"But it's addictive, man, like Angry Birds," Barry says, and we rise and fall and ride the crests home.

Somewhere far to the east of us, over the horizon, there is an all-women's team, the first ever, and from what we can make out on the radio, they've been taking many, many fish. But it's hard to know for sure; sandbagging and gamesmanship are a big part of the competition. You never want anyone to know your real numbers until the fish are totaled on Sunday. For now, the women and their lionfish are a distant rumor.

We're back at the dock just before sunset. We might have speared more than 400 lionfish. Or we might not have. I am asked to keep mum on the matter. We are met by a couple of marine biologists. These tournaments are a terrific resource for scientists. Tonight, they're checking the females for egg sacs, researching effective ways to interrupt that prodigious lionfish reproductive cycle. They'll be at it for hours, well into darkness, and will handle every one of those fish.

As it says on Barry's Zookeeper, LEAVE NO LIONFISH BEHIND.

Saturday

It's so windy today, and the surf so much worse, that most teams do not go back out. We do not go back out.

The women's team goes back out. No one has seen them yet. They remain a whisper filled with static, a ghost across the horizon, a figment. Talk of their courage and their madness is a near constant for the day.

For the rest of us, it's a hot sun and calypso on the loudspeakers and 700-horsepower pickup trucks in the parking lot.

The point of the dry-land portion of the tournament, the weekend-long lionfish festival in the small park out on the Plaza de Luna, is educational. Informational. And tasty. Once you see the banners in the little park, you begin to understand the statewide strategy for lionfish management.

"Eat 'em to beat 'em"

"Edible Invaders"

"Be the Predator"

"Remove—Eat—Report"

The exhibition tents and displays are evenly divided between things you can read and things you can eat. There are lionfish cooking demonstrations all day, given by well-known local chefs, and long lines to taste the samples. This morning it's Asian wraps done up with lionfish tenders. By noon it's a ten-minute wait to try one. One tent over, Capt. Robert Turpin of the Escambia

County Marine Resources Division is delivering an informational presentation to the crowd. "Remember folks," he says into the wind noise, "lionfish are venomous, not poisonous."

This is a central tenet of the "Eat 'em to beat 'em" master plan. Consumers don't know lionfish very well. Even though a lionfish sting is sharp and painful, the meat of the fish itself is safe to eat. Unlike fugu, Japan's riskiest delicacy, lionfish is harmless. The fish has to be handled carefully when caught and when filleted, but for customers in a restaurant or at the seafood counter of their local grocery, lionfish is no more of a threat than salmon or flounder or cod. Venomous, not poisonous, is the drumbeat of the whole weekend.

Because the only way to control the lionfish invasion in this hemisphere will be to create a market large enough to turn them into a national cash fish.

But you can't do that by spearing them one at a time. Especially not at depths greater than commercial divers can safely and routinely cull them. You need to start harvesting them in large, dependable numbers. And for that, you need to figure out how to trap them. Or kill them with submersibles, drones, or remote-operated vehicles.

Walk this way to the tent of Steve Gittings, chief scientist for NOAA's National Marine Sanctuary System. If you were asked to paint the portrait of a distinguished, thoughtful, slightly-gray-at-the-temples National Oceanic and Atmospheric Administration PhD, he'd be your guy. On his display table are a number of models of a bell trap, a kind of semiautomated snare that rests on the sea bottom, then closes over, catches and hoists up lionfish in quantity.

I asked him to thumbnail Florida's lionfish problem, just so we know.

"I think it boils down to two levels of activity that lionfish do. One is eating any small fish that they can eat, but that means those fish are not available for other fish to eat, commercial or otherwise, so that's a whole ecosystem-trophic effect. It's a collapse. Could be a collapse."

"On the other end of the spectrum," he goes on, "they're eating juveniles of the fish that would become commercially available. So, why are people not yet saying, 'There's no more grouper. There's no more snapper'? Well, it might be the juveniles of those species have not reached adulthood—and won't, because they're being eaten by lionfish. So if lionfish are eating a lot of juveniles of snapper, grouper, there's all of a sudden going to be a collapse at the level of species entering the adult phase. That will eventually show up as no more snapper-grouper."

That's it, that's the lionfish apocalypse. But Gittings is an optimist.

"I'm still hopeful that it'll be a non-apocalypse because I hope nature will figure it out. But, at least, as far as the evidence goes . . . so far, apocalypse. It could be.

"But, I have to trust in nature, because for a lot of previous invasive species, land or sea, nature eventually figures it out. With disease, with parasites, with predators. So something's going to get these things. Right now, they're taking over. They reproduce better than rabbits, eat like crazy, and nothing eats them.

"There are these places, though, where you just go, 'Where are the lionfish?' So, does that mean nonapocalypse, or does that mean they haven't gotten here yet? Does it mean they will? Does it mean they won't? Does it mean local control is taking care of the problem? I think it's that in large measure.

"Local control does do a lot of good. You hear people here talk about how they are not finding lionfish near shore. That's probably because people are shooting them. The farther offshore you get, the more fish you see.

"So, I think we have to treat it like an apocalypse, but even as a scientist I think it's going to work itself out, and become some kind of balance of nature."

And the deep-water traps?

"You can talk about local control in shallow water using divers. That's doing a good job. I think we ramp it up as much as possible to minimize anything that inhibits that from happening. But that helps us down to that depth.

"But now we've got to tackle the deep water problem. And do regional control. And how do you do that? You've got to engage lots of people, and maybe lots of different ways. I believe the fishing communities, they answer to that. I don't think that conservation people like myself can buy a bunch of ROVs and go down and shoot them and do things. The fisherman who has a good ROV or some other way of catching lionfish might do that, and that's a good thing, because they get to (A) kill fish and (B) sell fish and make money. And take the pressure off the other species while they're doing it.

"So that's why I got into the thinking about traps to deal with deep-water populations. My logic was, Let's design traps that fishermen would be comfortable with, which is mechanical. Fully mechanical, easily deployed, easily retrieved, you can put a bunch of them on a fishing boat. And then we've got to deal with the regulatory matters related to that."

In the next tent over, there's a beautiful mermaid in a chaise longue talking to children about ecology and our collective responsibility to the environment. There's a long line of kids—and their dads—waiting to speak to her.

Around the corner, I talk to Brian Asher, a diver and spearman, and one of the directors of SEALEG, a nonprofit trying to grow the lionfish business into sustainability.

"As a business problem, we have this incredible supply of lionfish. They're breeding rapidly. And on the other end, you have restaurants and grocery stores. You have this huge demand, and there's really no efficient way of connecting the two right now.

"The traps, though, haven't been available until the last two or three months when NOAA published the plans, and that's an inexpensive, easily deployable trap design. Taking commercial fishing operations, and having them focus on this would be . . . I mean, just huge gains can be made out of that. But it's convincing that fishing community, and then, on the flip side of that, convincing the public that, hey, this is something good to eat. And there's still a lot of resistance in the public."

Hence all the tastings. And "Venomous, not poisonous."

"Right, and again, we enjoy diving, we enjoy our reefs. The first time I pulled up a lionfish, and it had a shovelhead lobster baby in its stomach, it was like, all right, game on. I want to go down, and I want to spearfish for my allotment of snapper or grouper, or I want to pick up spiny lobster—those little bastards are eating what I am, eating my stuff! Well, someone needs to do something to fix that and it might as well be us."

One of the ways to break through with the public would be to get a big national retailer on board. Guess who's here this weekend with their own tent? Whole Foods Market.

Dave Ventura is the grocery chain's Florida regional seafood coordinator. The stores have been rolling lionfish out on a test basis for the last two years or so. The response has been overwhelmingly positive.

"Our customers here in Florida are very well educated about our ecosystem, our environment, are passionate about protecting them. They're very happy to hear that the Whole Foods in Florida has taken the lead on trying to be part of the solution to remove the lionfish from the water.

"What I can say is we've been selling lionfish for fifteen months and I'm happy to report we've sold over 30,000 pounds.

"You know, everybody seems to realize that the good news is we scratched the surface. We developed a market, we know there's a market. Now it's like, hey, how do we get it on scale? How do we remove the lionfish in large volume? Once we accomplish that, then I think I can say confidently that we are making a dent, making a difference. Right now, I think we've been very successful in creating a public awareness."

And Whole Foods is developing its own product lines, too, like smoked lionfish. There are a million ways to prepare it. In fact, do an image search for "whole fried lionfish." It's a centerpiece showstopper at several local restaurants, with the fins fanned golden brown in all directions. At the end of the meal, they hand out the spines as toothpicks.

So we're going to fight the rapaciousness of one species with the bottomless appetites of another. Ours. Lionfish in this hemisphere have only one enemy. Us.

But it's going to take some doing.

Because "venomous, not poisonous" sounds like something Truman Capote might have said about Gore Vidal on *The Dick Cavett Show*.

In Which I Speak to the Mermaid

Saturday night, and there's a lionfish tasting.

This is upstairs at the Bodacious Olive, a restaurant and event space on a charming old-town stretch of brick storefronts not far from the park and the tournament tents, across from a Pilates studio.

The wind howls and low clouds worry the rooftops, but inside the Edison bulbs glow and the wineglasses sparkle and the test kitchen is as snug and clean as a catalogue layout. There are forty or so of us here, sponsors and spear hunters and dive masters, wives and husbands and scientists, captains and mates and mermaids. Celebrity Flora-Bama "chef-advocate" Jon Gibson is making lionfish tacos and lionfish sashimi and talking about sustainability and lionfish deliciousness.

There's Captain Andy, and there's Allie and Brian and John and Steve. Barry isn't here. He's across town at Pensacola State for a screening of the documentary *Reef Assassin*, produced by Mark Kwapis and edited by Maribeth Abrams. It's all about the lionfish invasion, but thanks to a scheduling wormhole these two events are happening at the same time. Some of the people *at* the movie should be here. Some of the people *in* the movie are standing right in front of me. Confused, I talk to the mermaid. Her name is Moira Dobbs. She is from Plano, Texas—where she runs a mermaid school.

I'm in italics, and a business suit.

Do you find that the kids retain the things you tell them about lionfish?

"Absolutely. And what's so great is Coast Watch Alliance not only does amazing things for the lionfish invasion issue, but they also are big into marine debris awareness and cleanup. When I do these in-character performances, if they're a birthday party, if they're an event, I bring balloons, straws, fishing line, different things that I pick up at the bottom of the ocean as a diver, and I say, 'Hey, it was so nice to meet you, when I go home look at all these things that are all over my house,' and I watch it wash over these kids. And it's creating little eco-warriors."

She looks just about exactly how you'd picture a mermaid. Pale. Pretty. Lots of auburn hair. In fact, think of Ariel easing out of her twenties, on her way to a job interview, and you'll have it. But out there under the tent, on her chaise, sun bright and the bay sparkling, wearing the tail and her magnificent fin, talking to children, the illusion is complete.

So how long have you been doing this?

"Professionally, a couple years now. I host a full-time year-round professional mermaid school, that's actually in land-locked DFW, Texas."

Do you get a lot of good turnout, in Dallas-Fort Worth?

"We do, and many walks of life, for mermaid school, and that also allows me to establish a great performance troupe that does the same kind of in-character performances that I do. Birthday parties, ocean education, library readings, stuff like that."

Are you a lionfish hunter on your own time?

"I am, I am. Yes."

So you know all these guys?

"Yes. As a mermaid and a diver."

I was going to say, do a lot of the dads hit on the mermaid, when they bring the kids over?

"We get the 'Hey, speaking mythologically, I don't know if mermaids wear tops!' We call those 'merverts.' But yes, I'm all about the banter."

So the tail . . .

"That thing I was wearing today is a free-diving mono-fin embedded inside forty pounds of platinum Dragon Skin silicone. Yeah. So you can free-dive in the ocean in that thing."

Hot, though, on land.

"Yes. It is hot. It's neutrally buoyant, and really wonderful to swim in the ocean, or pool. But it's a little rough after a few hours. I do dry out. Every two to three hours, I take a thirty-minute break. You need to. Your feet are inside of that really heavy fluke. The fluke is the bottom of the tail that you see. It's kind of like being en pointe, in ballet."

So if you could tell America one last thing, as the mermaid spokesperson—

"Yes . . ."

—on behalf of the lionfish invasion awareness—

"Yes . . ."

—What would you say?

"Seek, find, and destroy, man."

• • •

Truth is, lionfish tastes pretty great. The raw flesh of the fish is opalescent, fine-grained and smooth and nearly translucent, with a flavor to match. On the tongue, uncooked, it melts fast and tastes faintly of the sea—a memory of salt rather than salt itself. Baked, broiled, fried, poached, grilled, seared, or blackened, the meat of the fish is firm and white and buttery. It takes and holds whatever flavors you throw at it, whether you're making ceviche or fish and chips. It stands up to Cajun rub and to citrus and to wasabi and to remoulade and cilantro and garlic and ginger and cumin and aioli. It won't back down from red peppers or green chilies. It is as fearless as the person cooking it.

Everyone lines up for samples. Lip-smacking ensues.

"Don't be afraid of it," Jon Gibson says low and sweet to us all. "This is a versatile fish." He's slicing fillets so thin you could read a newspaper through them if anyone still read newspapers. "Just remember, everybody, the fish is venomous, not poisonous."

And out we all go into that windy evening.

Sunday

Most of the tents were blown down overnight, so the park looks forlorn as folks work to reset for the big day. There's Captain Andy picking up chairs and tables while Adele rolls in the deep on the PA. The early crowd is sparse, but by midmorning, even under threat of rain, the little plaza is filled again, and the music rises with the smoke from the grills and the waves pound the seawall and the crowd waiting for lionfish-stuffed jalapeno poppers is as long as the line for the crawfish boil.

You hear fragments on the wind, from the chefs and the experts and the kids and their parents . . .

"they reproduce every three or four days"

"these are fantastic"

"it's really good"

"aren't they poisonous?"

"venomous"

"go tell your restaurants you want lionfish"

"there's not much I won't eat"

Early in the afternoon, it's time for the count and the presentations to the winners. Captain Andy handles the microphone and the afternoon is an inventory of his gratitude and his enthusiasm. He and the crowd are stoked.

Biggest fish speared was a little over seventeen inches.

Our boat, "Team Niuhi," finishes third, with 539 lionfish. "Full Stringer," a crew from up the road, is second, with 859 fish. Team "Hang On"—the all-women's team—wins going away, with 926 lionfish. The crowd roars and many tears are shed. Allie won't stop hugging people. For several hours.

There's a presentation of plaques and prize money and prizes, many of them quite nice, from dive gear to drones to nights out on the town, but it's pretty clearly pride everyone competes for.

Rachel Bowman is first among equals on the women's team. She is a commercial spear fisher down in the Keys and appears to be the lean, inked, freckled, and clear-eyed apex predator for the entire state of Florida.

She shoots and sells lionfish every day.

"I've got about a forty-mile range that I work, from Alligator Reef to American Shoals, and I have my spots. I have secret spots. I have public spots. The commercial fishermen in the Keys have been amazing as far as sharing their numbers with me, especially the commercial lobster guys. They know where there's big piles of rubble that other people don't know about because their traps get smacked on them. They really appreciate what I'm doing, and they help me out as much as possible. I like to think that the Whole Foods thing has made them more money because now the lionfish in their traps, they're not worth two dollars a pound anymore. Now they're worth six. dollars"

You're fighting them to a draw down there.

"Yeah, I've got commercial trap guys that tell me that last year, the lionfish numbers kind of stopped going up, and this year they've actually gone down a little bit.

"I know Dr. Stephanie Green with Oregon State University has been doing some research with the organization REEF. They found, on isolated coral heads in the Bahamas, that not only is there a decline in the lionfish population, but there's actually a resurgence of the native fish populations. What we're doing—we're never going to get rid of them—but I have to believe we're making a difference. She and I measured fish today and the whole table was covered in egg sacs. Those are egg sacs that are never going to have a chance to do any kind of damage."

What do you think of Doc Gittings's traps?

"Well, I've got a brother-in-law who's a commercial lobster trapper, and this year in three months, he pulled up 6,000 pounds of lionfish in his lobster traps. That's in sandy bottom, 200–300 feet, where divers can't go. So, maybe if he was allowed to deploy those traps when lobster season is closed, then that's another possibility."

Rachel Bowman has a diver-down flag enameled on her big toenail. She is the real reef assassin.

Grayson Shepard is the Panhandle charter captain who masterminded the women's team. Like Captain Andy, it is impossible to judge his age. He is sun-red and fit and rawboned and could be 35 or 235. He is now the Red Auerbach of lionfish, and we sat for a while to talk in the Florida Fish and Wildlife Conservation Commission motor home.

"I put together this little dream team that are just hardcore and fun as hell to hang out with. And they are dedicated and they are killers of the deep. They went with me in four-foot seas the past two days where a lot of men would not have gone. Several of my fellow charter captains canceled trips and they were freaking out. I'm like, I'm going. The girls are like 'go go go!' My buddies were on the radio like, 'Are you OK?' 'Are you all right?' I'm like, man we're fine. We're kicking ass out here."

I explained to Captain Shepard about the throwing up.

"Well they didn't throw up. The girls suited up and went down. Over and over and over again."

Captain Shepard is himself a little bit of a sentimental badass.

"This crazy little lionfish has brought together so many incredibly cool people. We all have the same screw loose in our head. That same screw makes you an interesting, easygoing kind of person. It's a little community. We all have this common obsession with lionfish. You could put all of us in a van and drive us across the country. We would get along like peas and carrots. We're best friends. When you meet us, we're all like of the same tribe. It gives us the chills."

.　　　.　　　.

Even with most teams canceling their Saturday fishing, the tournament still brought in nearly 4,000 lionfish. Turns out the only thing more rapacious on earth than a lionfish is you and me.

So I ask folks as they leave, "You think eating them might be able to help stop the invasion?"

And they'll say, "It's fantastic, I hope it helps."

or

"Fingers crossed!"

or

"It ain't gonna hurt. It's gonna help a little bit, I guess, but I don't know. That's a big Gulf out there. That's all they can do to try and stop it? I don't see how that's going to stop it."

.　　　.　　　.

For the last hour or two of the afternoon, everyone puts their feet up. After three days of work and worry and nausea, six-foot surf and hundred-foot bounces, there's finally time to sit around the tents and the trailers and drink spiced rum and tell some lies. This everyone does with great relief.

Music plays and the wind eases and the bay is a luminous green.

Andy says, "I think it went great. We had some tough obstacles and I was a little bit nervous that maybe we wouldn't have the best turnout and you know, under the circumstances, with the tough weather and all, I think we did a fantastic job and everybody really came together and they went out and worked real hard at getting their fish. They came in and they were all very supportive and they all had an awesome time and I think everything went very smoothly. I think it came out fantastic. I've been on the water long enough to know that you cannot predict the weather and even when you do, you're wrong."

Allie is still hugging people.

"Let's go eat," Andy says.

The Big Finish

So, quiet and tired, everyone caravans to the Sake Café, a sushi place a couple of neighborhoods over, eating what they speared, now set out on two long tables full of hand rolls and sashimi, chopsticks and wasabi and cold beer. The kitchen bustles, but the place isn't crowded. It's early yet, even for Sunday dinner in Pensacola. At the head of the longest table Andy's wearing that enigmatic smile, that sidewise Andy smile, but Barry is the one who stands to speak.

He thanks everyone for their hard work and for their excellent spearfishing skills and for fighting this good fight. He thanks the event sponsors for their contributions and the restaurant for making dinner. He talks about what all this means to the environment and to Florida and to him. When he talks about the camaraderie of the divers and the friendship and yes, the love, he surprises himself by choking up. He gathers himself and goes on just a little longer.

"You gotta eat 'em to beat 'em," he says at the end.

And everyone applauds.

Dolly back, roll credits, that's the last scene in your Hollywood movie.

But if you're writing a magazine story, maybe you don't end it there. Not like that. Not with sushi and a speech. Too upbeat. Too certain.

Nor can your story end with that unremarkable wind steady off the bay, not with the striking of the tents and boxing of the leftover brochures, not with the loading of the vans or the vendors rolling up their banners or emptying their grills, and not with the stragglers wandering back to the parking lot under a Sunday sky as flat and gray as gunmetal.

What you want is something to remember them all, a way to think of Florida and that crazy light and that water and those men and those women and those fish.

So maybe you'll look back, no matter where you go or what you do, and see them all forever at the dock that Friday night, the whole wrung-out, laughing, groaning boatload, Andy and Allie and Barry and John and Carl and Alex and those scientists gathered around those big boxes of fish, those big coolers filled with ice and fins and Japanese fans, the sun faltering in the west, tangled in the trees, shadows long on the ground, and the sky a low flame up there in the spreaders and the shrouds. One of the marine biologists leans down into the cooler and gingerly plucks up another lionfish. "I've got you now," she says to herself and for a second you don't know if she means one fish or the whole species and anyway you can barely hear her because Andy's got the stereo cranked on the boat and Van Halen is playing "Hot for Teacher." It's all a trick of the light, sure, too sentimental and too droll, but it's also true and that's the beauty of it.

It's a long fight. And maybe the lionfish win.

Maybe that's your ending.

Virginia Quarterly Review

FINALIST—ESSAYS
AND CRITICISM

Writes Leslie Jamison, "This is heartbreak: Rupture is huge in your heart, while the rest of the world is checking on scattered showers. Your ex can't stand the fact of your existence in the world, and your dad wants to know if you saw the Knicks game last night." And this is what the National Magazine Awards judges had to say: "Formally inventive, deeply insightful, 'The Breakup Museum' depicts the poignant sorrows of broken relationships while celebrating the plodding joys of longterm commitment." Jamison is a novelist as well as an essayist; she is now the director of the graduate nonfiction program at the Columbia University School of the Arts. Her latest collection of essays, Make It Scream, Make It Burn, was published in September 2019. "The Breakup Museum" appeared in the spring 2018 edition of Virginia Quarterly Review, one of three issues that won VQR its second National Magazine Award for General Excellence.

Leslie Jamison

The Breakup Museum

Exhibit 1: Clamshell necklace
Florence, Italy
It's a simple necklace: a tiny, brown-striped clamshell tied to a black leather cord. The shell was gathered from a beach in Italy, and attached to the cord by means of two holes drilled into the shell with a dental drill. The person who made the necklace for me was a dental student in Florence at the time. He did it secretly, in one of his classes, while he was supposed to be learning how to make crowns. I wore that necklace every single day, until I didn't anymore

The Museum of Broken Relationships is a collection of ordinary objects hung on walls, tucked under glass, backlit on pedestals: a toaster, a child's pedal car, a modem handmade in 1988. A wooden toilet paper dispenser. A positive pregnancy stick. A positive drug test. An axe. They come from Taipei, from Slovenia, from Colorado, from Manila, all donated by strangers, each accompanied by a story: In the fourteen days of her holiday, every day I axed one piece of her furniture.

One of the most popular items in the gift shop is the "Bad Memories Eraser"—an actual eraser sold in several shades—but in truth the museum is something closer to the psychic opposite of an eraser. Every one of its objects insists that something *was*, rather than trying to make it disappear. Donating an object to the museum permits surrender and permanence at once. You get it out of your home, and you make it immortal. "She was a regional buyer for a grocer and that meant I got to try some great samples," reads the caption next to a box of maple and sea salt microwave popcorn. "I miss her, her dog, and the samples, and can't stand to have this fancy microwave popcorn in my house." The donor couldn't stand to have it, but he also couldn't bear to throw it away. He wanted to put it on a pedestal instead.

When it comes to breakups, we are attached to certain dominant narratives of purgation, liberation, and exorcism: the idea that we're supposed to want to get the memories out of us, free ourselves from their grip. But this museum recognizes that our relationship to the past—its pain and ruptures and betrayals—is often more fraught, more vexed, full of ebb and pull. When I visited its permanent home in Zagreb, Croatia—housed in a baroque aristocratic home perched at the edge of Upper Town—I was on my own, though almost everyone else had come as part of a couple. The lobby was full of men waiting for wives and girlfriends who were spending longer with the exhibits. I imagined all these couples steeped in schadenfreude and fear: This isn't us. This could be us. In the guest book, I saw one entry that said simply: "I should end my relationship, but I probably won't," and fingered my own wedding ring—as proof, for comfort—but couldn't help imagining the ring as another exhibit, too.

Before flying to Zagreb, I'd put out a call to my friends—*What object would you donate to this museum?*—and got descriptions I couldn't have imagined: a mango candle, a penis-shaped gourd, the sheet music from Rachmaninoff's Piano Concerto no. 3, a clamshell drilled by a dental student, an illustration from a children's book that an ex had loved when he was young—showing a line of gray mice with thought bubbles full of the same colors above their heads, as if they were all dreaming the same dream.

The objects my friends described all reached toward these obsolete past tenses: *that time we dreamed the same dream*. They were relics from those dreams, as the museum exhibits were relics from the dreams of strangers—attempts to insist that they had left some residue behind.

Walking through the museum felt less like voyeurism and more like collaboration: Strangers wanted their lives witnessed, and other strangers wanted to witness them. I felt strangely useful, as if my attention offered proof—to the strangers who had donated these objects—that their thwarted love deserved attention. There was a deeply democratic vibe to the place, which seemed to insist that anyone's story was worth telling, and worth listening to. The donors weren't distinct, in any meaningful sense, from the observers. By contributing an item, any observer—anyone with a toaster or a toilet paper dispenser—could easily become an author. The curatorial notes quoted Roland Barthes: "Every passion, ultimately, has its spectator . . . (there is) no amorous oblation without a final theatre." The caption beside a small travel bottle of conditioner described a man named Dave: He had been "welcomed" into the open marriage of Mr. and Mrs. W.— Mrs. W., in fact, had left the conditioner behind after a weekend visit to his cabin—but after she and Mr. W were killed in a car crash, Dave was left with "no public forum to grieve." The caption seemed to be addressing me directly when it said: "You are giving Dave his public forum."

Exhibit 2: Shopping list
Princeton, New Jersey
I spent the first seven years of my twenties in serious long-term romantic relationships, and then I got my heart broken when I was 27 and never dated again. Ten years into my singleness, having moved four times since my last break-up, gotten a PhD and a job, gained 40 pounds, I was going through a box of old too-small summer clothes and slipped my hand into the back

pocket of some abbreviated jean shorts and felt a scrap of paper which turned out to be a shopping list in my heartbreaking ex's handwriting: "batteries, lg. black trash bags, Tide (small) bleach alt., g. onion." I suddenly remembered his gratuitous use of periods—oddly, always after he signed his name, every email and every letter ending with a punctuation mark of finality.

This museum of breakups began with a breakup of its own. Back in 2003, after Olinka Vištica and Dražen Grubišić ended their relationship, they found themselves in the midst of a series of difficult conversations about how to divide their possessions. As Olinka put it: "The feeling of loss . . . represented the only thing left for us to share." Over the kitchen table one night, they imagined an exhibit composed of all the detritus from breakups like their own, and when they finally created this exhibition, three years later, its first object was one salvaged from their own home: a mechanical wind-up bunny they'd called "honey bunny."

Just over a decade later, the story of their breakup has become the museum's origin myth. "It was the strangest thing," Olinka told me over coffee one morning. "The other day I was getting out of my car, right outside the museum, and I heard a guide telling a group of tourists about the bunny. He said: 'It all started with a joke'!" Olinka wanted to tell him that it hadn't been a joke at all, that those early conversations had been deeply painful, but she realized that the story of her own breakup had become a public artifact, subject to the retellings and interpretations of others. People took whatever they needed from it.

Two years after they'd moved out of their shared apartment, Dražen called Olinka with the idea of submitting their breakup installation to a local Zagreb art festival. They were rejected the first year but accepted the next, given only two weeks to plan the installation, and told they wouldn't be given space inside the gallery itself. So they got a shipping container delivered from Rijeka, a port city on the Adriatic Sea, and spent the next two weeks collecting objects. At first they were worried they wouldn't find enough, but everyone who heard about the idea responded. *I might have something for you.* Olinka met a woman under the clock tower in Ban Jelačić Square who arrived with her husband but brought an old diary filled with the name of her former lover; she met an elderly man in a bar—a wounded vet—who pulled a prosthetic leg out of a shopping bag and told the story of the social worker who'd helped him get it during the early nineties, when sanctions during the Balkan Wars made prosthetics nearly impossible to obtain. The prosthetic had lasted longer than their relationship, he said: "made of sturdier material."

When Olinka and Dražen finally found a permanent exhibition space, four years after that first exhibit, the space was in terrible shape: the first floor of an eighteenth-century palace in utter disrepair, perched near the top of a funicular railway. "We were a little bit crazy," Olinka said. "We had tunnel vision. Like when you fall in love." Dražen finished the floors and painted the walls, restored the brick arches. He did such a great job that people asked Olinka: "Are you sure you wanted to break up with this guy?"

That's the pleasing irony of the museum's premise: that in creating a museum from their breakup, Olinka and Dražen ended up forming an enduring partnership. Sitting in the museum coffee shop, Olinka and I could see the mechanical bunny in its glass case: presiding mascot and patron saint. "People think that the bunny is our object," Olinka said. "But really the museum is our object. Everything that it's become."

EXHIBIT 3: A COPY OF *WALDEN*, BY HENRY DAVID THOREAU

BUCHAREST, ROMANIA

R. and I both started reading *Walden* in the beginning of our relationship. It takes a certain amount of solitude to grow fond of *Walden*, and our relationship was a vessel where we could put both our isolations while keeping them separate, like water and oil. We were living together, but decided to sleep in different rooms, both reading *Walden* before falling asleep. It was our proxy: our bodies were separated by the wall in between our rooms, but our minds were converging towards the same ideas. By the time we broke up, neither of us had finished. Nevertheless, we continued reading it.

Every caption at the museum was an education in the limits of my vision. What looked like an Uno game was never just an Uno game. It was the Uno game that an American soldier had planned to give to his long-distance girlfriend—an Australian army widow, herself in the service, raising two small kids—but when they were finally done with their tours, and he came to Australia to meet her flight from Afghanistan, she told him she wasn't ready for a commitment. Years later, when he stumbled across this museum full of the detritus of lost loves, he decided to donate the Uno game they'd never played. He'd been carrying it with him all that time.

Some of the exhibits conjured grand historical dramas, like the love letter written by a thirteen-year-old boy escaping Sarajevo under fire in 1992: a note he'd written to Elma—who was stuck in the same convoy, in the car next to his—but hadn't had the courage to give her. He'd just given her his favorite Nirvana tape, since she'd forgotten to bring her own music. But the objects that moved me most were the ordinary ones, the toaster and wooden toilet paper dispenser, because their ordinariness suggested that every love story—even the most familiar, the most predictable, the least dramatic—was worth putting in a museum. The museum's former manager, Ivana Družetić, called it a descendant of the curiosity cabinet: "Since the discovery of that which is the smallest and the reaching of that which is the furthest, the criteria no longer seem to be craving the extreme, but rather attempting to capture all that which falls in between."

The museum's objects understood that a breakup is powerful because it saturates the banality of daily life, just as the relationship itself did: every errand, every annoying alarm-clock chirp, every late-night Netflix rental. Once love is gone, it's gone everywhere: a ghost suffusing daily life just as powerfully in its absence. A man leaves his shopping lists scattered across your days, cluttered with his personality tics and gratuitous periods, poignant in their specificity: *lg. black trash bags* summoning that time the trash bags were too small, or *g. onion*, the type necessary for a particular fish stew prepared on a particular humid summer evening. The exhibits were all vocabulary words drawn from private shared languages that I would never entirely understand—the beaten-up pot, the plastic bin—or relics from civilizations that no longer existed: a wooden toilet paper dispenser conjuring days when a young couple was constantly running out.

Some objects felt less like relics from the past and more like artifacts from unlived futures. A crumbling gingerbread cookie endured as stale eulogy for a one-day flirtation with an engaged man, one giddy afternoon spent at an Oktoberfest in Chicago, before a text arrived the next day: *It is hard for me to say this to you as you are a great girl but . . . please don't phone or text as I fear it would only cause trouble.* It was so seemingly inconsequential—the chance encounter, the dismissive text—something you'd never expect to find immortalized. And yet there it was. A single Oktoberfest mattered enough to make a woman save a gingerbread cookie until its frosting had gathered into pale broken scabs, and these scabs held the essence of the museum itself—its commitment to the oblique sadness of the "one-day thing," to attachments that might not seem worthy of commemoration, to the act of mourning what never happened rather than what did. Which is part of any breakup: grieving the enduring relationship that never came to pass, the hypothetical relationship that could have worked, the glimmering potential inside whatever actually happened. One wool sock with a regimental number came from a soldier's twenty-year affair, with a caption from his lover: "I had two children with him and we never shared a real conversation. I always thought that, one day, it would begin."

One journal at the museum, kept by a woman during one of her lover's bipolar episodes, was full of phrases repeated like mantras: *I am keeping my heart open* and *I am living in the now*, written over and over again. It was the triteness of those phrases that moved me. They weren't brilliant. They'd simply been necessary.

Exhibit 4: Envelope with single human hair
Karviná, Czech Republic
In 1993 I graduated college and taught English for a year in a coal mining village on the Polish/Czech border, a depressed, polluted, communist city in which I experienced loneliness like I'd never known before or since. The summer before I left, I met a Scottish boy named Colin at the amusement park in Salisbury Beach where he was running the ferris wheel. After the summer, we wrote letters to each other, and sometimes a letter from him was the only thing that got me through my day. He had auburn curls I adored and once when the familiar airmail-blue envelope arrived in my box I saw he had taped the flap and a single piece of his curly hair got trapped under the tape: A part of his body, his DNA, what would one day be shared with our children. After he dumped me in a pretty cowardly way—just stopped writing—I still checked my box every day and wept, then returned to my sad communist flat and wept, then looked at the envelope that held his single curly hair and wept some more.

"The museum has always been two steps ahead of us," Olinka told me, explaining that it seemed to have a will of its own from the start, an impulse to exist that lived outside of her and Dražen. It was as if all these stories had just been waiting all around them—like humidity in the air, a sky ready to rain. Immediately after their shipping-crate exhibition, Olinka and Dražen got a call from a Japanese quiz show that wanted to film an episode in their museum. But there was no museum. It was like that: people believing in the thing, wanting the thing, before it existed.

In the decade since that first shipping crate, the museum has taken many shapes: permanent installations in Zagreb and Los Angeles; a virtual museum comprising thousands of photographs and stories; and forty-six temporary installations all over the world—from Buenos Aires to Boise, Singapore to Istanbul, Cape Town to South Korea, from the Oude Kerk in Amsterdam's red-light district to the European Parliament in Brussels, all locally sourced, like artisanal grocers, stocked with regional heartbreak.

Olinka told me that the Mexico City exhibit was flooded with more than 200 donations in the first twenty-four hours, and that the French donors often narrated their own captions in the third person, while American narratives usually featured strong characters and prominent first person storylines, like little movies playing out in front of you—that all-American *I*. American curators were also much more likely to use the first-person when they talked about their exhibitions: *My collection; the donations I've gathered.* She and Dražen tried not to. It took a few years before they even explicitly introduced the backstory of their own breakup into the public narrative of their museum. They always believed the project belonged to something much larger than them, something larger than their private pain.

Objects make private histories public, but they also grant the past a certain integrity. Whenever memory conjures the past, it ends up papering over it: replacing the lost partner with memories and reconstructions, myths and justifications. But an object can't be distorted in these ways. It's still just a box of popcorn or a toaster, a hoodie that got drenched with sudden rain one night in 1997.

At another Zagreb exhibit I saw that week, this one devoted to the 1991 Serbian-Montenegrin attacks on Dubrovnik, it was the objects that felt most powerful: not the massive photographs showing pale stone forts exploded into plumes of smoke, but the small grenade shaped like a miniature black pineapple, and the crude cross a family had fashioned from pieces of an exploded artillery shell that hit their home. A soldier's pink flashlight sat beside a piece of shrapnel, a square of gauze stained with his blood, and a photo of him lying in a hospital bed with a bandage over one eye, rosary against his bare chest. His name was Ante Puljiz. Those words meant nothing to me. But that piece of shrapnel—it had been lodged inside his body.

Exhibit 5: Four black dresses
Brooklyn, New York

I would donate to the museum the four black dresses hanging in my closet: a shirtwaist, a sundress, a ribbed turtleneck, and an A-line of raw silk. Two of these dresses were given to me by my ex, and two I bought myself, but they all date from a time in my life when I imagined I could become the person I wanted to be by adopting a uniform. I thought—we both thought—that the problem of my un-femininity, my lack of interest in clothes, my general un-hipness, could be solved by my becoming one of those literary party regulars who dresses in black, makes cutting comments, and writes bestsellers. Two months before we broke up, this man said to me, "I'm just waiting to see if you become famous, because then I think I might fall in love with you." A horrible thing to say, clumsy in its attempt at honesty—yet I did see how this was what, on some level, I'd been promising him, the fantasy of a public self we'd been co-constructing. I would donate these dresses to the museum—except that I still wear them. All the time. It's just that I wear other dresses—purple, floral, geometric, pink—as well.

When I was young, before my parents split up, I believed that divorce was a ceremony just like marriage, only inverted: The couple walked down the aisle of a church, holding hands, and then—once they reached the altar—they unclasped their hands and walked away from each other. After a family friend ended her marriage, I asked her: *Did you have a nice divorce?* It seemed like a polite question. An ending seemed like something important enough to justify a ritual.

When performance artists Marina Abramović and her partner, Ulay, decided to end their twelve-year relationship—as lovers and artistic collaborators—they marked its ending by walking the length of the Great Wall of China. "People put so much effort into starting a relationship and so little effort into ending one," Abramović explained. On March 30, 1988, Abramović started walking from the eastern end of the Great Wall, the Gulf of Bohai on the Yellow Sea, and Ulay began walking from the western edge, in the Gobi Desert, and they each walked for ninety days, covering roughly 2,500 kilometers, until they met in the middle, where they shook hands to say goodbye. At a retrospective of Abramović's work in Stockholm, two video screens showed scenes from *The Lovers: The Great Wall Walk*. One screen showed Abramović walking past camels on hard dirt covered with snow, while the other showed Ulay hiking with a walking stick over green hills. The tapes were running on a continuous loop, and it seemed beautiful to me that on those screens, years after their breakup, these two lovers still walked constantly toward each other.

If every relationship is a collaboration—two people jointly creating the selves they will be with each other—this collaboration can sometimes feel like tyranny, forcing the self into the shape that might coax love, and it can sometimes feel like birth: *The self you make possible.* Sometimes the comet trail left behind—the dresses you wore, the lipstick you tried, the books you bought but never read, the bands you pretended to like—can feel like broken shackles, but sometimes it's beautiful anyway: a dress reclaimed from costume, turned into silk skin for a Saturday night.

In truth, I've been obsessed with breakups since before I was ever in a relationship. I grew up in a family thick with divorces and overpopulated by remarriages: Both sets of grandparents divorced, my mother's twice; both my parents married three times; my eldest brother divorced by forty. Divorce never seemed like an aberration so much as an inevitable stage in the life cycle of any love. But in my family the ghosts of prior partners were rarely vengeful or embittered. My mother's first husband was a lanky hippie with the kindest eyes who once brought me a dream catcher. My beloved aunt's first husband was an artist who made masks from the driftwood palm fronds he gathered from the beaches. These men enchanted me because they carried with them not only the residue of who my mom and aunt had been before I knew them, but also the spectral possibilities of who they might have become. Seventeen years after their divorce, my own parents had become so close that my mom, an Episcopal deacon, officiated my father's third marriage.

Which is all to say: I grew up believing that relationships would probably end, but I also grew up with the firm belief that even after a relationship was over, it was still a part of you, and that wasn't necessarily a bad thing. When I asked my mother what object she would contribute to the museum, she chose a shirt she had bought in San Francisco, years before I was born, with the woman she had loved before she met my father.

I grew up with the sense that a broken relationship always amounted to more than its breakage—because it might have an aftermath and also because everything that happened before it ended wasn't invalidated by the fact of it ending; because those memories, the particular joys and particular frictions and particular incarnations of self it had permitted, hadn't disappeared, though the world didn't always make room for them. To speak

of an ex too much was seen as the sign of some kind of pathol-
ogy, and the gospel of serial monogamy could have you believe
that every relationship was an imperfect trial run, useful only as
preparation for the relationship that finally stuck. In this model,
a family full of divorces was a family full of failures. But I grew
up seeing them as something else, grew up seeing every self as
an accumulation of its loves, like a Russian nesting doll that held
all of those relationships inside.

Exhibit 6: Paisley shirt
San Francisco, California
It was sometime in 1967. We bought our paisley shirts from
an outdoor rack in Haight-Ashbury. This was in the early
heady days of our relationship; for me all the more intoxicat-
ing as it was my first lesbian love affair. Our shirts almost
matched, but not quite, mine was psychedelic pink and hers
purple. They were definitely first worn at a Jefferson Airplane
concert, though the shirt carries memories of places it never
went: a year backpacking and picking crops in Europe, leading an olive picker strike in Provence, a camping trip in Death
Valley where we watched the sun set on one horizon while the
moon rose on the other. It was all so good and right and full
of hope, until it wasn't. I never understood why we ended,
although my wanting children probably had something to do
with it. The last time I saw her was at Gay Pride Day in Washington D.C. in 1975. That's a long time ago but the paisley shirt
has stayed with me. It reminds me who I once was.

When I was a kid, I loved a book called *Grover and the Everything
in the Whole Wide World Museum*. In the Whole Wide World
Museum, Grover visits "The Things You See in the Sky Room"
and the room full of "Long Thin Things You Can Write With,"
where a carrot has mistakenly ended up, so he returns it to an

elegant marble pedestal in the middle of the otherwise empty "Carrot Room." As Grover reaches the end of the exhibits, he wonders: "Where did they put everything else?" That's when he reaches the wooden door marked: "Everything Else." When he opens it, of course, it's just the exit.

When I left the Museum of Broken Relationships, everything on the streets of Zagreb seemed like a possible exhibit, an object that had been part of a love affair or that might be someday: a garden gnome grinning in front of lace curtains; purple modeling clay formed into uneven balls on a windowsill; orange plastic ash trays near the top of the funicular railway; every toothpick sticking out of the sausages roasting on an outdoor griddle in Strossmarket; every cigarette butt in the clogged metal street grate on Hebrangova ulica; the scab as large as an apple on an old man's exposed shin, as he rode a motorbike with an old woman gripping his waist. Perhaps someday she would wish she'd saved that scab as something to remember him by.

The cloudless Zagreb day held possible heartbreak like a distant ticking bomb. Every stranger carried the coiled history of his own great loves, opaque and untold: the old man with a white beard in Ban Jelačić Square, cranking by hand a wooden contraption that spun children in four woven baskets. What heartbreak had he known? Or the three young men walking down Radićeva ulica, eating identical ears of steaming corn—all tall and blond, like fairy-tale brothers, unbreakable. How had they been broken? I paused at the Stone Gate, a tunneled crook in the road with an extravagant gated altar to the Virgin Mary and a set of wooden pews facing its trough of candles, where elderly women sat with closed eyes or knelt to make the sign of the cross. It smelled like wax and smoke. What were these women praying for? Every silent stranger concealed a thousand secret needs or wounds, invisible and consuming, as she ushered her own private prayers up to God.

When I saw a man and woman sharing a bag of popcorn in Zrinjevac Park, she sitting on his lap with her legs wrapped around his waist, I wondered if someday, once everything was broken, they would remember the accessories of this particular day like soil samples: her sunglasses, his sneakers. I imagined their popcorn on a pedestal, with a spotlight shining on it—*Bag of popcorn; Zagreb, Croatia*—captioned by the story of another woman or another man or simply another year, how it dimmed exuberance into routine.

I could summon my own lost loves as an infinite catalogue: a pint of chocolate ice cream eaten on a futon above a falafel shop; a soggy tray of chili fries from the Tommy's at Lincoln and Pico; a plastic vial of pink-eye medicine; twenty different T-shirt smells; beard hairs scattered like tea leaves across dingy sinks; the three-wheeled dishwasher tucked into the Iowa pantry I shared with the man I thought I would marry. But perhaps the deeper question is not about the objects themselves—what belongs in the catalogue—but about why I enjoy catalogueing them so much. What is it about the ache that I enjoy, that etched groove of remembering an old love, that vein of nostalgia?

After breaking up with my first boyfriend, when we were both freshmen in college on opposite sides of the country, I developed a curious attachment to the sadness of our breakup. It was easier to miss the happiness of being together when we were no longer together. It was certainly easier than muddling through what our relationship had turned into: something strained by distance, and the gap between the different people we were becoming. Rather than sitting through stilted phone conversations and the hard work of trying to speak to each other, I could smoke my cigarettes outside at night in the bitter Boston cold, alone, and miss Los Angeles, and what it had been like to fall in love there: warm nights by the ocean, kissing on lifeguard stands. I was more comfortable mourning what the relationship had been than I'd been inhabiting the relationship itself. I loved the way sadness felt pure and ascetic: smoking a lot and eating nothing and listening to sad songs on repeat. That sadness felt like a purified bond, as if I was more connected to that man in missing him than I'd ever been while we were together. But it was more than that, too: The sadness itself became a kind of anchor, something I needed more than I'd ever needed him.

Exhibit 7: Steel guitar slide
Fayetteville, West Virginia

The most potent relationship object in my possession is an old steel guitar slide from the 1920s. It's a bar slide—or tone bar— meaning a simple chunk of chromed steel or brass, its original manufacture stamp worn away by constant fretting. My ex, a person of both exceptional musical ability and unusually destructive behavior, gave it to me (probably in a fit of the latter). I think it might have been his most prized possession, and he didn't tend to have many possessions. We were together for six years when I was very young, and the whole thing ended with me in a battered women's shelter. I can't quite manage to get rid of the tone bar, though, and of course I think about all the blues that have poured through it over time: his, mine by way of his. It still seems more his than mine, though—my fingers don't even fit its edges—and I'd gladly return it to him if he wanted it back.

Olinka believes that "melancholy has been unjustly banished from the public space" and told me she mourns the fact that it has been driven into ghettos, replaced by the eerie optimism of Facebook status updates. A guitar slide can hold the blues, *his and mine by way of his*, or a museum can hold the blues, insisting we need to make room for them. Olinka has always imagined museums as "civic temples where melancholy has the right to exist," where sadness can be understood as something other than a feeling meant to be replaced. She doesn't like when people praise her own museum's "therapeutic value." It suggests that sadness needs curing and denies its beauty. Her resistance made me think of a short story by Denis Johnson, the moment when its narrator hears the screaming of a woman whose husband has just died and thinks: "She shrieked as I imagined an eagle would shriek. It felt wonderful to be alive to hear it! I've gone looking for that feeling everywhere."

For fifteen years of my life, between my first breakup and my last one, I'd been committed to a belief in sadness as a rarefied state—a kind of affective distillery that could summon the strongest and purest version of me. But walking through Zagreb that week, two-and-a-half years married and two months pregnant, I was not looking for places to smoke quietly and feel lonely, scraping out my insides with the raw tobacco of unfiltered European cigarettes. I was looking for fresh fruit that might satisfy my sudden and overwhelming cravings: a paper bag of cherries from the market, or donut peaches so ripe their juice spilled onto my dress the moment my teeth punctured their skin.

I'd always given up on relationships once they seemed to lose their early states of unfettered love and unbridled passion. I found the aftermath of that early glow muddy and compromised. But getting married had felt like a commitment to another kind of beauty: the striated beauty of continuity, letting a relationship accrete its layers over the years, showing up to love in all of its evolving states, in its difficulty as well as its giddiness, staying inside something long enough to hold its past rough patches like talismans: *This has another side.*

Back in my hotel room, my phone buzzed with a message from a friend who was waiting at an airport in Colorado to meet the flight of a man she was falling in love with, and then a text from another friend: *We just broke up. Are you around? Just don't want to be alone all weekend.* The world is always beginning and ending at once: Icarus falls from the sky while someone else swipes right.

At the museum's pop-up installation in Boise, one man donated an answering machine that played a message from his ex—cursing him out, calling him an asshole—and then a message from his dad, talking about something as ordinary as the weather, and then another message from his ex, calling him an asshole all over again. This is heartbreak: Rupture is huge in your heart, while the rest of the world is checking on scattered showers. Your ex can't stand the fact of your existence in the world, and your dad wants to know if you saw the Knicks game last night. *We just broke up. Are you around? Just don't want to be alone all weekend.* The appeal of the museum is also about this: wanting company, wanting to turn the experience of becoming solitary into something social instead.

French conceptual artist Sophie Calle explained the premise of her 2007 installation *Take Care of Yourself* like this:

> I received an email telling me it was over.
> I didn't know how to respond
> . . .
> It ended with the words, "Take care of yourself."
> And so I did.
> I asked 107 women . . . to interpret this letter.
> To analyze it, comment on it, dance it, sing it.
> Dissect it. Exhaust it. Understand it for me.

The exhibition was composed of the chorus of their reactions: A "researcher in lexicometry" noted a lack of agency in the breakup e-mail's grammar. A proofreader highlighted its repetitions. A lawyer deemed the ex guilty of deceit. A criminologist diagnosed him as "proud, narcissistic, and egotistical."

Witnessing breakups and asking mine to be witnessed have been part of every deep friendship of my life, the act of collaborating as close readers, soothsayers, tea-leaf translators, alternate-narrative-makers: *darlin, can i beg you for a read on this?* a friend wrote once, forwarding an e-mail from a man she'd just broken up with. *i'm struggling to be sure i'm not being a hysterical*

woman . . . could just use someone else's eyes on this exchange, for
total sense of closure. crazy grateful for you . . . The breakup as
social experience isn't kiss-and-tell so much as a desire not to be
alone in facing a story that's now ended: Kicked out as character,
you become a reader, parsing the wreckage. It feels so much better not to read alone.

EXHIBIT 8: BOTTLE OF CRYSTAL PEPSI
(EXHIBIT MISSING)
QUEENS, NEW YORK

After my big broken love—the ending I knew would be my
biggest, the life I realized I wouldn't live—I met a wonderful
man who lived in Queens. He took me to trivia night at his
local bar in Astoria. He took me to a Christmas party at his
law offices in midtown. He took me to the Blazer Pub, near
his childhood home upstate, where we ate burgers and played
shuffle bowling. I knew he wasn't "the one" but also suspected
I no longer believed in "the one"—not because I'd never met
him, but because I thought I had met him, and now we were
done. The lawyer was an experiment in all the things I'd never
thought I wanted. He made me laugh. He made me feel comfortable. We ate comfort food. We made pancakes with rasp-
berries and white chocolate chips and watched movies on
weekend mornings. He found old re-runs of *Legends of the
Hidden Temple*, the stupid kids' game show we'd both loved
when we were young, and gave me a ten-year-old bottle of
Crystal Pepsi he'd found online—my favorite soda back in the
nineties, discontinued for years. He was remarkable, but
I couldn't ever quite see him—or see that—because I never
really believed in us. The constancy of his devotion started to
feel like a kind of claustrophobia. Nothing about us made
me feel challenged. It was like he taught me how much I
struggled to live inside love—to understand something as
love—without difficulty.

I thought of donating my bottle of Crystal Pepsi to the museum, as a memento of my last breakup before marriage, but I never put it in my luggage. I just left it at home, on my bookshelf. Why did I keep it there? It had something to do with wanting to acknowledge the man who'd given it to me: I hadn't given him enough credit while we were together, and keeping his last gift was a way of granting him credit in the aftermath. I wanted to acknowledge how our relationship had given me giddiness after years of fighting a relationship that wasn't working; how it had suggested that the things I'd always thought I wanted—charisma, elusiveness—weren't necessarily the things I needed.

For all the objects donated to the Museum of Broken Relationships—more than 3,000, over the years—I also wonder about the invisible ghost museum lurking in its margins, with vast halls full of all the objects people couldn't stand to part with. If I'm honest with myself, keeping that bottle of Crystal Pepsi isn't just about honoring the man who gave it to me or what we shared. It also has to do with enjoying that glimpse of sadness and rupture, with holding on to some reminder of the pure, riveting feeling of being broken.

These days, my life is less about the sublime state of solitary sadness or fractured heartbreak, and more about waking up each day and making sure I show up to my commitments: skyping my husband from Zagreb and e-mailing a good-morning video to my stepdaughter. These Zagreb days are not about making myself skinny to articulate my inner anguish but about eating when I'm hungry, feeding the fetus inside me: *istrian fuži* with truffles, noodles in thick cream; seabream with artichokes; something called a domestic pie; something called a vitamins salad. These days are less about the drama of thresholds and more about continuance, showing up and muddling through; less about the grand drama of ending and more about the daily work of salvage and sustenance.

I keep the Crystal Pepsi because it's a souvenir from those fifteen years I spent in a cycle of beginnings and endings, each one an opportunity for self-discovery and reinvention and transformative emotion; a way to feel infinite in the variety of possible selves that could come into being. I keep the Crystal Pepsi because I want some reminder of a self that felt volcanic and volatile—bursting into bliss or into tears—and because I want to keep some proof of all the unlived lives, the ones that could have been.

McSweeney's

WINNER—ASME AWARD
FOR FICTION

"Skinned" was one of three works of short fiction—the others were "Vinegar on the Lips of Girls," by Julia Dixon Evans, and "Unsound," by Maria Reva—that won McSweeney's the 2019 ASME Award for Fiction. The Ellies jury said these stories "explore the imprisonment of young women by social convention" and described them as "crisp" and "melodic." Arimah's first collection of short stories, What It Means When a Man Falls from the Sky, was published in 2017; she is now working on a novel. Founded in 1998 by Dave Eggers, McSweeney's was praised by the judges for "its assured spirit—and its commitment to surprise." The 2019 jury was led by Karolina Waclawiak, an executive editor at BuzzFeed News who is the author of three novels, including the forthcoming Life Events. After the judging she exchanged e-mails with the managing editor of McSweeney's, Claire Boyle, about the role of the editor. Their conversation immediately follows Arimah's story.

Skinned, by Lesley Nneka Arimah, *and* A Conversation with Claire Boyle and Karolina Waclawiak

Skinned, by Lesley Nneka Arimah

The unclothed woman had a neatly trimmed bush, waxed to resemble a setting sun. The clothed women sneered as she laid out makeup and lotion samples, touting their benefits. "Soft, smooth skin, as you can see," she said, winking—trying, and failing, to make a joke of her nakedness. Chidinma smiled in encouragement, nodding and examining everything Ejem pulled out of the box. Having invited Ejem to present her wares, she would be getting a free product out of this even if none of her guests made a purchase.

Ejem finished her sales pitch with a line about how a woman's skin is her most important feature and she has to take care of it like a treasured accessory. The covered women tittered and smoothed their tastefully patterned wife-cloth over their limbs. They wore them simply, draped and belted into long, graceful dresses, allowing the fabric to speak for itself. They eyed Ejem's nakedness with gleeful pity.

"I just couldn't be uncovered at your age. That's a thing for the younger set, don't you think?"

"I have a friend who's looking for a wife; maybe I can introduce you. He's not picky."

Ejem rolled her eyes, less out of annoyance than to keep tears at bay. Was this going to happen every time? She looked to Chidinma for help.

"Well, I for one am here for lotions, not to discuss covered versus uncovered, so I'd like this one." Chidinma held up the most expensive cream. Ejem made a show of ringing it up, and the other women were embarrassed into making purchases of their own. They stopped speaking to Ejem directly and began to treat her as if she were a woman of the osu caste. They addressed product questions to the air or to Chidinma, and listened but did not acknowledge Ejem when she replied. Ejem might have protested, as would have Chidinma, but they needed the sales party to end before Chidinma's husband returned. It was the only stipulation Chidinma had made when she'd agreed to host. It was, in fact, the only stipulation of their friendship. *Don't advertise your availability to my husband.* Chidinma always tried to make a joking compliment of it—"You haven't had any kids yet, so your body is still amazing"—but there was always something strained there, growing more strained over the years as Ejem remained unclaimed.

The woman who had first addressed Chidinma instead of Ejem, whom Ejem had begun to think of as the ringleader, noticed them glancing at the clock, gave a sly smile, and requested that each and every product be explained to her. Ejem tried, she really did, whipping through the product texts with speed, but the clock sped just as quickly and eventually Chidinma stopped helping her, subdued by inevitable embarrassment. Before long, Chidinma's husband returned from work.

Chance was all right, as husbands went. He oversaw the management of a few branches of a popular bank, a job that allowed them to live comfortably in their large house with an osu woman to spare Chidinma serious housework. He could even be considered somewhat progressive; after all, he had permitted his wife's continued association with her unclothed friend, and he wasn't the sort to harass an osu woman in his employ. True, he insisted on a formal greeting, but after Chidinma had bowed to him she raised herself to her tiptoes for a kiss and Chance indulged her, fisting his hands in the wife-cloth at the small of her back.

But he was still a man, and when he turned to greet the women his eyes caught on Ejem and stayed there, taking in the brown discs of her areolae, the cropped design of hair between her legs, whatever parts of her went unhidden in her seated position. No one said anything, the utter impropriety of an unclaimed woman being in the house of a married man almost too delicious a social faux pas to interrupt. But as Chidinma grew visibly distressed, the ringleader called the room to order and the women rose to leave, bowing their heads to Chance, giving Chidinma's hands encouraging little squeezes. No doubt the tale would make the rounds—"the way he *stared* at her"—and Chidinma wouldn't be able to escape it for a while. The women walked by Ejem without a word, the message clear: Ejem was beneath them.

Chidinma tried to distract her husband by asking about his day. Chance continued to stare at Ejem while he answered. Ejem wanted to move faster, to get out as quick as she could, but she was conscious of every sway of her breasts, every brush of her thighs as she hurried. Chance spoke to Ejem only as she was leaving, a goodbye she returned with a small curtsy. Chidinma walked her to the door.

"Ejem, we should take a break from each other, I think," she said with a pained air of finality, signaling that this break wasn't likely to be a temporary one.

"Why?"

"You know why."

"You're going to have to say it, Chidinma."

"Fine. This whole thing, this friendship, was fine when we were both uncovered girls doing whatever, but covered women can't have uncovered friends. I thought it was nonsense at first, but it's true. I'm sorry."

"You've been covered for thirteen years and this has never been a problem."

"And I thought by this time you'd be covered, too. You came so close with that one fellow, but you've never really tried. It's unseemly."

"He's only seen me this *once* since you made it clear—"

"Once was enough. Get covered. Get claimed. Take yourself off the market. Until then, I'm sorry, but no."

Chidinma went back inside the house before Ejem could respond. And what could she say anyway? *I'm not sure I ever want to be claimed*? Chidinma would think her mad.

Ejem positioned her box to better cover her breasts and walked to the bus stop. Chidinma hadn't offered her a ride home, even though she knew how much Ejem hated public transportation—the staring as she lay the absorbent little towel square on her seat, the paranoia of imagining every other second what to do if her menstrual cup leaked.

At the stop, a group of young men waited. They stopped talking when they saw Ejem, then resumed, their conversation now centered on her.

"How old you think she is?"

"Dude, old."

"I don't know, man. Let's see her breasts. She should put that box down."

They waited and Ejem ignored them, keeping as much of herself as possible shielded with the box and the cosmetic company's branded tote.

"That's why she's unclaimed. Rudeness. Who's gonna want to claim that?"

They continued in that vein until the bus arrived. Even though the men were to board first, they motioned her ahead, a politeness that masked their desire for a better view. She scanned the passengers for other uncovered women—solidarity and all that—and was relieved to spot one. The relief quickly evaporated. The woman was beautiful, which would have stung on its own, but she was young, too, smooth-skinned and firm. Ejem stopped existing for the group of young men. They swarmed the woman, commenting loudly on the indentation of her waist, the solid curve of her arm. The young woman took it all in stride, scrolling a finger down the pages of her book.

Ejem felt at once grateful and slighted, remembering how it had been in her youth, before her waist had thickened and her ass drooped. She'd never been the sort to wear nakedness boldly, but she'd at least felt that she was pleasant to look at.

The bus took on more passengers and was three-quarters full when an osu woman boarded. Ejem caught herself doing a double take before averting her gaze. It wasn't against the law; it just wasn't done, since the osu had their own transport, and the other passengers looked away as well. Embarrassed. Annoyed. Even the bus driver kept his eyes forward as the woman counted out her fare. And when she finally appeared in the center aisle, no one made the polite shift all passengers on public transportation know, that nonverbal invitation to take a neighboring seat. So even though there were several spots available, the osu woman remained standing. Better that than climb her naked body over another to sit down. It was the type of subtle social correction, Ejem thought, that would cause a person to behave better in the future.

But as the ride progressed, the osu woman squeezing to let by passengers who didn't even acknowledge her, Ejem softened. She was so close to becoming an unseen woman herself, unanchored from the life and the people she knew, rendered invisible. It was only by the grace of birth that she wasn't osu, her mother had said to her the very last time they spoke. "At least you have a choice, Ejem. So choose wisely." She hadn't, had walked away from a man and his proposal and the protection it offered. Her parents had cut her off then, furious and confounded that she'd bucked tradition. She couldn't explain, not even to herself, why she'd looked at the cloth he proffered and seen a weight that would smother her.

At her stop, Ejem disembarked, box held to her chest. With the exception of a few cursory glances, no one paid attention to her. It was one of the reasons she liked the city, everybody's inclination to mind their own business. She picked up the pace when she spotted the burgundy awning of her apartment building. In the elevator, an older male tenant examined her out of the corner of his eye. Ejem backed up until he would have had to turn around to continue looking. One could never tell if a man was linked or not, and she hated being inspected by men who'd already claimed wives.

In her apartment she took a long, deep breath, the type she didn't dare take in public lest she draw unwanted attention. Only then did she allow herself to contemplate the loss of Chidinma's friendship, and weep.

When they were girls, still under their fathers' covering, she and Chidinma had become fast friends. They were both new to their school and their covers were so similar in pattern they were almost interchangeable. Ejem remembered their girlhood fondly, the protection of their fathers' cloth, the seemingly absolute security of it. She had cried when, at fifteen, her mother had come into her bedroom and, stroking her hair, told Ejem that it was time to remove her cloth. The only people who could get away with keeping their daughters covered for long were the wealthy, who often managed it until the girls could secure wife-cloth. But Ejem's father had grown up a poor man in a village where girls were disrobed as early as possible, some even at age ten, and it was beyond time as far as he was concerned. He knew what happened to the families of girls who stayed covered beyond their station, with the exception of girls bearing such deformities that they were permitted "community cloth" made from donated scraps. But if a girl like Ejem continued to be clothed, the town council would levy a tax that would double again and again until her father could not pay it. Then his girl would be disrobed in public, and her family shamed. No, he couldn't bear the humiliation. Things would happen on his terms.

The day Ejem was disrobed was also the day her father stopped interacting with her, avoiding the impropriety of a grown man talking to a naked girl. Ejem hadn't wanted to go to school or market or anywhere out of the house where people could see her. Chidinma, still under her father-cloth, told her (horrified, well-off) parents that she, too, felt ready to disrobe so that she and Ejem could face the world together, two naked foundlings.

Chidinma's parents had tried to spin it as piousness, a daughter disrobed earlier than she had to be because she was so dedicated to tradition. But it'd had the stink of fanaticism and they'd lost many friends, something for which, Chidinma confided, her parents had never forgiven her.

A part of Ejem had always believed they'd be claimed at the same time, but then Chidinma had secured a wife-cloth at twenty, with Ejem as her chief maid. And then Chidinma gave birth to a boy, then two girls, who would remain covered their entire lives if Chidinma had anything to say about it. And through it all, Ejem remained uncovered, unclaimed, drifting until the likelihood passed her by.

She downed a mug of wine in one huge gulp, then another, before sifting through yesterday's mail. She opened the envelope she'd been avoiding: the notice of her upcoming lease renewal, complete with a bump in monthly rent. With the money she'd earned today, she had enough to cover the next two months. But the raised rent put everything in jeopardy, and Chidinma's abandonment meant Ejem could no longer sell to her wealthy set. If she couldn't secure income some other way, a move to a smaller town would soon be a necessity.

When she'd first leased the apartment, Ejem had been working at the corporate headquarters of an architecture firm. Though her nakedness drew some attention, there were other unclaimed women, and Ejem, being very good at what she did, advanced. Just shy of a decade later, she was over thirty, the only woman in upper management, and still uncovered.

Three months ago, Ejem was delivering a presentation to a prospective client. As usual, she was the only woman in the room. The client paid no attention to her PowerPoint, focusing instead on what he considered to be the impropriety of an unclaimed woman distracting from business matters. Ejem was used to this and tried to steer the conversation back to the budget. When the man ignored her, none of her coworkers bothered to censure him, choosing instead to snicker into their paperwork. She walked out of the room.

Ejem had never gone to human resources before; she'd always sucked it up. The HR manager, a covered woman who was well into her fifties, listened to her with a bored expression, then, with a pointed look at Ejem's exposed breasts, said, "You can't seriously expect a group of men to pay attention to pie charts or whatever when there is an available woman in the room. Maybe if you were covered this wouldn't happen. Until you are, we can no longer put you in front of clients."

Ejem walked out of the building and never returned. She locked herself away at home until Chidinma came knocking with a bottle of vodka, her youngest girl on her hip, and a flyer for home-based work selling makeup.

Now that lifeline was gone, and it would be only a matter of time until Ejem exhausted her savings. She switched on the TV, and flipped channels until she reached an uncovered young woman relating the news. The woman reported on a building fire in Onitsha and Ejem prepared dinner with the broadcast playing in the background, chopping vegetables for stir-fry until she registered the phrase "unclaimed women" repeated several times. She turned up the volume.

The newscaster had been joined by an older man with a paternal air, who gave more details.

"The building was rumored to be a haven of sorts for unclaimed women, who lived there, evading their responsibilities as cloth makers. Authorities halted firefighters from putting out the blaze, hoping to encourage these lost women to return to proper life. At least three bodies were discovered in the ashes. Their identities have yet to be confirmed."

That was the other reason Ejem wanted to remain in the metro area. Small towns were less tolerant of unclaimed women, some going so far as to outlaw their presence unless they were menials of the osu caste. They had a certain freedom, Ejem thought—these osu women who performed domestic tasks, the osu men who labored in the mines or constructed the buildings she'd once designed—though her envy was checked by the knowledge that it was a freedom born of irrelevance. The only place for unclaimed women, however, as far as most were concerned, was the giant factories, where they would weave cloth for women more fortunate than they.

The town's mayor appeared at a press conference.

"This is a decent town with decent people. If folks want to walk around uncovered and unclaimed, they need to go somewhere else. I'm sorry about the property loss and the folks who couldn't get out, but this is a family town. We have one of the world's finest factories bordering us. They could have gone there." The screen flipped back to the newsman, who nodded sagely, his expression somehow affirming the enforcement of moral values even as it deplored the loss of life.

Ejem battled a bubble of panic. How long before her finances forced her out into the hinterlands, where she would have to join the cloth makers? She needed a job and she needed it fast.

•   •   •

What sorts of jobs could one do naked? Ejem was too old for anything entry-level, where she'd be surrounded day after day by twentysomethings who would be claimed quickly. Instead, she looked for jobs where her nudity would be less of an issue. She lasted at a nursing home for five weeks, until a visiting relative objected to her presence. At the coffee shop she made it two and a half hours until she had to hide in the back to avoid a former coworker. She quit the next day. Everywhere she went heightened how sheltered she'd been at her corporate job. The farther from the center of town she searched, the more people stared at her openly, asking outright why she wasn't covered when they saw that she didn't bear the mark of an osu woman. Every once in a while Ejem encountered osu women forced outside by errands, branded by shaved heads with scarification scored above one ear. Other pedestrians avoided them as though they were poles or mailboxes or other such sidewalk paraphernalia. But Ejem saw them.

As her search became more desperate, every slight took a knife's edge, so that Ejem found herself bothered even by the young girls still covered in their father-cloth who snickered at her, unaware or not caring that they, too, would soon be stripped of protection. The worst were the pitying *Oh, honey* looks, the whispered assurances from older covered women that someone would eventually claim her.

After a while, she found work giving massages at a spa. She enjoyed being where everyone was disrobed; the artificial equality was a balm. Her second week on the job, a woman walked in covered with one of the finest wife-cloths Ejem had ever seen. She ordered the deluxe package, consisting of every single service the spa offered.

"And may I have your husband's account number?"

"*My* account number," the woman emphasized, sliding her card across the counter.

The desk girl glared at the card, glared at the woman, then left to get the manager. Everyone in the waiting room stared.

The manager, a woman close to Ejem's age, sailed in, her haughty manner turning deferential and apologetic as soon as she caught sight of the client. "I'm so sorry. The girl is new, still in father-cloth. Please excuse her." The finely clothed one remained silent. "We will, of course, offer you a significant discount on your services today. Maria is ready to start on your massage right away."

"No," the woman said firmly. "I want *her* to do it." Ejem, who'd been pretending to straighten products on the shelves, turned to see the woman pointing at her.

Soon she was in one of the treatment rooms, helping the woman to disrobe, feeling the texture of the cloth, wanting to rub it against her cheek. She left to hang it and encountered the manager, who dragged her down the hall and spoke in a harsh whisper.

"Do you know who that is? That is Odinaka, *the* Odinaka. If she leaves here less than pleased, you will be fired. I hope I'm clear."

Ejem nodded, returning to the massage room in a nervous daze. Odinaka was one of a handful of independently wealthy women who flouted convention without consequences. She was unclaimed, but covered herself anyway, and not in modest cloth, either, but in fine, bold fabric that invited attention and scrutiny. She owned almost half the cloth factories across the globe. This unthinkable rebellion drew criticism, but her wealth ensured that it remained just that: words but no action.

Odinaka sat on the massage table, swinging her legs. At Ejem's direction, she lay on her stomach while Ejem warmed oil between her hands. She coated Odinaka's ankles before sliding up to her calves, warming the tissue with her palms. She asked a few casual questions, trying to gauge whether she was a talker or preferred her massages silent. She needn't have worried. Not only did Odinaka give verbose replies, she had questions for Ejem herself. Before long, she had pried from Ejem the story of how she'd come to be here, easing muscle tensions instead of pursuing a promising career as an architect.

"It doesn't seem fair, does it, that you have to remain uncovered?"

Ejem continued with the massage, unsure how to reply to such seditious sentiments.

"You know, you and I are very similar," Odinaka continued.

Ejem studied the woman's firm body, toned and slim from years of exercise. She considered the other ways in which they were different, not least that Odinaka had never had to worry about a bill in her life. She laughed.

"You are very kind, but we're nothing alike, though we may be of the same age," she responded, as lightly as she could, tilting the ending into a question. Odinaka ignored it, turning over to face her.

"I mean it; we are both ambitious women trying to make our way unclaimed in male-dominated fields."

Except, Ejem didn't say, *you are completely free in a way I am not, as covered as you wish to be.*

"Covering myself would be illegal—" she started.

"Illegal-smeagle. When you have as much money as I do, you exist above every law. Now, wouldn't you like to be covered too?"

•   •   •

Odinaka was her savior. She whisked Ejem away from her old apartment, helping her pay the fee to break her lease, and moved her into a building she owned in one of the city's nicest neighborhoods.

Ejem's quarters, a two-bedroom apartment complete with a generously sized kitchen, had the freshness of a deep clean, like it had been long vacant, or had gone through a recent purge, stripped of the scent and personality of its previous occupant. The unit had a direct intercom to the osu women who took care of the place. Ejem was to make cleaning requests as needed, or requests for groceries that later appeared in her fridge. When Ejem mentioned the distance from the apartment to her job, Odinaka revealed that she didn't have to work if she didn't want to, and it was an easy choice not to return to the spa. The free time enabled her to better get to know the other women in the building.

There was Delilah, who seemed like a miniature Odinaka in dress and mannerisms, but in possession of only half as much confidence. Doreen, a woman close to forty, became Ejem's favorite. She owned a bookstore—one that did well as far as bookstores went—and she had the air of someone who knew exactly who she was and liked it. She eschewed the option to self-clothe.

"Let them stare," Doreen would declare after a few glasses of wine. "This body is a work of art." She would lift her breasts with her hands, sending Ejem and the other women into tipsy giggles.

The remaining women—Morayo, Mukaso, and Maryam—were polite but distant, performing enough social niceties to sidestep any allegations of rudeness, but only just. Ejem and Doreen called them the three M's or, after a few drinks, "Mmm, no," for their recalcitrance. They sometimes joined in Odinaka's near-nightly cocktail hour, but within a few weeks the cadre solidified into Odinaka, Delilah, Doreen, and Ejem.

With this group of women, there were no snide remarks about Ejem's nakedness, no disingenuous offers to introduce her to a man—any man—who could maybe look past her flaws. Odinaka talked about her vast business, Doreen about her small one, and they teased each other with terrible advice neither would ever take. Ejem talked some about the career she'd left behind, but didn't have much to add. And for the first time, her shyness was just shyness, not evidence of why she remained unclaimed, nor an invitation to be battered with advice on how she could improve herself.

Besides, Odinaka talked enough for everyone, interrupting often and dominating every topic. Ejem didn't mind, because of all of them, Odinaka had had the most interesting life, one of unrelenting luxury since birth. She'd inherited the weaving company from her father when he retired, almost a decade ago, which had caused an uproar. But if one of the wealthiest dynasties wanted a woman at the helm, it was a luxury they could purchase. And if that woman indulged in covering herself and collecting and caring for other unclaimed women, who had the power to stop her?

"I imagine creating a world," Odinaka often said, "where disrobing is something a woman does only by choice."

On Ejem's first night in the building, Odinaka had brought a length of cloth to her, a gift, she said, that Ejem could wear whenever she wanted. Ejem had stared at the fabric for hours. Even in the confines of the building, in her own unit, she didn't have the courage to put it on. At Odinaka's cocktail hour, Doreen would sit next to her and declare, "It's us against these bashful fuckers, Ejem," setting off an evening of gentle ribbing at everyone's expense.

"You really go to your store like that?" Ejem asked Doreen one afternoon. "Why don't you cover yourself? No one will say anything if they know you're one of Odinaka's women, right?" She was trying to convince herself that she, too, could don the cloth and go out in public without fear.

Doreen stopped perusing invoices to give Ejem all her attention. "Look, we have to live with this. I was disrobed at age ten.

Do you know what it feels like to be exposed so young? I hid for almost a decade before I found myself, my pride. No one will ever again make me feel uncomfortable in my own skin. I plan to remain unclaimed and uncovered for as long as I live, and no one can say a damn thing about it. Odinaka rebels in her own way, and I in mine. I don't yearn for the safety of cloth. If the law requires me to be naked, I will be naked. And I will be goddamned if they make me feel uncomfortable for *their* law."

·   ·   ·

The weeks of welcome, of feeling free to be her own person, took hold and, one night, when Ejem joined the other women in Odinaka's apartment, she did so covered, the cloth draped over her in a girl's ties, the only way she knew how. Doreen was the first one to congratulate her, and when she hugged Ejem, she whispered, "Rebel in your own way," but her smile was a little sad.

Odinaka crowed in delight, "Another one! We should have a party."

She mobilized quickly, dispensing orders to her osu women via intercom. Ejem had yet to see any of the osu at work, but whenever she returned to her quarters from Odinaka's or Doreen's, her bed was made, the bathroom mirror cleared of flecks, the scabs of toothpaste scrubbed from the sink, and the rooms themselves held an indefinable feeling of having only just been vacated.

In less than the hour it took Ejem and the other residents to get themselves ready for the party, Odinaka's quarters had become packed. Men and women, all clothed except Doreen, mingled and chatted. Doreen held court on the settee, sipping wine and bestowing coy smiles.

Ejem tried to join in, but even with the self-cloth, she couldn't help feeling like the uncovered woman she'd been her entire adult life. Odinaka tried to draw Ejem into her circle of conversation, but after Ejem managed only a few stilted rejoinders, she edged away, sparing herself further embarrassment. Ejem ended up in a corner watching the festivities.

She was not aware that she herself was being watched until a man she'd seen bowing theatrically to Odinaka leaned against the wall next to her.

"So, you're the newest one, huh?"

"I suppose I am."

"You seem reasonable enough. Why are you unclaimed?"

Ejem tensed, wary.

"What's that supposed to mean, 'reasonable'?"

He ignored the question.

"Do you know I have been trying to claim that woman ever since she was a girl?" He nodded toward Odinaka. "Our union would have been legendary. The greatest cloth weaver with the greatest cotton grower. What do you think?"

Ejem shrugged. It was really none of her business.

"Instead she's busy collecting debris."

Stunned by his rudeness, Ejem turned away, but he only laughed and called to someone across the room. Suddenly, every laugh seemed directed at her, every smile a smirk at her expense. She felt herself regressing into the girl who'd needed Chidinma's tight grip in hers before she could walk with her head high. She ducked out, intending to return to her quarters.

She ran into Delilah, who held a carved box under her arm, a prized family heirloom Ejem recognized from their many gatherings. It was one of the few objects Odinaka envied, as she could not secure one herself, unable to determine the origin of the antique. She was forever demanding that Delilah bring it out to be admired, though Delilah refused to let Odinaka have it examined or appraised, perfectly content to let her treasure remain a mystery.

Ejem didn't particularly like Delilah. She might have been a mini Odinaka, but unlike Odinaka, Delilah was pretentious and wore her fine breeding on her sleeve. Ejem's distress was visible enough that Delilah paused, glancing between her and the door that muted the soiree.

"Is everything okay?" she asked.

Ejem nodded, but a tight nod that said it was not. She watched Delilah's concern war with the promise of fun on the other side of the door. Delilah's movements, a particular twist in her shoulders, the way she clenched her fist, an angled tilt of her head, suddenly brought to Ejem's mind the osu woman on the bus. Something must have crossed her face because Delilah lifted a furtive, self-conscious hand to pat her hair into place—right where an identifying scar would have been if a government midwife had scored it into her head when she was six months old, and then refreshed it on return visits every two years until she turned eighteen. That practice was the extent of Ejem's osu knowledge. Her people lived side by side with the osu and they knew nothing of each other.

Looking at Delilah's box, it occurred to Ejem that an osu girl—if she were clever enough, audacious enough, in possession of impossibly thick hair—could take her most prized possession—say, a fine carved box that had been in the family for many generations—and sneak away in the middle of the night. She could travel farther than she had ever been in her life, to a city where no one knew her. And because she was clever, she could slip seamlessly into the world of the people she knew so well because she'd had to serve them all her life.

Before the thought could take hold, the uncertainty in Delilah's face was replaced by an artificial sweetness, and she patted Ejem's shoulder, saying, "Rest well, then," before escaping into the party.

Ejem was awoken at dawn by the last of the revelers leaving. She stayed in her apartment till eight, then took advantage of Odinaka's open-door policy to enter her benefactor's apartment. If she hadn't been there herself, she would never have believed it had been filled with partiers the night before. In three hours, someone, or several someones, had transformed the wreckage of fifty guests—Ejem remembered at least two spilled wineglasses and a short man who'd insisted on making a speech from an end table—back into the clean, modern lines preferred by one of the wealthiest women in the world. A woman who apparently collected debris, like her. She wasn't exactly sure what she wanted to say to Odinaka—she couldn't childishly complain that one of the guests had insulted her—but she felt injured and sought some small soothing.

She found Odinaka lounging in her bed, covers pulled to her waist.

"Did you enjoy yourself, Ejem? I saw you talking to Aju. He just left, you know." She wiggled her brows.

Well. Ejem couldn't exactly condemn him now. "We had an interesting conversation," she said instead.

"'Interesting,' she says. I know he can be difficult. Never mind what he said."

Odinaka pressed the intercom and requested a breakfast tray, then began to recap the night, laughing at this and that event she didn't realize Ejem hadn't been there to see.

After ten minutes, she pressed the intercom again. "Where is my tray?" she demanded, a near shout.

Catching Ejem's expression, she rolled her eyes.

"Don't you start as well."

Ejem opened her mouth to defend the osu women, but shut it just as quickly, embarrassed not only by the unattractive revolutionary bent of what she'd almost said, but also because it felt so much like a defense of herself.

"You are just like Doreen," Odinaka continued. "Look, I employ an army of those women. They have a job and they need to do it. You remember how that goes, right?" Odinaka turned on the television. A commercial advertised a family getaway that included passes to a textile museum where the children could learn how cloth was made. Ejem recalled a documentary she'd seen in school that showed the dismal dorms to which unclaimed women were relegated, the rationed food, the abuse from guards, the "protection" that was anything but. It had been meant to instill fear of ending up in such a place, and it had worked.

When the program returned, Odinaka turned up the volume until it was clear to Ejem she had been dismissed.

•   •   •

Ejem decided that her first foray in her new cloth would be to visit Doreen in her shop. Doreen would know just what to say to ease the restless hurt brewing inside her. She may even know enough of Delilah's history to put Ejem's runaway suspicions to rest. Doreen had invited her to visit the bookstore many times—"You can't stay in here forever. Come. See what I've done. See what an unclaimed woman can build on her own."

Wearing self-cloth in the safety of Odinaka's building was one thing. Ejem dawdled in front of the mirror, studying the softness of her stomach, the firm legs she'd always been proud of, the droop of her breasts. She picked up the cloth and held it in front of her. Much better. She secured it in a simple style, mimicking as best as she could the draping and belting of the sophisticated women she'd encountered.

For the first time in her adult life, no one stared at her. When she gathered the courage to make eye contact with a man on the sidewalk and he inclined his head respectfully, she almost tripped in shock. It was no fluke. Everyone—men and women—treated her differently, most ignoring her as yet another body on the street. But when they did acknowledge her, their reactions were friendly. Ejem felt the protective hunch of her shoulders smooth itself out, as though permission had been granted to relax. She walked with a bounce in her step, every part of her that bounced along with it shielded by the cloth. Bound up in fabric, she was the freest she'd ever felt.

Ejem was so happy that when she saw a familiar face, she smiled and waved before she remembered that the bearer of the face had disowned their friendship some months ago. Chidinma gave a hesitant wave in return before she approached Ejem, smiling.

"You're covered! You're claimed! Turn around; let me see. Your wife-cloth is so fine. I'm upset you didn't invite me to the claiming ceremony."

The words were friendly but the tone was strained, their last exchange still echoing in the air.

"There wasn't a ceremony. There was nothing to invite you to."

Chidinma's smile faded. "You don't have to lie. I know I was awful to you; I'm sorry."

"No, really, there wasn't." Ejem leaned closer, yearning to confide, to restore their former intimacy. "It's self-cloth. I covered myself."

It took Chidinma a moment to absorb this. Then she bristled, pulling back any lingering affection. Her smile went waxy and polite.

"You must be very happy with your husband."

"Chidinma, I don't have a husband. I'm covering myself."

Chidinma's look turned so vicious that Ejem stepped back, bumping into a man who excused himself.

"Are you, now? A self-cloth, is it? Someone from a good family like yours? I don't believe it." Unlike Ejem, Chidinma didn't lower her voice, earning startled glances from passersby. Ejem shushed her.

"Oh, are you ashamed now? Did something you're not entirely proud of?"

When Ejem turned to leave, Chidinma snatched her by the cloth. Now she whispered, "You think you're covered, but you're still naked. No amount of expensive 'self-cloth'—how ridiculous!—will change that."

It was a spiteful and malicious thing to say, meant to hurt, and it did. Ejem tried to pull her cloth from her old friend's fist, but

Chidinma didn't let go. She continued, her voice cracking with tears.

"You don't get to be covered without giving something up; you don't get to do that. It's not fair. After everything I did for you, it's not fair."

Chidinma cried openly now and Ejem used the opportunity of her weakened grip to twist away, near tears herself.

It had been easy, Ejem thought, in the opulence of Odinaka's house, to forget that they were breaking laws. Easy, too, to clink glasses night after night. What had some woman given up so that Ejem could have this cloth? Was she a weaver by choice or indentured, deemed past her prime and burdened to earn the care of the state? The fabric felt itchy now, as though woven from rough wire.

Ejem hurried back the way she had come, to the safety of Odinaka's building. On the verge of panic, she fumbled with the keys to her apartment and let herself in. Once inside, she leaned against the door and slid to the floor, head to knees, catching her breath. She felt . . . something, that made her look around, and that's when she saw the osu woman standing in the corner. Her skin was light, almost blending into the dusky beige of the wall, her scar a gristly, keloided mass on the side of her head. She appeared to be Ejem's age or older. She held a bottle of cleaning solution and a rag. She was naked.

It was clear by the hunch of her shoulders and the wary look in her eye that it was not a nakedness she enjoyed. How long had it been since Ejem had carried that very look on her own face? How long since she'd felt shame so deep she'd nearly drowned in it?

The day she'd lost her father-cloth, she'd pleaded with her father, fought him as he'd attempted to rip the fabric away. Her mother had cried to her to bear it with some dignity, but Ejem had gone mindless. When her father had finally taken all of the cloth, uncurling her fingers to snatch even the frayed strip she'd held on to, Ejem had curled into herself, making a cover of her appendages. Each day since had been a management of this panic, swallowing it deep in her belly where it wouldn't erupt.

The osu woman nodded to Ejem, then slipped through a panel in the wall and disappeared. The panel slid back into place soundlessly, and when Ejem went to the wall she could feel no seam. She clawed at it, bending and breaking her nails, trying to force a way in. Finding no entry from her side, she pounded and called out, seeking a welcome.

A Conversation with Claire Boyle and Karolina Waclawiak

KAROLINA WACLAWIAK: How long have you been at *McSweeney's*, and how did you get involved? It's a small outfit, so did you start out in your current position when you were hired? If not, what was your trajectory like?

CLAIRE BOYLE: I've been at *McSweeney's* for four years, have been editing the *Quarterly* for two. I came up the same way many of *McSweeney's* past did, which is first as an intern. I was an editorial intern, working on *The Believer* and *The Organist*, mostly. I'm surprised they hired me because as an intern I stole snacks from another organization in our office and got *McSweeney's* scolded for it. But they saw past that, and I came on staff, started doing sales and marketing, got my hands into editorial, and eventually took over the *Quarterly*, which I edit now along with books.

You interned at *The Believer* before eventually becoming an editor there, right? I imagine starting at *BuzzFeed* felt much different, in comparison. How'd you navigate that?

KAROLINA WACLAWIAK: Yep, I started at *The Believer* as an intern. I begged them to let me read their slush pile, basically. And that led me to associate editor, then deputy editor, etc. In my final years I was editing the bulk of the features we ran—four an issue. *BuzzFeed News* is totally different—and it was a huge learning curve. When I started at *BuzzFeed News*, Saeed Jones and I created an online culture magazine called *Reader*, and it became very tied to a busy news cycle—we covered mass shootings, the 2016 election, and Trump, alongside pop culture and cultural criticism and more evergreen features. And while I had a month (or several) to work on a stories at *The Believer*, I obviously didn't have that same luxury when we had to be responsive to cultural events. I now run *Reader* and we probably run five to ten essays a week and usually one feature. I also have a staff of writers and editors who are some of the smartest cultural thinkers I've met. They're adept at responding to what's happening in culture pretty quickly—but I've also been working on moving them into magazine features. Being able to juggle the type of stories I learned how to edit at *The Believer* and faster-turnaround pieces has been fun—and being able to write both is a skill I think writers need to have now. My only mandate is that the pieces we run need to have more depth than your average internet hot take. Whatever we're saying needs to be true and interesting in a week or month or even year later. I'm not interested in just running a content machine.

Do you feel an urgency to publish work that feels responsive to our current cultural moment? How do you find fiction that doesn't feel didactic?

CLAIRE BOYLE: This is something I think about a lot. The best of fiction is always a response, in some way or another, to what it is to be alive. And we're always looking for work that does that best—that is digesting, reflecting back some acute understanding of being a person. I feel strongly, though, that work written to explicitly express a certain conclusion—as with any work that knows exactly where it's going before it starts—risks limiting the story itself. It can become flat if it isn't allowed to surprise itself, to go in unexpected directions, which I think is where fiction gets much of its power.

That said, I absolutely don't think that means the work should be apolitical, either. And I don't think it can be—our experiences and beliefs are inextricably baked into us and so will and should always be part of our art.

KAROLINA WACLAWIAK: *McSweeney's* obviously has a distinct literary tradition. Do you feel like you've had an opportunity to make it your own in some way? What writers have you brought in that are new to the magazine?

CLAIRE BOYLE: Absolutely, that's the most exciting aspect of editing the *Quarterly*. It's really a treat to be able to work from a tradition that has created such a space for itself in these last twenty-one years, one that has been so important to many people. The *Quarterly*, at its inception, only accepted stories that had been rejected by other journals— it's no longer a requisite, of course, but the ethos remains that we're sifting the margins, finding writers out on the limbs who are trying things that might fail but that, when it doesn't, hits on something truly arresting. That's always the kind of work we'll be excited about. And I see my job as carrying that forward, helping that ethos to evolve. As the first female editor of the *Quarterly*, it's been important to me to emphasize the writing of nonbinary and women writers, along with all voices historically underrepresented in publishing.

I've been asking myself, what is today's equivalent of publishing work that's been overlooked by other publishers—what are the bold moves being made today that interest me most? The beautiful thing about that project is that, as our conception of risks we find interesting evolve, the magazine evolves. We'll always be looking for writers taking risks—it's just a question of what those risks look like.

As for new writers, a majority of the writers we've published since issue 49, which was the first issue I was at the helm for, have been new to the magazine, including the three recognized by this award—Lesley Nneka Arimah, Maria Reva, and Julia Dixon Evans, all of whom I deeply admire. We were also enormously excited to publish T Kira Madden, Laura van den Berg, and R. O. Kwon in our most recent issue, among many others.

KAROLINA WACLAWIAK: A big part of *McSweeney's* is discovering new voices and new talent. Are there people you have been really excited to launch, and what were some indications to you that they were going to be huge talent?

CLAIRE BOYLE: I wouldn't say I've seen a true "from oblivion to the stars" rise yet since I've been around, but we've published a number of more emerging writers who blew us away and are not surprised by the success they're finding. We were incredibly taken by the writing of Lisa Taddeo and Raven Leilani recently, whose names you'll know soon if you didn't already. Same goes for the extraordinary writer Emerson Whitney, whose memoir *Heaven* we're putting out early next year and I cannot wait to introduce to our readers. I'm also super excited to see what the Nigerian writer Adachioma Ezeano, who has a piece in the forthcoming issue 56, writes next—her prose is hugely original and propulsive. Discovering new writers is a huge motivator for us to do what we do. I'm curious how you guys go about finding new voices at *Buzzfeed*, what you look for and where you look for it.

KAROLINA WACLAWIAK: We actually post stories and essays that we admire in our Slack room daily. And we talk about them, and often I'll ask the editors to reach out to see if those writers have something to pitch us. We all read widely, and it's always exciting to discover a new voice elsewhere and pull them into the fold. I also ran an emerging writer fellowship for a few years—we're hoping to bring that back next year. And through that we found Niela Orr, who is now the interviews editor at *The Believer*, and Jen Choi, who is a brilliant essayist, among others. We have a lot of very smart emerging writers who have come through that internship, and I'm committed to finding new voices and building their careers. I also go to CalArts to speak to students every year and encourage new writers to pitch us wherever I meet them. What I look for is a distinctive point of view and someone who has a really strong voice. I also love writers who can pull a lot of threads together—for essays bringing in cultural context is crucial. Being able to contextualize what's happening today with events in the past, or even being able to show the lineage of where a pop star's work fits into is crucial to me. That shows me they're thinking deeply about whatever subject they're tackling and not just making superficial connections.

The publishing world has obviously gone through changes in the last few years and there are—in my mind—fewer places to have your fiction published. What do you think about the state of fiction today, especially short stories, and the role of literary magazines as a platform within the publishing industry?

CLAIRE BOYLE: It's true, I agree, though I do also think there are exciting presses popping up all the time. It's a shame that the industry is deemphasizing short stories— publishers are publishing fewer short-stories collections because they're thought of as less economically viable. And it bums me out to hear people talk about short-story collections as some kind of stepping stone for an author on their way to novels. Writing short stories involve notably different muscles, in my mind, than writing novels—it's about trying to evoke a universe in just a small space, about narrative selectivity, about each sentence holding an entire life. Being able to pack each sentence with that much life, to me, is what's so exciting about short stories, and to think of them as simply a means to novels is to miss out on some of the sharpest and most discerning voices—I mean look at Diane Williams and Lydia Davis and Lucy Corin. Literary magazines can hold that space, can assert that stories aren't important only to introduce new writers into the landscape, though there is that, but in their own right, as an explosive and exacting form that in many ways, given its length, enables more experimental and strange writing.

KAROLINA WACLAWIAK: I totally agree. There are things a short story can do that a novel never can. It's exciting to see what can be accomplished with such economy of language. And there's something really satisfying about reading a brilliant short story and it being over and thinking about it for weeks and months and years— how'd they do that? I have a deep admiration for short story writers. What kind of voices do you think are missing from more mainstream magazines that publish fiction?

CLAIRE BOYLE: There's an important conversation happening in publishing about representation, which is great, but we're only beginning to reckon with the biases the industry is built upon. There's a lot of ground to cover before magazines are properly representing work by writers of color, indigenous writers, economically disadvantaged writers, women, nonbinary, disabled, queer writers. Something I also think is missing, from mainstream but also all of publishing, is emerging writers who are older. We're used to expecting exciting new authors to be young, and I think that really limits the writing we focus on, the kind of experiences highlighted.

KAROLINA WACLAWIAK: It's true. So many literary awards are focused on youth—and have age cutoffs that perpetuate this anxiety that you need to have accomplished writing a book before thirty or be a discovered genius by the age of thirty-five or you essentially have missed the window of opportunity. I think that sense of anxiety probably drives people into MFA programs before they have had the kinds of life experiences that produce rich fiction. And so many author profiles push this narrative of young ingenue too! Which is why it was exciting to see Sigrid Nunez win the National Book Award for fiction last year. But even then she's branded as an overnight success when she's been writing books for decades! I could talk about the fetishization of the debut novel for 700 more hours, but let's get back to *McSweeney's*. How do you think being in San Francisco and not, say, a city like New York, where publishing is centered, impacts the kind of work *McSweeney's* looks for and publishes?

CLAIRE BOYLE: We're 100 percent impacted by not being in New York. Honestly, it's mostly because we're just blissfully unaware of what's going on over there in New York. We're gifted with space and also with dramatically fewer invites to cocktail parties, which means we get to create our own universe. Respond to what excites us, rather than what feels like it's picking up momentum, or competing to be ahead of the curve. We're spared the inside-baseball and industry chatter; spared the close attention to what everyone else is doing. It feels less like we're part of a business, an industry over here. If anything, the Bay Area publishing world feels more like a community—it's terrifically supportive, especially the women. We're in it together over here on our own very steep, tech-infested island. So we publish what moves us, and that's about it.

You're not in New York, either, but *Buzzfeed* seems so tuned in. With so many offices around the world, does each region bring in idiosyncratic work, or have you guys developed a common sensibility?

KAROLINA WACLAWIAK: I'm constantly looking for voices outside of New York because I do think it's easy to just focus on writers you see every day or meet at parties. But that can lead to a single perspective that leaves a lot of people out. But I think the internet has collapsed the need to live in New York in order to be a writer. Twitter has been a great place to find writers. Though sometimes I watch writers tweet themselves out of stories. Stop giving your ideas away for free on Twitter, people! However, if someone has an interesting idea they tweet out, we will often write to them to see if they have an essay in them. That's how we started working with the amazing essayist Hanif Abdurraqib—we saw him tweeting about something and reached out and now we work with him rather frequently. And he's Columbus, Ohio, based, so you really don't need to live in New York. You just need to be somehow engaged in the literary world. I am most interested in writers who have an interesting life experience or, really, have something deeply engaging to say that shifts how readers think about the world they live in.

Design is such an integral part of the *McSweeney's*. Why do you think it's important to have such a wild look and feel to the magazine?

CLAIRE BOYLE: We have our brilliant art director, Sunra Thompson, to thank for those wild designs. With each issue entirely redesigned and reimagined, the physicality of the magazine is really important to us. The joke is that people have come to expect to be surprised each issue (which leads to the conclusion that we should just start publishing uniform, sober, linen-bound issues if we want to surprise people). But in reality, there's a level of reverence that a sumptuous, beautifully designed object gives to the writing inside that I find really important—especially at this time when short stories are in peril. It also can function as a Trojan horse of sorts—you come for the book designed to look like a bag of party balloons, you stay for the remarkable writing inside.

The other thing that the elaborate, ever-shifting design of the magazine does is it keeps us editorially inventive. Each new design keeps us from falling into patterns— they generate fresh story ideas, themes, ways to present writing. As with water, the journal's content often takes the form of the container. And we get to imagine the most interesting ways to do that. The designs and editorial themes often come hand in hand, and it's not uncommon for an issue's editorial theme to be born from a design idea. It's a quarterly challenge for us to surprise and push ourselves, to find new ways to present and imagine how writing can be found, presented, conceived.

Permissions

Contributors

MARK ARAX is an author and journalist whose writings on California have won numerous awards for literary nonfiction. *The Atlantic Monthly* compared Mark's last book, *West of the West*, to the great social portraits by Steinbeck, Didion, and Saroyan. His other books include the memoir *In My Father's Name* and the best-selling *The King of California*, which won a California Book Award and was named a top book of 2004 by the *Los Angeles Times* and the *San Francisco Chronicle*. His newest book, *The Dreamt Land: Chasing Water and Dust Across California*, has been hailed by critics as one of the most important books ever written about the West.

LESLEY NNEKA ARIMAH's stories have been honored with a National Magazine Award, a Commonwealth Short Story Prize, and an O. Henry Award. Her work has appeared in *Granta*, *Harper's*, *McSweeney's*, and the *New Yorker* and has received support from the Elizabeth George Foundation and MacDowell. She was selected for the National Book Foundation's 5 Under 35, and her debut collection, *What It Means When a Man Falls From the Sky*, won the 2017 Kirkus Prize and the 2017 New York Public Library Young Lions Fiction Award and was selected for the PBS NewsHour–New York Times book club, among other honors. Arimah is a 2019 United States Artists Fellow in Writing. She lives in Las Vegas and is working on a novel about you.

REGINALD DWAYNE BETTS is a husband and father of two sons. A poet and memoirist, he is the author of three books: the recently published *Bastards of the Reagan Era*, the 2010 NAACP Image Award–winning memoir *A Question of Freedom*, and the poetry collection *Shahid Reads His Own Palm*. Betts is currently enrolled in the Ph.D. in law program at Yale Law School. He has earned a JD from Yale Law School, an MFA from Warren Wilson College, and a BA from the University of Maryland.

CLAIRE BOYLE is an editor and writer based in San Francisco. She is the managing editor of *Timothy McSweeney's Quarterly Concern*.

KASEY CORDELL is *5280* magazine's features editor. She writes and edits service features, departments, and long-form stories and contributes to 5280.com. An avid traveler and athlete, Cordell often writes about travel and the outdoors, as well as the military and veterans. In 2019, Cordell and *5280* deputy editor Lindsey Koehler earned *5280*'s first National Magazine Award for their November 2018 feature story "The Art Of Dying Well," which won the Personal Service category. The previous year Cordell was a National Magazine Awards finalist in the Leisure Interests category for "The 5280 Guide to Four Corners." In 2018, Cordell embedded with the U.S. Army in Afghanistan to write about one of the first gender-integrated howitzer crews sent to war ("13 Bravo"). The story was a finalist in the reporting category for the City and Regional Magazine Association awards. Cordell's previous work has also been recognized as a finalist in various CRMA categories. The Oregon native joined *5280* in 2013 after stints at the Boulder *Daily Camera*, *National Geographic Adventure*, and *Portland Monthly*. Her writing has also appeared in *Monocle*, the *New York Times*, and *Sunset*. Cordell studied psychology as an undergraduate at Lewis and Clark College and holds two master's degrees: one in Irish studies from Queen's University Belfast and another in journalism from the University of Colorado.

HANNAH DREIER covers immigration for *ProPublica*. She won the 2019 Pulitzer Prize in Feature Writing for a series of stories she wrote about a botched police crackdown on the gang MS-13 on Long Island. Previously, she served as the Associated Press's Venezuela correspondent for three years. Her Venezuela reporting won a Gerald Loeb Award, the James Foley Medill Medal for Courage in Journalism, and the Overseas Press Club Hal Boyle Award. She also covered California politics and the business of gambling for AP. Her reporting has led to the passage of new laws and the implementation of international sanctions. Her work has also been recognized by the Hillman Prizes, the John Jay College/Harry Frank Guggenheim Excellence in Criminal Justice Reporting Awards, and the Peabody Awards. Dreier grew up in San Francisco and now lives in Brooklyn.

CAITLIN FLANAGAN is a contributing editor at *The Atlantic*. She is the author of *Girl Land* and *To Hell with All That*.

FRANKLIN FOER is a staff writer for *The Atlantic*. He is the author of *World Without Mind: The Existential Threat of Big Tech* and *How Soccer Explains the World: An Unlikely Theory of Globalization*.

LESLIE JAMISON, a *VQR* editor at large, is the author of the nonfiction books *The Recovering* and *The Empathy Exams* and the novel *The Gin Closet*. She directs the graduate nonfiction program at Columbia University. Her next book, the essay collection *Make It Scream, Make It Burn*, is forthcoming in 2019.

LINDSEY B. KOEHLER edits service packages, nontraditional feature packages, long-form narrative features, and the magazine's Getaways and Great Outdoors departments for *5280*. Koehler also writes narratives and service packages. She is a three-time National Magazine Award finalist. Along with Kasey Cordell, Koehler wrote "The Art Of Dying Well," which won the 2019 Ellie for Personal Service. Her "Earth, Wind, and Water" feature was selected as a 2017 National Magazine Award finalist in the

Leisure Interests category. Koehler also cowrote, with Natasha Gardner, "Low on O2," which was an ASME finalist in the Personal Service category in 2010. Her 2015 fly-fishing story, "Hooked," won the City and Regional Magazine Association award for Leisure/Lifestyle Interests. In 2011 her feature "Gone"—a look at a local police detective searching for a missing child—was selected as a finalist in the Feature Story category by the City and Regional Magazine Association. Her narrative "Undefeated," which focused on a friend's encounter with the Denver serial rapist Brent J. Brents, was selected as the winning profile story at the 2006 Maggie Awards. Koehler was born in Charleston, West Virginia, spent more than a decade in suburban Atlanta, and moved to Colorado in 2001. She has a degree in magazine journalism from the Grady College of Journalism at the University of Georgia.

JOHN J. LENNON has written for *The Atlantic, Esquire, New York,* the *New York Times,* and the *Marshall Project,* where he is a contributing writer. Currently, he is incarcerated in Sing Sing Correctional Facility, in Ossining, New York. He will be eligible for parole in 2029.

JILL LEPORE, a staff writer, has been contributing to the *New Yorker* since 2005. Her books include *The Name of War*, which won the Bancroft Prize; *New York Burning*, which was a finalist for the Pulitzer Prize for History; *The Story of America*, which was shortlisted for the PEN Literary Award for the Art of the Essay; *Book of Ages*, a finalist for the National Book Award; and *The Secret History of Wonder Woman*. Her latest book, *These Truths: A History of the United States*, came out in September 2018. Lepore received her Ph.D. in American studies from Yale in 1995 and is the David Woods Kemper '41 Professor of American History at Harvard University. In 2012 she was named a Harvard College Professor in recognition of distinction in undergraduate teaching.

JEFF MACGREGOR is writer at large for *Smithsonian Magazine*. Over the years he has written for *Esquire*, the *New York Times*, *Sports Illustrated*, and many others and is the author of the critically acclaimed book *Sunday Money: Speed! Lust! Madness! Death! A Hot Lap Around America with Nascar.*

ADAM MOSS served as editor in chief of *New York* from 2004 to 2019. During his tenure, he was responsible for the revitalization of the now fifty-year-old print magazine, the relaunch of nymag .com, and the creation of five highly successful digital publications, *The Cut, Grub Street, Intelligencer, The Strategist,* and *Vulture.* Under Moss's leadership, *New York* won forty-one National Magazine Awards, including the 2013 award for Magazine of the Year, six awards for General Excellence in print, and seven for overall excellence for nymag.com. In addition, the magazine won the Society of Publication Designers award for Magazine of the Year and the American Society of Magazine Editors award for Cover of the Year three times each. In 2017, *Advertising Age* named *New York* magazine of the year and Moss editor of the year, an honor he also received in 2001 and 2007. In 2016, *Adweek* named Moss editor of the year and *New York* magazine of the year. In 2005, Moss was awarded an honorary doctor of humanities degree from his alma mater, Oberlin College, and in 2012 the Missouri Honor Medal for Distinguished Service in Journalism. Before joining *New York*, Moss was the editor of the *New York Times Magazine* and assistant managing editor of the newspaper, overseeing the *New York Times Book Review* and style and culture coverage as well as the magazine. Moss was the founding editor of *7 Days*, a New York weekly magazine, which won the National Magazine Award for General Excellence. Before that, he worked at *Esquire* in a variety of positions, including those of managing editor and deputy editor. Earlier he worked at *Rolling Stone.* In 2019, Moss was elected by ASME to the Magazine Editors' Hall of Fame.

LAURA PARKER is a staff writer at *National Geographic* who specializes in covering climate change and marine environments. She is the lead writer on *National Geographic*'s campaign to educate its global audience about plastic pollution.

JERRY SALTZ is the senior art critic at *New York* magazine and its entertainment site, *Vulture*; a leading voice in the art world at large; and an innovative user of social media. He joined the magazine's staff in 2007, and his writing ranges from cover stories to reviews to quick online commentaries. He won the Pulitzer Prize for Criticism in 2018, the National Magazine Award for Leisure Interests in 2019, and the National Magazine Award for Columns and Commentary in 2015, having been a finalist for the same award in 2011. Saltz was previously the senior art critic at the *Village Voice*, where he was a finalist for the Pulitzer Prize for Criticism in 2001 and 2006 and was the recipient of the 2007 Frank Jewett Mather Award for Art Criticism from the College Art Association. A frequent guest lecturer at major universities and museums, Saltz was also the sole adviser on the 1995 Whitney Biennial. Saltz has written for *Arts*, *Art in America*, *Flash Art*, *Frieze*, *Modern Painters*, *Parkett*, *Time Out New York*, and many others. His *Village Voice* columns were compiled into a book, *Seeing Out Loud: The Village Voice Art Columns, 1998–2003*. A second volume of his criticism, *Seeing Out Louder*, was published by Hardpress Editions. Saltz appeared as a judge on Bravo's *Work of Art: The Next Great Artist* for the show's two seasons and has been a guest on *CBS This Morning*, NPR, and other news outlets.

DOREEN ST. FÉLIX has been a staff writer at the *New Yorker* since 2017. Previously, she was a culture writer at MTV News. Her writing has appeared in the *The Fader*, *New York*, the *New York Times Magazine*, *Pitchfork*, and *Vogue*. In 2016, St. Félix was named one of *Forbes*'s 30 Under 30 in Media. In 2017 she was a finalist for a National Magazine Award for Columns and Commentary; in 2019 she won in the same category.

ERIC SULLIVAN is a senior editor for *Esquire*, where he writes and edits features. Before joining Hearst in 2015, he spent five years at *GQ*. He grew up in upstate New York, went to Wesleyan University, and lives in Brooklyn. A story he edited about the crackdown on gay culture in Russia, "Behind the Iron Closet," by Jeff Sharlet, won the 2015 Ellie for Reporting.

BEN TAUB joined the *New Yorker* as a staff writer in 2017. He has written for the magazine about a range of subjects related to jihadism, crime, conflict, and human rights, mostly in Africa, Europe, and the Middle East. In 2017 his work on Syria, which was supported by the Pulitzer Center on Crisis Reporting, was short-listed for a National Magazine Award and won the Livingston Award for International Reporting, the Robert F. Kennedy Award for International Print reporting, and the Overseas Press Club Award for Investigative Reporting. Taub also received the ASME Next Award for Journalists Under 30 and was named one of *Forbes*'s 30 Under 30 in Media. In 2018 his work on a convergence of crises in the Sahel won the George Polk Award for Magazine Reporting and the Prince Albert II of Monaco and U.N. Correspondents Association Global Prize for coverage of climate change. In 2019 his reporting on Iraq's post-ISIS campaign of revenge won the National Magazine Award for Reporting and the George Polk Award for Magazine Reporting.

NAHAL TOOSI is a foreign affairs correspondent at *Politico*. She joined *Politico* from the Associated Press, where she reported from or served as an editor in New York, Islamabad, Kabul, and London. She was one of the first foreign correspondents to reach Abbottabad, Pakistan, after the killing of Osama bin Laden. Before joining the AP, Toosi worked for the *Milwaukee Journal Sentinel*, where she mostly covered higher education but also managed to report from Iraq during the U.S. invasion in 2003, as well as from Egypt, Thailand, and Germany.

KAROLINA WACLAWIAK is the author of the critically acclaimed novels *How to Get Into the Twin Palms* and *The Invaders*. Her third novel, *Life Events*, will be published in spring 2020. Formerly an editor at *The Believer*, she is now the executive editor, culture, at *BuzzFeed News*.

ROBERT WRIGHT is a research assistant at the Center for Justice at Columbia University. He is a published author who combines personal experience and research to develop informed opinions about social injustice, mass incarceration, and prison reform. Wright, while incarcerated, received a bachelor's degree in behavioral science from Mercy College. Since joining the Center for Justice, Wright has participated in a number of panel discussions regarding social injustice, designed educational curriculums for adults and youth either involved or at risk of being involved with the criminal justice system, and researched the effects of trauma and punitive practices in urban communities. Next year, Robert will work towards a Ph.D. in social psychology.